A GRAMMAR OF MODERN CORNISH

Third edition

WELLA BROWN

Kesva an Taves Kernewek

(The Cornish Language Board)

First Published in 1984 by

THE CORNISH LANGUAGE BOARD

Second Edition January 1993

with the aid of a grant from the Task Force, Human Resources, Education, Training and Youth of the Commission of the European Communities.

Third Edition January 2001

Supported by a grant from 'Awards for All' (National Lotteries Board

Copyright © W. Brown

All rights reserved. No part of this publication may be reproduced, stored in a retrieval system or transmitted, in any form or by any means, electronic, photocopying, recording or otherwise, without prior permission of the publishers.

ISBN 1-902917-00-6

Printed by Penwell Ltd.

Callington, Cornwall

CONTENTS   PAGE

Prefaces	v
Abbreviations	viii
Phonology	1
Nouns	19
Pronouns	49
Adjectives	67
Numerals	81
Prepositions	98
Verbs	143
Adverbials	205
Prefixes	218
Verbal Particles	223
Conjunctions	230
Sentences	240
Subordinate Sentences	272
Interjections	295
General Index	297
Index of Verbs	316

Dhe bub huni,
Kerneweger kyn fo po na vo,
hag a gar an yeth kernewek

PREFACE TO THE SECOND EDITION

In compiling the second edition of this book I have followed the same guidelines as those used in the first edition, that is to say I have tried to provide a reasonably complete account of the Cornish language as currently used by most speakers and writers. Since the revived language is based on that of the classical texts the book will be equally serviceable to students of those works.

The treatment is a traditional grammatical one based on a step-by-step description of parts of speech and going on to the syntax of the whole sentence although points of syntax will necessarily be dealt with in the earlier parts of the book also.

There is a full general index and a separate index of verbs. Copious cross-references are included to help the user of the book to find a comprehensive description of any topic and because of this a certain amount of repetition in the text is inevitable. Those who have used the first edition of this book will find that the paradigms of the verbs have been simplified.

Cornish is a complex language, capable of expressing every style from the simplest everyday statement to the most involved and abstract poetical idea and it is hoped that this book will enable users of the language to exploit this richness to the full.

Most statements in this book are supported by examples based on the texts mentioned above but I have kept to a minimum direct quotations from those works.

In the translations of the examples the meaning assigned to any given word is that applicable in that particular context. As stated in the appropriate sections, the English usage for the second person is followed for singular and plural, 'you' representing both the Cornish *ty* and *hwi*.

In the introduction to the first edition of this grammar I anticipated that further research and the use of computer techniques would add to our knowledge of Middle Cornish and allow us to improve our modern language, particularly as to its phonology, the grammar and its vocabulary, expanded to meet modern needs, being adequately understood. This forecast has been fulfilled by the work of Dr Ken George whose doctoral thesis, *A Phonological History of Cornish*, Brest, 1984, followed by *The Pronunciation and Spelling of Revived Cornish*, 1986, provided for the first time a comprehensive evaluation of the sound system used in Cornish at any given stage and the evolution of those sounds from the age of the first written records to the time of the demise of the language at the end of the eighteenth century. An improved system of pronunciation and spelling having been thus described, the Cornish Language Board decided in 1987 to adopt it as representing a considerable advance, having the twin merits of greater accuracy than the Unified system in use up to that time, and of enabling learners to read Cornish without the use of the special diacritical marks which the former dictionaries had to employ. The changes are important but are not drastic and those accustomed to the older, Unified, system will have no difficulty in following the newer one. Conversely learners of the new system will not find Unified hard to read. The reformed system is usually referred to as Common Cornish *(Kernewek Kemmyn)*, a name suggested by John King. A full description of the system will be found in the works referred to above.

I repeat here my acknowledgement of the work of the pioneers of the language movement, Henry Jenner, R. Morton Nance, A.S.D Smith, E.G. Retallack Hooper, without whom Cornish would not be the living language it is today. The advances made in recent years in no way invalidate the achievements of those who laid the foundations of the revival and the changes now introduced are to be seen as a continuous development of all that they did. My thanks are due to a number of people who have examined the manuscript in whole or in part or who have offered suggestions based on their use of the first edition. I hope that they will accept this acknowledgement of the considerable help which they have given. Special mention must be made however of Graham Sandercock and Dr Ken George who have scrutinised almost every word of the book and have thus contributed to its accuracy. Spellings are taken from those given in Dr Ken George's *Gerlyver Meur* and every effort has been made to ensure complete agreement. In the event of a discrepancy, the authority of the *Gerlyver Meur* takes precedence, of course. Any shortcomings and errors in the book remain however the responsibility of the author.

I am glad to be able to take this opportunity also to express my thanks to my wife whose support over the many months during which this new edition has been in preparation has been invaluable.

Wella Brown

Mis Genver 1993

PREFACE TO THE THIRD EDITION

A third edition of the *Grammar of Modern Cornish* having been called for, the opportunity has been taken of correcting errors and of rewriting and expanding a number of sections. My thanks are again due to all those who in using the book have made suggestions for improvement, in particular those resulting from Ray Edwards' researches into the classical texts and published in his *Notennow Kernewek*.

The publication of Ken George's *Gerlyver Kres* has provided a few minor changes in spelling, for example: wor'tu to **war-tu** 'towards'; tryga to **triga** 'dwell' (and derivatives); trelya to **treylya** 'turn'; plu to **plyw** 'parish'.

The valuable review of verbal forms made by Ray Edwards in his *Verbow Kernewek* (Cornish Language Board 1995 and subsequent editions) expands the information given in this book. The examination of the subjunctive forms in the classical texts By Dr Ken George and which formed the subject of his paper to Harvard University in October 2000 has enabled me to make the table given in §182 more accurate.

Cornish like all living languages is developing, evolving its own idioms and vocabulary as it does so, yet it needs to retain its individual character and I hope that this book will continue to be of use to those who are involved in that development and who seek to preserve that character.

I am grateful to David Balhatchet for his detailed scrutiny of the manuscript thus enabling me to eliminate numerous typographical and other errors. I am deeply indebted to Graham Sandercock whose painstaking transference of the original computer language into a more modern format has contributed to the improved layout of the text. My wife, Liz, undertook the tedious task of helping to check the index and I thank her not only for that but for her continued support throughout.

Wella Brown

Mis Du 2000

ABBREVIATIONS and REFERENCES

adj. *adjective*
adv. *adverb*
BM. *Bywnans Meriasek, Whitely Stokes, London 1872; Cornish Language Board, 1996*
B. *Breton*
compl. *complement*
conj. *conjunction*
C. *Cornish*
CEMN. *Cornish-English Dictionary, FOCS, 1938*
CFA. *Cornish for All, Morton Nance, 3rd ed., 1958*
CS. *Cornish Simplified, A.S.D. Smith, 2ed., 1965*
d. *dual*
def. *definite*
def.art. *definite article*
exclam. *exclamation, exclamative*
f. *feminine*
F. *French*
George, *The Pronunciation and Spelling of Revived Cornish, 1986*
HMSB. A *Historical Morphology and Syntax of Breton, Roparz Hemon, Dublin, 1975*
imperf. *imperfect*
imperv. *imperative*
indic. *indicative*
interj. *interjection*
interr. *interrogative*
LHB. *Language and History in Early Britain, Jackson, Edinburgh 1953*
lit. *literally*
LP. *A Concise Comparative Celtic Grammar, Lewis and Pedersen, Göttingen, 1974*
m. *masculine*
MC. *Mount Calvary, The Passion Poem, Kesva an Taves Kernewek, 1972*
neg. *negative*
n./nns. *noun/nouns*
nom. *nominal*

num. *number/numeral*
opt. *optative*
OM. *Origo Mundi, ed. Norris, 1859*
part. *participle/particle*
PD. *Passio Domini, Nance and Smith, ed. Sandercock, 1982*
perf. *perfect/perfective*
plup. *pluperfect*
p./pl. *plural*
poss. *possessive*
pref. *prefix*
prep. *preposition*
pres. *present*
p./f. *present/future*
pres. part. const. *present participle construction*
pret. *preterite*
pron. *pronoun*
ref. *referring to, with reference to*
rel. *relative*
RD. *Resurrexio Domini, Nance and Smith, ed. Sandercock, 1984*
sent. *sentence*
s./sing. *singular*
sub. *subordinate*
subj. *subjunctive*
suff. *suffix*
Supp. *Supplements to Cornish Simplified, Retallack Hooper, An Lef Kernewek*
vb. *verb, verbal*
v.n. *verbal noun*
voc. *vocative*
W. *Welsh*
WG. *Welsh Grammar, Morris Jones, 1970*
1 *first person*
2 *second person*
3 *third person*
0 *impersonal*
* *assumed form*
/ *indicates alternative forms*

PHONOLOGY

§1 **The phonemic system** A system of orthography is phonemic when each significant unit of sound (phoneme) is uniquely represented by a single written unit (grapheme). Thus the sound /m/ is always expressed by the letter <m>, the sound /x/ is written <gh> and these letters or combinations of letters always represent those same sounds. Modern Cornish, as described in this book, uses a phonemic orthography. The exception is the letter <y> which represents either the vowel /I/ or the semi-vowel /j/.

§2 **The alphabet and spelling** The Cornish alphabet is:

| a | b | ch | d | e | f | g | h | i | j | k | l | m | n | o | p | r | s | t | u | v | w | y |

These letters are used to represent the sounds of Cornish as follows:

Vowels

| a | e | eu | i | o | oe | ou | u | y |

Diphthongs

| aw | ay | ew | ey | iw | ow | oy | yw |

Semi-vowels

| w | y |

Consonants

| b | bb | ch | d | dd | dh | f | ff | g | gg | gh | ggh | h | hw | j | k | kk |
| l | m | mm | n | nn | p | pp | r | rr | s | ss | sh | t | tt | th | tth | v |

The letter **c** is used only in the digraph **ch** and the doubled forms of **ch**, **gh** and of **th** are **cch**, **ggh** and **tth** respectively. The digraph **sh** occurs in a few English borrowings with its English value. In native words the letters represent distinct sounds.

Several schemes for naming the Cornish alphabet have been proposed. The following with minor amendments is that of George Ansell. The names are pronounced as ordinary Cornish words.

Letter	Name	Letter	Name	Letter	Name	Letter	Name
A	a	G	ge	M	em	T	te
B	be	H	ha	N	en	U	u
CH	cha	I	I	O	o	V	ve
D	de	J	je	P	pe	W	we
E	e	K	ka	R	er	Y	ye
F	ev	L	el	S	es		

PRONUNCIATION

In the descriptions of individual sounds which follow, the Cornish symbol is given first and then a comparison is made between the Cornish sound and the nearest English one. Occasionally another language is used for comparison when there is no near English value. These descriptions are condensed from the full accounts provided in *The Pronunciation and Spelling of Revived Cornish*, K. George, 1986 (George). Vowel length is discussed in §7 but in general refers to the duration of the sound rather than to any change in quality.

§3 **Vowels**

a   when long is like the E. exclamation 'ah!' and when half long or short is the sound of 'a' in the E. dialect of East Cornwall.
e   is the 'e' in E. 'bet'.
eu   is the 'eu' in French 'peu'.
i   is like the 'ee' in E. 'beet' but somewhat closer.
o   when long is the 'ou' in E 'sought'. When short it is the 'o' in E. 'sot'.
oe   when long is the 'oa' in 'boat' in the E. dialect of West Penwith or the sound of the F. word 'eau'. When short it is unrounded and is the 'u' of words like 'cut' in the E. dialect of West Penwith, but slightly closer.
ou   when stressed is the 'oo' of E 'boot'.
u   is the 'u' of F. 'tu'.
y   is the 'i' of E. 'bit' but somewhat extended.

§4   **Semi-vowels** The semi-vowels stand alone or form the second element of the diphthongs as described in §5.

w   is the 'w' of E. 'wet'.
y   the 'y' of E. 'yet'. This letter also represents a full vowel, as described above in §3. It is a semi-vowel when followed in the same word by a full vowel or by a diphthong: **yagh** 'healthy'; **redya** v.n. 'reading'; **yeyn** 'cold'.

§5 Diphthongs

A diphthong is a vowel of continually changing quality. The two letters of the digraph which represent the diphthong mark approximately the points at which it begins and ends.

- **aw**   is the 'ow' in E. 'how'.
- **ay**   is the 'y' in E. 'by'.
- **ew**   is the 'ew' in W. *tew* 'fat' or the diphthong heard in the dialectal pronunciation of 'cow' in Mid- and West Cornwall.
- **ey**   is the 'ei' of E. 'veil' with a closer first element.
- **iw**   is the 'iw' of W. *lliw* 'colour' or the 'ew' of E. 'brew' with a closer first element and not like English 'you'.
- **ow**   is a sound between E. 'owe' and 'awe'.
- **oy**   is the 'oy' of E. 'boy'.
- **yw**   is like the 'ew' in E. 'flew'. Not like E. 'you'.

§6 Consonants

- **b**   'b' as in E. 'bell'.
- **ch**   'ch' as in E. 'church'. In loan words only, with the exception of **chi** 'house'.
- **d**   'd' as in E. 'dog'. A **d** in final position and the double form **dd** would be found in loan words only.
- **dh**   as the 'th' in E. 'these'.
- **f**   'f' in E. 'fin'. With **m, n, l, r**, or a vowel before and after the **f**, it is partly voiced to a sound between **v** and **f**. Examples: **an fos** 'the wall', **mar freth** 'so fluent', **avel fros** 'like a stream'. This change is purely phonetic and without grammatical significance.
- **g**   'g' in E. 'gap'. The double form **gg** is found in a few loan words only.
- **gh**   When final and in the group **-ght**, like the 'ch' in Scottish 'loch'. When, between vowels and in the groups **-lgh-, -rgh-** between vowels, it is a strongly stressed **h** as in the English exclamation 'aha!' It is not found in initial position. The doubled form is written **ggh**.
- **h**   'h' in E. 'hat'. It is always distinctly sounded.
- **hw**   An aspirated **w**, so written to preserve the influence of **h**.
- **j**   'j' in E. 'jam'.
- **k**   'k' in E. 'kin'.
- **l**   In the E. word 'level' the first **l** is described as 'clear' and the second as 'dull'. The **l** in Cornish is always clear.
- **m**   'm' in E. 'man'. A final single **m** occurs in loan words only. When doubled and following a stressed vowel, the sound is prolonged as in E. 'mummy'. In these circumstances the first **m** may be denasalised to give the group **bm**.

n	'n' in E. 'not'. When doubled and following a stressed vowel, it is prolonged as in E. 'cannot'. In these circumstances, as in the case of **mm**, the first element may be denasalised to give the group **dn**.
p	as 'p' in E. 'pat'. A number of loan words with final **-pp** are thus spelt in order to indicate that the preceding vowel is short.
r	should always be sounded as a clear trip or roll with the tip of the tongue against the upper gum behind the teeth. It should not be allowed to affect the quality of the preceding vowel, even when this is short, or omitted as in some forms of E.
s	's' as in E. 'sat'. When between **m, n, r, l**, or a vowel, whether within a word or externally at word boundaries, it may be partly voiced to a sound beween **s** and **z**. Examples; **an son** 'the sound', **avel sagh** 'as a sack', **asyn** 'an ass'. This change is purely phonetic in nature and has no grammatical significance.
sh	as 'sh' in E. 'ship'. In loan words only. Otherwise the sounds are distinct: **palshe (pals-he** 'increase'(§187)).
t	as 't' in E. 'top'.
th	'th' as in E. 'thick'. The doubled form is spelt **tth**.
v	as 'v' in E. 'vat'.

As shown in §2, a number of the consonantal sounds can be doubled within a word. This means that the position of the speech organs, the articulators, is held for a rather longer period than would be the case with a single sound. Compare the English phrases 'lay down' and 'laid down', both being said without a pause between the two words.

§7   **Vowel length**   The term 'vowel length' refers simply to the duration of the sound of the vowel. Cornish has long, half-long and short vowels but the contrast is most marked between a long and a short vowel, e.g. **mel** /me:l/ 'honey' and **mell** /mel/ 'joint', where the double 'l' shows that the vowel is short. In the table below can be read off, for each of the vowel lengths, long, half-long or short, the situation in which each is found.

Conversely the table shows for each situation what quantity is to be given to each vowel.

Length	Situation	Examples
The vowel is long /e:/	in words of one stressed syllable ending in one consonant	**del** /de:l/ 'foliage'

The vowel is half-long /e./	in stressed syllables ending in one consonant in words of more than one syllable	**delenn** /ˈde.len/ 'leaf'
The vowel is short /e/	in all unstressed syllables whether the syllable ends in one or two consonants, as well as in words of one stressed syllable ending in two consonants.	**delennik** /deˈlen.nik/ 'leaflet' **pell** /ˈpel/ 'far'

Certain common monosyllables which are unstressed nevertheless end in one consonant: **pan** 'when', **kyn** 'although', **an** 'the'. A vowel which is unstressed will tend in normal speech to lose some of its distinctiveness. Compare the 'a' in 'man' with the 'a' in 'woman', the 'i' in 'villa' with the 'i' in 'devil'. Similarly the Cornish vowels 'i', 'y' and 'u' all tend to become like the 'i' in E. 'pin' when unstressed.

STRESS

§8 **General** A stressed syllable is shown by the mark ˋ placed before it. A secondary stress is marked ˋˋ. The stress in Cornish normally falls on the penultimate syllable of a word: **gosˋlowes** 'listen'; **diheveˋlepter** 'dissimilarity'.

Monosyllables are stressed, with the following exceptions:

(1) The definite article **an** 'the'.

(2) The verbal particles **a**, **y**, **re**, **ny**, etc. (§274 to §281).

(3) The possessive adjectives **ow** 'my', **dha** 'thy', **y** 'his, its', **hy** 'her, its' (§51).

(4) The suffixed pronouns **vy** 'me', **ty** 'thee', etc., except the doubled forms which have a secondary stress on the second syllable: **ˋdhymmo eˋˋvy** 'to me' (§64(2)). When used with the word **go** 'woe' however the suffixed pronoun takes the stress: **goˋvy** 'unlucky me!' (§68).

§8(5)   Phonology

(5) The demonstrative enclitics **ma** 'this', **na** 'that' (§50(5)).

(6) Conjunctions in general: **ha** 'and', **pan** 'when', **mar** 'if', etc.

(7) The preposition **dhe** 'to' (§141).

§9   **The stress in compound words**   When prefixes or suffixes are added to a word or when it combines with other words, the compound is usually perceived as a unit and is stressed accordingly. For a fuller discussion see §60, §61.

(1) Prefixes: **mab** 'son', **`anvab** 'childless'; **mamm** 'mother', **`lesvamm** 'stepmother'; **pleth** 'pliant', **`hebleth** 'rather pliant, flexible'.

(2) Adjectives: **tas** 'father', **`hendas** 'forefather'; **lamm** 'leap', **`droglamm** 'mishap'.

(3) Numeral prefixes: **leuv** 'hand', **`diwleuv** 'a pair of hands'; **gweyth** 'occasion', **`unnweyth** 'once'; **liw** 'colour', **`unnliw** 'monochrome'.

(4) Suffixes including verbal endings: **tewes** 'sand', **tew`esek** 'sandy'; **`ugens** 'twenty', **u`gensves** 'twentieth'; **sugal** 'rye', **su`galdir** 'ryefield'; **`diwes** 'drink', **di`wotti** 'pub, drinking-house'; **`lyver** 'book', **ly`verva** 'library'; **kommol** 'clouds', **kom`molenn** 'a cloud', **kommo`lennow** 'individual clouds' **`gweres** v.n. 'help', **gwe`resav** 'I help'.

In the following cases there is no change in the original stress:

(5) With the prefixes **ke-** 'with'; **di-/dis-** 'without': **ke`haval** 'similar' (**haval** 'like'); **ke`hys'** 'of the same length' (**hys** 'length'); **kem`mys** 'so much' (**my(n)s** 'amount') and **kekem`mys**, a double form with the same meaning; **ke`par** 'in the same way' (**par** 'equal'); **di`gnas** 'unnatural' (**gnas** 'nature'); **di`son** 'soundless' (**son** 'sound'); **dis`liw** 'colourless' (**liw** 'colour'); **dis`len** 'dis-loyal' (**len** 'loyal').

(6) With the prefix **keth** 'same' which is often assimilated to the second word of the compound: **kef frys** 'as well' (**prys** 'occasion') and **kekef frys** with the same meaning; **ket`tell** 'as soon as' (**dell** 'as'); **ket`toth** 'as soon as' (**toth** 'speed'). **Kem`mysk** 'mixture' is similarly treated but has a different origin.

(7) The various forms of the suffixed pronouns (§64) have no effect on the stress of the original word: **a`wrussowgh-hwi** 'did you?' **y dhre`hevel e``ev** 'building it'. A secondary stress appears in this last example; (§8(4)).

§11   Phonology

(8) The demonstrative enclitics **ma** and **na** do not affect the stress: **an `lowarth ma** 'this garden'; **an `bibenn na** 'that pipe' (§50(5)).

(9) The compounds of **Dy**'(= **dydh**) 'day' and **mis** 'month' keep the stress on the name of the day or of the month: **Dy `Sul** 'Sunday'; **mis `Me** 'May'; **mis Gwynn`gala** 'September'. Similarly: **dy`goel** 'holiday'; **dy`gweyth** 'a working day, a weekday'.

(10) When a preposition forms a compound with a noun to make another preposition or an adverb, the compounded noun retains its own stress in the new word: **war-`lergh** 'behind' (**lergh** 'track'); **war-dhe`lergh** 'behind' (**de`lergh** 'rear'); **a-`bervedh** 'within' (`**pervedh** 'interior'); **a-dhiwar-`leur** 'up off the floor' (**leur** 'floor'). A few adjectives are made in the same way: **a-dhe`vis** 'exact' (**de`vis** 'plan'); **a-`wartha** 'at the top'(**gwartha** 'top').

(11) When a preposition forms a compound with another preposition, however, the last retains the stress: **a-`rag** 'before', **dhe`rag** 'before', **a-dhe`rag** 'before'; **di`worth** 'from off', **a-dhi`worth** 'from off'.

(12) Verbs formed by the addition of the reflexive and reciprocal prefix **om-** 'self' (§273) are accented normally on the penultimate syllable: **om`weres** 'help oneself' (`**gweres** 'help'); `**omwul** 'make oneself out to be' (**gul** 'make').

In some verbs however the stress remains on the final syllable: **om`ri** 'give oneself up' (**ri** 'give'); **om`dowl** 3s.p./f. of **om`dewlel** 'wrestle' (**tewlel** 'throw').

In a few verbs several meanings are distinguished by the stress: `**omdhoen** 'conceive a child', **om`dhoen** 'bear oneself, behave' (**doen** 'carry'); **om`ladha** 'kill oneself', `**omladh** 'fight', with the loss of an **a**, from **ladha** 'kill' (§232).

(13) Verbs formed by the addition of the suffix -**he** to a stem retain the stress on the syllable beginning with this -**h**: **berr`he** v.n. 'shorten', **berr`hav** 'I shorten', **berr`hasons** 'they shortened', **berr`hes** past part. 'shortened' (§187).

§10 **The stress with following adjectives** An adjective following a noun takes the stress: **moes `hir** 'a long table'; **pows `velyn** 'a yellow dress'. If the noun has two or more syllables, it keeps its own stress as a secondary one: ``**dalleth `da** 'a good start'; ``**gwydhenn `varow** 'a dead tree'.

§11 **The stress in the genitive construction** When a noun defines another noun standing before it (§55), the main stress falls on the second noun: **garr**

§11 Phonology

`margh '(the) leg of a horse'; **jynn-`skrifa** 'typewriter'. If the first noun has two syllables or more, it keeps its own stress as a secondary one: ``**alhwedh** `daras '(the) key of a door'. Similarly, when the second, defining, noun is itself defined in some way, the first noun has a secondary stress: ``**mab y** `das '(the) son of his father'; ``**leur an** `chambour '(the) floor of the bedroom'.

§12 Irregular stress

(1) The following words of more than one syllable are nevertheless stressed on the final syllable:

a`ges	'than'	dre`mas	'good man'
a`hwer	'sorrow'	drog-at`ti	'epilepsy'
an`drow	'afternoon'	e`ghan	'alas!'
(for an`derow)		go`dhor	'mole'
an`koth	'unknown'	god`ramm	'cramp'
an`kres	'disquiet'	goel`dheys	'harvest festival'
at`tal	'repayment'	mygh`tern	'king'
a`vel	'as'	na`hen	'any other'
a`weyl	'gospel'	na`meur	'much at all'
bo`ban	'grotesque image'	nammny`gen	'just now'
bo`ken (poken)	'or else'	na`moy	'any more'
bul`horn	'snail'	na`neyl	'nor'
bys`mer	'infamy'	piwpy`nag	'whosoever'
bytte`gyns	'nevertheless'	po`ken	'or else'
bytte`le	'nevertheless'	py`gans m.	'wherewithal'
de`goedh	'(it) behoves'	py`nag	'whatever'
di`hwans	'eagerly'	py`seul	'how many'
a-dhi`hwans		seula`brys	'just now'
dem`mas	'good man'	seula`dhydh	'some time ago'
de`vri	'indeed'	sow`eth	'alas'
yn te`vri		toet`ta	'at high speed'
di`ank v.n.	'escape'	war-`barth	'together'
di`barth	'separation'	y`ma	'there is', etc.
di`berth v.n.	'separate'	y`mons	'they are'
doha`jydh	'afternoon'	yn`wedh	'as well'
do`los v.n.	'pretend'	y`tho	'so, then'

(2) In the following words the stress comes before the penultimate:

`arader	'plough'	`kenedhel	'nation'
`aradror	'ploughman'	ke`niterow	'female cousin'

dy`gynsete	'day before yesterday'	**`klabytter**	'bittern'
		`lelduri	'loyalty'
`kelegel	'chalice'	**`lenduri**	'honesty'
`kenderow	'male cousin'	**`tulyfant**	'turban'

Obvious borrowings from other languages keep their original stress: **`hardigras** 'vengeance'; **`oratri** 'oratory'; **`trayturi** 'treachery'; **de`vis** 'device, idea'.

§13 **Loss of final consonants** In unstressed final syllables a terminal -v may be dropped: **ena** for **enev** 'soul'; **diwla** for **diwleuv** 'a pair of hands' (cf. §20 (3)).

VOWEL AFFECTION

§14 **Origin** The word **mab** 'son' has the plural **mebyon**. In this plural word the original **a** of **mab** has been affected by the **y** of the next syllable. This process of vowel affection in any syllable is brought about by the speaker's anticipation of the close forward position of the tongue which is required for the pronunciation of **i, y** or **e**. (George, 5.6, LP. p.106 fol., LHB. p.573 fol.). Such changed forms are now part of the lexicon and new formations should conform to the pattern: **tonn** 'wave', **tennik** 'wavelet, ripple'; **fols** 'split', **felsik** 'crack'.

§15 **Vowels affected** Under the influence of the close vowels mentioned above, **a** becomes **e**, **e** becomes **y**, **o** becomes **e**. There is in addition an enhanced affection of **a** to **y** in certain parts of verbs the verbal nouns of which end in **-a** or **-ya**: **kara** v.n. 'love', **kyrriv** 1s. pres.subj. 'I may love'. Certain other verbs have in the 3s.p./f.indic. **y** for **a**: **kavoes** v.n. 'find', **ev a gyv** 'he finds' (§192).

§16 **Examples** Vowel affection will be noted as it occurs in various classes of words but some examples are given here:

	Unaffected	Affected
Plural	**sagh** 'sack'	**seghyer** 'sacks'
Diminutive	**tamm** 'bit'	**temmik** 'a little bit'
Abstract n.	**prov** 'proof'	**prevyans** 'proving'
Past part.	**maga** 'nourish'	**megys** 'nourished'
Verbal n.	**sorr** 'anger'	**serri** 'be or make angry'
Verb	**kara** 'love'	**keryn** 'we love'

§17 OMISSION, ADDITION AND CHANGE OF SEGMENTS

§17 In normal utterance a sound rarely occurs in isolation. Usually it has to be accommodated to the flow of speech and to do so with economy of effort either the segment itself or the surrounding segments (a segment, phonetically, is a point in the production of a sound) may have to be omitted altogether or be modified in some way. Such changes may take the form of the omission or addition of syllables or of assimilation (§18-§20) and are made equally within words or at their points of contact with each other, especially if the words involved are closely associated, forming a unit within the sentence, e.g. a noun with its following or preceding adjective, or a preposition and its noun, etc.

(1) Omission of one of two adjacent vowels, usually the second, or of a consonant between two vowels occurs in certain common phrases or combinations: **ha** + **an** = **ha'n** 'and the'; **dhe** + **an** = **dhe'n** 'to the'; **yma** + **an** = **yma'n ...** 'the ... is' (§50(2)); **ha** + **agan** = **ha'gan** 'and our'; **yn** + **aga** = **y'ga** 'in their' (§52). Other, less regular, contractions, are exemplified by **nevr'** for **nevra** before vowels.

(2) A consonant between one **s** and another may be dropped in parts of certain verbs: **les'sa** for **lestsa** 'he had prevented' (§196).

(3) A **w** before an **s** may be written but not pronounced in parts of certain verbs: **lanwsa** 'he had filled', pronounced as /lansa/ (§193).

(4) A vowel of accommodation may be introduced into certain nouns and adjectives: **hanow** 'name' but **henwyn** 'names'; **garow** 'rough' but **garwa** 'rougher' (George, 5.7) and into certain verbal forms: **restra** v.n. 'make tidy' but 3s.p./f. indic. and 2s. imperv. **rester** (§194-§195); **lenwel** v.n. 'fill' but **lenow** 3s.p./f. indic. (§193).

ASSIMILATION

Assimilation is a change in a sound, generally by its being voiced or unvoiced, either within a word or at word boundaries, under the influence of an adjacent sound. The degree of change will vary between none at all in slow and careful speech to complete assimilation of one sound to the other in rapid speech.

§18 **Voiced and unvoiced consonants**

(1) The following are always voiced:

§20(3)   Phonology

| bb | dd | gg | l | ll | m | mm | n | nn | r | rr |

(2) The following are always voiceless:

| k | kk | p | pp | t | tt |

(3) The following are voiced when a vowel or **l**, **m**, **n**, **r** precedes or follows:

| b | d | dh | g | j | v |

(4) The following may be partially voiced when a vowel or **l**, **m**, **n**, **r** precedes or follows (new lenition; see §22):

| ch | f | gh | h | s | sh | th |

§19 **Unvoicing in like pairs of consonants** There are six pairs of consonants which are alike in terms of place of articulation, one of the pair being voiced, the other voiceless. They are, the voiced member first:

| b/p | d/t | dh/th | g/k | j/ch | v/f |

When the members of a pair come together in any combination, they are both unvoiced: **heb palas** 'without digging' is pronounced in speech of medium speed as /hep palas/; **shap berr** 'a short shape', as /shap perr/; **kok gwag** an empty fishing boat', as /kok kwag/; **rag gul** 'in order to do', as /rak kul/.

§20 **Unvoicing in unlike pairs of consonants**

(1) A voiced consonant is unvoiced when it comes before a voiceless consonant. This occurs most frequently when the second consonant is **h** or **s**: **yn-medh hi** 'said she', pronounced as /yn meth hi/; **mab souder** 'the son of a soldier', /map soudor/. There are other possibilities: **heb falladow** 'without fail', /hep falladow/; **drog chons** 'an evil chance', /drok chons/.

(2) A voiced consonant is unvoiced when it comes after a voiceless consonant. This most commonly occurs after **s** and **th**: **kres Dyw** 'the peace of God' is thus pronounced /kres tyw/; **treth garow** 'a rough beach' as /treth karow/.

(3) An initial consonant **v** in most cases results from the soft mutation of **b** or **m**: **vydh** as a suffix with permanent mutation 'at all' from **bydh**. The abstract

or local suffix **-va** assimilates an **-s** or **-t** before it in some words: **hes** 'shoal' + **-va** = **hevva** 'a swarming'; **skoes** 'shield' + **-va** = **skovva** 'shelter' (32(12), 34(4)). The 1s. suffixed pronoun **-vy** causes the loss of the verbal ending **-v**: **ny vynnav vy** 'I will not' /ny vynna vy/. A **v** in absolute final position is pronounced as **f**: **na vynnav** '(no) I will not' /na vynnaf/. A **v** followed by an **f** is unvoiced: **ny vynnav fia** 'I will not flee' /ny vynnaf fia/.

(4)   The above rules of assimilation apply equally within words and with compounds: **redsyn** 2p.pret. 'we read' tends towards the pronunciation /retsyn/; **godhvos** 'knowledge' towards /gothfos/ or even /goffos/ in rapid speech.

MUTATIONS

Assimilations of the type described above were produced at a former stage of the language and have been reduced to a system affecting the initial consonant of a word in certain grammatical situations.

These systematic changes are called 'mutations'. The several kinds of mutation are named after the type of phonetic change which takes place.

§21   The systems of mutation

The table below sets out the mutations numbered as follows:

1   The original consonant

2   Lenition or 'soft' mutation

3   The spirant or 'breathed' mutation

4   Provection or 'hard' mutation

5   Lenition and provection or 'mixed' mutation

Key to symbols in the following table:

-   No mutation takes place

*   No change after **s, th**

+   In 2nd and 5th state mutations, as though from original **gw-**

KR or KL not affected

§22 **The table of mutations**

1	2	3	4	5	5
Unmutated	Soft	Breathed	Hard	Mixed Normal	Mixed After 'th
B	V	-	P	F	V
CH	J	-	-	-	-
D	DH	-	T	T	T
GA	The G is	-	KA	HA	HA
GE	dropped	-	KE	HE	HE
GI	and the	-	KI	HI	HI
GL	next letter	-	KL	-	-
GR	becomes	-	KR	-	-
GW	the	-	KW	HW	W
GY	initial	-	KY	HY	HY
GO+	WO	-	KO	HWO	WO
GU+	WU	-	KU	HWU	WU
GRO+	WRO	-	KRO	HWRO	WRO
GRU+	WRU	-	KRU	HWRU	WRU
K	G*	H#	-	-	-
M	V	-	-	F	V
P	B*	F	-	-	-
T	D*	TH	-	-	-

There are also a few instances of a nasal mutation (§27).

Gnas 'nature' mutates as words with initial **gl-**, **gr-** except in the compound **dignas** 'unnatural'.

Omitted from this table is any reference to 'new lenition', the partial voicing of **f** and **s** in certain situations (see under these letters in §6). New lenition and its omission from the table of formal mutations is discussed fully in George 5.1.

§23 **Causes of second state mutation** (softening, lenition)

(1) Words causing the softening of the initial consonant of the next word (section references are given) are:

a	rel.part.	'who, which', etc.	§278
a	interr.part.		§277
a	voc.part.	'O!'	§352(7)

§23(1)   Phonology

a	prep.	'of, from'	§126
a-ban	conj.adv.	'since'	§294
a-dhann	prep.	'from under'	§169
a-dhia	prep.	'from, since'	§130
assa	exclam.part.	'how!'	§281
dell	conj.adv.	'as'	§297
dew/diw	num.	'two'	§96
dha	poss.adj.	'thy'	§51
dhe	prep.	'to'	§141
dre	prep.	'through, by means of'	§268
erna	conj.adv.	'until'	§295
fatell	conj.adv.	'how'	§77
hedra	conj.adv.	'while'	§295
hwi	voc.pron.	'you!'	§352(7)
kettell	conj.adv.	'as soon as'	§295
malbew	interj.	'pest!'	§352(3)
mar	adv.	'so'	§84
mil	num.	'thousand'	§103
na	neg.verb.part.	'not'	§291
na	neg.rel.part.		§276(6)
nammna	conj.adv.	'almost'	§267
ny	neg.verb.part.	'not'	§275
pan	conj.adv.	'when'	§295
pana	interr.pron.	'what'	§74(3)
pur	adv.	'very'	§267
re	adv.	'too'	§267
re	opt.part.	'may!'	§229(1)
re	perf. part.		§279
re	prep.	'by!' (oath)	§156
seul	adv.pron.	'so much', etc.	§72(13)
ty	voc.pron.	'thou!'	§352(7)
war	prep.	'on'	§161
y	poss.adj.	'his/its'	§51(5)
yn-dann	prep.	'under'	§168
yn unn	adv.pres.part.		§243(5)

(2) **Words causing second state mutation in some cases only**

an	def.art.	'the' before fem.s.nns. and masc.pl. nns. denoting persons (§50(3a,b))
an	def.art.	'the' before **dew**, **diw** 'two' (§50(3c))

14

bys	prep.	'until' (§140)
heb	prep.	'without' (§148)
keth	adj.	'same' before f.s.nns. but **k-**, **p-**, **t-** are not affected (§83(5c))
meur	adv.	'great' before adj. (§57(2a))
pan	interr.pron.	'what?' as **an** above (§74(2))
unn	num.	'one' before f.s.nns. (§95(3))

A number of prefixes cause incomplete second state mutation (see under separate entries in the chapter on prefixes).

(3) **Constructions in which second state mutation occurs**

(a) Adjectives are mutated:
   - after fem.s. nns. (§83(2a)).
   - after masc.pl.nns denoting persons (§83(2b)).
   - after dual nns. of both genders (§83(2d)).
   - after **onan** 'one' when used as a pron. and referring to fem.s.nns. (§95(1)).
   - after **an huni** 'the one' referring to a fem.s.n. (§72(1)).
   - when forming part of a personal name: **Wella Goth** 'Old Will', **Yowann Verra** 'John (the) Shorter'.
   - when females are addressed and an epithet is added: **Maria ger** 'Dear Mary!' (§352(7)).
   - after **an** 'the' when they are prefixed to, or precede, a fem. s.n. or a masc.pl.n. denoting person; **an debelvenyn** (**tebel**) 'the wicked woman', **an dhrogwesyon** (**drog**) 'the evil fellows' (§83(4b)).

(b) Verbs formed by prefixing an adjective have the verbal stem mutated: **kammdybi** (**tybi**) 'think wrongly'. The adjective is then treated as an integral part of the new stem (§83(4c)).

(c) Compound nouns may have mutation of the second noun (§61(1d, 2e)).

(d) Phrases which have become a conventional unit often show mutation: **gul vri** (**bri**) 'hold in esteem'; **vydh** (**bydh**) 'at all' as suffixed to a noun, etc., **den vydh** 'any man'; **hedhyw vyttin** (**myttin**) 'this morning', **Dy' Gwener vyttin** 'Friday morning', **Kemmer with!** 'Take care!' etc.

(e) Prefixes in general cause mutation, usually lenition, of the word to which they are affixed. As mentioned in (2) above, these mutations are often incomplete.

§23(3f)   Phonology

(f) Tenses of the verb **bos** 'be' change initial **b-** to **v-** when the complement precedes the verb without a verbal particle intervening: **parys veu ev** 'he was ready' (§333(4a)).

(g) The personal pronouns **my** 'I/me', **ty** 'thou/thee' are mutated to **vy, sy/jy** when suffixed (§64(1)).

(h) Proper names of places and persons which are felt to be Celtic are subject to mutation but other, non-Celtic names, may not be: **dhe Gammbronn** (**Kammbronn**) 'to Camborne' but **a Birmingham** 'from Birmingham'; **A Vighal!** 'O Michael!' **dhe Varia** 'to Mary'. To some extent this is a matter of personal taste.

(i) Nouns in appositional genitive when fulfilling the function of adjectives: **bran dre** 'rook' from **bran** 'crow' and **tre** 'homestead' (§23(3a), §55).

(j) Prefixed nouns used as adjectives: **penndhyskador** 'head-teacher' from **penn** and **dyskador** (§61(1d)).

(4) **Anomalies and exceptions**

The word **gorsedh** 'a gathering of bards' becomes **an orsedh** and not the expected *an worsedh. The words **gew** 'woe' and **gyw** 'spear' are respectively **wew** and **wyw** when mutated. Certain borrowings from English are treated as though they were from an original which has been mutated and a back formation restores the supposed original consonant: **bilen** 'villainous' and **bileni** 'villainy' as though **vilen** and **vileni** were mutated forms. Conversely the verbs **desta** and **dustunia** 'testify' have what seems a permanent mutation from **testa** and **tustunia**.

§24 **The breathed (spirant) mutation** involves the change of **k** to **h**, **p** to **f** and **t** to **th**. This mutation is caused by the following words:

(1) poss.adjs. **ow** 'my'; **hy** 'her'; **aga** 'their' (§51(1)(6)(8)).

(2) nums. **tri/teyr** 'three' (§97).

(3) **na-** 'some', a variant of **neb** 'some, any'. It mutates comparative adjs. and **kyns** 'before', **ken** ; 'other'(§83(7)).

(4) **Dy'**, a curtailed form of **dydh** 'day', mutates the word **Kalann** 'Kalends, 1st of the month' to give **Dy' Halann Me** 'May Day', **Dy' Halann Ebryl** '1st April', etc.

§25 **The hard mutation** (provection) is the change of **b** to **p**; **d** to **t**; **g** to **k**; **j** to **ch** (not shown in the table in §22). It is therefore an unvoicing of voiced sounds and the converse of the second state (soft mutation or lenition). Hardening is caused by:

(1) the present participle particle **ow** which is derived from the preposition **orth** (§152(10) and §243).

(2) conjunctions **mar, mars, mara , maras** and **a** 'if' (§292).

§26 **The mixed mutation** involves the following changes: **b** becomes **f**, **d** becomes **t**, **g** becomes **h**, and **gw** becomes **hw**. Initial **go, gu, gro, gru** are mutated as though from an original **gwo, gwu, gwro, gwru**; **m** becomes **f**; **gl** and **gr** are not affected. The 2s. poss.adj. and 2s. infixed pron. **'th** 'thy, thee' differs from this scheme in that **b** and **m** become **v**, and **gw** becomes **w**. However the several tenses of the verbal phrase **y'm beus** 'to have' retain the **b** to **f** mutation: **re'th fo** 'may you have' (§198).

Mixed mutation is caused by:

kyn	conj. adv.	'though' §293
maga	adv.	'as' §84
may	conj. adv.	'that' §291, 'where, when'
ple	interr. adv.	'where?' §74(12)
p'eur	interr. adv.	'when?' §74(15)
py	interr. adv.	'where?' §75
'th	poss. adj. and infixed pron.	'thy' §51(4) 'thee' §65(2)
y	verb. part.	§274
yn	adv. part	§92

§27 **Nasal mutation** occurs in a few words in Cornish: **an dor** 'the earth, the soil, the ground' becomes **an nor** when it means 'the world' as contrasted with **an nev** 'heaven'. Similarly when compounded with **bys** 'world' to give **an norvys** 'the world, the terrestrial globe'. **Unnek** 'eleven' from **unn** + **deg** shows a nasal mutation. **Davas** f. 'sheep' regularly mutates to **an dhavas** 'the sheep' but the form **an navas** is found.

An opposite but not regular tendency is found in the double nasal groups -**mm**- and -**nn**- when these follow a stressed vowel. The first element is denasalised by some speakers to give -bm-, -dn-: kabm (**kamm**) 'wrong', pedn (**penn**) 'head'.

§28

§28   A mutation of **dydh** 'day' is found after words ending in -**n** and the initial **d**- is mutated to **j**-: **dydh** 'a day' but **an jydh** 'the day', **yn jydh** 'in a day'. If the adjective **keth** 'same' intervenes, the mutation is retained: **an keth jydh** 'the same day', etc. The plural **dydhyow** is not mutated: **yn dydhyow tremenys** 'in past days'. Normal mutation obtains in other cases: **dew dhydh** 'two days'.

§29   **Irregular, anomalous or missed mutations**, chiefly in the second state, occur in the classical texts and in place names, so that in such cases the above statements may seem not to apply. For a fuller exposition of the structure of place names, see P.A.S. Pool, *The Place-Names of West Penwith*, 1973, p.11 and O.J. Padel, *Cornish Place-Name Elements*, 1985.

NOUNS

FORM AND FUNCTION

§30 **Forms of the noun** Nouns can be classified as to their form into roots and derived nouns. The words **kusulya, kusulyans, kusulyas, kusulyador, omgusulya, omgusulyans,** are made up of the root **kusul** 'advice' with one or more affixes: **-ya, -yans, -yas, -yador, om-,** each of which has a meaning apart from that of **kusul**. Any further division of this root **kusul** would be into units of sound and not into units of meaning. The word **meyn** 'stones' can be said to be derived from the singular form **men** by the change of the internal sound from **e** to the diphthong **ey** and the noun **seghyer** 'sacks' can be made from the singular **sagh** by an internal vowel change and the addition of a suffix **-yer**.

These changes in form are thus linked to changes in meaning or function, and in the sections which follow, the forms taken by abstract nouns, nouns of instrument or of agency, nouns of place, diminutives and some others are described.

Verbal nouns, which are true nouns associated with verbs, are discussed more conveniently in §233.

§31 **Abstract nouns associated with verbs**

(1) **-ADOW**. A plural form with an abstract meaning (§43(3)): **dannvonadow (dannvon)** 'sending a message'; **difennadow (difenn)** 'prohibition'; **falladow (fyllel)** 'failure'; **kemmynnadow (kemmynn)** 'bequeathing'. In spite of the plural form, referring pronouns are singular (§71): **Difennadow na vokker, anodho ny'm deur kammenn** 'Prohibiting one from smoking, it's nothing to me'.

(2) **-ANS**. Abstract nouns from verbs with the verbal noun ending in **-he** have **-ans** as the ending: **kovheans (kovhe)** 'remembrance'; **gwellheans (gwellhe)** 'improvement', **iselheans (iselhe)** 'lowering' (§187).

Abstract nouns from verbs of the form **annia** with the stem ending in **-i** and with the verbal noun ending in **-a** have an abstract noun ending in **-ans**: **provians (provia)** 'provision' (§186).

The abstract noun **tristans** 'sadness' is from the adjective **trist** 'sad'.

§31(2)

The abstract nouns **bywnans** 'life' and **mernans** 'death' associated with the verbal nouns **bywa** 'live' and **merwel** 'die' have the letter -n- inserted before the ending.

(3) -YANS. Abstract nouns formed from verbs with the verbal ending -ya end in -yans: **redyans** (**redya**) 'reading'; **spedyans** (**spedya**) 'progress' (§188).

No rule connects other forms: **dyskans** (**dyski**) but **mollethyans** (**mollethi**) 'cursing'; **kargans** (**karga**) 'loading' but **megyans** (**maga**) 'nurture, culture'.

§32 **Abstract nouns associated with nouns and with adjectives**

(1) -A. From nouns and adjectives. The ending -a is a reduced form of -edh (§32(3)): **lowena** (**lowen**) 'happiness'; **noetha** (**noeth**) 'nakedness'; **gormeula** 'praise'.

(2) -DER/-TER. From adjectives. The form -der is used after a final -dh, -l, -m, -n, -r, -v, -w. The form -ter is used elsewhere and final -g becomes -k: **pellder** (**pell**) 'distance'; **toemmder** (**toemm**) 'warmth'; **efander** (**efan**) 'spaciousness'; **heudhder** (**heudh**) 'joyfulness'; **hirder** (**hir**) 'length'; **krevder** (**krev**) 'strength'; **bywder** (**byw**) 'liveliness'; **syghter** (**sygh**) 'dryness'; **muskokter** (**muskok**) 'madness'; **palster** (**pals**) 'abundance'; **onester** (**onest**) 'propriety'; **serthter** (**serth**) 'steepness'; **drokter** (**drog**) 'vice'; **karadewder** (**karadow**) 'lovableness'; **kasadewder** (**kasadow**) 'hatefulness'.

(3) -EDH. From adjectives: **euveredh** (**euver**) 'futility'; **keweredh** (**kewar**) 'accuracy'; **meuredh** (**meur**) 'greatness'; **stlavedh** (**stlav**) 'lisping'. **Gwiryonedh** 'truth' is from **gwiryon** 'righteous'.

(4) -EDHES. From adjectives: **plosedhes** (**plos**) 'foulness'; **podredhes** (**poder**) 'corruption'.

(5) -ES. From adjectives and nouns: **peghes** (**pegh**) 'sin'; **sawes** (**saw**) 'soundness'; **syghes** (**sygh**) 'thirst'; **yeghes** (**yagh**) 'health'.

(6) -ETH/-OLETH. From adjectives and nouns: **hireth** (**hir**) 'longing'; **kigereth** (**kiger**) 'butchery'; **ansansoleth** (**ansans**) 'impiety'; **kosoleth** (**kosel**) 'calmness'; **sansoleth** (**sans**) 'piety'.

(7) -IETH/-ONIETH. From nouns and denoting an art or science, belief, status: **falghunieth** (**falghun**) 'falconry'; **medhygieth** (**medhyk**) 'medicine'; **deynieth** (**deyn**) 'deanery'; **mynsonieth** (**myns**) 'geometry'; **losonieth** (**los**) 'botany'; **gwasonieth** (**gwas**) 'servitude'.

§33(1) Nouns

(8) **-NETH**. From adjectives: **furneth (fur)** 'wisdom'; **gokkineth (gokki)** 'foolishness'; **hirneth (hir)** 'long time'; **Kristoneth (Kristyon)** 'Christianity'; **sygerneth (syger)** 'sluggishness'.

(9) **-NI**. From adjectives: **klofni (klof)** 'lameness'; **krefni (kraf)** 'avarice'; **kothni (koth)** 'old age'.

(10) **-SES**. From nouns: **pergherinses (pergherin)** 'pilgrimage'; **skolheygses (skolheyk)** 'scholarship'; **unnses (unn)** 'unity'; **uvelses (uvel)** 'humility'; **yowynkses (yowynk)** 'youth'.

(11) **-URI**. From adjectives derived from loan words: **falsuri (fals)** 'falseness'; **lelduri (lel)** 'loyalty'; **lenduri (len)** 'faithfulness', these last two examples with an intrusive -d- .

(12) **-VA**. From nouns: **ankovva (ankov)** 'forgetfulness'; **diberthva (diberth** v.n.) 'separation'; **kollva (koll)** 'loss'; **skoellva (skoell)** 'waste'; **tremenva (tremen)** 'passing'.

(13) **-VANN**. From adjectives and nouns: **loskvann (losk)** 'burning'; **poethvann (poeth)** 'scorching'.

(14) **-YJYON**. From adjectives: **golowyjyon (golow)** 'radiance'; **poesyjyon (poes)** 'oppression'; **yeynyjyon (yeyn)** 'cold'.

(15) **-YNSI**. From nouns: **ankombrynsi (ankombra** v.n.) 'embarrassment'; **sherewynsi (sherewa)** 'depravity'.

(16) **-YS**. From adjectives: **henys (hen)** 'old age'; **kenys (kan)** 'singing'.

By far the most common abstract nouns are those with the endings -der/-ter, -edh/-neth and -eth/-oleth. The forms in -ieth/-onieth are less common and the other forms mentioned above are represented by comparatively few items in the lexicon.

§33 Nouns of instrument and of agency

(1) **-ELL**. An instrument or tool: **gwynsell (gwyns)** 'fan'; **kravell (krava** v.n.) 'scraper'; **reknell (rekna** v.n.) 'calculator'; **tardhell (tardh)** 'vent'; **yeynell (yeyn)** 'refrigerator'. This is the form preferred for new terms.

§33(2)   Nouns

(2)   **-ER/-YER**. The forms in **-yer** correspond to the verbal nouns in **-ya**. Instrument, machine or mechanical device: **kantoler (kantol)** 'chandelier'; **kolmer (kolm)** 'binder for papers'; **trogher (treghi** v.n.) 'coulter of plough'; **draylyer (draylya)** 'trailer'.

(3)   **-ER/-YER** and **-OR/-YOR**. Agent or doer. The forms in **-yer/-yor** correspond to verbal nouns in **-ya**. Those in **-er/-yer** are preferred for this usage: **gwrier** (verbal stem **gwr-** of **gul** 'to do, make') 'maker, doer'; **spiser** (**spisa** m.) 'grocer'; **moldrer (moldra** v.n.) 'murderer'; **nedher (nedha** v.n.) 'spinner'; **redyer (redya** v.n.) 'reader'; **telynnyer (telynnya** v.n.) 'harpist'; **kuhudhor (kuhudha** v.n.) 'accuser'.

(4)   **-OUR**. This suffix is used almost entirely in loan words denoting an agent or in a few cases an instrument: **brybour** 'vagabond'; **doktour** 'doctor'; **mentenour** 'supporter'; **trompour** 'trumpeter'; **sallyour** 'salt-cellar'; **tallyour** 'serving dish'.

(5)   **-YAS**. Agent. The plural of these nouns is in **-ysi**: **gwithyas (gwitha** v.n.) pl. **gwithysi** 'guardian'; **kevywyas (kevywya** v.n.) 'partygoer'; **oferyas (oferya** v.n.) 'priest'; **riyas (ri** v.n.) 'donor'.

(6)   **-YDH**. Agent: **breusydh (breusi** v.n.) 'judge'; **lywydh (lywyas** v.n.) 'director, president'.

Different forms of the noun of agency may denote different functions: **breusydh** 'arbitrator', **breusyas** 'judge, a member of the judiciary'.

§34 **Nouns of place**

(1)   **-EK**. Denotes a place where some natural product or material is abundant. The plural of these nouns is in **-egi**: **hornek (horn** 'iron') 'iron-bearing ground'; **kowlek (kowl** 'cabbage') 'cabbage patch'; **kelynnek (kelyn** 'holly') holly grove; **lusowek (lusow** 'ashes') 'ash-pit'; **onnek (onn** 'ash trees') pl. **onnegi** 'ash-grove'.

(2)   **-JI/-DI/-TI** 'house' implies a building of some sort. The form in **-ji** is regular; **-di** is found as an alternative to **-ji** or **-ti** after final **-gh, -n** or a vowel; **-ti** is used after final **-gh, -k, -p, -s, -t, -th**: **alusenji (alusen** 'alms') 'almshouse'; **bowji (bow-** 'cow') 'byre'; **klavji (klav** 'sick person') 'hospital'; **lyverji (lyver** 'book') 'bookshop'; **mirji (mir** 'look') 'gallery'; **skolji (skol** 'school') 'school-house'; **kiji (ki** 'dog') 'kennel'. **Meyndi (meyn** 'stones') 'stone-house'; **moendi (moen** 'ore') 'ore store'; **greji/gredi (gre** 'herd') 'cattle-shed'.

§35(3) Nouns

Managhti (**managh** 'monk') 'monastery'; **kleghti** (**klegh** 'bells') 'belfry'; **koskti** (**kosk** 'sleep') 'dormitory'; **popti** (**pob-/pop-** 'bake') 'bakehouse', but **pryntji** (**prynt** 'print') 'printing-office'; **gwithti** (**gwith** 'custody') 'museum'. A final -s in the root element is usually changed into -t-: **abatti** (**abas** 'abbot') 'abbey'; **arghantti** (**arghans** 'money') 'bank'; **devetti** (**deves** 'sheep') 'sheep-cote', but **burjesti** (**burjes** 'burgher') 'guildhall'. Note also **batti** (**bath** 'coin') 'mint' with like assimilation.

(3) -LA. A suffixed variety of **le** 'place': **dornla** (**dorn** 'hand') 'handle'; **magla** (**maga** v.n. 'rear') 'place where something is reared'; **troesla** (**troes** 'foot') 'pedal'.

(4) -VA. A mutated version of -**ma** 'place': **ankorva** (**ankor** 'anchor') 'anchorage'; **esedhva** (**esedha** v.n. 'sit') 'seat'; **gwariva** (**gwari** 'game') 'playhouse'; **kerdhva** (**kerdh** m. 'walk') 'footpath, parade'; **lyverva** (**lyver** 'book') 'library'; **milva** (**mil** 'animal') 'zoo'; **medhygva** (**medhyk** 'doctor') 'surgery, clinic'. Several examples of the assimilation of the final letter of the root word to the -v- of the suffix are found: **marghasva** (**marghas** 'market') 'market place', but **skovva** (**skeus** 'shadow') 'shade'; **soedhva** (**soedh** 'office, post') 'office', but **kovva** (**kudh** v.n. 'hide') 'hiding place'.

§35 Diminutives

These forms are used to denote a smaller or younger state of something, or as terms of familiar address.

(1) -IK. Causes vowel affection in some stems (§14): **mammik** (**mamm** 'mother') 'mummy'; **mynnik** (**mynn** 'kid') 'kidlet'; **plemmik** (**plomm** 'lead') 'plummet'; **tasik** (**tas** 'father') 'daddy'; **tellik** (**toll** 'hole') 'little hole, puncture'. For the plurals of forms in -ik see §43(13).

(2) -ELL: **kornell** (**korn** 'corner') 'nook'; **krugell** (**krug** 'mound') 'little mound'; **loerell** (**loer** 'moon') 'satellite'; **spavnell** (**spavenn** 'quiet interval') 'lull'; **torthell** (**torth** 'loaf') 'small loaf'.

(3) -ENN: **baghenn** (**bagh** 'cell') 'small cell'; **benowenn** (**benow** 'female') 'wench'; **hwegenn** (**hweg** adj. 'sweet') 'darling, sweeting'; **kennenn** (**kenn** 'skin') 'film'; **lostenn** (**lost** 'tail') 'skirt'; **pibenn** (**pib** 'pipe') 'tube'; **skethenn** (**sketh** 'strip') 'small strip'; **towlenn** (**towl** 'throw, plan') 'programme'. It should be noted that this form is identical with that of the singulative (§44), so that in some instances the word may be assigned to either class: **trethenn** (**treth** 'sand, sand-beach') 'patch of sand'.

(4) **-YNN**: **blewynn** (**blew** 'hair') 'a small hair'; **godolghynn** (**godolgh** 'rise in the ground') 'tump'; **hwegynn** (**hweg** adj. 'sweet') 'sweetmeat'; **kroenegynn** (**kroenek** 'toad') 'little toad'; **ponsynn** (**pons** 'bridge') 'little bridge'; **skennynn** (**skenna** 'sinew') 'tough bit of meat'. There are several doublets in these last two classes of diminutives: **hwegenn/hwegynn**, with meanings as above; **tegenn** 'trinket, jewel'; **tegynn** 'trinket, toy'.

§36 Miscellaneous forms

(1) **-AS**. Action or the result of action and derived from a verbal stem, noun or adjective: **boksas** (**boks** 'blow') 'flurry of blows'; **gorheras** (**gorher** 'lid') 'covering'; **gwias** (**gwia** v.n. 'weave') 'web'; **mynnas** (**mynn-** v. stem 'wish') 'wish'; **trigas** (**trig-** v. stem 'dwell') 'stay'.

(2) **-AS**. The capacity of anything, English '-ful': **bollas** (**bolla** 'bowl') 'bowlful'; **breghas** (**bregh** 'arm') 'armful'; **chias** (**chi** 'house') 'houseful'; **dornas** (**dorn** 'hand') 'handful, fistful' and so 'thump, blow'; **hanafas** (**hanaf** 'cup') 'cupful'; **loas** (**lo** 'spoon') 'spoonful'. Note here that **hanaf-te** is 'tea-cup' and **lo-de** is 'tea-spoon' but **hanafas te** is 'a cup of tea' and **loas te** is 'a spoonful of tea' (§59). Some derived nouns are compounds of two nouns. See further examples in §61.

(3) **-(G)WEYTH**. 'Time, occasion': **androweyth** (**androw** 'afternoon') 'afternoon-time'; **unnweyth** (**unn** 'one') 'once'; **Sulweyth** (**Sul** 'Sunday') '(on) a Sunday'. For the use of this suffix in the formation of adverbial numbers see §121(1).

(4) **-(G)WEYTH**. 'Work, craft': **brosweyth** (**brosya** v.n. 'stitch') 'embroidery'; **meynweyth** (**men** 'stone') 'stonework'; **priweyth** (**pri** 'clay') 'pottery'.

(5) **-REYDH**. 'Sex, kind': **benynreydh** f. (**benyn** 'woman') 'female'; **gorreydh** m. (**gor(ow)** 'male') 'male'; **kemmyskreydh** m. (**kemmysk** 'mixture') 'hybrid, mongrel'.

GENDER

In respect of gender, all Cornish nouns fall into one of two classes, masculine or feminine. There are a few doubtful or ambiguous cases (§40).

§37 **The meaning of gender** Gender refers to the noun in context when any one of the following conditions obtains.

§38(6)

(1) The singular noun is mutated by lenition (softening) after **an** 'the' or **unn** 'one' (§23(2)): **benyn** 'woman' **an venyn** 'the woman', **unn venyn**, 'one woman' (feminine).

(2) The noun being singular, an adjacent qualifying word undergoes mutation by lenition (§23(3a)): **ploumenn las (glas)** 'a blue plum' (feminine).

(3) The noun is the referend of one of the pronouns **ev, y, 'n, hemma, henna** (masculine); **hi, hy, 's, homma, honna** (feminine).

(4) The noun is the referend of one of the cardinal numbers **dew, tri, peswar** (masculine); **diw, teyr, peder** (feminine).

Apart from these considerations, gender has no significance and has no implication in respect of the thing named when this is a living creature. Grammatical gender is an aspect of the word in context, sex is a biological characteristic of a living thing. However nouns which refer unambiguously to male or female persons are masculine or feminine respectively.

§38 Masculine nouns

Classed as masculine are:

(1) Abstract nouns ending in **-adow,-ans, -yans, -der/-ter**: **plegadow** m. 'inclination'; **sians** m. 'fancy'; **kuntellyans** m. 'gathering'; **ewnder** m. 'rightness'; **braster** m. 'greatness, size' (§31(1)(2)(3), §32(2)).

(2) Most abstract nouns ending in **-edh**: **euveredh** m. 'futility'; **keweredh** m. 'accuracy'; **meuredh** m. 'greatness'; **stlavedh** m. 'lisping'.

(3) Nouns of instrument ending in **-er/-yer**: **kolmer** m. 'binder for papers'; **trogher** m. 'coulter of plough' (§33(2)).

(4) Nouns of agency ending in **-er/-yer, -or/-yor, -yas, -ydh**: **pregowther** m. 'preacher'; **kuhudhor** m. 'deceiver'; **hembrenkyas** m. 'leader'; **lywydh** m. 'president' (§33(3)(5)(6)).

(5) Nouns of agency or instrument ending in **-our**: **doktour** m. 'doctor'; **sallyour** m. 'salt-cellar' (§33(4)).

(6) Nouns from adjectives ending in **-ek, -yek, -yk** when these denote persons: **kloppek** m. 'lame person'; **sevelyek** m. 'bystander'; **diskryjyk** m. 'unbeliever' (§79(1)(6)(7)).

(7) Nouns of place formed from **-ji/-di/-ti, -la**: **gwerthji** m. 'shop'; **gredi** m. 'cattle-shed'; **marghatti** m. 'market-house'; **dornla** m. 'handle' (§34(2)(3)).

(8) All diminutives in **-ik** and in **-ynn** which are derived from original masculine nouns: **godolghynn** m. (**godolgh** m. 'rise in ground') 'tump'; **kokynn** m. (**kok** m. 'fishing boat') 'small boat'; **meppik** m. (**mab** m. 'son') 'small son' (§35(1), §35(4)).

(9) Names of crafts in **-gweyth/-weyth**: **priweyth** m. 'pottery' (§36(4)).

(10) All verbal nouns: **bos** v.n. '(the state of) being, existence'; **kerdhes** v.n. '(the act of) walking'; **ri** v.n. '(the act of) giving' (§235(2)).

(11) Nouns which refer uniquely to males: **gour** m. 'man, husband'; **tas** m. 'father'; **tarow** m. 'bull'.

§39 Feminine nouns

Classed as feminine are:

(1) Abstract nouns derived from adjectives and ending in **-a**: **lowena** f. 'happiness'; **noetha** f. 'nakedness' (§32(1)).

(2) Abstract nouns ending in **-eth/-neth**: **kigereth** f. 'butchery'; **furneth** f. 'wisdom'; **glasneth** f. 'blueness'; **sansoleth** f. 'piety', **genesigeth** f. 'time of birth' (§32(6)(8)).

(3) Abstract nouns ending in **-ieth/-onieth** and denoting an art, science, belief, status: **bardhonieth** f. 'poetry'; **dororieth** f. 'geology'; **godhonieth** f. 'knowledge, science'; **gwasonieth** f. 'slavery'; **medhygieth** f. 'medicine'; **perghennieth** f. 'ownership' (§32(7)).

(4) Abstract nouns ending in **-va**: **bosva** f. 'existence'; **kabolva** f. 'mix-up' (§32(12)).

(5) Nouns of instrument and diminutives in **-ell**: **gwynsell** f. 'fan' (§33(1)); **torthell** f. 'small loaf'.

(6) Nouns of place in **-ek**: **glowek** f. 'coal-field'; **heligek** f. 'willow grove' (§34(1)).

(7) Nouns of place ending in **-va**: **kuntellva** f. 'meeting place'; **milva** f. 'zoo' (§34(4)).

§40(4)   Nouns

(8) All diminutives in **-enn** and those in **-ik** from an original feminine noun: **pollenn** f. 'puddle'; **kathik** f. 'kitten' (§35(3), (1)).

(9) Singulative nouns formed by adding **-enn** to a collective noun to denote an individual of a class: **fionenn** f. (**fion** 'narcissus' as a species) 'a narcissus plant'; **pluvenn** f. (**pluv** 'feathers') 'a feather' (§44(2)).

(10) Names of settlements, towns and rivers by analogy with **tre** f., **avon** f.: **Kernow** f. Cornwall; **Karesk** f. Exeter; **Tamer** f. Tamar.

§40 **Ambiguous cases**

(1)   **TRA** 'thing' is treated as follows:

As masculine
- accompanying numerals have the masculine form: **peswar tra** 'four things'.
- referring pronouns are the masculine forms: **Kemmer an dra ma! My a'n kemmer** 'Take this thing! I take it'.

As feminine
- mutation takes place after **an** 'the' and **unn** 'one': **an dra** 'the thing', **unn dra** 'one thing'.
- accompanying adjectives are mutated: **tra vyghan** 'a small thing'.

(2)   **POBEL** 'people' is treated in all respects as a feminine singular noun except that referring pronouns and verbs are plural: **an bobel** 'the people'; **diw bobel** 'two peoples' but **An bobel a sevis. Ena y kansons aga han** 'The people stood. Then they sang their song'. **Pobel** has a plural, **poblow**: **poblow Afrika** 'the peoples of Africa'.

(3)   **TUS** 'people' is used as the plural of **den** 'person'. The word is treated as a feminine singular in that it is mutated after **an** 'the' and is followed by a mutated adjective: **an dus** 'the people'; **tus vas** 'good people'. Referring pronouns and verbs are plural: **Ow thus a biw an chi hogen ny drigons ynno** 'My family own the house but they don't live in it'. The adjective **arall** has its plural form after **tus**: **Mir orth an dus erell!** 'Look at the other people!'

(4)   A few nouns are regarded as being either masculine or feminine: **nev** 'heaven'. Other examples will be found in the dictionaries where however a preferred gender will be indicated.

GENDER AND SEX

As stated above (§37(4)), grammatical gender is an aspect of the word as a unit of language and biological sex is an aspect of the object as a living being.

§41 The feminine suffix **-es** may be added to a masculine noun referring to a male person to make a feminine noun referring to a female. This suffix is added to:

(1) Nouns of agency in **-er/-yer**, **-or/-yor**, in **-yas** (the **-s-** in this latter case becomes **-d-**) and in **-ydh**: **brosyores** f. (**brosyer** m.) 'embroideress'; **toellores** f. (**toeller** m.) 'deceiver'; **trethyades** f. (**trethyas** m.) 'passenger across water'; **breusydhes** f. (**breusydh** m.) 'female judge' (§33(3)(5)(6)).

(2) Other nouns: **elses** f. (**els** m.) 'step-daughter'; **kentrevoges** f. (**kentrevek** m.) 'female neighbour'; **managhes** f. (**managh** m. 'monk') 'nun'; **meres** f. (**mer** m.) 'mayoress' or 'woman mayor'; **myghternes** f. (**myghtern** m.) 'queen'; **tioges** f. (**tiek** m.) 'farmer's wife' or 'woman farmer'.

§42 Terms denoting kinship and names of domestic and familiar animals usually employ different words to distinguish the sexes.

(1) Kinship:

tas	'father'	**mamm**	'mother'
mab	'son'	**myrgh**	'daughter'
broder	'brother'	**hwoer**	'sister'
ewnter	'uncle'	**modrep**	'aunt'
noy	'nephew'	**nith**	'niece'
kenderow	'male cousin'	**keniterow**	'female cousin'
gour	'husband'	**gwreg**	'wife'
hwegron	'father-in-law'	**hweger**	'mother-in-law'
deuv	'son-in-law'	**gohydh**	'daughter-in-law'

(2) Familiar animals:

badh	'boar'	**banow**	'sow'
bogh	'billy-goat'	**gaver**	'nanny-goat'
hordh	'ram'	**davas**	'ewe, sheep'
karow	'stag'	**ewik**	'hind'
ki	'dog'	**gast**	'bitch'
kulyek	'cock'	**yar**	'hen'

§42(6) Nouns

| margh | 'stallion' | kasek | 'mare' |
| tarow | 'bull' | bugh | 'cow' |

In some of these cases the noun, masculine or feminine, may represent the species in general or any individual, regardless of sex: **ki** m. 'dog'; **margh** m. 'horse'; **gaver** f. 'goat'; **davas** f. 'sheep'.

The same remark applies to many names of animals, the noun having its own gender regardless of the sex of the animal.

Masculine		*Feminine*	
gryll	'cricket'	**garan**	'crane'
hok	'hawk'	**godh**	'mole'
goedhvil	'wild beast'	**sarf**	'serpent'
sim	'ape'	**pedresyf**	'newt'
etc.		*etc.*	

If it is necessary to distinguish between the sexes of animals, it may be done in several ways.

To denote the female of a species:

(3) The suffix **-es** (§41) is added to the masculine word: **bleydhes** f. (**bleydh** m.) 'she-wolf'; **golvanes** f. (**golvan** m.) 'hen-sparrow'; **konines** f. (**konin** m.) 'doe-rabbit'; **lewes** f. (**lew** m.) 'lioness'; **lowarnes** f. (**lowarn** m.) 'vixen'; **orses** f. (**ors** m.) 'she-bear'.

(4) The adjective **benow** is added to the masculine word. Note that the word remains grammatically masculine although referring pronouns and demonstrative pronouns are feminine: **Ott yn-hons dew er benow, onan anedha owth ystynna hy diwaskell!** 'See over there two she-eagles, one of them spreading her wings!'

To denote the male of a species:

(5) The adjective **gorow** is added to the feminine word. Note again that the gender of the noun remains grammatically feminine and that referring pronouns and demonstratives are masculine: **An sarf worow yw brassa es y vata** 'The male snake is larger than his mate', with lenition of **gorow** to **worow** (§23(3a)).

(6) The noun **gour** m. 'male' is prefixed to the feminine word: **gour-gath** m. (**kath** f.) 'tom-cat'; **gour-logosenn** m. (**logosenn** f.) 'male mouse'. Note that in

29

these cases the grammatical gender is that of the governing word **gour**: **tri gour-gath**, **tri** being the masculine form of the numeral: **An gour-logosenn a dheuth diworth y doll.** 'The he-mouse came away from its hole', **y** being the masculine possessive adjective.

(7) The word **goedh** f. 'goose' has **kulyek-goedh** m. from **kulyek** m. 'cock' and other similar compounds may be made when referring to male birds. The compound is masculine in gender.

NUMBER

Number in Cornish comprises singular, plural, collective, singulative and dual forms of the noun.

§43 **Plurals** The plurals of nouns are formed from their corresponding singulars in a number of ways.

(1) by the addition to the singular form of one these endings:

Ending	Example	
-ow	**koesow**	'woods'
-yow	**luyow**	'armies'
-yon	**mebyon**	'sons' (with vowel affection (§14))
-on	**ladron**	'thieves'
-yer	**prennyer**	'pieces of wood'
-i	**profoesi**	'prophets'
-es	**ewntres**	'uncles'
-ens	**noyens**	'nephews'
-edh	**eledh**	'angels'
-ys	**rewlys**	'rules'
-s	**resons**	'reasons'

Of these endings, **-ow** and **-yow** are by far the most common. The endings **-ys** and **-s** are used with borrowings from English: **paynys** (**payn**) 'pains'; **gytterns** (**gyttern**) 'guitars'. Remarks on some of these forms now follow.

(2) The form **-ow** provides a plural for abstract nouns in **-ans** (§31(2)) and **-yans** (§31(3)) when such nouns are to be given a concrete meaning: **tybyans** 'thought' in the abstract sense, **tybyansow** 'thoughts, opinions' as applied to the results of the activity; **redyans** 'reading', the ability or process as a concept, **redyansow** 'readings', particular acts or occasions of doing so.

§42(10) Nouns

(3) Conversely, the plural form in -adow is used as an abstract noun: **falladow** 'failure' (§31(1)).

(4) When a feminine noun denoting a female has been formed by the addition of the ending -es (§41) to the corresponding masculine noun, the resultant word has its plural in -ow: **kanoresow** (**kanores** f. from **kaner** m.) 'female singers'.

(5) The noun **tra** 'thing' (§40(1)) has the plural **traow** which means 'things' in general, whether concrete or ideal. The plural noun **taklow** has the narrower meaning of 'gear, stuff': **taklow-krambla** 'climbing gear'. **Genes dog dha daklow!** 'Bring your stuff with you!'

(6) The ending -yon is added to singular forms to make the plurals of nouns of agency in -er/-yer, -or/-yor (§33(3)): **kasoryon** (**kasor**) 'warriors'; **holyoryon** (**holyer**) 'followers'; **gwrioryon** (**gwrier**) 'makers, doers'; **formyoryon** (**formyer**) 'creators'. Note that the -e- of the singular ending becomes -o- in the plural.

(7) The same ending -yon is used to make the plurals of nouns ending in -ek, -yk from adjectives with the same endings (§79(1)(7), §90). The -e- of the singular ending becomes -o- in the plural: **edhommogyon** (**edhommek**) 'needy ones'; **diskryjygyon** (**diskryjyk**) 'unbelievers'.

(8) The ending -es is commonly but not exclusively used to make the plurals of names of animals and birds: **hordhes** (**hordh**) 'rams'; **miles** (**mil**) 'beasts'; **puskes** (**pysk**) 'fish(es)'. This form should not be confused with that made when the ending -es which converts a masculine noun denoting a male being is added to a feminine noun to denote the corresponding female (§42(3)).

However there are relatively few cases where this ambiguity can arise: **broghes** (**brogh**) 'badgers' or 'female badger'. The presence or absence of mutation may distinguish the two,: thus **an broghes** pl. 'the badgers', **an vroghes** f. 'the female badger'. Examples of nouns not referring to animals are: **bysyes** (**bys**) 'fingers'; **ewntres** (**ewnter**) 'uncles'.

(9) Nouns of place in -ek (§34(1)) denoting a place of abundance have their plurals in -i: **glowegi** from **glowek** (**glow**) 'coal-fields'; **onnegi** from **onnek** (**onn**) 'ash-groves'.

(10) This same plural ending -i may cause vowel affection in some words: **arlydhi** (**arloedh**) 'lords'; **brini** (**bran**) 'crows'; **gisti** (**gast**) 'bitches'.

§42(11) Nouns

(11) Plurals in -s- and -ys. Most of the words with one of these endings are of English origin. No comprehensive rule can be given as to which words have one or other of these endings. Many Cornish speakers today use a plural in -ow, or -yow for some of these words: **stret, stretow/stretys;** cf. the usage in Welsh and Breton. Vowel affection does not occur before -**ys** in these cases.

(a) Plurals in -**s** are formed from words ending in -**l**, -**m**, -**n** or -**r** preceded by a vowel:

Singular	Plural	Meaning
konsel	**konsels**	'councils'
kwarel	**kwarels**	'claims'
pompyon	**pompyons**	'pumpkins'
skantlyn	**skantlyns**	'templates'
avoutrer	**avoutrers**	'adulterers'
pomster	**pomsters**	'quack-doctors'
spalyer	**spalyers**	'mine-labourers'
spenser	**spensers**	'butlers'
spiser	**spisers**	'grocers'

Exceptions:

In some words of this pattern the vowel of the last syllable of the singular is dropped before adding the plural ending -**ys**:

korbel	**korblys**	'brackets'
trobel	**troblys**	'troubles'
reken	**reknys**	'accounts'
	(also **reknow**)	
tokyn	**toknys**	'tickets'
	(also **tokynyow**)	
menyster	**menystrys**	'ministers'
naker	**nakrys**	'kettledrums'
soudor	**soudrys**	'soldiers'
	(also **soudoryon**)	

The suffix -**ys** is also added, exceptionally, to the following words which end in -**l**, -**n** or -**r**:

kanell	**kanellys**	'taps, spigots'
desir	**desirys**	'desires'
enor	**enorys**	'honours'

§42(11d)   Nouns

(b) Loan words ending in -nt drop the -t and add -s:

garlont	garlons	'garlands'
	(or garlontow)	
marchont	marchons	'merchants'
tulyfant	tulyfans	'tulips, turbans'

Exceptions:

The following words add -s/-ys directly to the singular:

entent	ententys	'purposes'
remenant	remenants	'remains'
sand	sandys	'courses of a meal'

(c) Other borrowed words which add -ys to the singular:

chalys	chalysys	'chalices'
ertach	ertajys	'heritages'
lett	lettys	'hindrances'
	(also lettow)	
offis	offisys	'functions'
pokk	pokkys	'pockmark'
polat	polatys	'fellows'
rewl	rewlys	'rules'
	(also rewlow)	
sloj	slejys	'sledgehammers' (with vowel affection)
tid	tidys	'tides'
trumach	trumajys	'passages by water'

Note however with -s:

degre	degrys	'degrees, ranks'
gyglet	gyglets	'wanton persons'
papynjay	papynjays	'parrots'
vertu	vertus	'powers'

(d) Loan words with the singular ending in -a drop this -a and add -ys:

challa	challys	'jawbones'
chymbla	chymblys	'chimneys'
	(or chymblow)	

33

§42(11d)   Nouns

gaja	gajys	'forfeits'
mata	matys	'mates'
popa	popys	'puffins'
skala	skalys	'bowls'
skila	skilys	'reasons'
spera	sperys	'spears'
tylda	tyldys	'tents'
	(or **tyldow**)	

(e)   The word **kastell** has the plural form **kastylli** when the meaning is 'castle' but **kastyllys** when the meaning is 'village'. **Kestell** 'castle' is plural in form but usually singular in meaning. Both **kastell** and **kestell** may mean 'tor' (O.J. Padel, *Cornish Place Name Elements*, Eng. Place Name Soc. 1985, p.42).

(12) Plurals are also formed by a change in the internal vowelling of the singular: **breder (broder)** 'brothers' (note also the form **brederedh** 'brotherhood'); **deves (davas)** 'sheep'; **elergh (alargh)** 'swans'; **gever (gaver)** 'goats'; **gwer (gour)** 'men, husbands'; **mergh (margh)** 'horses'; **mels (mols)** 'wether sheep'; **meyn (men)** 'stones'; **ydhyn (edhen)** 'birds'.

Change in the vowelling may also accompany the addition of an ending: **brini (bran)** 'crows'; **gwragedh (gwreg)** 'wives'; **mebyon (mab)** 'sons'; **mowesi (mowes)** 'girls'; **tavosow (taves)** 'tongues'.

(13) Diminutives ending in -**ik** (§35(1)) may add -**ow** to the singular ending or -**igow** to the original plural: **meppigow** or **mebyonigow (meppik, mebyon)** 'little boys'; **myrghigow** or **myrghesigow (myrgh, myrghes)** 'little girls'; **lewigow** or **lewesigow (lewik, lewesigow)** 'lion cubs'; **fleghigow** or **fleghesigow** 'little children'.

(14) The singular/plural opposition is expressed in a few cases by the use of different words: **den/tus** 'person/people' (§40(3)); **ki/keun** 'dog/dogs'; **ojyon/oghen** 'ox/oxen'.

§44   **Collectives and singulatives**

(1)   Collective nouns denote a class or a group. They are most common in names of living things such as plants or animals but other types occur: **derow** 'oak-trees'; **gwydh** 'trees'; **lusow** 'ashes'; **meskel** 'mussels'; **nedh** 'nits'; **niwl** 'fog'; **niver** 'number'; **onn** 'ash-trees'; **pluv** 'feathers'. For referring pronouns and verbs see §71(2).

§46(2) Nouns

(2) Singulatives are formed from collective nouns by the addition of the ending -**enn**, giving the meaning 'an individual of the group, a single specimen'. Thus from the examples in (1): **derwenn** 'an oak-tree'; **gwydhenn** 'a tree'; **lusowenn** 'a cinder'; **mesklenn** 'a mussel'; **nedhenn** 'a nit'; **niwlenn** 'a fog bank, patch of mist'; **niverenn** 'a numeral'; **onnenn** 'an ash-tree'; **pluvenn** 'a feather'. Exceptions are: **gwarthek** 'horned cattle' and **mogh** 'swine' which do not make singulatives.

(3) The singulative may itself be given a plural with the addition of the ending -**ow** and this plural will mean 'a number of individuals of the species or class: **ster** 'stars'; **sterenn** 'a star'; **sterennow** 'a number of individual stars'.

§45 **The dual** The numeral **dew** m., **diw** f. 'two' prefixed to a singular noun forms a dual in the case of names of paired parts of the body. The compound word refers to one person: **dewlagas** (**lagas** m.) 'a person's eyes'; **dewdroes** (**troes** m.) 'a person's feet'; **diwlin** (**glin** f.) 'a person's knees'; **diwarr** (**garr** f.) 'a person's legs'. The texts sometimes use the plural where the dual would be expected: **dewdroes Yesus karadow** 'the feet of dear Jesus' but **korf ha penn, treys** (pl.) **ha diwla** 'body and head, feet and hands (of Jesus)'; **Yosep dhe Grist a ewnas y arrow** (pl.) **ha'y dhiwvregh hweg** 'Joseph for Christ put straight his legs and sweet arms' MC. 232.1/2. The duals **dewdroes** and **diwarr** would have been regular in these cases.

For the use of the dual with plural possessive adjectives, see §50(3).

For referring pronouns, see §71(2).

For mutations associated with the dual, see §23(3a), §83(2d) and §96.

§46 **Count nouns and mass nouns**

(1) Count nouns denote separate entities which can be counted and which can therefore be preceded by numerals or words which imply number and which are regularly used in a plural form: **kador**, 'a chair', **teyr hador** 'three chairs', **kadoryow** 'chairs', **lies kador** 'many chairs'.

(2) Mass nouns are not preceded by numerals or by words which imply number and do not occur in the plural except with a special meaning which is described below: **bara** 'bread'; **bryv** 'bleating of sheep'; **bros** 'great heat'; **busel** 'cattle dung'; **daffar** 'gear'; **dowr** 'water'; **gwara** 'ware'; **hoelan** 'salt'; **hwarth** 'laughter'; **kewer** 'weather'; **kosk** 'sleep'; **oyl-men** 'petrol'. If a word which implies number does precede a mass noun or if a plural or a singulative

is formed, it is to be read as meaning 'sort, kind, type': **dew vara** 'two (sorts of) bread'; **Yma oylyow-men nag yns gwiw rag an karr ma** 'There are some (types of) petrol which are not suitable for this car'; **buselenn** 'a cow-pat'.

CASE

§47 Syntactic relationships in Cornish are shown in a number of ways. Nouns and pronouns are not declined to indicate case.

(1) Subject and object (nominative and accusative) are identified by word order, by the relationship of the appropriate words to the verb and its particles (§301).

(2) The English possessive 'of', etc. (genitive) is expressed in Cornish by the simple apposition of nouns with or without a determiner (§50-§52) before the last noun. Alternatively the preposition **a** 'of, from' is used. These constructions represent various ideas: possession, constitution, social relationships, as well as grammatical function (§55-§58).

(3) The indirect object (dative) is represented by the use of various prepositions, chiefly **dhe** 'to' (§141) and **rag** 'for' (§154). The infixed pronouns are in a few cases used as indirect rather than direct objects (§65(7)).

(4) The particle **yn** with a noun denotes manner or means (ablative): **yn attal** 'in repayment'; **yn kettep onan/penn/gwas** 'every one'; **yn ober** 'as a fact, in fact'; **yn prov** 'as a proof'; **yn ro** 'as a gift'; **yn tokyn** 'as a record'; **Myghtern ov ... yn henna y feuv genys** 'A king I am ... as that I was born' PD. 2020-1; **yn skorjys prennyer esa** 'for whips there were sticks' MC. 131.1 (§257(3)).

DEFINITION AND DETERMINERS

§48 **Definite and indefinite nouns** Certain nouns without any formal definition refer uniquely to one individual and are therefore definite by virtue of their meaning. These are the proper nouns of traditional grammar, comprising names of people, places, etc.: **Meryasek, Kammbronn**.

Other nouns are used in a general, indefinite sense: **dowr** 'water'; **kerensa** 'love'; **kummyas** 'permission'; **lowena** 'happiness'; cf. mass nouns (§46(2)).

Between these extremes most common nouns when left undefined refer to any one of the members of a class. Cornish has no indefinite article corresponding

§49(5)   Nouns

to the E. 'a/an': **gwreg** 'wife, a wife'; **moes** 'table, a table'; **bleydh bras** 'a big wolf'; **gwell fordh** 'a better way'; **oes a gres** 'an age of peace'.

However, **unn** 'one' may sometimes be interpreted as an indefinite article (§49(1)).

§49 Limited indefiniteness can be expressed in several ways.

(1) The numeral **unn** 'one' in the sense of 'a certain' is put before the noun: **unn chi** 'a certain house'; **unn venyn** 'a certain woman'; **unn gour da** 'a certain good man' (§95(3)).

(2) The indefinite adj., pron. **neb** may be used, sometimes separately, sometimes as a prefix, in common compounds: **neb chi** 'a certain house'; **neb den** 'some person or other'; **nebonan** 'someone'; **nep-prys** 'sometime'; **neppyth** 'something'. **Neb** may be followed by a plural noun: **neb fordhow** 'certain ways'; **neb lavarow** 'some statements or other' (§72(7)).

(3) The word **vydh** (**bydh**) is put after the noun in cases where a negative is expressed or implied to mean '(not) any': **Ny welis golow vydh** 'I didn't see any light'; **heb gwaya vydh** 'without any movement' (§266).

(4) There is an increasing tendency to extend the use of the expression **pypynag** 'whatever' to indicate indefiniteness: **py towl pynag a vo plegadow genes** 'whatever plan pleases you'; **Py benyn bynag a weli ev, nyns o my!** 'Whatever woman he saw, it wasn't me!' (§72(11)).

(5) The expressions **mab dha dhama, mab dha vamm** 'your mother's son, yourself' and, to a female, **myrgh dha dhama, myrgh dha vamm** 'your mother's daughter, yourself', with a casual, disrespectful or critical implication, are, in the 3rd person, **mab y dhama, mab y vamm** m. and **myrgh hy dama, myrgh hy mamm** f., and equivalent to the English 'so-and-so, someone or other, some man or woman': **An damaj a veu gwrys gans mab y dhama** 'The damage was done by someone or other'.

Formal definition is associated with:

    the definite article **an** (§50);
    the possessive adjectives (§51) which are together classed as determiners;
    the appositional genitive construction (§55).

§50 The definite article

(1) The definite article **an** comes directly before its noun except that the superlative form of the adjective and certain common adjectives may intervene (§84(8)), (§83(4)(5)): **an ladron** 'the thieves'; **an gwella gwas** 'the best servant'; **an hager awel** 'the bad weather'.

(2) **An** is shortened to **'n** after a vowel in certain common combinations: **a'n** 'of the'; **dhe'n** 'to the'; **ha'n** 'and the'; **na'n** 'nor the'; **re'n** 'by the' (oath); **y'n** 'in the'. Other contractions are occasionally found: **dre'n** 'through the'; **yma'n** 'the ... is' (§17(1)).

(3) Mutation by softening (lenition) of the initial consonant of the following word takes place after the article in certain cases (§23(2)).

(a) With feminine singular nouns: **an vre (bre)** 'the hill'; **an dhyskadores (dyskadores)** 'the female teacher'; **an wodh (godh)** 'the mole'; **an wlas (gwlas)** 'the country'; **an grib (krib)** 'the crest'; **an vyrgh (myrgh)** 'the daughter'; **an desenn (tesenn)** 'the cake'.

(b) With masculine plural nouns denoting persons: **an vugeledh (bugeledh)** 'the shepherds'; **an dhellyon (dellyon)** 'the blind persons'; **an wonisogyon (gonisogyon)** 'the workers'; **an withysi (gwithysi)** 'the guardians'; **an gusuloryon (kusuloryon)** 'the counsellors'; **an vestrysi (mestrysi)** 'the masters'; **an brofoesi (profoesi)** 'the prophets'; **an dus (tus)** 'the people'. There is no mutation of the initial t- in **an tasow (tasow)** 'the fathers'.

Two plurals mutated though not referring to persons are: **an vergh (mergh)** 'the horses' and **an veyn (meyn)** 'the stones'.

Clear English borrowings are not mutated: **an doktours (doktours)** 'the doctors'.

(c) With the numerals **dew** m., **diw** f. 'two': **An dhew dhen** 'the two persons'; **an dhiw venyn** 'the two women'. Following this usage the dual is mutated after **an** (§45): **Kemmerewgh e er an dhew dhorn!** 'Take him by the two hands!' **an dhiwskovarn** 'the two ears'. The form **dewdhek** 'twelve' (§100) in the expression **an dewdhek** with the special meaning of 'the twelve' (apostles or jurymen) is not mutated nor are **dewgens/dew ugens** 'forty' (§101(2)) or **dew kans** 'two hundred' (§101(6)).

(4) The definite article **an** is used with some words in Cornish where it is not

§51(4)   Nouns

used in English: **a'n penn dhe'n troes** 'from head to foot'; **dhe'n mernans** 'to death'; **dhe'n nev** or **dhe nev** 'to heaven'.

(5) **An** and a noun, singular or plural, may be followed by one of the enclitics **ma/na** to give the meaning 'this/these', 'that/those': **oll an bys ma** 'all this world'; **Gweres an fleghes ma!** 'Help these children!' **an bows na** 'that coat'; **an dus na** 'those people'. With the pronoun **re** 'some' a plural demonstrative pronoun is formed: **an re ma** 'these (ones)'; **an re na** 'those (ones)' (§72(12)).

§51 **The possessive adjectives** These are as follows:

1s.	ow, am, 'm	'my'	1p.	agan	'our'
2s.	dha, 'th	'thy, your'	2p.	agas	'your'
3s.m.	y	'his/ its'	3p.	aga	'their'
3s.f.	hy	'her/its'			

Remarks on the possessive adjectives:

(1) 1s. **ow** causes breathed (spirant) mutation (§24): **ow hyst (kyst)** 'my box'; **ow hweth (kweth)** 'my garment'; **ow fenn (penn)** 'my head'; **ow thas (tas)** 'my father'.

(2) The abbreviated form **'m** is used after certain monosyllables ending in a vowel (§52). The full form **am** is not now used but is found in the texts: **gans am kar** 'with my father', MC. 93.6. There is no mutation after these forms.

(3) 2s. **dha** causes mutation by softening (lenition) (§22): **dha vos (bos)** 'your being'; **dha dhyskans (dyskans)** 'your lesson'; **dha worthyp (gorthyp)** 'your answer'; **dha weles (gweles)** 'your seeing' = 'seeing you'; **dha golonn (kolonn)** 'your heart'; **dha gwarel (kwarel)** 'your claim'; **dha vamm (mamm)** 'your mother'; **dha begh (pegh)** 'your sin'; **dha droes (troes)** 'your foot'.

(4) The abbreviated form **'th** is used after certain monosyllables ending in a vowel (§52). This word is followed by a modified 'mixed' mutation (§26). Changes are:

from	b-	d-	ga-	ge-	gi-	go-	gro-	gru-	gu-	gw-	gy-	m-
to	v-	t-	ha-	he-	hi-	wo-	wro-	wru-	wu-	w-	hy-	v-

Examples: **dhe'th vodh (bodh)** 'according to your will, as you wish'; **My a'th wel (gwel)** 'I see you'; **Hwans a'n jeves a'th wul (gul) y skrifennyas** 'He wishes to make you his secretary'; **y'th torn (dorn)** 'in your hand'.

§51(4) Nouns

For the reference of **dha**, **'th** see §71(1). Note however that the English translation is given in the plural as 'your, yours'.

(5) 3s.m. **y** mutates by softening (lenition) (§22): **y gavoes** (**kavoes**) 'finding it', lit. 'its finding'; **y vyrgh** (**myrgh**) 'his daughter'. For the reference of **y** see (§71(3a)).

(6) 3s.f. **hy** causes the breathed (spirant) mutation as **ow** 'my' above (1). **hy hador** (**kador**) 'her chair'; **hy helli** (**kelli**) 'losing it'; lit. 'its losing'. For the reference of **hy** see (§71(3b)).

(7) 1p. and 2p. **agan** and **agas** do not mutate the initial consonant of the following word. In combination with certain monosyllables ending with a vowel the initial **a-** is dropped: **ha'gan** 'and our'; **y'gas** 'in your' (§52).

Note that in the texts a contracted form of the 2p. is found, as for **agas**: **rag as lavur** 'for your work', OM. 2766; **war as fleghes** 'on your children', PD. 2643; cf. infixed pronouns (§65).

(8) 3p. **aga** 'their' causes breathed (spirant) mutation as **ow** in (1) above: **aga fobel** (**pobel**) 'their people'; **aga hwartenn** (**kwartenn**) 'their quarter'. Initial **a-** is dropped with certain monosyllables ending with a vowel (§52). For the reference of the 3p., see §71(2).

§52 **Table of contracted forms of the possessive adjectives**

1s.	**ha'w/ ha'm** and my	**na'w/ na'm** nor my	**a'w/ a'm** from/of my	**dh'ow/ dhe'm** to my	**re'w/ re'm** by my	**yn ow/ y'm** in my
2s.	**ha'th** and your	**na'th** nor your	**a'th** from/of your	**dhe'th** to your	**re'th** by your	**y'th** in your
3s.m.	**ha'y** and his/its	**na'y** nor his/its	**a'y** from/of his/its	**dh'y** to his/its	**re'y** by his/its	**yn y** in his/its
3s.f.	**ha'y** and her/its	**na'y** nor her/its	**a'y** from/of her/its	**dh'y** to her/its	**re'y** by her/its	**yn hy** in her/its
1p.	**ha'gan** and our	**na'gan** nor our	**a'gan** from/of our	**dh'agan** to our	**re'gan** by our	**yn agan/ y'gan** in our
2p.	**ha'gas** and your	**na'gas** nor your	**a'gas** from/of your	**dh'agas** to your	**re'gas** by your	**yn agas/ y'gas** in your
3p.	**ha'ga** and their	**na'ga** nor their	**a'ga** from/of their	**dh'aga** to their	**re'ga** by their	**yn aga /y'ga** in their

§55(1)   Nouns

Remarks on the contracted forms:

(1)   The first singular forms **ow, 'm** are used indifferently (§51(2)).

(2)   The full forms **yn ow, yn dha, yn y, yn hy, yn agan, yn agas, yn aga** are acceptable alternatives to the contracted forms **y'm**, etc. In these two-syllable contracted forms the stress falls on the second syllable: y`gan, etc.

(3)   In the 2s. **dhe dha** 'to your' is rarely used: **dhe dha anow mynnav amma** 'I will kiss your mouth', BM. 64.

(4)   **A'y** 'from, of his/its' and **re'y** 'by him/its' have an apostrophe although no letter is omitted, to show that two words are involved. They are spoken as one syllable. In **ha'y, na'y** the final -g of **hag** has been dropped (§283, §284). The 3s.f. forms are written with an apostrophe to mark the omission of the **h-** of **hy**.

§53   A plural possessive adjective followed by a singular or a dual noun has a distributive sense, the 'something' of each individual: **treghi aga briansenn** 'cutting their throats', i.e. the throat of each one; **Klyw agan lev!** 'Hear our voice!' i.e. the voice of each one of us; **I a shakyas aga fenn** 'They shook their heads', i.e. each one did so; **sywya aga bodh** 'following their (own) inclination'; **War aga dewlin yth e ... re erell** 'On their knees ... went others', MC. 195.1. Followed by a plural noun however these expressions have a collective sense: **Ni a gren agan barvow** 'We shall shake our beards' i.e. all together as a group; **Y hwolghas aga garrow** 'He washed their legs', where the emphasis is on the totality of the action.

§54   A possessive adjective is repeated before each noun to which it refers: **Ny leveris mann na dh'y wreg na dh'y fleghes** 'He said nothing either to his wife or to his children'; **Kemmer dha wreg ha'th fleghes** 'Take your wife and your children'; **Gans ow thas ha'm mamm yth eth** 'With my father and my mother I went'. This applies to verbal nouns also: **I a ylli agan gweles ha'gan klywes** 'They were able to see and hear us'. As the examples show, a preposition associated with the possessive adjective need be repeated only if there is to be particular emphasis on its repetition.

§55   **The appositional genitive**   The second noun of a pair may be taken as defining the first which is not then preceded by **an** 'the': **to an chi** 'THE roof of the house'. The status of the second noun itself can be:

(1)   Indefinite: **penn margh** 'the head of a horse'.

§55(2)

(2) A general term: **kost bywnans** 'the cost of living'.

(3) A proper noun: **gour Pamela** 'the husband of Pamela' (= 'Pamela's husband').

(4) Defined by a possessive adjective: **kows ow howeth** 'the speech of my friend'.

(5) Defined by the definite article: **dornla an daras** 'the handle of the door'.

There can be several defining nouns linked by conjunctions: **dyller an lyver ha'y ystynnans** 'the publisher of the book and its supplement'.

The sequence can have a chain of terms, each defined by its successor: **alhwedh daras an chi** 'THE key of THE door of THE house'; **enep dowr an lynn** 'THE surface of THE water of THE lake'; **dor lowarth kares ow gwreg** 'THE soil of THE garden of THE friend of my wife' ='my wife's friend'.

§56 **The range of ideas expressed by the second noun** The ideas expressed by the second, defining, noun, can be put into categories but the classification so made is not exhaustive and some of the categories clearly overlap.

The second noun names:

(1) The subject or doer of the action implied in the first noun: **dre worthyp an flogh ma** 'through the answer of this child'; **wosa bos an den omma** 'after the man was here' lit. 'after the being of the man here'; **bodh an kaderyer yw** 'the wish of the chairman is'; **awos difenn y berghennek** 'in spite of the prohibition of its owner' (§139(9)).

(2) The object of an action implied in the first noun: **own koedha** 'the fear of falling'; **gwrier an jynn** 'the maker of the machine'; **rag mentons an laghow** 'for the maintenance of the laws'; **gul y hwans gwir** 'making his wish (come) true'; **truedh gweles an dra yndella** 'a pity to see the thing so' (§240(1)).

(3) The thing or person possessing the quality or attribute named by the first noun: **klerder an dowr** 'the clearness of the water'; **hys dha bal** 'the length of your spade'; **bywnans souder** 'the life of a soldier'; **galloes an wask** 'the power of the press'; **mynnas an werin** 'the will of the common people'; **hanow dha hwoer** 'the name of your sister'.

§57(2a)   Nouns

(4) The whole of something, the first noun naming a part: **gwartha y benn** 'the top of his head'; **bys yn kres an dre** 'right to the centre of the town'; **tenewenn an garth** 'the side of the yard'; **goeles an nans** 'the bottom of the valley'. If however the first noun is a noun of quantity or of number, the construction with the preposition **a** 'of' is regularly used (§57(2)).

(5) The object of a social relationship: **mab Davydh** 'David's son'; **myrgh pyskador** 'the daughter of a fisherman'; **teylu Mighal** 'Michael's family'; **linyeth myghtern** 'the offspring of a king'; **tus Peder** 'Peter's people'; **kerens y vamm** 'his mother's relations'; **kowethes Kerensa** 'Kerensa's friend'; **lywydh an Konsel** 'the leader of the Council'; **penndhyskador an skol na** 'the head-teacher of that school'.

(6) Origin, the place with which something or someone is associated: **epskop Kernow** 'the bishop of Cornwall'; **pobel an wlas** 'the people of the country'; **mer Pennsans** 'the Mayor of Penzance'.

(7) The possessor of a thing: **chi y genderow** 'his cousin's house'; **dre dhorn estren** 'by the hand of a stranger'; **pyth krav** 'the property of a miser'; **gwerthji Mtr Jones** 'Mr Jones's shop'; **kolonn flogh** 'the heart of a child'.

§57 The preposition **a** 'from, of' (§126) can be used to express several of the relationships described above thus allowing the first noun to be left either undefined or defined in some way.

(1) The possession of a quality or attribute (§56(3)): **hys a'th pal** 'a length of your spade'; **an klerder a'n dowr** 'the clearness of the water'; **sywyans a'n gwrians** 'a result of the action'; **an sywyans a'n gwrians** 'the result of the action'.

(2) When the first noun of a pair denotes some part of a thing named by the second noun and is a noun of number or of quantity, the preposition **a** is used to connect them (§56(4)): **rann vras a'n ober** 'a large part of the work'; **an lyha rann a'n mater** 'the least part of the matter'; **meur a dus** 'many people'; **an bush bras a fleghes** 'the big group of children'; **onan a'th lyvrow** 'one of your books'; **trihans peuns a vona** 'three hundred pounds of (in) money'; **hanter a'n fordh** 'a half of the road'. Certain common words however form an exception to this practice, as follows:

(a) **MEUR** 'much, many, great' has the following constructions, conveniently summarised here.

§57(2a)   Nouns

As a noun connected to the following word by the preposition **a** as in the regular examples above: **meur a boenvos** 'much trouble'; **meur a dus** 'many people'.

As an adjective meaning 'great' directly before its noun and causing mutation: (§83(4)): **meur dros** 'a great noise'.

As an adjective standing after its noun and mutated in accordance with the usual rule (§83(2)): **trygh meur** 'a great victory'; **an fordh veur** 'the main road' lit. 'the great road'.

Note also the expressions **meur a anes** (**anes** adj. 'troubled', m. 'uneasiness') 'very ill at ease': **Meur a anes gyllys on** 'We are become very ill at ease', BM. 2904 and **meur a skant** 'very scarce' (**skant** adj. 'scarce', adv. 'scarcely') : **Dowr yw meur a skant omma** 'Water is very scarce here', BM. 658.

(b)   **NEBES** 'a few, some, little' is placed directly before its noun, plural if it is a count noun, singular if it is a mass noun (§46): **nebes moesow** 'a few tables'; **nebes kloesyow** 'some hurdles'; **nebes sugra** 'some sugar'; **nebes glaw** 'a little rain'. Cf. §72(6).

(c)   **OLL** 'all, the whole of', when preceding its noun, is not linked to it by the preposition **a**: **oll dha gerens** 'all your relations'; **oll an kadoryow** 'all the chairs'.

(3)   Connection with a place, origin (§56(6)): **an epskop a Gernow** 'the bishop of Cornwall'; **an ost a'n chi** 'the landlord of the house'; **an ganoryon a Vreten Vyghan** 'the singers of Brittany'; **benyn a Lannstefan** 'a woman of Launceston'; **myghtern a Bow Sows** 'a king of England'.

§58   The construction with **a** is necessarily used in certain cases:

(1)   When the second noun names a quality or attribute possessed by a person or thing. This is then the opposite sense to that described in §56(3): **dowr a glerder** 'water of clearness' = 'clear water'; **poynt a skians** 'a point of wisdom', **an poynt a skians** 'the point of wisdom'; **den a vri** 'a man of renown', **an den a vri** 'the man of renown'; **gwrians a falsuri** 'an act of treachery', **an gwrians a falsuri** 'the act of treachery'; **ser a gonnyk** (**konnyk** 'skill') 'a skilful craftsman'.

(2)   If the second noun names the material of which something is made, its composition: **dornla a vrest** 'a handle of brass' = 'a brass handle', **an dornla a vrest** 'the handle of brass' = 'the brass handle'; **morthol a ven** 'a stone

§59(4)   Nouns

hammer', **an morthol a ven** 'the stone hammer'; **an garlont a vrialli** 'the garland of primroses'.

By an extension of the same idea, this construction denotes the contents of a vessel or container: **skudellas a iskell** 'a dishful of soup'. The same ideas may be conveyed by simple apposition (§59(4)).

§59   Simple apposition

Nouns or phrases occurring in succession in the same statement, retaining the same syntactical relationship to the rest of the sentence, may present a number of ideas all applying to the same thing: **My a welas ow howeth Mighal, skrifennyas an kessedhek** 'I saw my friend Michael, the secretary of the committee', where the three terms, **ow howeth**, **Mighal**, and s**krifennyas an kessedhek** are equally in the relationship of direct object of the verb and are all attributes of the same being; **lader kleves** 'a thief (in the form of) a disease' = 'a wasting disease'. Thus in the following usages:

(1)   In the names of places: **an avon Tamer** 'the river Tamar'; **an menydh Everest** '(the) mount Everest' = 'Mount Everest'; **an wlas Kernow** 'the country (of) Cornwall'; **an Ynys Vreten** 'the British Isle'. These are equivalent to **an avon henwys Tamer** 'the river called Tamar', etc.

(2)   Titles in which the second element is a personal name: **Sen Pyran** 'St Perran'; **Myghtern Margh** 'King Mark'; **Pab Yowann** 'Pope John'. The definite article can be used if required: **an myghtern Margh** 'the king Mark'; **an pab Yowann** 'the pope John', the orthography then requiring a lower case initial as shown.

(3)   Certain conventional expressions of time: **Dy' Sul** 'Sunday'; **mis Me** '(the) month (of) May', 'May' (§111); **prys te** 'tea-time'.

(4)   Here too may be placed constructions in which the second noun denotes the material of which something is made, its composition, the contents of a container (§58(2)). Thus:

With **a**	Simple apposition	
dornla a vrest	**dornla brest**	'a brass handle'
an dornla a vrest	**an dornla brest**	'the brass handle'
kals a veyn	**kals meyn**	'a heap of stones'
an kals a veyn	**an kals meyn**	'the heap of stones'
kelornas a dhowr	**kelornas dowr**	'a bucketful of water'
an kelornas a dhowr	**an kelornas dowr**	'the bucketful of water'

COMPOUND NOUNS

§60 Compound words in general are usually formed of two elements. Such a compound is called 'proper' if the resultant word is of the same class as the second word of the compound. Thus **gwerthji** 'shop' is a proper compound because it is a noun, as is **ji** (**chi**), the second word. If the compound word is of a different class from that of the second element, the compound is called 'improper'. The word **a-denewenn**, an adverb, 'to one side' is improper because the second word is the mutated form of **tenewenn**, a noun, 'side'.

A further distinction is between close and loose compounds. In close compounds the derived term is written as one word and accented normally: `hirgylgh m. 'oval'; ly`verva f. 'library'. A loose compound on the other hand retains the accents of the original terms, one being secondary: ``war-dhe`lergh adv. 'to the rear'; ``karr-`tan m. 'motor-car'; gwynn-`rudh adj. 'pink' lit. 'white-red'. In this latter case the two elements may be written either as one word or hyphenated as in the examples given.

§61 Compound nouns are proper compounds in the sense defined above. They may be either close ('strict' in some authors) or loose compounds.

(1) Close compounds use the first element rather as a prefix with an adjectival function: **mammvro** f. 'motherland'; **dornlyver** m. 'handbook'. The following points are to be noted:

(a) The two elements are written as one word.

(b) The compound is treated as a single word and takes the appropriate stress: **argh`antti** 'bank'; **dorn`lyver** m. (**dorn** m. 'hand', **lyver** m. 'book') 'handbook'.

(c) It is the second element which determines the gender and plural of the compound: **dowrlann** f. **dowrlannow** pl. (**dowr** m., **glann** f.) 'waterside'.

(d) Mutation (lenition) of the initial letter of the second noun takes place whatever the gender of the nouns involved, unless inhibited by a final -s or -th in the first noun (§22): **minvlew** 'facial hair' (**min** m. 'face', **blew** coll. 'hair'); `kaskyrgh m. kas`kyrghow pl. (**kas** f. 'war', **kyrgh** m. 'way') 'campaign'.

(e) Common elements in the first place are: **DORN** 'hand': **dornla** m. (**le/la** 'place') 'handle'; (§34(3)); **DOWR** 'water': **dowrgi** m. (**ki** 'dog') 'otter';

§61(2d)   Nouns

MAMM 'mother': **mammskrif** m. (**skrif** 'writing') 'manuscript'; **MOR** 'sea': **morvleydh** m. (**bleydh** 'wolf') 'shark'; **PENN** 'head, chief': **penndhyskador** m. (**dyskador** 'teacher') 'head-teacher'.

Note however **penn-bloedh** 'anniversary'; **penn-tir** 'headland' in which **penn** 'head, end' is the principal word, the compounds being loose ones, the plurals of which are **pennow-bloedh** and **pennow-tir**; see (2) below.

(f) Common elements in the second place are: **GWEYTH** f. 'time' (§36(3)): **dydhweyth** f. (**dydh** m. 'day') 'daytime'; **nosweyth** f. (**nos** f. 'night') 'night-time'; **GWEYTH** m. 'work': **priweyth** m. (**pri** 'clay') 'pottery'; **GWAS** m. 'man, servant': **skrifwas** m. (**skrif** 'writing') 'clerk'; **JI/TI/DI** m. 'house, building' (§34(2)): **krowji** m. (**krow** 'shed') 'shed'; **batti** m. (bath 'coin') 'mint'; **LENN** f. 'cloth, fabric': **leurlenn** f. (**leur** m. 'floor') 'carpet'; **LES** m. 'plant, wort': **bo`reles** m. (**bora** m. 'dawn') 'daisy'; **koskles** m. (**kosk** m. 'sleep') 'poppy'; **trenkles** m. (**trenk** adj. 'sour') 'rhubarb'. In some cases the word **les** is in the first place and then forms a loose compound: **lesloes** m. (**loes** adj. 'grey') 'horehound'; **lesparos** m. (**paros** m. 'wall') 'pellitory'; see (2) below.

(g) Close compounds are also formed by joining an adjective to a following noun. A list of such prefixed adjectives is given in §83(4): **gowle`verel** v.n. (**gow** 'lie', **leverel** v.n. 'saying') 'speaking falsely'; **kamm`dybyans** m. (**kamm** 'wrong', **tybyans** 'opinion') 'wrong opinion, mistake'.

(2) Loose compounds put the defining noun in the second place and therefore are examples of the genitive of apposition (§55, §56). This second noun is often a verbal noun.

Points to note are:

(a) Words are usually joined by a hyphen. The second word retains the main stress with a secondary stress in the first word: ``jynn-`skrifa** m. 'typewriter'.

(b) Either of the words joined may be plural: **bugel-deves** m. (**bugel** m. 'shepherd', **deves** pl. of **davas** 'sheep') 'shepherd'; **eskelli-kroghen** m. (**eskelli** pl. of **askell** 'wings', **kroghen** 'skin') 'bat'.

(c) It is the first element which determines the gender and plural of the compound: **bran-dre** f., **brini-tre** pl. (**bran** 'crow', **tre** 'homestead') 'rook'.

(d) The compound is treated as a single word and can be preceded by the

§61(2d) Nouns

definite article **an** or by a possessive adjective or be itself a defining word: **an vran-dre** f. 'the rook'; **ow jynn-amontya** m. 'my computer'; **penn eskelli-kroghen** 'the head of a bat'.

(e) Since the second, qualifying, word is effectively an adjective, then its initial letter undergoes the appropriate mutation (lenition) in the same way, that is to say after feminine singular nouns or masculine plural nouns referring to persons (§83(2)). Thus:

	Singular		Plural	
f.	**kador-vregh**	(**bregh** 'arm')	**kadoryow-bregh**	'armchair(s)'
f.	**mamm-wynn**	(**gwynn** 'white')	**mammow-gwynn**	'grandmother(s)'
m.	**mab-gwynn**		**mebyon-wynn**	'grandson(s)'

Mutation of some initial letters is inhibited when the final sound of the first word is -s or -th: **pows-dhemmedhyans** (**pows** f. 'gown', **demmedhyans** 'marriage') 'wedding-gown' but **pows-kosk** (**kosk** 'sleep') 'nightdress'; **kweth-wolghi** (**kweth** f. 'cloth', **golghi** 'washing') 'dishcloth', but **pows-kroghen** (**kroghen** 'skin') 'coat of skin' (§22).

(3) Improper compounds formed by the association of a noun and adjective follow the same rules: **spern-du** (**spern** coll., **du** 'black') 'blackthorn' but **spernenn-dhu** (**spernenn** sing.) 'a blackthorn tree'; **den-da** (**den** 'person', **da** 'good') 'relative by marriage' but **tus-dha** (**tus** pl.) 'relatives by marriage'.

For adjectival phrases see §89.

For compounds formed with prefixes see §268 to §273.

❖ ❖ ❖ ❖ ❖ ❖

PRONOUNS

§62 **The forms of the personal pronouns** The following table shows the forms of the personal pronouns and includes for completeness the possessive adjectives (= dependent possessive pronouns).

	1s.	2s	3s.m.	3s.f.	1p.	2p.	3p.
Independent	my	ty	ev	hi	ni	hwi	i
Suffixed single	-vy	-jy	-ev -e	-hi	-ni	-hwi	-i
Suffixed double	-evy	-tejy	-eev	-hyhi	-nyni	-hwyhwi	-ynsi
Suffixed reduced	-ma -a	-ta -a	-va -a	-	-	-	-
Infixed	'm	'th	'n	's	'gan 'n	'gas 's	's
Dependent possessive (poss. adjs. see §52)	ow	dha	y	hy	agan	agas	aga

§63 **Independent pronouns** The independent forms are used as equivalent to nouns in the following cases:

(1) As the subject of a nominal sentence (§303). The pronoun heads the sentence and the following verb is 3s. whatever the person and number of the pronoun: **My a grys** 'I believe'; **Ty eth** 'You went'; **Hwi yw** 'You are' **I re dhothya** 'They had come'.

(2) An independent pronoun can stand before the verb in a verbal sentence (§302); thus drawing attention to the subject implied in the verbal ending by anticipating it: **Hwi kyn hyllowgh y wul, neb ken a'n gwra** 'Although you are able, someone else does it'; **Ty a-ban gewssys, pub huni a woer konvedhes an dra** 'Since you spoke, everyone can understand the matter'.

(3) Negative sentences, being verbal sentences, can have a similar anticipatory subject: **Ty, ny wodhes** 'You, you didn't know'; **Ni ny yllyn mos** '(As for us) we cannot go' (§302(6)).

(4) An independent pronoun before a verbal phrase, having an infixed pronoun as its object, anticipates and draws attention to that object: **Ev pan y'n gwelav** '(As to him) when I see him'; **ni mar ny'gan menegsens** 'if they had not mentioned us'.

§63(5) Pronouns

(5) The complement of the verb **bos** 'be' is sometimes an independent pronoun (§331(3)), §333(3)): **Yw my henna?** 'Am I that one?' MC. 43.4. **My ywa** 'It is I'. **Yw hwi eus omma?** 'Is it you (who) are here?' **Henna yw ev** 'That one is he'.

(6) An independent pronoun can be the subject of the construction conveniently called the infinitive construction, consisting of the preposition **dhe** 'to' with the verbal noun: **ty dhe vynnes ow gweres** '(that) you will help me', lit. 'you to wish to help me'; **ev dhe dhos omma** '(that) he came here', lit. 'he to come here'. For the uses of this construction see §141(19) and §334(3).

(7) Certain descriptive phrases begin with the conjunction **ha** 'and' and a noun or dependent pronoun. The verbal element of such phrases is expressed through an adjective, a past participle or the present participle construction. The English equivalent in this last case is a phrase beginning with 'as' or 'while': **ha my gwann** 'I being weak'; **hag ev gwarnyes** 'and he (having been) warned'; **hag i ow kortos** 'as they (are/were) waiting'. The notion of time has to be supplied by the context: **Ughel y harmsons hag i ow kul ges anedhi** 'Loudly they shouted as they were making fun of her' (§351).

(8) Equative comparisons in some cases have **ha** 'and' before the second term of the comparison and this second term may be an independent pronoun: **kepar ha my** 'like me'; **kehys hag i** 'the same length as they (are)' (§287).

(9) The pronoun object of some prepositions is the independent form: **war-tu ha ty** 'towards you'; **a-der ni** 'without us'.

§64 **Suffixed pronouns** in their various forms are enclitics. They are attached to nouns in the possessive construction, to inflected verbs and to pronouns with personal endings, and reinforce or emphasise a previously expressed pronoun or one implied in the verbal or personal ending. They are particularly used in interrogative sentences: **Ple'th eth ev?** 'Where did he go?'

The single and the double forms are written separately. The reduced forms are joined to the previous word, when this is a verb, with an apostrophe in place of the dropped verbal ending: **aga soedh i** 'their job'; **Piw osta?** 'Who are you?; **A vynn'ta mos?** 'Will you go?'

The pronoun is joined to an adjective following a noun: **dha gusul vas ty** 'your good advice'.

Remarks on the several forms of the suffixed pronouns now follow:

50

§64(3) Pronouns
(1) Single forms

1s.   -**vy**, is the mutated form of **my**.
2s.   -**jy**, has undergone a double change, -**ty** to -**dy** to -**jy**.
3s.m. -**e** is a reduced form of -**ev**.

(2) Double forms (emphatic). These pronouns, like the single suffixed forms, are attached to a noun in the possessive construction, an inflected verb, or a preposition with a personal ending. A secondary stress falls on the final syllable (§8(4)): `**ganso e**``**ev** 'with him'; **ow deuv** `**hweg e**``**vy** 'my dear son-in-law'. The difference between the significance of the single forms and that of the double forms is one of emphasis, thus: **ow lyver** 'my book'; **ow lyver vy** '*my* book'; **ow lyver evy** 'MY book'.

(3) Reduced forms. The reduced forms consist of the first element of the double form. For example the original 1s. double form **mevy** became **me vy** and then, with the loss of the second element, **me**, usually written as part of the verb. This was interpreted as **ma**. A further reduction gave the form **a**, common to all the singular forms. The plural forms are not reduced.

These reduced pronouns are used only with commonly occurring verbs such as **bos** 'be' (§197) and the auxiliaries **gul** 'do, make' (§225), **mynnes** 'will' (§226), **galloes** 'be able' (§227), **godhvos** 'know, understand' (§200). The verb itself is often shortened and the suffix is written with it as one word.

1s.   MA/A. The -**v** of the verbal ending -**av** is dropped: **gwra'ma** (= gwrav + ma) 'I do'; **o'ma** (= ov + ma) 'I am'; **a'ma** (= av + ma) 'I go'.

2s.   TA/A. The verbal endings -**dh**, -**ydh** are often dropped and -**sys**, -**ses** become -**s**: **mars osta/o'ta** 'if you are'; **A wre'ta ?** (= wredh, 2s. p./f. of **gul** + ta) 'do you?' **gwruss'ta** (gwrussys, 2s. pret. of **gul** + ta) 'you did'; **gwruss'ta** (gwrusses, 2s. plup. of **gul** + ta) 'you had done'; **gyll'ta** (gyllydh, 2s. p./f. of **galloes** + ta) 'you can', but **beusta** (beus, 2s. pret. of **beus** + ta) 'you were'.

3s.   VA/A: **ywa** (yw + a) 'he/it is'; **gwruga** (gwrug, 3s. of **gul** + a) 'he did'; **ymava** (= yma + va) 'he/it is'; **ova** (o 3s. imperf. of **bos** + va) 'he/she/it was'; **bova** (bo 3s. pres.subj. of **bos** + va) 'he/she/it may be'.

The reduced forms have lost their emphasising force and are now virtually equivalent to verbal endings: **Oma vy?** 'Am I?' **Pandr'ra'ma vy?** 'What am I to do?' **A wre'ta jy neuvya?** 'Do you swim?' **A yll'ta jy lamma mar bell?** 'Can you jump so far?' **Prag na'n gwith'ta jy?** 'Why don't you look after it?' **Ple'mava ev?** 'Where is he?' **Yn Lannstefan ymava ev** 'He is in Launceston'.

§65 Pronouns

§65 Infixed pronouns are so called because they come between a verbal particle and the verb. Remarks on their form and uses follow.

(1) The apostrophe which precedes the pronoun is a writing convention. Hyphens have been used but the apostrophe is more usual: **my a'n gwel** (my a-n gwel) 'I see him/it'.

(2) Only the 2s. causes mutation (mixed) (§26, §52(3)): **mar ny'th welav (gwelav)** 'if I don't see you'.

(3) The 1p. and 2p. have in literary usage alternative, shorter forms; **'n**, **'s**: **hwi a'n pys** 'you ask us'; **my a's gwarnyas** 'I warned you'.

(4) The infixed pronoun is in most cases the direct object of the verb: **neb re'n gwerthas seulabrys** 'who has already sold it'.

(5) The infixed pronoun sometimes refers back to a direct object already mentioned: **an vleujenn pan y's torras hi** 'the flower when she picked it'; **i kettell y's pysis an venyn** 'they as soon as the woman asked them'. It is not however obligatory to insert the infixed pronoun in such constructions: **an vleujenn pan dorras hi; i kettell bysis an venyn** are also used.

(6) Infixed pronouns can be reinforced by a suffixed pronoun: **My a'n lett ev** 'I prevent him'; **An medhyk re's sawyas hi** 'The doctor has cured her'.

(7) In several cases the infixed pronoun represents an indirect object (dative).

(a) In forms of the verbal phrase **y'm beus** 'I have', etc. (§198). The verbal element in these phrases is the 3s. of a tense of **bos** 'be' and so the literal meaning is 'there is to me', etc.

(b) The defective verb **deur** 'it concerns', used only in this, the 3s. present: **ny'm deur** 'it matters not to me', 'I do not care'; **ny'th teur** 'it doesn't concern you' (§246(3)).

(c) With the verbs **darvos** (§203), **hwarvos** 'happen' (§202) instead of the preposition **dhe** 'to' and a personal ending: **Bythkweyth ny'm darva** 'It never happened to me' (§141(6)).

§66 Pronouns with the imperative A pronoun with the imperative expresses either the subject or the object, as follows:

§67 Pronouns

(1) The subject of the second person imperative is implied by the form of the verb but may be reinforced by a separate pronoun, either an independent form before the verb or a suffixed form after it. Singular: **Ke!**; **Ty ke!**; **Ke jy!**; **Ke dhejy**; **Ty ke jy!**; **Ty ke dhejy!** 'Go!' Plural: **Ewgh!**; **Hwi ewgh!**; **Ewgh hwi!**; **Ewgh hwyhwi!**; **Hwi ewgh hwi!**; **Hwi ewgh hwyhwi!** 'Go!' **Sevewgh!**; **Hwi sevewgh!**; **Hwi sevewgh hwi!** 'Stand!' The first expression in each series is the least, the last the most, emphatic.

(2) The subject of the other persons is the appropriate suffixed pronoun: **Gwren ni mos!** 'Let's go!' **Kemmeres ev an piwas** 'Let him have the prize!' **Bedhens i furra nessa!** 'Let them be wiser next (time)!'

(3) The object of the verb is expressed in a number of ways.

(a) By a suffixed pronoun (§64): **Holyewgh vy!** 'Follow me!' **Hwi holyewgh vy!** 'Follow me, you!' **Synsyn e!** 'Let's grab him/it!' **Gwereses hi!** 'Let him help her!' **Daskorr i dhodho!** 'Return them to him!' Note that the form of the 3s.m in these cases is **e**.

(b) Occasionally by an independent pronoun before the verb: **Ev gwra!** 'Do it!'

(c) More rarely, in a literary style, by the use of an infixed pronoun (§65) between the particle **a** and the verb: **A'gan gwereses!** 'Let him help us!' **A's gwelyn ni!** 'Let us see them!' **A'n klywens!** 'Let them hear him!'(§278(2c)). The negative particle is **na**: **Na's shyndyens i!** 'Let them not hurt them!' (§276). Note that the verb **gasa** 'let, allow, leave' would be employed to provide the phrase **Na's gas dh'aga shyndya** 'Don't let them hurt them!' The same verb is used to make a 1s. imperative (§183).

(4) A linking pronoun is necessarily used when a noun object has preceded the verb: **An bleujennow ma, rester i** 'These flowers, arrange them!'

(5) Verbs with the verbal ending **-ya** (§188) normally drop the ending in the 2s. of the imperative but when followed by the independent forms **e** 'he/it' and **i** 'they', the **-y** is retained: **Red an lyther!** 'Read the letter!' but **Redy e!** 'Read it!'

§67 **OTTA/AWOTTA, OTT/AWOTT** (the latter pair preferred before vowels) 'see!' 'behold!' 'lo!' are interjections, but have the verbal force of an imperative. The pronominal endings are as follows:

§67   Pronouns

ottavy	'here I am!'	ottani	'here we are!'
ottajy	'there you are!'	ottahwi	'there you are!'
ottava/ottensa	'there he/it is!'	ottensi	'there they are!'
ottahi/ottensi	'there she/it is!'		

The second form given for the 3s.m. and 3s.f. is the conjunctive form of the pronoun as is the 3p. These forms were originally used to contrast the person or thing indicated with another already mentioned but in modern usage they are merely alternatives.

These words are used to call attention to someone or something. They may have the adverbs **omma** 'here, now', **ena** 'there, then' attached as a suffix or separately written. Any of the forms given above may be so used: **Ottomma, awotta omma,** 'See here, now!' **Ottena, otta ena** 'See there, then!' **Omma ottaty golghys!** 'Now see you are washed!' BM. 1832; **Ottensi omma!** 'Here she is!' (§352(7)).

§68 **GO**, an exclamative form of **gew** m. 'woe', cf. §88, is combined with pronouns thus: **go vy**; **go jy**; **go ev**; **go hi**; **go ni**; **go hwi**; **go i**. The meaning is 'unlucky me!' 'poor old me!' 'woe betide!' etc. All are pronounced as two syllables and stressed on the last. The cause of the sorrow, distress, if stated, is expressed by the use of one of the following constructions:

(1) A clause introduced by a conjunction: **Go ev pan y'n synssiv!** 'Woe betide him when I catch him!'

(2) A relative clause: **Go i a wra dha serri!** 'Bad luck to those who make you angry!' **Go ev na worfenn y hwel!** 'Woe betide him who doesn't finish his work!'

(3) A verbal noun with or without a possessive adjective to denote the object: **Go hi trebuchya mar boes!** 'Unlucky her (to) stumble so heavily!' **Go vy y vones ow eskar!** 'It's unfortunate for me that he's my enemy' lit. 'his being my enemy'.

(4) A clause introduced by the preposition **rag** 'for' (§154): **go ni rag esedha y'n tyller na!** '(It's) unfortunate for us (that) we sat in that place!'

DEMONSTRATIVE PRONOUNS

Some demonstrative pronouns are always independent. Others are used either dependently or independently.

§69 **Independent demonstrative pronouns are singular or plural**

(1) Singular are **hemma** m., **homma** f. 'this'; **henna** m., **honna** f. 'that'. Of these, **hemma** and **homma** refer to persons or things near at hand, present at the time of speaking, and **henna**, **honna** denote persons or things not near at hand, not present at the time of speaking: **Deber hemma!** 'Eat this!' **Gallas honna tramor** 'That one (woman) has gone overseas'.

All four forms are shortened before **yw** 'is' and **o** 'was', but not elsewhere, to **hemm, homm, henn, honn**: **Hemm yw ow chi** 'This is my house'; **Honn o gokki** 'That (female) was silly'.

(2) The plural forms are, **an re ma** 'these'; **an re na** 'those': **An re ma a worthybis** 'These replied' (§72(12)).

(3) **AN KETH** 'the same' (§83(5c)) is often combined with the above expressions to give the meanings 'the one/ones mentioned', 'the same one/ones': **an keth homma** f. 'this same one'; **an keth henna** m. 'that same one'; **An keth re na a sevis orto** 'Those same ones opposed him'.

§70 Dependent or independent are the demonstratives which signify alternatives.

(1) **AN EYL** as an independent pronoun means 'the other, the latter, the last of several things just mentioned': **Hwans a'm beus a redya pella ha hwans a'm beus a vos dhe goska, an eyl a vynnav y wul** 'I wish to read longer and I wish to go to sleep, I will do the latter'; **Keffrys Bretonek ha Kernewek yw yethow keltek; an eyl a gowsav** 'Both Breton and Cornish are Celtic languages; I speak the latter'; **Piw yw henna a dheu dhe'n dre ... ow mos war-tu ha'n Templa? My a grys y kemmersa hwath an eyl kyns es merwel** 'Who is that who comes townward ... going towards the Temple? I believe he will have taken this (the Temple) yet before he dies', PD. 320-4.

(2) As independent alternatives the following sets are employed:

§70(2)   Pronouns

For the nearer or last mentioned item		For the remoter or first mentioned item	
AN EYL	'the one, this one'	Y GILA m.	kila 'fellow'
HEMMA m.	'this'	HY BEN	ben f. (cf. benow 'female')
HOMMA f.	'this'	AN KYNSA	'the first'
AN NESSA	'the nearer'	AN ARALL	'the other'

Only if both terms are feminine in gender is **hy ben** used. Thus in referring to two books (**lyver** m.): **Kemmer an eyl mes gas y gila** 'Take this one but leave the other'; to two children, a boy and a girl: **Yma dhyn dew flogh, Petrek ha Tamsyn; an eyl yw peswar bloedh ha'y gila yw hwegh bloedh** 'We have two children, Petrock and Tamsyn; the latter is four years old and the former is six years old'. Speaking of two women: **An eyl yw kottha es hy ben a dri bloedh** 'This second one is older than the other by three years'; **My a dell toll rag an eyl (leuv** f.) … **My a dell toll rag hy ben** 'I will bore a hole for the one (hand) … I will bore a hole for the other' (second and third executioners) PD. 2743-49.

(3)   **AN ARALL** 'the other' is also used as an independent pronominal and can be paired with an appropriate alternative term: **Hemm o chi ow thas gwynn, an arall o an chi may triga y vroder** 'This was my grandfather's house, the other was where his brother lived'.

(4)   Used dependently, **an eyl** is paired with the adjective **arall**, pl. **erell** (§81): **Ni a war an eyl fordh ha hwi, kewgh war an fordh arall!** 'We go by the one road and you, go by the other!; **An eyl re a vynna mos mes an re erell a's tevo own** 'These were willing to go but the others were afraid'.

§71   **Reference of pronouns and possessive adjectives**

(1)   Second person. In direct address the pronouns of the second person are used having regard to the number of people spoken to. Thus Modern Cornish uses the singular to individuals and the plural to groups. In accordance with the usual English practice, both forms are rendered in translation as 'you, your'.

Singular: **An aval, ty, kemmer, tann!** 'The apple, you (thou) take it!' **My a'th pys** 'I ask you (thee)'; **Ev a aswonn dha das** 'He knows your (thy) father'.

Plural: **Ha hwi, gwrewgh e, ytho!** 'And you, do it, then!' **Lowena re'gas bo!** 'May you have happiness!' **Yw hemma agas lyver?** 'Is this your book?'

In the texts an individual is sometimes addressed in the plural as a mark of respect: **Hwi hag oll agas pobel** 'You and all your people' (Duke of Brittany to

King Conan, BM. 242); **Agas pysi y fynnav** 'I will beseech you' (Meriasek as a youth to the Bishop of Kernow). This practice is subject to variation. A messenger addresses the Duke of Brittany: **Arloedh, dha vodh a vydh gwrys** 'Lord, thy will will be done', BM. 37. Veronica uses both the singular and the plural forms in speaking to the Emperor of Rome: **Kyn teffo y'gas golok** 'Though he should come into your sight' but **Oll a'th kleves** 'All of thy disease', RD. 1696 and 1861.

(2) Plurals. Plural pronouns and possessive adjectives refer to plural nouns, collective nouns and duals: **An palyow o ufer. I re bia terrys** 'The shovels were useless. They had been broken'; **Der an del** (coll.) **y kerdhi, orth aga skoellya dhe denewenn** 'Through the leaves he would walk, scattering them to the side'; **Dha dhiwleuv!** (dual). **Ke! Golgh i!** 'Your (two) hands! Go! Wash them!'

(3) Gender. The pronouns of the 3s. are used as follows.

(a) Masculine

For nouns of masculine gender with the exception of those mentioned in the next paragraph: **An lyver** (m.) **ma plos y vaylyer** 'This book with a dirty cover' lit. 'dirty its cover'.

For male animate beings, even if the grammatical gender of the noun is feminine: **An tiek a vagas an margh** (m.) **orth y witha dour** 'The farmer reared the horse, looking after it carefully'; **Y teuth an gannas** (f.) **ha'n vyghternes a'n degemmeras yn hegar** 'The ambassador came and the queen received him kindly'; **An edhen** (f.) **worow a vydh liwekka ages y vata fest yn fenowgh** 'The male bird is more colourful than his mate very often' (§42(6)).

For facts, verbal action and the result of action: **Prag na glywis hemma kyns?** 'Why did I not hear this before?' **Da via genev mos lemmyn. Bia. Ev a via an gwella kusul oll** 'It would be well for me to go now. It would. It would be the best plan altogether'; **My a'n ambos** 'I promise it' (that something will be done); **Ni a yll y wul** 'We can do it' (some action); **rag hemma/henna** 'because of this/that' (some fact).

(b) Feminine

For nouns of grammatically feminine gender with the exception of those mentioned in the next paragraph: **Py liw yw hi?** (**an voes** f.) 'What colour is it? (the table)'.

§71(3b)   Pronouns

For female animate beings even if the grammatical gender of the noun is masculine: **An venyn a leveris hi dhe brena re** 'The woman said that she had bought too much'; **An flogh m. a's teves anwoes warnedhi** 'The child (female) has a cold'; **An lyfans m. a dhedhow hy oyow yn poll pur** 'The (female) toad lays her eggs in a clear pool' (§42(2)).

For time, weather, circumstances, conditions: **Py eur yw hi?** 'What time is it?' **Diwedhes yw hi** 'It's late'; **Hi a wra glaw** 'It's raining'; **ow tybi y fedha hi y'n fordh ma** 'thinking it (circumstances) would be thus'; **Hi yw dhe well** 'It's (the condition of something) better'. Thus in BM. 3287 both usages are found together: **Dar! Deuva hi dhe henna?** 'What! Has it (the state of affairs) come to this?' (the action of a page in refusing to carry out an errand).

For towns, settlements and rivers (**tre** f. 'settlement' and **avon** f. 'river' understood): **Honna a vydh gelwys Godran** 'This (town) will be called Godran', BM. 2289; **Yn Lysteuder ... honna yma** 'In Lestowder ... this (settlement) is', BM. 2284-85; **an Loveni ha'n koesow rybdhi** 'the (river) Loveny and the woods beside it'. Note that the word **tra** f. 'thing' is feminine in gender but referring pronouns are masculine (§40(1)): **Y synsi an dra ma rag y witha. Ev o drudh dhodho** 'He held on to that in order to protect it. It was precious to him'. The word **pobel** 'people' (§40(2)) is similarly treated as feminine singular but referring pronouns are plural: **An bobel re dhewisas aga lywydh** 'The people have chosen their leader'.

The definite article **an** 'the' is properly a demonstrative and is dealt with in §50. The enclitic demonstratives are described more particularly in §50(5).

§72 **Pronominals** As well as the pronouns which refer to definite individuals and things, there is a group of general, indefinite pronominal words. They are of various origins and some have other functions, as adjectives, adverbs or nouns. Many are used as the antecedent to a relative sentence or stand at the head of a nominal sentence (§303). They are described in the following paragraphs.

(1)   **HUNI** 'one' is used after **lies** 'many', **pub** 'every': **Yndella yw lies huni** 'Many a one is like this'; **Pub huni a woer henna** 'Everyone knows that'. The use of **huni** may be extended by putting **an** 'the' or a possessive adjective before it to contrast something with a thing or person already mentioned or known to the hearer: **Gwell yw genev an huni rudh** 'I prefer the red one' (as distinct from those of other colours); **An huni hir yw y vroder** 'The tall one is his brother' (not any of the others); **Ow huni o terrys** 'Mine was broken' (others were not).

§72(7) Pronouns

(2) **KEMMYS** and **KEKEMMYS** 'as many, all (who), as much': **kemmys re wrug y redya** 'all who have read it'; **Kemmys na worthyb, aga hanow a vydh defendys a'n rol** 'All who don't answer, their names will be deleted from the list'; **Ny welsys kekemmys hag a welis vy** 'You didn't see as many/as much as I saw'. These words also function as adjectives: **kemmys boes hag a yllir y dhybri** 'as much food as one can eat'.

(3) **KEN** 'other' (§83(5b)): **Gwall veu, ny veu ken** 'It was an accident, it was nothing else' lit. 'it was not other'; **Ny leveris hi ken** 'She didn't say anything else'; **Piw a ylli gul ken?** 'Who could do otherwise?' For **ken** as an adjective see §83(5b). See also **hepken** (§148(2)(6)) and **nahen** (§83(7)).

(4) **KENIVER** 'as many, all (who)': **Keniver a dheuth a dhegemmeras dynnargh** 'As many as came received a welcome'; **Dhe geniver na yllons dos y tannvonav an negys ma** 'To all who cannot come I send this message'. This word is also used as an adjective with a singular noun although subsequent nouns may be plural: **keniver best eus y'n tir, ydhyn, ha puskes keffrys** 'as many animal(s) as there are on earth, birds, and fishes too', OM. 1215-16.

(5) **MYNS** m. 'size, number' is used as a pronoun, 'as much, as many as, all who, whoever': **dhe vyns a vynn** 'to as many as will'; **myns a'n jeves charj** 'all who have responsibility'; **myns yw unnver ganso** 'whoever is in agreement with him'. When followed by **may** and an oblique relative sentence (§342) it has the meaning 'to the extent to which, as far as, as much as': **Dhe beub, gweres myns may hylli** 'Help everyone as much as you can'; **Nyns yw da ev dhe lavurya myns may hwra** 'It is not good that he works to the extent that he does'. **Myns** can be used adjectivally before a singular noun: **myns den** 'as many men', OM. 983.

(6) **NEBES**. This word is related to **neb**; see (7) below. It means 'some, a few, little, a little, something': **Nebes a woer an gwiryonedh** 'A few know the truth'; **Deber nebes ha bos yagh** 'Eat little, and be healthy'; **My a'm beus nebes dhe leverel dhis** 'I have something to say to you'.

As an adjective **nebes** stands before its noun which is plural if it is a count noun, singular if it is a mass noun (§46): **nebes niverennow** 'a few numbers'; **nebes keus** 'a little cheese'.

For the use of **nebes** as an adverb see (§267).

(7) **NEB** 'someone, something, anyone, anything': **neb eus ow triga gensi** 'someone who is living with her'; **neb na gar redya** 'anyone who does not love

§72(7)   Pronouns

reading'. Used independently as in these examples, **neb** usually refers to persons but it should be noted that although commonly found as the antecedent to a relative sentence, **neb** is not itself the relative pronoun. Dependently before a noun **neb** denotes either persons or things: **neb flogh** 'some child'; **neb chi** 'some house, a certain house' (§49(2)); **neb tu** 'somewhere'; **neb plas** 'some place', and the compounds: **nebonan** 'someone', **neptra, neppyth** 'something'; **nep-prys** 'sometime'. **Neb** can be the object of a preposition: **dhe neb** 'to someone' (§340(10)).

(8) **OLL** 'all' is used independently or dependently: **Oll re fyllis** 'All have failed'; **An perghennek a werthas oll** 'The owner sold all'.

As a dependent form it precedes or follows the expression it qualifies (§57(2c)). In the first case it is in the appositional genitive construction: **oll dha gerens** 'all (of) your relations'; **oll an re na** 'all (of) those', and in the second case **oll** is in simple apposition: **henna oll** 'all that'; **ha'n pow bras oll** 'and all the large country'.

It precedes an independent personal pronoun **oll ni** 'all (of) us' but follows a preposition with a personal ending: **dhyn oll** 'to us all'; **warnedha i oll** 'on them all'.

Oll is used in combination with **pub** 'every' (see (10) below): **pub eur oll** 'every hour, always'; **Ens pub oll!** 'Let everyone go!' **pub studhyer oll** 'every student'; **pub onan oll** 'every one'. Used as an adverb, **oll** has the sense 'completely': **Yma ev y honan oll** 'He is completely alone'; **oll euver** 'completely useless'; **oll warbarth** 'completely together'.

(9) **ONAN** 'one' has a pronominal role: **Onan a omros, onan a heryas orthyn hwath** 'One gave himself up, one defied us still'. An accompanying adjective is mutated if **onan** refers to a feminine noun: **Yth esa kuntellva, onan vras** 'There was a meeting place, a large one'. The compound **nagonan** 'anyone' cf. (§83(7)) is used with a negative either expressed or implied: **Eus nagonan vydh synsys?** 'Is no one taken?' = 'is there (not) anyone?'

(10) **PEUB** 'all, every'. As an independent form this word is spelt as shown: **peub a dyb yndella** 'Everyone thinks so'; **Peub a esedh war an fos na** 'Everyone sits on that wall'.

As a dependent form with an adjectival role it is spelt **pub** indicating a different pronunciation: **pub tre** 'every town'; **pub huni** 'every one' (see (1) above). In compounds: **pubonan** 'everyone'; **puptra** 'everything'; **pup-prys** 'every time, always'.

§73(1) Pronouns

(11) **PYNAG, PYPYNAG,** 'whatever, whatsoever', **PIWPYNAG** 'whosoever, whomsoever' **PYLEPYNAG** 'wheresoever', **PYNEYLPYNAG** 'whichever one (of two)' are all forms derived from the interrogative pronoun **py** (see §74(1)) and a negative particle *nag/nak (see LP. sec. 380 and WG. sec. 163 vi). The meaning is therefore equivalent to the English 'what not?' i.e. 'anything at all'. These words are sometimes described as indefinite relative pronouns although they are in fact indefinite antecedents to relative sentences (§340(8)): **Y'fydh pynag a vynni** 'You shall have whatever you will'; **Piwpynag a dherivis henna a gammleveris** 'Whoever reported that said wrongly'; **Pylepynag yth ello, yth av vy ynwedh** 'Wheresoever he goes, I go also'; **Kav pyneyl pynag oll yw gwell genes** 'Take whichsoever of the two you prefer'. When used adjectivally, a noun associated with these words comes between the two elements: **py lyver pynag** 'whatever book'; **py benyn bynag** 'whatever woman' (§49(4)).

(12) **RE** 'some' (people, things): **re a'n Gernewegoryon** 'some of the Cornish speakers' (§57(2)): **My a vynn doen re genev** 'I will take some with me'.

(13) **SEUL** 'such, as many' is used independently as antecedent to a relative sentence: **Seul a dhe'n varghas Sulweyth a gammwra** 'Such as go to the market on a Sunday, do wrong'; **Seul a allo kana, gwrens kana!** 'As many as can sing, let them sing!' **Seul** also precedes comparative adjectives, causing mutation: **Seul voy ankow!** 'So many more deaths!' BM. 2351. For its use in denoting parallel increase in a quality see §87.

INTERROGATIVE PRONOUNS

These words are used independently or in close association with another word. Brief remarks on their syntactical relations are included below but these are more fully discussed in §320-§330. All are used to introduce either direct or indirect questions.

§73 **Personal interrogatives**

(1) **PIW** 'who' stands independently at the head of a nominal sentence, forming a question: **Piw a dhiskwedhas hemma dhis?** 'Who showed you this?' **Piw a yll ev bones?** 'Who can he be?' **Piw yw neb a hwilowgh hwi?** 'Who is it you are looking for?' **Ny wonn piw eus omma devedhys dhe'm gweles** 'I don't know who there is here (who has) come to see me'. **Piw yw** and **p'yw** are both 'who is?' **P'ywa** is used as an interjection, 'what! who!'

§73(2)   Pronouns

(2) **PIW** lit. 'to whom is?' is made up of the dative of the interrogative pronoun **piw** and a reduced form of **yw** 'is'. It is used as a transitive verb with the meanings 'own, possess, win', although it has no verbal noun. The word **piwas** m. means 'reward, entitlement, penalty'. The other tenses of the verb are made up of **piw** and inflected forms of **bos** 'be' (§197, §252).

§74 A number of interrogatives are based on the simple form **py** 'what' which together with its compounds is described in the paragraphs which follow.

(1) **PY** 'what' is a dependent form which precedes its noun without causing mutation except in a few common phrases: **Py lyver?** 'What book?; **Py fosow yw kreffa es an re ma?** 'What walls are stronger than these?' **Ny wodhons py dydh y teuthons** 'They don't know (on) what day they came'.

A former usage in which the pronoun preceded a preposition associated with it is referred to where appropriate (§147(4), §154(2), §157).

(2) **PAN** (perhaps py + an = 'what the') 'what' is also a dependent form which mutates its noun as does **an** (§50(3a,b)): **pan ki?** (ki m.) 'what dog?' **pan gath?** (kath f.) 'what cat?' **pan mowesi?** (mowesi f.p.) 'what girls?' **pan vebyon?** (mebyon m.p.) 'what boys?'

(3) **PANA** (py + an + a 'what the of') 'what?' may be considered as **pan** (2) with the addition of the preposition **a** 'of'. Because of the preposition embedded in it, it softens all following nouns (§126): **Pana dra a ynnowgh hwi warnodho?** 'What do you urge upon him?' MC. 99; **Pana vre yw honna?** 'What hill is that?' **Lemmyn y hwelav pana ji ywa** 'Now I see what house it is'.

Like other interrogative pronouns **pan** and **pana** may be used in an exclamative sense: **Pan gwel brav ywa!** 'What a fine view it is!' **Pana vater bras o henna!** 'What a great matter that was!'

(4) **PANDRA** (py + an + dra 'what the thing') 'what' stands as an independent form and is followed by a nominal sentence which completes the question. The final -a usually drops before parts of the verb **bos** 'be' which start with a vowel: **Pandr'yw a vynnowgh hwi?** 'What is it that you wish?' **Pandr'yma gans Meryasek?** 'What's with Meriasek?' i.e. 'What about Meriasek?' BM. 3814. The vowel is also dropped before the verbal particle **a**: **Pandr'a allav vy y wul?** 'What can I do?' **Pandr'a yll henna dhe vos?** 'What can that be?' The pronoun may also make compounds with the tenses of the verb **gul** 'do, make': **Pand'ra vy?** (**pandra a wrav vy**) 'What do I do?'

Pand'rug ev? (**pandra a wrug ev**) 'What did he do?' **Pand'ren dhodho?** (**pandra a wren**) 'What shall we do to him?' It will be seen that in these cases the whole section, -**ra a w**- is dropped.

As an exclamative: **Pandra! Glaw a wra hi!** 'What! It's raining!' and with the meaning 'why': **Pandra, ny vynn'ta kewsel?** 'Why won't you speak?' lit. 'What (is the reason), you won't speak?'

(5) **PYTH** (**py** + **pyth** 'what thing') is an independent form which introduces a nominal sentence as a question. The particle **a** is often omitted but the consequent soft mutation is retained. **Pyth** is most common before parts of the verb **bos** 'be' which start with a vowel, **pandra** (4) above, being used elsewhere but not exclusively so: **Pyth yw hemma?** 'What is this?' **Pyth yw gwell dhe vos gwrys?** 'What is best to be done?' **Pyth o an gusul wella?** 'What was the best plan?' **Pyth a vynnowgh hwi y wul?** 'What do you wish to do?' **Ny wonn pyth wrav** 'I don't know what to do'. **An pyth** is used as an antecedent to a relative sentence (§340(7)).

(6) **PY RE, PANA RE** 'what things, what ones, what persons'. These expressions are used as independent forms in nominal sentences: **Py re a wels'ta?** 'What things did you see?' **Lavar dhymm pana re a dyv gwella omma** 'Tell me what things grow best here' (§72(12)).

(7) **PYNEYL** (**py** + **an** + **eyl**) (§70(1)) 'which of two'. Independent or dependent: **Pyneyl yw an hirra?** 'Which is the taller?' **Pyneyl chi o gwell ganso; an huni a-dal an eglos po an huni yn Stret an Grows?** 'Which house did he prefer; the one opposite the church or the one in Cross Street?' The pronoun may be linked to its noun by the preposition **a** 'of': **Pyneyl a'y dhewdroes a veu shyndys?** 'Which of his feet was injured?'

(8) **PYGEMMYS** (**py** + **a** + **kemmys** 'of what quantity? (§72(2)). 'How much?, How many?' Either independent or dependent: **Pygemmys a dhugons tre?** 'How much did they carry home?' As dependent it is followed by a singular or plural count noun or by a mass noun: **Pygemmys chambour(s) eus y'n ostel na?** 'How many bedrooms are there in that hotel?' **Pygemmys prevyans a'n jevo ev?** 'How much experience had he?'

(9) **PY LIES** 'how many' (§83(5e)) is either independent or dependent. An accompanying count noun is singular: **Py lies a'th eus, mar pleg?** 'How many have you got, please?' **Y fydh govynnys, "Py lies peuns?"** 'It will be asked, "How many pounds?"' **Py lies gweyth? py lies termyn? py lies treveth?** 'how often?'

§74(10) Pronouns

(10) **PY SEUL** 'how many, how much' is an independent form: **Py seul a niversons i?** 'How many did they count?' **Py seul yw dha wober?** 'How much is your wage?'

(11) **PY EGHENN, PY KINDA, PY PAR, PY SORT**, all meaning 'what kind (of)'. They occur as independent or dependent forms: **Py sort a bleg genowgh?** 'What kind do you like?' lit. 'What kind pleases you?' **Py eghenn kewer yw hi?** 'What sort of weather is it?' **My a woer bos karr nowydh dhodho, mes py par yw ev?** 'I know he has a new car, but what kind is it?' **Py kinda pystri o henna?** 'What sort of trickery was that?'

(12) **PLE** (**py le** 'what place' or perhaps **py yn le** 'in what place') 'where', adds **-th** before vowels in the verbs **bos** 'be' and **mos** 'go' but not elsewhere. An independent form used before a verb with only an infixed pronoun intervening, it causes mixed (fifth form) mutation (§26): **Ple hwruss'ta terri an froeth na?** 'Where did you pick that fruit?' **Ple'th esos jy?** 'Where are you?' **Ple esedhsowgh hwi de?** 'Where did you sit yesterday?' **Ny wonn ple'th av** 'I don't know where I shall go'; **Ple'n jevydh chi?** 'Where will he get a house?' **Py le/la** and **py yn le** are independent adverbial forms: **Gyllys yns, ny wonn py le** 'They're gone, I don't know where'. The common phrase **ple'ma** 'where is?' consists of **ple** with the addition of the syllable **-ma**, a shortened form of **yma**, the 3s.pres. of **bos** 'be'. The plural is **ple'mons** 'where are?': **Ple'ma Morwenna?** 'Where is Morwenna?' **An paperyow-nowodhow, ple'mons i?** 'The newspapers, where are they?' (§332(7)).

(13) **A BLE** 'from what place, whence'. The construction is as for **PLE** (12), causing mixed mutation in the following verb: **A ble'th esosta?** 'Where are you from?' **A ble sordyas an tros na?** 'Where did that noise arise from?' **A by le/la** are independent adverbial forms: **Devedhys yw hi mes ny wonn a by le** 'She's arrived but I don't know from where'.

(14) **PY KOST, PY PLAS, PY TYLLER** 'in what place, where'. These phrases are used as independent forms before a verbal sentence introduced by the particle **y(th)**: **Py kost yma hi?** 'Where is she?' **Py tyller y's kudhas?** 'Where did he hide them?'

(15) **P'EUR** (**py + eur** 'what hour, what time) 'when' introduces a verbal sentence and causes mixed mutation, or rather, the particle **y** being dropped, the mutation it causes remains. The particle is re-introduced if an infixed pronoun occurs: **P'eur fydh an kuntellyans?** 'When will the meeting be?' **Ny wonn p'eur y'n metyav** 'I don't know when I shall meet him' (§326). The question 'What time is it?' is in Cornish **Py eur yw hi?** (§112).

§77   Pronouns

(16) **PRAG** (**py** + **rag** 'what for') 'why' (§324) is an example of a preposition following the word it is combined with (cf. **pygans** m. = **py gans** 'what with, wherewithal, means, requisites'). **Prag** is followed by the verbal particle **y**(**th**), negative **na**(**g**) (§274, §276): **Prag y toellsys dha vroder?** 'Why did you deceive your brother?' **Prag yth yns mar skwith?** 'Why are they so tired?' **Prag na dheu'ta nes?** 'Why didn't you come nearer?' **Prag nag eus denvydh omma dh'gan degemmeres?** 'Why is there no one here to receive us?' **My a gonvedh prag y'n gwrug** 'I understand why he did it'.

Nominal forms are **prag**, **praga**, **pyraga**, all masculine and meaning 'the reason why, the cause': **Ny gavas prag may feu res y dhampnya** 'He found no cause why he should be condemned'; **Gyllys yw hi - praga?** 'She's gone - why?'

§75 **PY** 'where, whither' (§326) is used as **ple** (§74(12)) but is much less common. It comes directly before its verb unless an infixed pronoun is involved. It adds **-th** before initial vowels in tenses of the two verbs **bos** 'be' and **mos** 'go' and causes mixed mutation (§26). Combination with **-ma** 'is' and comparison with **ple'ma** above gives the forms **py'ma** 'where is?' and **py'mava** 'where is he/it?' (§326): **Ny wonn pyth av lemmyn** 'I don't know where I shall go now'; **Py hallas an re ma mos?** 'Where could those (ones) go?' **Ny wodhon pyth en** 'We don't know where to go'; **Dha lyver, py'mava?** 'Your book, where is it?' **Py'ma neb a vynn dha guhudha?** 'Where is the one who will accuse you?' **Py'ma ow frisner fiys?** 'Where is my prisoner fled?'

§76 **PES** 'how many' is a dependent form and perhaps from **py lies** 'what amount?' It is used especially with singular nouns of space or time (§328): **Pes mildir alemma dhe Bennsans?** 'How many miles from here to Penzance?' **Pes mis y hwre'ta triga ganso?** 'How many months are you going to stay with him?' **peskweyth?** 'how often?' **pes termyn?** 'how long?' (§324). These two latter words may also be used as demonstratives (§328); **pes bloedh?** 'how many years old? how old?' (§114).

§77 **FATELL** 'how', an interrogative adverb, may be mentioned here. It stands independently before an inflected verb and causes mutation by softening. If an infixed pronoun occurs, **fatell** is followed by a particle: **Fatell welsons i an lyther?** 'How did they see the letter?' **Lavar fatell y'n kevsys** 'Say how you found it'. **Fatell** corresponds to the English 'how is it, what is it like?': **Fatell yw an chambour? Brav yw.** 'What is the bedroom like? It's fine' (§323).

The general interrogative particle is **a**. It is discussed in §320.

RELATIVE PARTICLES

Relative sentences are introduced by one of several words which are better described as relative particles than as relative pronouns. They are dealt with in the chapter on verbal particles, §274-§281, and in the sections on relative sentences, §339-§343.

❖ ❖ ❖ ❖ ❖ ❖

ADJECTIVES

Adjectives, like nouns, may be put into one of two groups. In the first group are words which cannot be broken down into meaningful parts: **hel** 'hospitable'; **lover** 'leprous'; **melyn** 'yellow'; **teg** 'fair'.

§78 **Derived adjectives** Derived adjectives consist of a stem which is usually a noun, singular or plural, or another adjective, with a suffix or a prefix attached. Prefixes for the most part have the effect of modifying the basic meaning of the stem by adding the ideas of negation, of deprivation, of repetition, of intensity, and they are discussed in the chapter on prefixes (§268-§273).

A few adjectives are formed by the combination of the prepositions **a** 'of, from' and **dhe** 'to' with nouns: **a-dhevis** (**devis** 'device') 'exact'; **a-ves** (**mes** 'open country') 'outside'; **a-vann** (**bann** 'height') 'on high'; **a-wartha** (**gwartha** 'summit') 'upper'; **a-woeles** (**goeles** 'bottom') 'lower'. From another adjective: **a-dhiwedhes** (**diwedhes** 'late') 'tardy'; **dhe les** (**les** 'profit') 'useful'; **dhe wari** (**gwari** 'play') 'at liberty'. Other prepositions are also used: **yn** is found in the combination **yn-tenn** (**tenn** 'pull') 'taut', lit. 'in a state of tension'; **a** in the compound preposition **a-rag** 'before' which is used as an adjective: **an daras a-rag** 'the front door'. These forms are usually written with a hyphen: **derivas a-dhevis** 'an exact statement'; **Dyw a-vann** 'God on high'; **an ebrenn a-wartha** 'the sky above'. Most of these compounds also serve as adverbs (§257-§267).

§79 **Suffixes** Adjective-forming suffixes are attached to nouns, singular or plural. Such derived adjectives may in turn function as nouns and form a plural (§90).

(1) **-EK** gives the meaning, 'appertaining to, relating to, having a property'. When applied to bodily characteristics such adjectives imply an exaggeration of the quality: **hornek** (**horn** 'iron') 'made of iron'; **hwansek** (**hwans** 'desire') 'desirous'; **knowek** (**know** 'nuts') 'nutty, with nuts'; **menydhek** (**menydh** 'mountain') 'mountainous'; **mellek** (**mell** 'joint') 'jointed'; **ownek** (**own** 'fear') 'fearful'; **sterennek** (**sterenn** 'star') 'starry, astral'; **tasek** (**tas** 'father') 'paternal'; **tellek** (**tell** 'holes') 'with holes'; **tollek** (**toll** 'hole') 'with a hole'; **tewesek** (**tewes** 'sand') 'sandy'; **boghek** (**bogh** 'cheek') 'big-cheeked'; **elek** (**el** 'chin') 'having a big chin'; **lagasek** (**lagas** 'eye') 'with big eyes' or 'sharp-eyed'.

These same forms serve as nouns denoting a place where some natural product

§79(1)   Adjectives

is abundant: **elowek** (**elow** 'elms') 'a stand of elms'. The plural is in **-egi**: **redenegi** (**reden** 'bracken') 'areas of bracken' (§34(1), §43(9)).

(2)   **-EL/-YEL**: **brithel** (**brith** 'streaked') 'mackerel' = 'streaked'; **deverel** (**dowr** 'water') 'watery'; **floghel** (**flogh** 'child') 'childish'; **goethel** (**goeth** 'stream') 'watery'; **gourel** (**gour** 'man') 'virile'; **gwydhyel** (**gwydh** 'trees') 'wooded'; **kadoryel** (**kador** 'chair') 'chair-like'.

(3)   **-IK/-ESIK**: **heudhik** (**heudh** 'joy') 'joyful'; **keudhesik** (**keudh** 'sorrow') 'sorry, contrite'; **unnik** (**unn** num. 'one') 'solitary'. This ending applied to colour terms especially gives the meaning of the English '-ish': **loesik** (**loes** 'grey') 'greyish'; **rudhik** (**rudh** 'red') 'reddish'.

(4)   **-OW** Some stems have this ending: **garow** 'rough'; **marow** 'dead'; **medhow** 'drunk', but the form **-adow** gives a gerundive meaning to an adjective derived from a verbal noun and equivalent to the English '-able': **aradow** (**aras** v.n. 'plough') 'arable'; **karadow** (**kara** v.n. 'love') 'lovable'; **kasadow** (**kasa** v.n. 'hate') 'hateful'; **servadow** (**servya** v.n. 'serve') 'serviceable, provisional, draft'.

(5)   **-US** Added to nouns or to other adjectives this ending frequently has the meaning 'giving rise to': **didhanus** (**didhan** 'amusement') 'amusing'; **hwarthus** (**hwarth** 'laughter') 'laughable'; **prederus** (**preder** 'thought') 'careful, thoughtful'; **tarosvannus** (**tarosvann** 'ghost') 'ghostly'; **yaghus** (**yagh** 'healthy') 'healthful'.

(6)   **-YEK**: **estrenyek** (**estren** 'stranger') 'foreign'; **konneryek** (**konnar** 'rage') 'rabid'; **sevelyek** (**sevel** v.n. 'stand') 'standing'.

(7)   **-YK**: **diskryjyk** (**diskrysi** v.n. 'disbelieve') 'disbelieving'.

(8)   **-YS**: **flerys** (**fler** 'stink') 'stinking'; **marthys** (**marth** 'wonder') 'wonderful'. This is also the ending of the past participle of the verb: **terrys** (**terri** v.n. 'break') 'broken' (§244(1)).

The ending **-ek** is by far the most common adjectival suffix. Adjectives in **-ik**, and **-us** are much less common. Other forms listed above are comparatively rare.

§80   The dictionaries list as occurring in the source texts some hundred or so adjectives of obvious English or French form and origin: **fast** 'firm'; **preshyous** 'precious'; **prout** 'proud'; **sertan** 'certain'.

§82(1)   Adjectives

They should be treated in all respects as Cornish. Thus **perfeyth** 'perfect' has the comparative form **perfeyttha** 'more perfect'; a mutated initial, **an venyn berfeyth** 'the perfect woman' and takes a prefix, **anperfeyth** 'imperfect'.

§81 **Gender and number of adjectives** Cornish adjectives do not mark the gender of the noun they accompany. As to number, only **arall** 'other' has a true plural form, **erell**: **a'n barth arall** 'on the other side'; **gwreg arall** 'another woman'; **tus erell** 'other people'; **re erell** 'other ones'. Only if the noun or pronoun itself is plural is **erell** used: **lies ki arall** 'many other dogs'; **keun erell** 'other dogs'. After a dual noun **erell** is to be preferred but **arall** can be used: **a pe diwleuv erell/arall** 'if there were another pair of hands'.

Plurals of adjectives used as nouns are numerous (§90).

§82 **Comparative and superlative forms of the adjective** The forms of the adjective used in the comparative or in the superlative sense end in a suffix **-a**. Doubling or hardening or both may occur in the end consonants.

(1) Change of final consonant:

b	>	pp	kr	>	kkr	rdh	>	rth
bl	>	ppl	l	>	ll	rg	>	rk
br	>	ppr	ld	>	lt	rj	>	rch
ch	>	cch	ldr	>	ltr	rv	>	rf
d	>	tt	lv	>	lf	s	>	ss
dh	>	tth	m	>	mm	sh	>	ssh
dhl	>	tthl	mbl	>	mpl	sl	>	ssl
dhr	>	tthr	mbr	>	mpr	sn	>	ssn
dhw	>	tthw	n	>	nn	sw	>	ssw
dr	>	ttr	nd	>	nt	t	>	tt
f	>	ff	ndl	>	ntl	th	>	tth
g	>	kk	ndr	>	ntr	thl	>	tthl
gh	>	ggh	ng	>	nk	thr	>	tthr
gl	>	kkl	ngr	>	nkr	tl	>	ttl
gn	>	kkn	nj	>	nch	v	>	ff
j	>	cch	p	>	pp	vn	>	ffn
k	>	kk	r	>	rr	vr	>	ffr
kl	>	kkl	rd	>	rt			
kn	>	kkn	rdr	>	rtr			

Thus: **glyppa** (**glyb**) 'wetter'; **tekka** (**teg**) 'finer'; **syggha** (**sygh**) 'drier'; **moenna** (**moen**) 'thinner'; **poettha** (**poeth**) 'much hotter'; **kreffa** (**krev**) 'stronger'.

§82(1) Adjectives

Apart from the above there is no change: **trenka (trenk)** 'more bitter; **yowynka (yowynk)** 'younger'; **glewa (glew)** 'sharper'; **sleya (sley)** 'cleverer'. Positive forms ending in a vowel remain unchanged and make their comparative forms by the use of **moy** 'more', **moyha** 'most': **moy bysi** 'busier'. This is the case also with past participles in **–ys** and polysyllables: **moy brewys** ' more crushed'; **an moyha kasadow** 'the most hateful (§267).

(2) A vowel in the last syllable of the positive form is elided in adjectives ending in -ow: **garwa (garow)** 'rougher'; **salwa (salow)** 'safer'. A similar usage is found before a final -l, -n, -r. In these cases the penultimate consonant changes as in (1) above: **appla (abel)** 'abler'; **leffna (leven)** 'smoother'; **hakkra (hager)** 'uglier'; **metthwa (medhow)** 'drunker'; **pottra (poder)** 'more rotten'.

(3) Irregular are **diwettha (diwedhes)** 'later'; **esya (es)** 'easier'; **har'ha** for **harttha (hardh)** 'bolder'; **hena (hen)** 'older'; **duha (du)** 'blacker'.

(4) The comparative and superlative forms of some common adjectives are supplied by different words.

byghan	'small'	**le**	'less'	**lyha**	'least'
da *or* **mas**	'good'	**gwell**	'better'	**gwella**	'best'
drog	'bad'	**gweth** *or* **lakka**	'worse'	**gwettha**	'worst'
isel	'low'	**isella** *but in place names* **is**	'lower'	**isella** **isa**	'lowest'
-	-	**kyns**	'former'	**kynsa**	'foremost, first'
meur	'much, great'	**moy**	'more, greater'	**moyha**	'most, greatest'
nebes	'little'	**le** *(in quantity or number (§72(6))*	'fewer, less'	**lyha**	'fewest, least'
ogas	'near'	**nes**	'nearer'	**nessa**	'nearest'

In modern usage a regularly formed comparative of **byghan, byghanna**, provides an alternative to **le** to specify the meaning 'smaller, smallest': **Nyns yw gwir an byghanna pors dhe synsi an lyha arghans** 'It is not true that the smallest purse holds the least money'.

In the same way the comparative **brassa (bras)** 'bigger' refers particularly to size whilst **moy/moyha** imply quantity and number: **an brassa gwydh** 'the biggest trees'; **moyha froeth** 'most fruit'.

§83(2d)   Adjectives

For the use of the comparative/superlative adjective as a noun see §90.

§83 **The position of adjectives** Adjectives either follow or precede the noun.

(1) Attributive adjectives usually follow the noun which they qualify: **towl fur** 'a wise plan'; **dowr kler** 'pure water'.

Two adjectives in this position may be linked by **ha** 'and' or the conjunction may be omitted: **den rych ha bysi** 'a rich and busy man'; **drehevyans bras nowydh** 'a big new building'.

Similarly with pairs of nouns in the appositional genitive (§55), each noun is followed by its appropriate adjective: **dowr ylyn an gover** 'the clear water of the brook'; **dowr an gover ylyn** 'the water of the clear brook'.

(2) When an adjective thus follows its noun, mutation (softening) of the initial of the adjective takes place as follows:

(a) After a feminine singular of any meaning: **golok lew** (**glew**) 'a bright look'; **an vugh worm** (**gorm**) 'the dun cow'.

(b) After a masculine plural noun denoting persons and after the pronoun **re** 'ones' when referring to masculine persons or to a mixed group: **gowleverysi dhrog** (**drog**) 'wicked liars'; **an oberoryon bals** (**pals**) 'the numerous workers'; **an re goth** 'the old ones' (men or a group of men and women);

(c) After a noun of any gender when preceded by **dew/diw** 'two': **an dhew dhen vrav** (**brav**) 'the two fine men'; **diw grog dynn** (**tynn**) 'two sharp tugs'.

(d) Thus after the dual of any gender: **dewlagas las** (**glas**) 'two blue eyes'; **y dhiwskoedh ven** (**men**) 'his two strong shoulders'.

The mutations described above only take place if the adjective immediately follows the noun: **kan dhistyr** 'a meaningless song' but **kan hager distyr** 'an unpleasant, meaningless song'; **dewlagas las bras** 'two big blue eyes'.

The mutation of the adjective is inhibited after a final **-s**, **-th** if the initial consonant of the adjective is **k-**, **p-** or **t-** (§22): **eglos** (f.) **vyghan** (**byghan**) 'a small church', but **eglos koth** 'an old church'; **dewlagas** (d.) **las** (**glas**) 'two blue eyes', but **dewlagas teg** 'two lovely eyes'; **ewntres** (m.pl.) **dha** (**da**) 'good uncles' but **ewntres pals** 'numerous uncles'; **skath** (f.) **wynn** (**gwynn**) 'a white boat', but **skath terrys** 'a broken boat'.

§83(2d)   Adjectives

The adjective **mas** 'good, of service, of use' is used in the form **'vas**, possibly for **a vas** after a noun of either gender: **kusul** (f.) **'vas** 'good advice'; **tybyans** (m) **'vas** 'a useful thought'.

(3) The demonstrative enclitics **ma, na** (§50(5)) are attached to an adjective after a noun to which they refer: **an lyther hir ma** 'this long letter'; **an menydh ughel na** 'that high mountain'. In the phrases **an re ma/na** 'these/those' (things or persons) there is mutation of the included adjective when the things referred to are male persons or a mixed group, but not otherwise: **an re dhiek na** 'those lazy ones' (men or men and women); **an re diek na** 'those lazy ones' (women only); **an re gwynn ma** 'these white ones' (things) ((2b) above).

Similarly a suffixed pronoun (§64) comes after the adjective or adjectives: **ow lowarth byghan vy** 'my little garden'; **aga hwel bras, a-vern ynsi** 'their great, important work'.

(4) Certain common adjectives may either precede or follow the noun. They are:

berr	'short'	**gwir**	'true'	**leun**	'full'
bras	'big'	**hager**	'ugly'	**meur**	'great, much, many'
drog	'bad'	**hir**	'long'	**ogas**	'near'
ewn	'right'	**kamm**	'wrong'	**pur**	'pure, very'
fals	'false'	**kott**	'short'	**tebel**	'devilish'
fekyl	'false'	**kuv**	'kind'	**vil**	'vile'
gow	'lying'	**lel**	'loyal'	**war**	'careful'
gwann	'weak, bad'	**len**	'faithful'		

(a) When these adjectives precede the noun they mutate its initial consonant by softening, whatever its gender (but not initial **k-, p-** or **t-** after **-s, -th**): **berr dermyn** (**termyn**) 'a short time'; **leun golonn** (**kolonn**) 'full heart'; **hirgorn** (**korn**) 'long trumpet' but **fals tybyans** 'false opinion'; **ty fals jogler!** 'you false clown!' **hager bryv** (**pryv**) 'ugly reptile'; **meur byta** (**pyta**) 'great pity' (note that **meur** with the meaning 'much' is connected to its noun by **a** (§57(2a)): **pur ogas kar** 'a very close relation'.

(b) Adjective and noun may be written as one word to form a close compound (§61(1g)): **drogwas** (**gwas**) 'evil fellow, rogue', pl. **drogwesyon**; ``**gwirlev`eryas** 'speaker of the truth'. Such compounds follow the normal rules for mutation, i.e. f.s. nouns have soft mutation after **an** 'the' and **unn** 'one' and m.pl. nouns denoting persons have soft mutation after **an**. Similarly, following adjectives are mutated (§83(2)). The examples below demonstrate the

§83(5c) Adjectives

combination of **tebel** 'evil', **benyn** 'woman', **benynes** 'women', **borr** 'fat' and **gwann** 'weak, ineffectual', **gwikor** 'trader', **gwikoryon** 'traders' and **krav** 'grasping'.

benyn f.	gwikor m.
tebelvenyn	gwannwikor
tebelvenyn vorr	gwannwikor krav
an debelvenyn	an gwannwikor
tebelvenynes	gwannwikoryon
tebelvenynes borr	gwannwikoryon grav
an tebelvenynes	an wannwikoryon
an tebelvenynes borr	an wannwikoryon grav

(c) Any of the above adjectives may be joined to a verbal noun as a prefix and are retained throughout the inflected verb: **brasleverel** 'talk boastfully', **ev a vrasleveri** imperf.indic. 'he used to talk boastfully'; **meurgara** 'love greatly', **meurgerys** p.part. 'greatly loved'. So also **drokhandla** 'ill-treat'; **gwannrewardya** 'reward meagrely'; **lelservya** and **lelwonis** 'serve loyally'; **leunbysi** 'beseech earnestly'; **tebelwolia** 'wound badly' (§235(5)).

These adjectives precede in order to give particular emphasis to the adjectival element and are found for the most part in expressions of commendation or disparagement. When they follow the noun in the regular way, such emphasis is lost: **pur dhowr** 'real water' as against **dowr pur** 'pure water'; **an meur dhiskwedhyans** 'the great exhibition', pre-eminently so, contrasted with **an diskwedhyans meur** 'the great exhibition'.

(5) Adjectives which always precede the noun are the following:

(a) **HEN** 'old, former' softens the following consonant: **hendas** (**tas** 'father') 'forefather'; **hendra** (**tra/tre** 'settlement') 'old settlement'; **henfordh** (**fordh** 'road') 'old, superseded road'.

(b) **KEN** 'other' does not mutate the initial of its noun: **ken pow** 'another country'; **dhe gen tre** 'to another town'; **ken termyn** 'another time'; **ken tra** 'another thing'. Note however **hag oll ken** 'everything else', where **ken** is a noun or pronoun.

For the use of **ken** in comparisons see §85; for **nahen** see (7) below and for **poken** see §285.

(c) **KETH** 'same' causes the same mutations as does **an** (k-, p-, t- excepted)

§83(5c) Adjectives

and in the same circumstances: **an keth chi na** 'that same house'; **y'n keth vaner** (**maner** f.) 'in the same manner'; **an keth tra** (**tra** f. 'thing'); **an keth vyghternedh** (**myghternedh** m.pl. 'kings') 'the same kings'. For the use of **keth** in comparisons see §287.

(d) **KETTEP** 'each, every', no mutation: **kettep onan, kettep penn** 'every one'.

(e) **LIES** 'many' is used before a singular noun without mutation: **lies bleujenn** 'many flowers'; **lies lyver** 'many books'; **gans lies lev** 'with many voices'.

(f) **LOWER** 'many' is used as is **lies**, before a singular noun without mutation: **lower gover** 'many streams'; **lower le** 'many places'.

(6) The words **flour, lowr** and **pals** have some peculiarities.

(a) **FLOUR** 'perfect, flower, finest specimen' is used as an adjective or as a noun: **medhyk flour** 'an outstanding doctor'; **Lowena dhe flour an bys** 'Joy to the best in the world' (a messenger speaking to Pharaoh), OM. 1541. There is a derived word **flourenn** f. 'fine specimen'.

(b) **LOWR** 'enough' usually follows its noun but may come before it: **petrol lowr** 'enough petrol'; **kentrow lowr** 'enough nails', but **lowr pygans dhe vywa orto** 'enough to live on'.

(c) **PALS** 'many, plentiful' follows a plural noun: **geryow pals** 'many words'; **sybwydhennow pals** 'lots of fir trees'.

(7) **NA-** 'some, any'. This word, a variant of **neb** (§72(7)), is used before **ken** 'other' and comparative adjectives, usually in association with a negative, expressed or implied. It causes third state mutation (breathed, §24(3)) in **ken** 'other', **kyn/kyns** 'former'; **pella** 'further': **nahen diwes** 'any other drink'; **nahen skila** 'any other reason'; **nyns eus fordh nahen** 'there is no other way'; **der y alloes ha tra nahen** 'through his own ability and (not) anything else'; **nahyns** '(not) any sooner'; **ny vydh an kuntellyans nahyns** 'the meeting will not be any sooner'; **nafella** 'any further'; **Na gerdh nafella!** 'Don't walk any further!' The positive form **pell** is also used without mutation: **mar trigav omma na pell** 'if I stay here long at all (and I should not)'. **Namoy** 'any more': **namoy ny res** 'any more is not necessary'; **Mar strechyn omma namoy, y'gan bydh edrek** 'If we wait here any longer (and we should not), we shall regret it'; **heb na hirra lavarow** 'without any further words'.

§84   Adjectives

Note also **nameur** '(not) much at all': **Ny'n karav nameur** 'I'm not very fond of it', and the adverbs **nammenowgh** 'seldom', **na vydh** 'at all'. In **nagonan** 'anyone', cf. §72(9), the -**g** is probably added by analogy with **na(g)** conj. 'not' (§284). In permanent compounds the elements are joined as one word.

(8) The comparative/superlative adjective usually precedes its noun, in which case there is no mutation of the initial of the noun whatever the gender and number of the noun: **yma gwell fordh** 'there is a better way'; **kreffa den** 'a stronger person'; **an splanna del** 'the most splendid foliage'; **y gottha koweth** 'his oldest friend'. The adjective may follow to give special force to the expression: **fordhow gwell** 'better ways'; **ow mab kerra** 'my dearest son'; **an grassa brassa** 'the greatest thanks'. In this case the adjective is mutated regularly by softening after a feminine singular noun or a masculine plural noun denoting persons: **y'n fordh wella** 'in the best way'; **an dus vryntinna** 'the most noble people'.

It is the use of the determiner which gives the superlative meaning to the adjective as denoting a unique individual: **toemma** 'warmer'; **an toemma** 'the warmest'; **agan hirra gwydhenn** 'our tallest tree' but it need not always be expressed: **nessa dhe'n vyghternes** 'the nearest to the queen'. This is especially so in those cases where the superlative has a distinct form (§82(4)).

§84   **The equative** The first element of an equative statement which says that two items are equal in some respect ('as ... as') is introduced by **mar** or by **maga** 'so' preceding an adjective in the positive degree. **Mar** is followed by second state (soft) mutation, **maga** by fifth state (mixed) mutation: **mar wann** (**gwann**) 'so weak'; **maga town** (**down**) 'so deep'.

The second element of the comparison is introduced by **avel** 'as' before a noun, by **dell** 'as' before a verb (§297).

Avel takes pronominal endings as follows:

avelov	'as I'	**avelon**	'as we'
avelos	'as you'	**avelowgh**	'as you'
avello	'as he/it'	**avella**	'as they'
avelli	'as she/it'		

Note that the forms of the third person double the -**l** before the ending. Examples: **mar wynn avel an ergh** 'as white as the snow'; **mar leven avel moes** 'as level as a table'; **mar hweg avelos** 'as sweet as you'; **maga harow avella** 'as rough as they'; **kan mar deg dell wodhya** 'as lovely a song as he

§84 Adjectives

knew'; **maga noeth genys dell via** 'as naked as he had been born'.

The adjective may precede its noun as described in §83(4): **mar hir fordh** 'as long a road'.

The second part of the comparison can be omitted or merely implied by the context: **Pan wre'ta mar deg agan dyski** 'Since you teach us so well (as you do)'; **Mar ny gowssa mar veur ny'n jevia mar lies eskar** 'If he didn't speak so much (as he does) he would not have so many enemies'.

For the use of the conjunction **ha** 'and' in an equative statement see §287.

For the use of a comparative adjective with a tense of the subjunctive to form an equative clause see §348(5).

§85 Comparison The first element of a comparison contains an adjective in the comparative degree. The second element is introduced by **es/ages** 'than' and by **es dell/ages dell** before a verb. **Es/ages** has pronominal endings as follows:

(ag)esov	'than me'	(ag)eson	'than us'
(ag)esos	'than you'	(ag)esowgh	'than you'
(ag)esso	'than him/it'	(ag)essa	'than them'
(ag)essi	'than her/it'		

Note that the forms of the third person double the **-s** before the pronominal ending.

Examples: **gweth ages kroenek** 'worse than a toad'; **hwekka es mel** 'sweeter than honey'; **An diwedh o hakkra es an dalleth** 'The ending was worse than the beginning'; **Unn peuns yw moy es peswar-ugens diner** 'One pound is more than eighty pence'; **Nyns eus neskar dhymm ken agesos** 'I have no relation other than you'; **gwell via es y skoellya** 'it would be better than wasting it', lit. 'its wasting'; **Skwittha o de es dell ywa hedhyw** 'He was more tired yesterday than he is today'; **Ny yll hi gul ken es dell wra hi** 'She can do no more than she does'; **Moy poenvos yw hi pan weres es dell yw pan na weres ev** 'It's more trouble when he helps than when he doesn't help'.

§86 Increase Increase towards a higher degree of a quality is expressed by the use of the preposition **dhe** 'to' before the comparative adjective: **dhe lowenna my a vydh** 'the happier I shall be'; **ni a vydh dhe greffa** 'we shall be the stronger'; **ty a far dhe lakka** 'you will fare the worse'. The same function is served by **seul** 'so much' (§72(13)) before a comparative which it mutates:

§88(3c) Adjectives

Ena seul wynna i a vydh 'Then they will be so much whiter'.

§87 **Parallel increase** The terms mentioned above, **dhe** and **seul** when used in parallel clauses express dependent increase: **Dhe harttha vydh an rol ... dhe bella hi a vydh ow redya** 'The more exact the list be ... the longer it will be in reading', BM. 2842-44; **Dhe well an jydh, dhe well an gwrians** 'The better the day, the better the deed'; **Seul wanna y teu ha bos, seul lewa y teu y dybyans ha bos** 'The weaker he becomes, the clearer his thought becomes'; **Seul skaffa seul well** 'The sooner the better'.

§88 **The exclamative** An exclamation, 'how ...! what ...!' can be expressed in one of several ways.

(1) By the use of the verbal particle **ass/assa** 'how!' (§281) before a part of the verb **bos** 'be': **Ass on skwith!** 'How tired we are!' lit. 'How we are tired!' **Ass en vy hwansek a'th weles** 'How desirous I was of seeing you!' lit. 'How I was ...!' **Assa viens prederys** 'How worried they had been!' lit. 'How they had been ...!'

(2) It may be expressed by a compound made up of an adjective with **a** and a noun: **Dyw, drog a loes!** 'God, what an evil (of a) pain!' MC. 224.8; **Drog a le!** 'What an evil place!' **Splann a wel!** 'What a splendid view!'

(3) GWYNNVYS (**gwynn** 'fair', **bys** 'world') 'happy, fortunate', is used in an exclamative sense. The subject is a following noun or an indefinite pronoun in a nominal sentence or, rarely, the relative particle itself (§278(1b)). The cause of the joy, satisfaction, etc. is explained as follows:

(a) In the predicate of the sentence: **Gwynnvys an den a brenas chi kyns an kost dhe ughelhe!** '(How) fortunate the person who bought a house before the cost rose!'; **Gwynnvys neb a drikko y'n le na!** 'Anyone who lives there is lucky!' **Gwynnvys an re a's teves kusul dha!** '(How) fortunate (they are) who get good advice!' **Gwynnvys a'n jeffo termyn dhe bowes** 'Lucky (for) anyone who has time to rest!'

(b) A verbal noun is used: **Gwynnvys bywa y'n oes ma!** '(How) fortunate to be alive in this age!'

(c) A verbal noun with a possessive adjective as object is used (§240(1)): **Gwynnvys y gavoes wosa an termyn hir ma!** '(How) lucky to find it after this long time!'

(d) The infinitive construction (**dhe** with a verbal noun (§141(19)) may be employed: **Gwynnvys ty dhe seweni y'n tor' ma!** 'Good for you, succeeding this time!' **Gwynnvys an gewer dhe vos mar doemm!** 'It's fortunate that the weather is so warm!' lit. 'Fortunate the weather to be so warm'.

(e) A defining possessive adjective may be incorporated with **gwynnvys**: **Gwynn dha vys ty dhe seweni y'n tor' ma!** '(How) lucky you are to succeed this time!' **Gwynn y vys neb a woer hemma!** 'He who knows this is lucky!'

With these expressions compare the use of **go** with personal pronouns (§68) and see also interjections (§352).

§89 **Adjectival phrases** The construction mentioned in §88(3e) may be described as an adjectival phrase. Another such construction is formed from an adjective followed by a possessive adjective and its noun. The adjectival phrase thus formed refers to the noun to be described: **marner tewedhek y vin** 'a sailor with a weather-beaten face', lit. 'a sailor weather-beaten his face'; **kales y enep yw men a'n par na** 'hard-surfaced is stone of that sort'. So in the phrases cited above **gwynnvys** 'happy, fortunate': **mamm gwynn hy bys** 'a fortunate mother'.

Since the simple adjective does not refer directly to the principal noun, it is not mutated after feminine singular nouns or after masculine plural nouns denoting persons: **Benyn kuv hy gnas dell o, ny ylli hi perthi an dra** 'Kind-natured woman as she was, she could not bear the affair'; **tiogyon trist aga min** 'sad-faced farmers', lit. 'farmers sad their face'.

§90 **The adjective as a noun** Most adjectives, whether stems or derived forms, can be used as nouns and form a plural (§43(7)): **edhommek** adj. 'needy', m. 'a needy person', pl. **edhommogyon**; **klav** adj. 'ill', m. 'an invalid', pl. **klevyon**; **stlav** adj. 'lisping', m. 'one who lisps', pl. **stlevyon**; **termynek** adj. 'dawdling', m. 'a dawdler', pl. **termynogyon**; **lusowek** adj. 'ashy', f. 'ash-pit', pl. **lusowegi**; **pluvek** adj. 'feathery' f. 'pillow', pl. **pluvogow**.

Note also **an da** 'the good', **an drog** 'the bad': **diworth an da dhe wuthyl drog** 'from the good to do evil', MC. 21.3-4; **drog penn** 'a headache', lit. 'a bad (of) a head'; **drog dans** 'toothache'.

Superlative forms of the adjective are also used as nouns: **Ev yw an brassa** 'It is the biggest (one)'; **gorhemmynnadow a'n gwella** 'best wishes', lit. 'wishes of the best'; **avalow a'n brassa** 'the biggest of apples'.

§91 Adjectives

The construction with the preposition **a** 'of' is used when a second noun denoting a collection is added (§57(2)) **an hirra a'n wer** 'the tallest of the men'; **an yowynka ahanowgh** 'the youngest of you'.

Ordinal numerals may similarly function as either adjectives or as nouns: **an pympes a'n rew** 'the fifth in (lit. 'of') the row'; **an unnegves warn ugens a vis Me** 'the thirty-first of May'.
When adjectives are thus used as nouns, the normal rules for mutation apply: **A venynes oll, hi o an dekka** 'Of all women she was the fairest'; **an gevoethogyon** 'the mighty (ones)'.

§91 **The adjective as an adverb** An adjective can, without any change of form, be used adverbially: **da y hwonn** 'I know well'; **Y'n hembronkyas ughel** 'He led him high up'; **dyghtys dignas** 'treated unnaturally'. Comparative forms: **kewsel kuffa** 'speak more kindly'; **Ni a vynn kerdhes pella** 'We will walk farther'.

Forms with **na-** (83(7)): **mar tur na fella an gwari** 'if the play lasts any longer'.

With the use of **mar** or **maga** 'so' (§84): **ty dhe vynnes mar sempel** 'that you wish so simply'; **war-lergh koska mar dha** 'after sleeping so well'; **maga ta/magata** 'as well, also': **war an forn magata** 'on the stove as well'.

Certain adjectives are regularly used as adverbs to express intensity.

BRAS 'big'. A rare usage: **speshyal bras** 'most specially', MC. 110.8.
FEST 'fast': **fest yn ta** 'very well indeed'.
MARTHYS 'marvellous': **marthys goethus** 'very proud'.

There is no mutation after these three words.

PUR 'pure, perfect'. This is the most commonly used word. It causes mutation by softening of the following consonant: **pur boes (poes)** 'very heavy'; **pur barys** 'very readily'; **pur dha** 'very good'; **pur sewen** 'very successful'.

The comparative and superlative forms, **moy** 'more' and **(an) moyha** 'the most', of the adjective **meur** 'much' (§82(4)), are used adverbially before an adjective in the positive degree to express the comparative and superlative degree of that adjective: **moy logh** 'more remiss' instead of **loggha**; **an moyha dov** 'the tamest' in place of **doffa**. This is always the case when the adjective is a past participle (§245(5)): **moy kerys** 'more loved'; **Pyneyl o an moyha**

§91 Adjectives

synsys? 'Which (of the two) was the more beholden?' **moy skoellys es kyns** 'more scattered than before'. Similarly **le** 'less' and **(an) lyha** '(the) least' indicate a diminution of the quality: **le kempenn** 'less tidy'; **an lyha kempenn** 'the least tidy'; **le kerys** 'less loved'; **lyha kerys** 'least loved'.

§92 The particle **yn** can be used with adjectives to make adverbs. This particle causes fifth state (mixed) mutation (§26): **yn ta (da** 'good') 'well'; **yn fas (mas** 'good') 'well'; **yn splann (splann** 'splendid') 'splendidly'; **yn fen (men** 'strong') 'strongly'; **yn tynn (tynn** 'sharp') 'sharply'; **yn krev (krev** 'strong') 'strongly, quickly'; **fest yn krev** 'very strongly'; **yn tebel (tebel** 'evil') 'evilly'.

Such constructions may serve as the complement of **bos** 'be' and similar verbs with the meaning 'in a certain state': **Henn yw yn ta** 'That is in a good state/well'; **Ow holonn res eth yn klav** 'My heart has gone into a sick state'; **Ottomma pons yn koedhys** 'See here a bridge in a ruined state'. Cf. §245(6).

❖ ❖ ❖ ❖ ❖

NUMERALS

§93 The forms of the numerals, cardinal and ordinal, are given below together with the ordinal abbreviations as used in dates.

Counting is in twenties.

(1) The numerals from one to twenty

1	onan		11	unnek
	unn with nouns (§95(3))			
1a	kynsa		11ves	unnegves
2	dew m.		12	dewdhek
	diw f.			
2a	nessa		12ves	dewdhegves
3	tri m.		13	trydhek
	teyr f.			
3a	trysa/tressa		13ves	trydhegves
4	peswar m.		14	peswardhek
	peder f.			
4a	peswara		14ves	peswardhegves
5	pymp		15	pymthek
5es	pympes		15ves	pymthegves
6	hwegh		16	hwetek
6ves	hweghves		16ves	hwetegves
7	seyth		17	seytek
7ves	seythves		17ves	seytegves
8	eth		18	etek
8ves	ethves		18ves	etegves
9	naw		19	nownsek
9ves	nawves		19ves	nownsegves
10	deg		20	ugens
10ves	degves		20ves	ugensves

(2) The numerals from twenty-one to thirty-nine are compounds of the simple numerals and the phrase **warn ugens** 'on twenty' (§161(6)):

§93(2)

21	onan warn ugens	31	unnek warn ugens
21ens	kynsa warn ugens	31ens	unnegves warn ugens
22	dew warn ugens	32	dewdhek warn ugens
22ens	nessa warn ugens	32ens	dewdhegves warn ugens
23	tri warn ugens	33	trydhek warn ugens
23ens	trysa warn ugens	33ens	trydhegves warn ugens
24	peswar warn ugens	34	peswardhek warn ugens
24ens	peswara warn ugens	34ens	peswardhegves warn ugens
25	pymp warn ugens	35	pymthek warn ugens
25ens	pympes warn ugens	35ens	pymthegves warn ugens
26	hwegh warn ugens	36	hwetek warn ugens
26ens	hweghves warn ugens	36ens	hwetegves warn ugens
27	seyth warn ugens	37	seytek warn ugens
27ens	seythves warn ugens	37ens	seytegves warn ugens
28	eth warn ugens	38	etek warn ugens
28ens	ethves warn ugens	38ens	etegves warn ugens
29	naw warn ugens	39	nownsek warn ugens
29ves	nawves warn ugens	39ens	nownsegves warn ugens
30	deg warn ugens		
30ves	degves warn ugens		

(3)   The numerals from forty to ninety-nine are compounds of the simple numerals with a multiple of **ugens**. The linking word is **ha** 'and':

40	dew-ugens	50	deg ha dew-ugens
40ves	dew-ugensves	50ens	degves ha dew-ugens
41	onan ha dew-ugens	51	unnek ha dew-ugens
41ens	kynsa ha dew-ugens	51ens	unnegves ha dew-ugens
42	dew ha dew-ugens	52	dewdhek ha dew-ugens
42ens	nessa ha dew-ugens	52ens	dewdhegves ha dew-ugens
43	tri ha dew-ugens	53	trydhek ha dew-ugens
43ens	trysa ha dew-ugens	53ens	trydhegves ha dew-ugens
44	peswar ha dew-ugens	54	peswardhek ha dew-ugens
44ens	peswara ha dew-ugens	54ens	peswardhegves ha dew-ugens
45	pymp ha dew-ugens	55	pymthek ha dew-ugens
45ens	pympes ha dew-ugens	55ens	pymthegves ha dew-ugens
46	hwegh ha dew-ugens	56	hwetek ha dew-ugens
46ens	hweghves ha dew-ugens	56ens	hwetegves ha dew-ugens
47	seyth ha dew-ugens	57	seytek ha dew-ugens
47ens	seythves ha dew-ugens	57ens	seytegves ha dew-ugens
48	eth ha dew-ugens	58	etek ha dew-ugens
48ens	ethves ha dew-ugens	58ens	etegves ha dew-ugens
49	naw ha dew-ugens	59	nownsek ha dew-ugens
49ens	nawves ha dew-ugens	59ens	nownsegves ha dew-ugens

§93(5) Numerals

(4) The numerals from sixty to seventy-nine

60	tri-ugens	70	deg ha tri-ugens
60ves	tri-ugensves	70ens	degves ha tri-ugens
61	onan ha tri-ugens	71	unnek ha tri-ugens
61ens	kynsa ha tri-ugens	71ens	unnegves ha tri-ugens
62	dew ha tri-ugens	72	dewdhek ha tri-ugens
62ens	nessa ha tri-ugens	72ens	dewdhegves ha tri-ugens
63	tri ha tri-ugens	73	trydhek ha tri-ugens
63ens	trysa ha tri-ugens	73ens	trydhegves ha tri-ugens
64	peswar ha tri-ugens	74	peswardhek ha tri-ugens
64ens	peswara ha tri-ugens	74ens	peswardhegves ha tri-ugens
65	pymp ha tri-ugens	75	pymthek ha tri-ugens
65ens	pympes ha tri-ugens	75ens	pymthegves ha tri-ugens
66	hwegh ha tri-ugens	76	hwetek ha tri-ugens
66ens	hweghves ha tri-ugens	76ens	hwetegves ha tri-ugens
67	seyth ha tri-ugens	77	seytek ha tri-ugens
67ens	seythves ha tri-ugens	77ens	seytegves ha tri-ugens
68	eth ha tri-ugens	78	etek ha tri-ugens
68ens	ethves ha tri-ugens	78ens	etegves ha tri-ugens
69	naw ha tri-ugens	79	nownsek ha tri-ugens
69ens	nawves ha tri-ugens	79ens	nownsegves ha tri-ugens

(5) The numerals from eighty to ninety-nine

80	peswar-ugens	90	deg ha peswar-ugens
80ves	peswar-ugensves	90ens	degves ha peswar-ugens
81	onan ha peswar-ugens	91	unnek ha peswar-ugens
81ens	kynsa ha peswar-ugens	91ens	unnegves ha peswar-ugens
82	dew ha peswar-ugens	92	dewdhek ha peswar-ugens
82ens	nessa ha peswar-ugens	92ens	dewdhegves ha peswar-ugens
83	peswar ha peswar-ugens	93	trydhek ha peswar-ugens
83ens	trysa ha peswar-ugens	93ens	trydhegves ha peswar-ugens
84	peswar ha peswar-ugens	94	peswardhek ha peswar-ugens
84ens	peswara ha peswar-ugens	94ens	peswardhegves ha peswar-ugens
85	pymp ha peswar-ugens	95	pymthek ha peswar-ugens
85ens	pympes ha peswar-ugens	95ens	pymthegves ha peswar-ugens
86	hwegh ha peswar-ugens	96	hwetek ha peswar-ugens
86ens	hweghves ha peswar-ugens	96ens	hwetegves ha peswar-ugens
87	seyth ha peswar-ugens	97	seytek ha peswar-ugens
87ens	seythves ha peswar-ugens	97ens	seytegves ha peswar-ugens
88	eth ha peswar-ugens	98	etek ha peswar-ugens
88ens	ethves ha peswar-ugens	98ens	etegves ha peswar-ugens
89	naw ha peswar-ugens	99	nownsek ha peswar-ugens
89ens	nawves ha peswar-ugens	99ens	nownsegves ha peswar-ugens

§93(6)   Numerals

(6) Numerals from one hundred to one hundred and eighty

100	kans		160	eth-ugens
100ves	kansves		160ves	eth-ugensves
120	hwegh-ugens		180	naw-ugens
120ves	hwegh-ugensves		180ves	naw-ugensves
140	seyth-ugens			
140ves	seyth-ugensves			

(7) Numerals from two hundred to nine hundred

200	dew kans		600	hwegh kans
200ves	dew kansves		600ves	hwegh kansves
300	tri hans		700	seyth kans
300ves	tri hansves		700ves	seyth kansves
400	peswar kans		800	eth kans
400ves	peswar kansves		800ves	eth kansves
500	pymp kans		900	naw kans
500ves	pymp kansves		900ves	naw kansves

(8) Numerals from one thousand to ten thousand

1000	mil		6000	hwegh mil
1000ves	milves		6000ves	hwegh milves
2000	dew vil		7000	seyth mil
2000ves	dew vilves		7000ves	seyth milves
3000	tri mil		8000	eth mil
3000ves	tri milves		8000ves	eth milves
4000	peswar mil		9000	naw mil
4000ves	peswar milves		9000ves	naw milves
5000	pymp mil		10,000	deg mil
5000ves	pymp milves		10,000ves	deg milves

(9) Higher numerals

100,000	kans mil
100,000ves	kans milves
1,000,000	milvil
1,000,000ves	milvilves
3,000,000	tri milvil
3,000,000ves	tri milvilves
4,000,000	peswar milvil
4,000,000ves	peswar milvilves etc.

§94 **The numeral 0** A number of words are used in association with a negative to mean 'not anything, nothing' (§266). One of these, **mann**, has been adopted to stand for 'nothing, nought' in counting and reckoning: **Tri marnas tri yw mann** 'Three less three is nothing'. So in reading a number sequence such as 5061 by digits, one says, **pymp, mann, hwegh, onan** 'five, nought, six, one', and in other contexts the term **(an) niverenn mann** '(the) number nought, zero': **rew hir a niverennow mann** 'a long row of noughts'.

§95 **The numeral 1** The numeral 1 has the independent form **onan** which can be used as a pronoun: **Ny vynnav gasa onan** 'I will not leave one'.

(1) An adjective in agreement with **onan** as a pronoun is mutated if the noun referred to is feminine in gender (§72(9)).

(2) In the form **honan** the numeral is used with possessive adjectives to mean 'alone, self'.

ow honan	'I alone, myself'
dha honan	'you alone, yourself'
y honan	'he/it alone, him/itself'
hy honan	'her/it alone, her/itself'
agan honan	'we alone, ourselves'
agas honan	'you alone, yourselves'
aga honan	'they alone, themselves'

Examples: **My a vynn mos ow honan dhe Loundres** 'I wish to go alone to London'; **Ke ty dha honan dhe wari!** 'Go and play by yourself!' **Yndella yw par dell y'n redsyn agan honan** 'It is just as we ourselves read it'; **Gwell yw dhywgh hwyhwi mos agas honan** 'It is better for you to go yourself' (emphatic), RD. 641-2.

This is not, of course, the reflexive pronoun 'self' which in Cornish is rendered by the verbal prefix **om-** (§232, §273).

These same phrases in apposition to a possessive construction mean 'belonging to oneself, own': **ow fluvenn ow honan** 'my own pen'; **y'ga diwleuv aga honan** 'in their own hands'; **Ev a'n jeves y garyans y honan** 'He has his own transport'.

When the pronoun is the object of a preposition, this must be expressed: **dhe Yowann y honan** 'to John himself' so **dhodho y honan** 'to him himself'; **Na serrewgh orthowgh agas honan!** 'Don't be angry at yourselves!' and not *Na serrewgh orth agas honan.

§95(3)   Numerals

(3)   The dependent form of the numeral is **unn**: **Yma marth dhymm a unn dra** 'I wonder at one thing'; **Unn loas a vydh lowr** 'One spoonful will be enough'. This **unn** causes soft mutation of a following feminine singular noun as in the first example, so: **unn koweth** 'one male friend' but **unn gowethes** 'one female friend'.

Unn also functions as an adjective giving the meaning 'a certain' (§49(1)). Rarely it may be interpreted as the indefinite article 'a/an' (§49(1)).

Note the expressions **unn mab** 'one son, one boy': marnas **unn mab dhe'm cherya** 'only one son to cheer me' but **unn vab** in the special sense of 'only son': **dha unn vab ker** 'your only dear son'.

§96   **The numeral 2**   The numeral 2 has a masculine form, **dew**, and a feminine form, **diw,** and these are used, as are all the numerals, either independently: **Gorr an dhew ma y'n amari** 'Put these two in the cupboard!' or dependently: **Golgh an dhiw skudell kynsa!** 'Wash the two dishes first!'

Both forms cause second state mutation: **dew bons** (**pons** m.) 'two bridges'; **diw gyst** (**kyst** f.) 'two boxes'. Both numerals are themselves mutated after **an** 'the': **an dhew vrybour** (**brybour** m.) 'the two tramps'; **an dhiw vre** (**bre** f.) 'the two hills' (§50(3c)).

An accompanying adjective is also mutated: **dew wover vyghan** (**gover** m., **byghan** adj.) 'two small streams'; **an dhiw elestrenn velyn** (**melyn** adj.) 'the two yellow irises' (§83(2c)).

For **dew/diw** used to make a dual number of the noun see §45.

§97   **The numeral 3**   The numeral 3 also has a form for each gender, **tri** m., **teyr** f. and both aspirate a following **k-** to **h-**, **p-** to **f-** and **t-** to **th-** (§24): **tri margh** 'three horses'; **tri hans** (**kans** m.) 'three hundred'; **tri hwartron** (**kwartron** m.) 'three quarters'; **tri fenn** (**penn** m.) 'three heads'; **tri thenewenn** (**tenewenn** m.) 'three sides'; **teyr gwydhenn** 'three trees'; **teyr hador** (**kador** f.) 'three chairs'; **teyr hweth** (**kweth** f.) 'three cloths'; **teyr farth** (**parth** f.) 'three sides'; **teyr thro** (**tro** f.) 'three turns'.

§98   **The numeral 4**   The numeral 4 has a masculine and a feminine form, **peswar** m., **peder** f., neither of which causes mutation: **peswar le** 'four places'; **peder gre** 'four herds'.

Note **pedrek** adj. 'square' and **pedrenn** 'hindquarter'.

§99 The remaining numerals to 10 have no separate masculine and feminine forms nor do they cause mutation.

Note however **pym'woli** 'five wounds (of Christ)' as found in the texts is a close compound (§61(1)) and the -p of **pymp** is omitted with softening of the **g-** of the noun.

§100 From 11 to 19 the numerals are a compound of the digit and **deg** 'ten'. The **d-** of **deg** is softened in **dewdhek** 'twelve', **trydhek** 'thirteen', **peswardhek** 'fourteen'; hardened (§25) in **pymthek** with loss of -p-, in **hwetek** 'sixteen' with loss of -gh-, in **seytek** 'seventeen' and **etek** 'eighteen' with loss of -th-. In **unnek** 'eleven' the **d-** has dropped and in **nownsek** 'nineteen' it has converted to an -s- with a vowel change.

§101 From 20 upwards to 199 the procedure is as follows:

(1) Counting is in twenties and the second hundred carries on from the first after **kans** 'hundred' has been passed: **ugens** 'twenty'; **dew-ugens** 'two twenties, forty'; **hwegh ha tri-ugens** 'six and three score, sixty-six'; **kans hag unnek** 'one hundred and eleven'; **seyth-ugens** 'seven twenties, one hundred and forty'; **nownsek ha naw ugens** 'nineteen and nine twenties, one hundred and ninety-nine'; **deg warn ugens a vona** 'thirty (pieces) of money', PD.593; **ha tri-ugens moy** 'and sixty more', MC. 227.5; **eth-ugens flogh** 'one hundred and sixty children', BM. 1561.

(2) **Dew-ugens** 'forty' has a contracted form **dewgens**.

(3) **Hanterkans** 'half a hundred' is the usual form for an exact fifty. **Deg ha dewgens** is an alternative and is regular in the compounds: **hanterkans troeshys** or **deg troes-hys ha dewgens** 'fifty feet (length)'; **peswardhek ranndir ha dewgens** 'fifty-four districts'.

(4) Compound numbers from 21 to 39 are invariable in the order of their constituent parts, the smaller number being placed first and linked to the following **ugens** 'twenty' by the preposition **warn** 'on' §161(6): **tri warn ugens** 'three on twenty, twenty-three'; **trydhek warn ugens** 'thirteen on twenty, thirty-three'.

(5) Compound numbers from 41 to 199. The most common usage in modern Cornish is to put the smaller numerical element first: **onan ha dew-ugens** 'forty-one'; **peswardhek ha seyth-ugens** 'fourteen and seven twenties, one hundred and fifty-four'. The reverse order is rare: **dewgens hag onan**; **seyth-**

§101(5)   Numerals

ugens ha peswardhek. In both cases the two elements are joined by **ha(g)** 'and'.

(6)   **KANS** 'one hundred' causes no mutation but in several combinations it drops its -s, the following consonant then undergoing hardening in some cases: **kankweyth (kan(s), gweyth)** 'a hundred times'; **kangour** 'a hundred men'. Other compounded words are: **kansblydhen** f. 'a century', pl. **kansblydhynyow**; without loss of the -s; **kansplek** adv. 'hundredfold'; **kanspoes** 'hundred-weight'; **kansvil** 'one hundred thousand' with mutation of **mil** 'thousand' instead of **kans mil** (§93(9)).

The term for two hundred is **dew kans** without the expected mutation of the -k of **kans** (§96) in order, no doubt, to avoid confusion with **dew-ugens (dewgens)** 'forty'.

Spiration of the **k-** after **tri** gives **tri hans** (§97).

§102   From 200 on counting proceeds by hundreds and the intermediate groups of twenties: **dew kans ha seyth warn ugens** 'two hundred and seven on twenty, two hundred and twenty-seven'; **eth kans, pymthek ha dew-ugens** 'eight hundred, fifteen and two twenties, eight hundred and fifty-five'.

§103   **MIL** m. and its compounds (§93(8)(9)) soften a following consonant: **mil ji** 'a thousand houses'. **Milvil** 'a thousand thousand, a million' has an alternative, **milyon** m. 'a million'.

§104   Long complex numbers use the conjunction **ha(g)** only where necessary as an internal link in each numerical term, successive steps being separated in writing by a comma. To illustrate the points made in the foregoing sections several examples of longer numbers are appended with literal translations.

208	**dew kans hag eth**	'two hundred and eight'
281	**dew kans, onan ha peswar-ugens**	'two hundred, one and four twenties'
331	**tri hans, unnek warn ugens**	'three hundred, eleven on twenty'
476	**peswar kans, hwetek ha tri-ugens**	'four hundred, sixteen and three twenties'
1261	**mil, dew kans, onan ha tri-ugens**	'a thousand, two hundred, one and three twenties'
3350	**tri mil, tri hans ha hanterkans**	'three thousand, three hundred and half a hundred'

§105(3a) Numerals

64,794	peswar mil ha tri-ugens, seyth kans, peswardhek ha peswar-ugens	'four and three twenties (of) thousands, seven hundred, fourteen and four twenties'
240,903	dew kans mil ha dew-ugens, naw kans ha tri	'two hundred and two twenties (of) thousands, nine hundred and three'
5,500,000	pymp milyon ha hanter '	'five million and a half'
40,500,000	dew-ugens milyon, pymp kans mil	'two twenties (of) millions, five hundred thousands'

For an alternative way of rendering very large numbers see §105(3a).

§105 The noun denoting the objects numbered is associated with the numeral in the following ways:

(1) If the number is a single term or a simple multiple of twenty, a hundred, a thousand or a million, the noun follows it in the singular: **deg kador** 'ten chairs'; **trydhek aval** 'thirteen apples'; **hanterkans bloedh** 'fifty years of age'; **tri-ugens lath** 'sixty yards'; **dew kans benyn** 'two hundred women'; **mil beuns** 'a thousand pounds'; **peswar mil dhen** 'four thousand people'; **pymp mil strekys** 'five thousand strokes', MC. 227.3; **tri milyon owr** 'three million (pieces) of gold', RD. 2258.

(2) If the number consists of two numerical terms, the noun is singular and placed after the first term of the number: **unn jydh warn ugens** 'twenty-one days'; **deg lyvenn ha dew-ugens** 'fifty pages'; **hwegh blydhen ha dew-ugens** 'forty-six years'; **peswardhek diner hag eth ugens** 'one hundred and seventy-four pence'; **peswar kans bugh ha hanterkans** 'four hundred and fifty cows'; **naw kans flogh ha hwetek** 'nine hundred and sixteen children'; **mil nos hag onan** 'a thousand and one nights'. These elements are occasionally found in the reverse order to that given here but the same principle applies (§101(5)): **dew-ugens blydhen ha hwegh** 'forty-six years', PD.351.

(3) The number may be linked to a following plural noun by the preposition **a** 'of'. This is the simplest method in some cases.

(a) When the number has three or more terms: **kans, peswar warn ugens a dheves** 'one hundred and twenty-four sheep'; **dewdheg mil, hwegh kans, trydhek ha peswar-ugens a beunsow** 'twelve thousand, six hundred and ninety-three pounds'. Thus with the components of very large numbers (§104): **eth ha dew-ugens a vilyonow, seyth kans ha pymthek warn ugens a vilyow, kans hag onan a dus** 'forty-eight million, seven hundred and thirty-five thousand, one hundred and one persons'.

§105(3b) Numerals

(b) When the noun itself is qualified in some way: **tri mil ha dew kans a fleghes kottha es trydhek bloedh** 'three thousand, two hundred children older than thirteen years'; **pymp warn ugens a gerri flamm nowydh** 'twenty-five brand-new cars'.

(4) The noun is rarely put in the plural before the numeral, a poetic usage: **dinerow hwegh** 'pence six', BM. 3409; **peunsow kans** 'pounds one hundred', BM. 2579; **dagrennow tri** 'tears three', MC. 225.1. Note in this latter case that the number is to be regarded as a masculine noun whilst the preceding noun is feminine plural.

§106 The words **deg** m. **degow** pl. 'ten(s)'; **ugens** m. **ugensow** pl. 'twenty, twenties'; **kans** m. **kansow** pl. 'hundred(s)'; **mil** m. **milyow** pl. 'thousand(s)'; **milyon** m. **milyonow** pl. 'million(s)', may be used as common nouns: **Lies mil a grys henna** 'Many thousands believe that'; **My re welas kansow anedha** 'I have seen hundreds of them'; **Ugensow a varnoryon a veu beudhys** 'Scores of sailors were drowned'.

§107 **Forms of the ordinal numerals**

(1) **KYNSA** 'first' is a superlative adjective which may like other superlatives precede or, for special emphasis, follow, its noun (§83(8)): **an kynsa stevell** 'the first room'; **an sita gynsa** 'the first city'.

(2) **NESSA** 'second', lit. 'nearer, next' is also a superlative adjective (§82(4)): **an nessa dyskans** 'the second lesson'; **kemmer an nessa fordh!** 'take the next road!'

(3) **TRESSA** 'third' is formed by analogy with **nessa**, **TRYSA** being the true ordinal. **PESWARA** 'fourth' is also adjectival.

(4) **PYMPES** 'fifth' adds **-es** to the cardinal form.

(5) **HWEGHVES** 'sixth' is regular but the variations **hweghes**, **hweffes** are found in the texts.

(6) **SEYTHVES** 'seventh' and **ETHVES** 'eighth' are regularly formed but **seythes** and **ethes** occur occasionally.

(7) The remainder of the ordinals to 'twentieth' are formed by adding the suffix **-ves** to the cardinal numeral the final **-k** of which becomes **-g** in the compound: **unnegves** (**unnek**) 'eleventh'.

(8) From 'twenty-first' to 'thirty-ninth' the smaller numerical element alone has the ordinal form: **(an) kynsa warn ugens** '(the) twenty-first'; **an etegves warn ugens** 'the thirty-eighth'.

(9) From 'fortieth' upwards the smaller numerical element in a compound carries the ordinal suffix, whatever the order of the parts: **an kynsa ha dew-ugens** 'the first and two twenties, the forty-first' or less often **an dhew-ugens ha kynsa** 'the two twenties and first'.

(10) In all cases the final syllable of the ordinal element is used with a numeral as an abbreviation of the full ordinal: **kynsa, 1a**; **pympes, 5es**; **kansves, 100ves**; **hweghves warn ugens, 26ves**; **seyth ugensves, 140ves**; **mil, tri hans, nessa ha peswar-ugens, 1382a**.

§108 Constructions with the ordinals

(1) The noun regularly follows the ordinal part of the numeral: **an kynsa penn-bloedh warn ugens** 'the twenty-first anniversary', lit. 'the first anniversary on twenty'; **an trihans, pympes dydh ha tri-ugens** 'the three hundred and sixty-fifth day', lit. 'the three hundred, fifth day and three twenties'; **an dhew vilves blydhen** 'the two thousandth year'.

(2) In a partitive sense the ordinals are followed by **a** 'of' (§57(2)): **an hweghves mis a'n vlydhen** 'the sixth month of the year'; **an ugensves folenn a'n lyver** 'the twentieth page of the book'. Thus with pronouns: **an tressa rew anedha** 'the third row of them'.

(3) These expressions may be defined, as in some of the foregoing examples, by the definite article or by one of the possessive adjectives: **agan kynsa tybyans** 'our first thought'.

§109 Fractions

(1) HANTER m. 'half' is used directly before a noun: **hanter brykk ha hanter men** 'half brick and half stone'; **hanternos** 'midnight'; **hanterdydh** 'noon'; **hanterkans** 'half a hundred, fifty'. The word has an adverbial use also: **Nyns yw ev hanter da** 'It's not half good (enough)'.

(2) KWARTRON/KWARTER/KWARTENN m. 'quarter', plurals **kwartronys, kwartrys, kwartennow**: **dew gwartron**; **tri hwartron** 'three quarters'.

§109(3) Numerals

(3) **RANN** f. 'part, share' also occurs with an ordinal number: **teyr ethves rann a dhewdhek warn ugens** 'three eighths (parts) of thirty-two'. The word **rann** may be understood: **seyth degves** 'seven tenths'. In an idiomatic sense the phrase **diw rann** 'two parts' means 'two thirds'.

(4) Decimal fractions require the use of the word **poynt** 'point' or a similar term. The digits following the point are then given in order: **eth warn ugens, poynt onan, mann, dew, hwegh** 'twenty-eight point one, nought, two, six', 28.1026.

(5) Percentages. The value of the percentage is followed by the phrase **an kans** '(of) the hundred' or **kansrann: deg an kans/deg kansrann** 'ten per cent'.

§110 **The simpler arithmetic operations are as follows:**

(1) Addition. The terms are linked by the conjunction **ha** 'and': **Dew ha tri yw pymp** 'Two and three are five' or **Dew ha tri a wra pymp** 'Two and three make five'. The verb is **keworra** 'add': **Mar keworrir tri dhe eth an sywyans yw unnek** 'If three is added to eight, the result is eleven'.

(2) Subtraction as an operation makes use of the word **marnas** 'unless, save, exclusive of' (§151): **Deg marnas pymp yw pymp** 'Ten less five is five' or **Deg marnas pymp a wra pymp** 'ten less five makes five'; **Kans marnas seytek a wra tri ha peswar-ugens** 'A hundred less seventeen makes eighty-three'. The verbal expression is **kemmeres diworth** 'take away from': **Kemmer naw diworth dew-ugens! Unnek warn ugens!** 'Take nine from forty! Thirty-one!'

(3) Multiplication is simply expressed by the juxtaposition of the two numbers concerned: **Dew bymp yw/a wra deg** 'Two fives are/make ten'. For greater explicitness the word **gweyth** 'time' (§61(1f), §121(1)) may be used: **Tri dewdhek gweyth yw/a wra hwetek warn ugens** 'Three twelves are/make thirty-six'. The verbal phrase **lieshe/gweyth** 'increase/times' can be used: **Ena my a lieshas peswar teyrgweyth ha kavoes dewdhek** 'Then I multiplied four three times and got twelve'.

(4) The verbal participle **rynnys** 'shared' is used to describe division: **Kans rynnys ynter deg yw/a wra deg** 'One hundred divided into ten (parts) is/makes ten'; **Tri ha tri-ugens rynnys ynter pymp yw/a wra dewdhek ha tri gesys** 'Sixty-three divided into five (parts) is/makes twelve and three left (over)'. The operation is expressed by **ranna yntra/ynter** 'divide between'. **Rann dewdhek**

§112   Numerals

ha tri-ugens yntra eth! Pyth yw an sywyans? Naw! 'Divide seventy-two by eight! What is the result? Nine!'

§111   **The date**

(1)   The year is either counted in hundreds as in English: **etek kans, dew-ugens ha hwetek** 'eighteen hundred and fifty-six, 1856' or, with the thousand separately expressed, **mil, eth kans, dew-ugens ha hwetek**, the same date. The latter usage is more common.

(2)   **Day and month**   **Dy' Yow, an seythves warn ugens a vis Meurth** 'Thursday, the twenty-seventh of March', in abbreviated form, **an 27ens a vis Meurth**. The word **dy'** is put before the name of the day unless **an** 'the' is used: **an Yow** 'on Thursday(s)'. Before the name of the month **mis** is always used with a lower case initial: **mis Genver** '(the) month (of) January'.

§112   **Time of day**   The question 'What time is it?' **Py eur yw (hi)?** is answered by a numeral and the word **eur** f. 'hour'. The numeral will have a feminine form where appropriate: **peder eur** 'four o'clock' (§71(3b)).

Time after the hour is either the hour followed by the minutes: **diw eur ugens** 'two hours twenty' or the number of minutes with **wosa** 'after': **ugens (mynysenn) wosa diw (eur)** 'twenty (minutes) after two (hours)'. The quarter hour is **kwartron** (§109(2)): **unn eur kwartron** 'one hour a quarter' or (**unn**) **kwartron wosa unn (eur)** '(a) quarter after one (hour)'. The half hour is **hanter** (§109(1)): **pymp eur hanter** 'five hours (a) half, half-past five'.

Time before the hour is expressed either by the use of **marnas** (§110(2)): **teyr eur marnas kwartron** 'three hours less (a) quarter', or by the use of the preposition **dhe** 'to': **kwartron dhe deyr eur**, the same time; **unnek eur marnas pymp (mynysenn) warn ugens** 'eleven (hours) less twenty-five (minutes)' or **pymp mynysenn warn ugens dhe unnek (eur)** 'twenty-five (minutes) to eleven (hours)'.

Before and after noon is **kyns hanterdydh** 'a.m.' and **wosa hanterdydh** 'p.m.'.

The time at which something happens is expressed similarly with the addition of the preposition **dhe** 'to' (§141(12)): **dhe naw eur** 'at nine o'clock'.

The noun **eur** f. 'hour' denotes the time, as above, whereas the noun **our** m. is a span of time: **diw eur** 'two o'clock', **dew our** 'two hours' (of time): **My a dheuth dhe'n le ambosys dhe dhiw eur hag a wortas dew our** 'I came to the place arranged at two o'clock and waited (for) two hours'.

§113 **Duration of time** Duration of time is expressed without the use of a preposition except in a few conventional phrases: **dew-ugens dydh** '(for) forty days', OM. 1027; **Ev a driga ena ugens blydhen** 'He lived there (for) twenty years'; **Res o dhymm y wortos hanter our** 'I had to wait for him (for) half an hour'; **Hirneth y fywa hi hy honan** '(For) a long time she lived on her own'; **Hi a sevis berrdermyn ena yth eth** 'She stood (for) a short time then she went'.

With the preposition **rag** 'for' (§154(5)) in the phrases **rag nevra** 'for ever'; **rag an termyn** 'for the time (being)'.

§114 **Age** Age can be defined in several ways using **bloedh** 'year of age' or **oes** 'age': **Pes bloedh os jy? Tri bloedh warn ugens ov** 'How old are you? I am twenty-three years old'; **Pyth yw y oes?** 'What is his age?' **Dew-ugens bloedh yw ev** 'Forty years of age he is' or **Dew-ugens bloedh yw y oes** 'Forty (years) is his age'.

§115 **Linear measurement** Questions are introduced by phrases such as **Pygemmys hys yw?** 'How long is?' **Pygemmys les yw?** 'How wide is?' **Pygemmys ughelder yw?** 'How high is?' **Pygemmys downder yw?** 'How deep is?'

The appropriate units are: **meusva** f. 'inch', pl. **meusvedhi**; **troes-hys** m. 'foot', pl. **troes-hysyow**; **lath** f. 'yard', pl. **lathow**; **mildir** m. 'mile', pl. **mildiryow**; **milimeter** m. 'millimetre', pl. **milimetrow**; **sentimeter** m. 'centimetre', pl. **sentimetrow**; **kilometer** m. 'kilometre', pl. **kilometrow**.

Statements in reply to questions such as those above can contain the phrases: **a-hys** 'in length'; **a-les** 'in width'; **yn ughelder** 'in height'; **yn downder** 'in depth': **An gyst ma yw peswar troes-hys a-hys, tri throes-hys a-les ha dew droes-hys yn downder** 'This box is four feet long, three feet wide and two feet deep'.

§116 **Distance** Distance in the sense of 'how far is?' is expressed by **Py hys yw alemma/ahanan/alena dhe/bys dhe/bys yn?** 'How far is it from here, from there to?': **Py hys yw ahanan bys yn Lannstefan? Ugens mildir yw.** 'How far is it from here (from us) right into Launceston? Twenty miles'. The word **pes** with a noun may be used (§76): **Pes kilometer alena dhe Fowydh? Dewdhek** 'How many kilometres from there to Fowey? Twelve'.

§117 **Square measure** In square measure the units are followed by the word **pedrek** 'square in shape': **meusva bedrek** 'square inch'; **meusvedhi pedrek** 'square inches'; **deg mildir pedrek** 'ten square miles'; **tri meter pedrek** 'three square metres'. The idea of squaring a quantity is conveyed by the verb **pedrekhe** 'make square': **naw pedrekhes yw onan ha peswar-ugens** 'nine squared is eighty-one'.

§118 **Volume and size** Volume and size in general is suggested by **braster** 'bigness': **pygemmys braster yw?** 'What size (volume) is?' A cubic dimension is denoted by the numeral with **triflek** 'threefold' (§121(2)): **naw meusva driflek** 'nine cubic inches'. The verb is **triflegya** 'make three fold'.

§119 Other words with mathematical connotations are: **akont** m. 'account'; **akontya** 'count'; **akontyans** 'reckoning'; **amontya** v.n 'count, reckon'; **jynn-amontya** 'computer'; **awgrym** 'mathematics'; **musur** m. 'measure'; **musura** v.n. 'measure'; **niver** m. 'number'; **niverenn** f. 'numeral'; **nivera** v.n. 'count'; **niveryans** m. abs.n. 'counting'; **rekna** v.n. 'reckon', **reknell** f. 'calculator'.

§120 Miscellaneous numerical expressions with examples

(1) ONAN HAG ONAN 'one by one, singly': **tri ha tri** 'three by three, by threes', etc.

(2) AGAS PYMP 'you five, the five of you'; **agan tri** 'we three, the three of us'.

(3) AN TRI 'the three'; **an dhew** 'the two, both'. With **oll** 'all': **oll an peswar anedha** 'the whole four of them, all four of them'.

(4) PUB 'each': **pub kans** 'each hundred'.

(5) NEB KANS 'about a hundred, a hundred, more or less'.

(6) OGAS HA KANS 'about a hundred, nearly a hundred, getting on for a hundred'.

(7) MOY (AG)ES 'more than', LE (AG)ES 'fewer than': **moy es pymp warn ugens** 'more than twenty-five'; **le ages mil** 'fewer than a thousand'.

(8) ORTH NIVER 'in number': **tri mil orth niver** 'three thousand in number', BM. 1539; see §152(3).

§120(9) Numerals

(9) **PORAN** 'exactly, quite': **hanterkans poran** 'fifty exactly' (§267).

(10) 'PER' as a measure is expressed by the use of the preposition **orth** (§152(3)): **I a's gwertha a ugens diner orth an peuns** 'They sold them for twenty pence per pound'.

§121 **Adverbial numbers**

(1) Adverbs with the meaning 'a certain number of times' are compounds of numerals and the noun **gweyth** f.

unnweyth	'once'	hwegh gweyth	'six times'
diwweyth	'twice'	seythgweyth	'seven times'
teyrgweyth	'three times'	ethgweyth	'eight times'
pedergweyth	'four times'	naw gweyth	'nine times'
pympgweyth	'five times'	degkweyth	'ten times'

and thence, **unnek gweyth** 'eleven times', **dewdhek gweyth** 'twelve times, **trydhek gweyth** 'thirteen times', **lieskweyth** 'many times', etc. Note that in the first four items the compound is written as one word.

With **ugens** 'twenty' and **kans** 'hundred' the -s drops out and the **gw-** of **gweyth** is hardened to **kw-** : **ugenkweyth** 'twenty times'; **kankweyth** 'hundred times'. This usage is extended to compounds of these numbers: **seyth ugenkweyth** 'one hundred and forty times'; **tri hankweyth** 'three hundred times'; **Deg kankweyth dhis lowena!** 'Ten hundred times happiness to you!' PD. 574.

After **mil** 'thousand' there is softening: **milweyth** 'thousand times'; **teyr milweyth** 'three thousand times'.

(2) '-FOLD' in the numerical sense is rendered by **-plek** m.: **dewblek** 'twofold, double'; **triflek** 'threefold, triple'; **tri-ugens plek** 'sixtyfold'; **kansplek** 'a hundredfold'; **milblek** 'a thousandfold'. **I a sewen milblek gwell** 'They shall succeed a thousandfold better', OM. 523.

(3) **KEMMYS** 'the same measure' (§261) is compounded with numerals: **dewgemmys, trihemmys, peswar kemmys, unnek kemmys, mil gemmys** 'twice, three times, four times, eleven times, a thousand times as much': **Yma edhomm a dri hemmys a gadoryow** 'Three times as many chairs are needed'. These words are used in replies to questions with **pygemmys** 'how much' (§327): **Pygemmys moy y fydh lowr ragdho?** 'How much more will be

§122(6)   Numerals

enough for him?' **Trihemmys** 'Three times as much'. Comparisons are expressed through **ha** 'and' (§287): **Yma dewgemmys benynes ha gwer** 'There are twice as many women as men'.

(4)   **GWELL** 'better' and **GWETH** 'worse', comparative adjectives (§82(4)), are combined with **mil** 'thousand', the adjective undergoing softening of the initial: **milwell** 'a thousand times better, much better'; **milweth** 'a thousand times worse, much worse'.

(5)   **TERMYN** 'time' is used with ordinals with the sense, 'the -nth time': **an peswara termyn warn ugens** 'the twenty-fourth time'.

§122   **The decimal system of counting**

In Wales a decimal system of counting is in use alongside the Celtic method of reckoning by twenties. It has been suggested that a decimal system should be used in Cornwall and such a system is here described although to date it has found little favour.

(1)   One to ten. The feminine forms **diw**, **teyr**, **peder** are not used.

(2)   From eleven to ninety-nine the tens and units are separately counted: **unn deg unn** 'one ten one' = 11; **dew dheg tri** 'two tens three' = 23; **naw deg naw** 'nine tens nine' = 99.

(3)   The hundreds and the thousands are similarly treated: **dew gans** 'two hundred'; **tri mil** 'three thousand'.

(4)   Complex numbers evaluate each digit as above: **pymp mil, peswar kans, hwegh deg, naw** 'five thousand, four hundred, six tens, nine' = 5469.

(5)   The numeral is followed by **a** 'of' and a plural noun; **seyth a gentrow** 'seven nails'; **eth kans, seyth deg, tri a dus** 'eight hundred, seven tens, three of people' = 873 people.

(6)   No ordinals are used. Instead, a cardinal number follows the noun: **an tyller dew dheg eth** 'the place two tens eight' = 'the twenty-eighth place'.

❖ ❖ ❖ ❖ ❖

PREPOSITIONS

§123 Forms of the prepositions Some of the prepositions have simple forms. Others are compounds. Examples of these latter follow.

(1)   Preposition with another preposition: **a** + **rag** = **a-rag** 'before'; **dhe** + **rag** = **dherag** 'in front of'.

(2)   Preposition with a noun: **er** + **pynn (penn** 'head') = **erbynn** 'against'; **yn** + **le** = **yn le** 'in place of'.

(3)   Preposition with a noun and a conjunction: **war** + **tu** + **ha** = **war-tu ha** 'towards'.

(4)   Compound adverb with a simple preposition: **a** + **pervedh** m. 'interior' = **a-bervedh** adv. 'within', and this with the addition of the preposition **yn** gives the preposition **a-bervedh yn** 'inside'; **yn** + **mes** m. 'field' = **yn-mes** adv. 'outside', and with the simple preposition **a** this becomes **yn-mes a** 'outside of'.

§124 Government of the preposition In all but the few cases which are mentioned below the preposition comes directly before the noun which it governs as its object.

Only the prepositions **a** 'from, of', **dhe** 'to', **dre** 'through', **war** 'on', **yn-dann** 'under' regularly mutate the initial of the following word by softening. Government of a pronoun object is affected in one of several ways.

(1)   The pronoun object is represented by a personal ending to the preposition: **rag** 'for', **ragov** 'for me'.

(2)   The pronoun object is represented by a possessive adjective put before the last element of a compound preposition: **erbynn** 'against', **er ow fynn** 'against me'.

(3)   The pronoun object is represented by an independent pronoun: **troha** 'towards', **troha my** 'towards me'.

(4)   Some prepositions are not found with a pronoun object. These are mentioned, as they occur, in the sections below.

§125(1)   Prepositions

§125 **The personal endings of the prepositions** These may be classified according to the vowel which characterises the ending of the 1st and 2nd persons singular and the 1st person plural. The endings for the other persons are uniform.

1s.	-av	-ov -	-iv	The
2s.	-as	-os	-is	characteristic
3s.m	-o	-o	-o	vowel being
3s.f.	-i	-i	-i	-a, -o and -i (-y)
1p.	-an	-on	-yn	respectively.
2p.	**-owgh**	**-owgh**	**-owgh**	
3p.	-a	-a	-a	

The prepositions **dhe** 'to' (§141) and **gans** 'with' (§147) have endings peculiar to themselves.

The arrangement of the following sections describes the prepositions in alphabetical order except for a few cases of derivatives, e.g. **a-rag** follows **rag** and **diwar** follows **war**.

§126 **A** 'of, from' implies movement away from an object or location. It causes mutation by softening of the initial letter of the following noun.

The forms with pronominal endings.

1s.	**ahanav**	*of me*		1p.	**ahanan**	*of us*
2s.	**ahanas**	*of you*		2p.	**ahanowgh**	*of you*
3s.m.	**anodho**	*of him/it*		3p.	**anedha**	*of them*
3s.f.	**anedhi**	*of her/it*				

The meanings of **a**, principal and derived.

(1) Movement from a place or from an object: **Ev a dheuth a Sen Niot** 'He came from St Neot'; **A-dhistowgh y poenyas an gath a'n daras** 'Immediately the cat ran from the door'; **mar nyns edh a'y nagha** 'if you don't leave off denying it', lit. 'go from denying'.

So with expressions implying separation: **a-dre** 'away from home'; **pell a** 'far from' and with verbs of hindering, refusing, lacking, failing, saving. **Lettya**: **Ny'm lett a dhyski** 'He will not prevent me from learning'; **skonya**: **Piw a skon a dhos?** 'Who refuses to come?' but see §141(15j) when it takes **dhe**; **fyllel**: **Ny fyllons a arghans** 'They will not lack for money'; **Wostalleth kyn**

§126(1)   Prepositions

fallav a'y wul an dro ma, y tehwelav; 'Though I fail to do it at first, I will return'; **difres: Henna a'n difresas a brederi re** 'That saved him from worrying too much'.

Note however that **lesta** 'prevent' is constructed with **rag** (§154(4)) (also includes **lettya**).

(2) The point of departure: **a'n penn dhe'n troes** 'from (the) head to (the) foot'; **alemma** 'from here, from now'; **ahanan** 'from us, from here, from now'; **alena** 'from there, from then'; **a-ban (a + pan** 'when') 'since', lit. 'from when'; **a-ble, a-byle, a-byla** 'from where?, whence?' **a-dhia** 'from there, from yonder, since'; **a-dhann** prep. 'from under'.

(3) The source or origin: **drefenn an vertu a'n lavar Krist pan gowsas** 'because of the power of the words when Christ spoke' MC. 68.1-2; **a'y vodh y honan y feu hemma gwrys** 'according to his own intention this was done'; **Hi a worthybis a'y anvodh** 'She answered unwillingly; **mars yw hemma kusul an konsel** 'if this is te advice of the council'.

(4) Simple location, the implication of movement being lost: **a'n barth dheghow/kledh** 'on the right/left side'; **a'n barth kledh dhe'm chi** 'on the right side of my house'; **a bub tu** 'on every side'; **a neb tu** 'on some side or other'; **a'n eyl tu** 'aside, apart'; **Res vydh sevel a'n eyl tu a-dhiworta** 'It will be necessary to stand aside away from them'. Thus when some feeling or state is situated in the body or mind: **moy brew a'y gorf** 'more broken in his body'; **Gwenys veuv a'm troes** 'I was stung in my foot'; **a wel dhe** 'in the sight of'; **a wel oll dhe'n dus** 'completely in the sight of the people'.

So of posture and attitude applied to persons: **a'y esedh** 'sitting'; **a'y sav** 'standing'; **a'y worwedh** 'lying'. The possessive adjective varies with the person spoken of: **Yth esens a'ga gorwedh** 'They were lying down'.

Numerous compounds are thus formed with **a** as the first or the last element: see Adverbs, some adjectives (§78), and some prepositions (see below).

(5) The material of which something is made is named after **a** (§58(2)): **gwrys a bri** 'made of clay'. This remains the case when the material is, as it were, ideal and abstract: **den a vri** 'a man of reputation'; **benyn a dhynyta** 'a woman of dignity, a dignified woman'; **a'n par ma, a'n par na** 'of this kind, of that kind'; **skrifer a'th par** 'a writer like you'; **a-dhevis** 'excellent, first-rate'; **towl a-dhevis** 'an excellent plan'; **My yw epskop a-dhevis** 'I am a first-rate bishop', BM. 3916.

§126(8a) Prepositions

Verbs and other expressions meaning 'fill, full of' are therefore constructed with **a**: **leun a dhowr** 'full of water'; **Lanw e a dhor!** 'Fill it with earth!'

(6) The whole of which something is a part is indicated by **a**: **rann vras a'n penshyon** 'a large part of the pension'; **bush byghan a'n dus** 'a small group of the people'.

Thus with **meur a** 'much of, many of' (§57(2a)). The preposition is so used when the first noun is to remain indefinite in contrast to the genitive of apposition in which the first noun is necessarily defined (§55). For example the two words **fenester** 'window' and **chi** 'house' can be associated in four ways, each indicating that the one is part of the other.

Appositional genitive	With the preposition **a** 'of'
FENESTER AN CHI '(the) window of the house' **FENESTER CHI** '(the)window of a house'	**FENESTER A'N CHI** 'a window of the house' **FENESTER A JI** 'a window of a house' **AN FENESTER A'N CHI** 'the window of the house'

(7) The origin of an event is expressed through the use of **a**: **Hemm o dedhewys dhymm ganso a'y guvder** 'This was promised to me by him out of his kindness'; **Ny yllir re y wormel a'y weres** 'One cannot praise him too highly for his help'.

(8) The idea of location allows **a** to be used to indicate in a very general way the field of reference of a noun or other word, yielding expressions which can be translated by 'in respect of, with regard to, concerning, about, with reference to', etc.'

(a) General: **Yth esa dadhel a'n dowlenn** 'There was an argument with regard to the programme'; **Deriv dhymm a'th teylu** 'Tell me about your family'; **Piw a wodhya fatell via a'n den na?** 'Who knew how it had been with that person?' **istori a vywnans an sens** 'a history concerning the lives of the saints'; **Prederi a'n mater my a vynn** 'I will think about the matter'; **Pes da on a'gas kusul** 'We are very pleased with your advice'; **Ymons ow mones di a borpos** 'They are going there in respect of a purpose, with a purpose'; **Mar ger ywa ahanan** 'He is so dear to us'; **a'm godhvos** 'to my knowledge, as a fact'.

§126(8b)   Prepositions

(b) Phrases which have the meaning of regard, attention, concern: **Ny'm deur mann a dybyans denvydh** 'I don't care about anyone's opinion'; **Ny'm deur travyth ahanas** 'I care nothing at all about you'; **Ny wra ev vri anedha** 'He has no regard at all for them', lit. 'He makes no account of them'; **Ny synsav vy a'th krevder unn favenn goeg** 'I care not an empty bean for your might'.

(c) Certain verbs: **dannvon a** 'send ... to': **Ev re's dannvonas a hwilas gweres** 'He has sent them to look for help'; **erghi a** 'order to' (but more usually without a preposition): **An breusyas re'n erghis a be** or **An breusyas re'n erghis pe** 'The judge has ordered him to pay'; **gras/grassow a** 'thanks for': **Meur ras dhis a'th lyther** 'Many thanks for your letter' (for other constructions see §141(15e)): **kusulya a** 'advise to'; **My a'th kusul a omdenna** 'I advise you to withdraw'; **lenwel a** 'fill with'; **pysi a** 'ask someone to': **Ow gwreg a'gas pys a goena genen** 'My wife asks you to have supper with us' (for other constructions with **pysi** see §154(3), §161(9) and §229(3d)).

(d) Certain nouns are commonly found as the first element in phrases of this kind and the second element is often a verbal noun: **chons a** 'chance to'; **dout a** 'doubt about'; **Na borth dout ahanav!** 'Don't have any doubt about me!' **edrek a** 'regret': **I a's tevydh edrek bras a dhemmedhi** 'They will regret marrying very much'; **edhomm a** 'need of/to': **Nyns eus edhomm lemmyn a dhybri** 'There is no need now to eat'; **hwans a** 'desire of/to': **Yma hwans dhedha a gana** 'They want to sing'; **kummyas a** 'permission to' (occasionally with **dhe** (§141(18)): **Ro dhymm kummyas a skrifa dhodho!** 'Give me permission to write to him!' or **kummyas dhe**; **leun a** 'full of': **leun a dhowr** 'full of water'; **mall a** 'impatience, eagerness to': **Mall yw genev a dhalleth an goel** 'I am eager to start the holiday'; **marth a** 'wonder at': **a-ban eus marth dhodho a'n hwedhel** 'since he wonders at the story'; **meth a** 'shame, ashamed of': **Meth o gans an flogh a'y wrians** 'The child was ashamed of his action'; **own a** 'fear of': **Ni a'gan beus own a'n tewlder** 'We are afraid of the dark'; **prys a** 'time to': **Nans yw prys a worfenna** 'Now is the time to finish'.

Except with **edrek**, **marth** and **meth**, **a** may be omitted if the nouns come together: **edhomm dybri** or **edhomm a dhybri** 'need to eat' but **meth a oela** 'shame at crying', cf. §57 and §147(5b), §255.

(e) Expressions of mercy and/or pity are followed by **a** and a noun denoting the person to whom the feeling is directed: **Kemmer mersi a'm enev!** 'Take pity on my soul!' **ow kemmeres pyta a'n fleghes** 'taking pity on the children'; **Kemmer truedh a'n re voghosek!** 'Take pity on the poor!'

§129 Prepositions

(f) Exclamative phrases are formed of an adjective followed by **a** and a noun: **Teg a wel!** '(What a) fine (thing) of a sight!' **Drog a alar!** '(What an) evil (thing) of an affliction!' (§88(2)).

(9) The location can be regarded as representing a value, a standard against which something is judged: **Re hir o an estyllenn a hanter meusva** 'The shelf was too long by half an inch'; **Go hi! An lovan yw re gott a droes-hys** 'Drat it! The rope is too short by a foot'; **a verr dermyn** or **a dermyn berr** 'in a short time'; **a'y anvodh** 'against his will'. So with expressions of buying and selling to indicate the price: **My a'n gwerth a dhew beuns** 'I'm selling it for two pounds'; **Ena y prenir leth a bris isella** 'There one buys milk at a lower price'; **Gwerthes y huk dhe brena anedhi ... kledha!** 'Let him sell his cloak to buy (with its value) a sword!' PD. 922-23.

§127 **A-BARTH** 'on the side of'. From **a** and **parth** f. 'side'. This preposition governs a noun object directly and a pronoun object through **dhe** 'to'.

(1) 'On the side of': **kerens a-barth an tas** 'relatives on the father's side'; **kerens a-barth an vamm** 'relatives on the mother's side'; **genys ... a-barth tas ha mamm keffrys** '(well) born ... on both the father's and the mother's side', BM. 358-59; **a-barth a-woeles** 'on the bottom side, down below'; **a-barth a-wartha** 'on the top side, up above'; **a-barth dheghow** 'on the right-hand side'; **a-barth kledh** 'on the left-hand side'; **mars yw a-barth an re na's teves hwans a janjya** 'if he is on the side of those who don't want change'; **a-barth dhywgh** 'on your side'.

(2) 'In the name of, for the sake of': **A'n kaves a-barth y fleghes** 'Let him have it for the sake of his children'; **a-barth an Tas** 'in the name of the Father'; **A-barth dhedha ev re skonyas a assentya** 'For their sake he has refused to agree'; **A-barth dhymm na'n gwra!** 'For my sake do not do it!'

§128 **A-DAL** From **a** and **tal** m. 'brow' with the meanings 'opposite, facing'. It governs a noun directly or a pronoun through **dhe**: **Yma arghantti a-dal an eglos** 'There is a bank opposite the church'; **Piw yw henna usi owth esedha a-dal dhedhi?** 'Who is that (man) who is sitting facing her?'

§129 **A-DER** 'without, beyond, apart from, outside, away from, except'. **A-der** with a noun or an adjective denotes a negative alternative 'not': **Peder a yv gwin, a-der korev** 'Peter drinks wine, not beer'; **An vleujenn yw gwynn, a-der rudh** 'The flower is white not red'; **Galsa oll, a-der gortos dhe weres** 'All had gone, not waiting to help'; **An fleghes a warias y'n lowarth, a-der an chi** 'The children played in the garden, not (in) the house'.

§129 Prepositions

A-der is followed by a noun or by an independent pronoun: **Meur o an tros a-der ken** 'The noise was exceptionally great'; **Ev re wrug an hwel a-der my** 'He has done the work without me'; **Maria, a-der dha vregh dyllo dhymm dha vab Yesus!** 'Mary, from out of your arm give me your son Jesus!' BM. 3631-32. Used adverbially: **A-der medhelhes, bras owgh** 'Apart from being weakened you are (still) great'.

§130 **A-DHIA** 'from, since'. A compound from **a** and **di** adv. 'thither' (§259(3)): It causes soft mutation and is used with expressions of time or place and only with nouns: **a-dhia an dre** 'from the town'; **a-dhia naw eur** 'since nine o'clock'.

For **a-dhann** see §169.
For **a-dhiwar** see §162.
For **a-dhiworth** see §153.

§131 **A-DREUS DHE** 'athwart, across, contrary': **My a'n gorr a-dreus dhe'n kleudh ma** 'I will put it across this ditch'; **kyn hwrylli kows a-dreus dhyn ni** 'though you contradict us'.

§132 **A-DRO DHE** 'about, around': **a-dro dhe'n park** 'around the field'; **Oll a-dro dhywgh yma edhomm** 'All about you there is need'. In a transferred sense: **ger a-dro dhe Gernewek** 'a word about Cornish'; **Lavar dhymm a-dro dhodho!** 'Tell me about it!'

§133 **A-DRYV** 'behind' governs a noun directly or a pronoun through **dhe**: **Ny gewsyn a-dryv tus** 'I didn't speak behind people's backs', lit. 'behind people'; **pan sevis hi a-dryv dhodho** 'when she stood behind him'.

§134 **A-GOVIS** 'on account of, for the sake of, on behalf of'. The noun element is **govis** 'care, regard, attention'. Compare also **govijyon** 'care(s), sorrow(s)'.

This preposition is not used with nouns as object. Hence, for clarity, the basic form is shown without the expected mutation after **a**.

The government of pronouns is by the use of possessive adjectives before **govis**.

1s.	**a'm govis**	*for my sake*	1p.	**a'gan govis**	*for our sake*
2s.	**a'th wovis**	*for your sake*	2p.	**a'gas govis**	*for your sake*
3s.m.	**a'y wovis**	*for his/its sake*	3p.	**a'ga govis**	*for their sake*
3s.f.	**a'y govis**	*for her/its sake*			

§139(4)   Prepositions

Examples: **Saw gwra unn dra a'm govis!** 'Do just one thing for my sake!' **Na borth own a'm govis!** 'Don't be afraid on my behalf!' **Y'th pysav a'y wovis na ylli pella gans an mater ma** 'I ask you for his sake not to go further with this matter'; **An fleghes, a'ga govis, taw!** 'The children, for their sake, be quiet!'

§135 **A-JI DHE** 'within, inside': **Ny veu a-ji dhe Gernow** 'He was not in Cornwall'; **a-ji dhe'm lowarth** 'inside my garden'; **Ny dheuth a-ji dhe'n yet** 'He didn't come inside the gate'; **a-ji dhe our** 'within an hour'; **a-ji dhodho** 'inside it'. Cf. **yn chi** §167(1).

§136 **A-UGH** 'above'. Cf. **ughel** 'high'.

1s.	a-ughov	*above me*	1p.	a-ughon	*above us*
2s.	a-ughos	*above you*	2p.	a-ughowgh	*above you*
3s.m.	a-ughto	*above him/it*	3p.	a-ughta	*above them*
3s.f.	a-ughti	*above her/it*			

The meaning of **a-ugh** is 'at a point above': **neb a-ughon** 'someone (who is) above us'; **a-ugh y benn** 'above his head'; **a-ugh an gwydh** 'above the trees'; **Ni a yll nija a-ugh lies pow** 'We can fly above many countries'; **ughel a-ughon** 'high above us'.

§137 **A-VES DHE** 'outside': **A-ves dhe'n dre yth esa** 'Outside the town it was', MC. 162.3; **a-ves dhedhi** 'outside it'. Cf. **yn-mes a**, §175.

§138 **A-WOSA** 'after'. From *gosa mutated to **wosa** (cf. Breton *goude* 'after', *a c'houde* 'since' and Welsh *wedi* 'after'). This word is used chiefly as an adverb but it is also found as a preposition: **a-wosa mernans** 'after death'; **a-wosa hemma** 'after this'; **a'y wosa** 'notwithstanding, nevertheless', lit. 'after it' (§258(6)). See also **wosa** (§166).

§139 **AWOS** 'because', etc. Cf. Breton *evit* 'for, in order to'. **Awos** governs as follows:

(1)   A noun directly: **awos nown** 'because of hunger'.

(2)   An indefinite pronoun: **awos neppyth** 'because of something or other'.

(3)   A relative particle (rare): **awos a wredh** 'because of that which you do'.

(4)   A verbal noun with its dependent nouns or pronouns: **awos y vos an mester** 'because of his being the master'.

§139(5) Prepositions

(5) An 'infinite' construction, **dhe** with a verbal noun and dependent nouns or pronouns: **awos hwi dh'agan aswonnvos** 'because of your knowing us' (§141(19)).

These last two constructions are fully described in §346.

The meanings of **awos** are as follows:

(6) The cause from which something follows: **awos lavar leverys** 'because of something (which was) said'; **Nyns yw meth genev awos gul henna** 'I am not ashamed of doing that', lit. 'It is no shame with me because doing of that'; **awos bos yeyn** 'for (fear of) being cold'; **awos an hwedhel dhe vos re hir** 'because of the story being too long'.

(7) From the idea of cause comes the idea of intention: **awos gorfenna an hwel** 'in order to finish the work'; **Ny vedhav mos di awos leverel ger dhodho** 'I dare not go there to speak a word to him'.

(8) 'For the sake of, in the name of somebody or something': **awos unn den** 'for the sake of one man'; **Ny vynnsen gortos omma awos kans peuns** 'I wouldn't stay here for (the sake of) a hundred pounds'; **awos Dyw** 'for God's sake'; **awos eghenn, awos an bys, awos tra, awos travydh** 'at all, on any account'.

(9) As the equivalent of the English 'in spite of, notwithstanding, after all': **Ny vynn ev gasa awos myns a wren dhodho** 'He is not willing to leave in spite of all we do to him'; **Awos my dhe gewsel dhedha, ny grysons dhymm** 'Notwithstanding my speaking to them, they don't believe me'; **Awos y rowedh, ev a vydh kyrghys omma** 'In spite of (all) his importance, he will be brought here'; **Nyns yw skyllenn vydh awos oll an glaw** 'There's not a shoot, after all the rain'.

§140 **BYS** 'until, as far as, up to, even to' governs a noun directly or through one of the prepositions **dhe** or **yn**. Pronoun objects follow one of these prepositions. Mutation after **bys** is as follows:

b > v	g > -	k	all	d > t in close combination
m > v	gw > w	p	unchanged	
		t		

(1) **Bys dydh fin** 'until the last day'; **byttiwedh (bys + diwedh)** 'to the end, in fine, after all'; **bys pennvlydhen** 'to the end of the year, for a year'; **bys**

§141(2)   Prepositions

omma 'up to this point'; **bys ti (di)** 'thither, right there'; **mos hware bys ti** 'going there straight away'; **bys nevra** 'evermore'; **bys vykken, bys vynari** 'evermore'; **bys vynytha** 'for ever'.

(2) With **dhe** 'to': **Ke bys dhodho!** 'Go right up to him!' **Gortewgh bys dhe worfenn an troyll!** 'Stay till the end of the party!'

(3) With **yn** 'in' with the meanings 'unto, all the way to': **I eth bys yn Bronn Wennili** 'They went all the way to Brown Willy'; **pan dhothyen bys y'n yet** 'when we had come all the way to the gate'; **bys yn nyhewer** 'right up to yesterday evening'; **War nuk y kerdhas bys y'n hel** 'Immediately he walked right into the hall'.

(4) **Bys** is used before **pan** 'when' and **may** to emphasise these conjunctions (§295, §347(1), §350).

§141 **DHE** 'to'. This is one of the most important of the prepositions with a wide range of meanings and a number of syntactic functions. It has the primary meaning of motion towards an object and therefore the identification of the object as a fixed point. **Dhe** mutates by softening. The forms with pronominal endings are as follows:

1s.	**dhymm**	*to me*		1p.	**dhyn**	*to us*
2s.	**dhis**	*to you*		2p.	**dhywgh**	*to you*
3s.m.	**dhodho**	*to him/it*		3p.	**dhedha**	*to them*
3s.f.	**dhedhi**	*to her/it*				

(1) There are several longer forms, 1s. **dhymmo** and 2s. **dhiso** which have slight emphasis. Further emphasis is obtained when the suffixed pronouns are added (§64): **dhodho ev** 'to him'; **dhedhi hi** 'to her'. When this is the case, the long forms referred to above are always used: **dhymmo vy** 'to me'; **dhiso jy** 'to you'.

(2) Destination, which is often figurative, is denoted by **dhe**: **mones dhe-dre** 'going home'; **mones dhe'n dre** 'going to (the) town'; **Ni eth dhe Yowann** 'We went to John'; **hag a entras dh'y ji** 'and entered his house'; **hag ev a veu degys dhe'n krow** 'and it was brought to the shed'; **An avon a res dhe'n mor** 'The river runs to the sea'; **na vo gesys dhe goll** 'that it be not lost, lit. 'left to loss'; **Gorr e dhe'n pons!** 'Lead him to the bridge!' **Gallas an re na dhe'n fo** 'Those ones have fled away', lit; 'have gone to flight'; **An hanaf a wra terri dhe demmyn** 'The cup will break to pieces'; **Dhe'n dor arta ty a dreyl** 'You will turn again to (the) earth', OM. 64.

§141(3)   Prepositions

(3) Progression towards a greater degree of a quality is shown by the use of the preposition **dhe** with a comparative form of the adjective (§86): **rag ny vydhav dhe well** 'for I shall not be any the better'; **ha may fo dhyn ni dhe weth** 'and so it may be the worse for us'; **My a vydh dhe lowenna** 'I shall be the happier'.

(4) The recipient, the owner of a thing or quality: **Meur ras dhe gemmys re'gan gweresas** 'Many thanks to all who have helped us'; **Ow gorhemmynnadow dhywgh** 'My greetings to you'; **Sewena dhodho!** 'Success to him!' **Nyns eus par dhis yn dyskans** 'You have no equal in learning'; **rag yma govynn dhymm** 'for I have a question'; **Meur a folneth o dhodho** 'It was a great foolishness in him'; **Yma ken dhe Beder dhe grodhvolas** 'Peter has cause to grumble'; **Yma chi dhymm** 'I have a house'.

So with nouns expressing emotion, need, want, etc.: **edrek** 'regret', **edhomm** 'need', **dout** 'fear, doubt', **dughan** 'grief', **hireth** 'longing', **mall** 'eagerness, impatience', **marth** 'wonder', **meth** 'shame', **nown** 'hunger', **syghes** 'thirst', **hwans** 'wish', etc.

The action in such cases is denoted by the verbal noun with or without the preposition **a** before it (§126(8d)) or rarely by the verbal particle **y** and the subjunctive (§229(3)). The long form of **bos** 'be' is used. See also **gans** (§147(5b)): **Yma syghes dhymm** 'I am thirsty'; **Yth esa marth dhedhi a henna** 'She wondered at that', lit. 'There was wonder to her from that'.

For ownership in general, variously expressed, see §249-§256.

(5) Use, advantage, serviceability, importance, necessity, duty. In expressions of this nature **dhe** is used to show the person who benefits from the action: **Lemmyn pan yw agan kylgh kowlwrys dhyn** 'Now that our circle is completed for us'; **neb a vynn da dhodho** 'someone (who) wishes him good'; **Agas bos pell ahanan yw moy gweres dhymm** 'Your being far from us is more help to me'; **Rag yma boes pareusys dhis ha dhedha keffrys** 'For there is food prepared for you and for them also'; **An men ma dhyn ni piw a'n omhwelis?** 'This stone who overturned it for us?' MC. 253.7-8; **Bysi yw dhis bos war** 'It is important for you to be careful'; **Pur vysi hemma a vydh dhedha ha dhe gemmys a vydh gansa** 'This will be very important for them and for all who will be with them'; **Res o dhodho gasa y ober a-varr** 'He had to leave his work early'; **Dhyn ni ny dal mann** 'It matters to us not at all'; **Y lavarav dell dhegoedh dhymm** 'I say as I must'; **Py gober a goettho dhodho?** 'What wage would be due to him?' **Ri pyth dhiso dhymm ny vern** 'Giving wealth to you does not bother me', BM. 2586; **Nyns yw dhe denvydh agan**

§141(11)   Prepositions

toella 'It is not for anyone to deceive us'. Cf. **fyllel dhe** below (15c). See also §246-§248.

(6) Happening to, befalling. Verbs of this sort are constructed with **dhe**: **Pandr'eus hwarvedhys dhe'n alhwedhor?** 'What has happened to the treasurer?' **Bedhes gwrys dhodho dell vynn!** 'Let it be done to him as he wishes!' For infixed pronouns with the verb **hwarvos** see §65(7c).

(7) Causing, making something happen is **gul** 'do' followed by **dhe** and a verbal noun (or **may** with the subjunctive (§349)): **Gwra dhe'th flogh y dhybri!** 'Make your child eat it!' **mar kyllydh gul dhe'm karr mos** 'if you can make my car go'; **Pandr'a wrug dhe'n gorhel beudhi?** 'What caused the ship to sink?'

Gasa 'allow, let' has the permitted action expressed by **dhe** and a verbal noun: **My a asas dhedhi mos** 'I allowed her to go'. This construction is used to make a 1s. imperative. **Gas vy dhe goska!** 'Let me sleep!' (§183(1)).

(8) Terms of proximity are followed by **dhe**: **na mos ogas dhe'n wydhenn!** 'nor go near the tree!' **nessa dhe'n eglos** 'next to the church'. So also **a-ogas** and **yn ogas** 'near': **yn ogas dhe'n men** 'in the neighbourhood of the stone'. However **yn y ogas** 'near him/it', etc. is also used (§177).

(9) Likeness, similarity are expressed by words which are followed by **dhe**: **haval dh'agan tas** 'like our father'; **Nyns eus parow dhis y'n bys** 'There is no one like you in the world'.

Note that **haval** and similar words are also constructed with **orth** 'at' (§152(3)).

(10) The idea of conformity to, of being in accordance with, is denoted by **dhe** with nouns, singular or plural: **dhe'm tybyans** 'in my opinion'; **oll dh'y vodh** 'all according to his wish', MC. 248.6; **dhe'th arghadow** 'according to your orders'; **My a'n dre dhywgh tre dhe'th tannvonadow** 'I will bring it back to you according to your instructions'; **dhe'm galloes** 'according to my ability'. So also expressions such as **dhe-wir** 'according to the truth, truly'; **dhe blemmik** 'to the plumb, straight'; **dhe skwir** according to the pattern, standard'; **dour dhe borpos** 'strictly to plan'.

(11) Position relative to another thing may be denoted by **dhe**: **Ty a vydh a'n barth kledh dhe Beder** 'You will be on Peter's left'; **lywya a'n barth dheghow dhe'n fordh** 'driving on the right-hand side of the road'; **a wel dhe oll y gowetha** 'in the sight of all his friends'.

§141(11) Prepositions

Position at a place is usually shown by the preposition **yn** 'in, on' (§167(4)).

(12) A point in time: **dhe'n tressa dydh** 'on the third day' (also **y'n tressa dydh**); **dhe naw eur** 'at nine o'clock'; **dhe benn unn mis** 'at the end of one month'; **dhe gyns** 'first of all'. See also §112.

(13) Purpose: **dhe vires orth an diskwedhyans** 'to look at the exhibition'; **dhe gollenwel oll an tylleryow** 'to fill all the places'; **myrgh pronter dh'y bar** 'a clergyman's daughter for his mate'; **Tewlys os dhe vraster** 'You are meant for greatness'; **Y'th hwys lavur dhe dhybri** 'In your sweat labour to eat'; **Henn yw dhe vegyans myns a vyw** 'This is for the nourishment of everything which lives'. See also **rag** §154(2b).

Mos dhe and **dos dhe** thus translate the English 'go and' and 'come and': **mones dhe vires ow thas** 'going to see my father'; **Prag na dheuth dhe'm wolkomma?** 'Why didn't he come to welcome me?'

(14) The remoter or indirect object of many verbs is connected to the verb by **dhe**. Such verbs are those with the meanings of giving, granting, showing, telling, saying to, bringing, handing, promising, ordering, etc.: **Dhis y rov ow gwella ro** 'To you I give my best gift'; **Kummyas a wrontyav dhis** 'I grant you permission'; **Y'n diskwedhas dhodho** 'He showed it to him'; **Lavar dhymm!** 'Tell me!' **Ev a'n kampoellas dh'y hwoer** 'He mentioned it to his sister'; **pan dhegsa an dowr dhedhi** 'when he had brought the water to her'; **Ystynn dhymm an paper-nowodhow, mar pleg!** 'Hand me the newspaper, please!' **Piw a ambosas henna dhedha?** 'Who promised them that?' **Y worhemmynnadow dhe'n re ma o dell syw** 'His orders to them were as follows'.

(15) Certain verbs which in English govern a direct object have in Cornish an indirect object.

(a)   **AMMA** 'kiss': **My a vynn amma dhiso** 'I will kiss you'.

(b)   **DYSKI** 'teach', **dyski dhe nebonan** 'to teach (to) someone': **Piw a dhyskas dhis gul henna?** 'Who taught you to do that?' See also §147(7).

(c)   **FYLLEL** with the meaning 'lack' or 'be wanting' is linked by **dhe** to the noun denoting that which lacks the quality or thing: **Arghans a fylli dhodho** 'He lacked money'; **Ny fyll kowetha dhedhi** 'She doesn't lack friends'. With the meaning 'fail' the person affected is denoted by **dhe**: **Y nerth a fyllis dhodho** 'His strength failed him'; **Mar fyll dhis peub ken, ny fallav dhiso** 'If all others fail you, I shall not fail you'.

§141(15g)   Prepositions

(d)   GAVA 'forgive' has **dhe** before the name of the person to be forgiven: **Gav dhymm!** 'Forgive me! I beg your pardon!' The action for which forgiveness is sought is either the direct object of the verb or a phrase after the preposition **awos** (§139): **Ev a vynn gava dhis dha fowtow** 'He will forgive your faults'; **Gevewgh dhyn agan bos helergh!** or **Gevewgh dhyn awos bos helergh!** 'Forgive us (for) being late!' **Ny ylli hi gava hy mamm awos hy dh'y lettya a dhemmedhi** 'She was not able to forgive her mother for preventing her from marrying'.

(e)   GRASSA 'thank' has the person thanked after the preposition **dhe** and the reason for the gratitude as the direct object of the verb: **Dhis y hwrassav an gusul** 'I thank you for the advice', lit. 'I thank to you the advice'; **Grass e dhe Dhyw!** 'Thank God for it!' **Dhodho y'n gressyn** 'We thank him (for) it'. In the passive: **Bedhes gressys dhodho!** 'Let him be thanked for it!, lit. 'Let it be thanked to him!' The noun **gras** m., pl. **grassow** can be used after the verbs **aswonn(vos)** and **godhvos** (§200), both with the meaning 'know', but although the name of the person thanked follows **dhe** as before, the cause of the gratitude is denoted by **a** 'of' before a noun (§126(8c)) or by the present participle construction naming an action: **Y hwonn meur ras (gras) dhis a'th kuvder** 'I thank you very much for your kindness'; **Yth aswonnav gras dhodho ow tos omma hedhyw** 'I thank him (for) coming here today'. Note that the verbal particle **Y(th)** is often omitted in these expressions: **Gonn gras dhis a'th lavar** 'Thank you for your speech' (§274(5)).

The abridged forms **meurastajy** (singular) and **meurastahwi** (plural) from **meur ras dhe** are quite common and have the same construction as the full forms: **Meurastajy ow kul hemma!** 'Thanks for doing this!' **Meurastahwi a'gas rohow!** 'Thanks for your presents!' **Ras** (plural **rasow**) is a permanently mutated form of this word, **gras**, with the meanings 'grace, blessing, value': **dhe ras, gans meur a ras** 'excellently'; **mab ras** 'favourite son'; **a gemmys ras** 'of so much worth', MC. 235.3.

(f)   GREVYA 'trouble, afflict, oppress' is connected to its object by **dhe**: **Ny rev an glaw dhyn** 'The rain doesn't trouble us'; **Yma neppyth ow krevya dhedhi** 'There is something troubling her'.

(g)   GWERES 'help' takes either a direct or an indirect object to indicate the person helped. The action for which help is needed is expressed by the use of the present participle construction: **Gweres Yowann ow kul tan!** 'Help John to make a fire!' **Mar mynn'ta, ty a yll gweres dhymm** 'If you will, you can help me'; **Ev a'n gweresas ow chanjya an vonden wenys** 'He helped him change the punctured tyre'; **Kyn hwresso dh'y vroder, ny'n jeves mall a wul**

§141(15g)   Prepositions

travydh 'Though he may help his brother, he is not eager to do anything'.

(h)   **KRYSI** 'believe'. When there is a personal reference, the preposition is used: **Ny allav krysi dhodho** 'I can't believe him'; **Ny grysis dh'y lavarow** 'I didn't believe his words'. If there is no personal reference, the preposition is omitted: **Ny grysowgh an gwiryonedh** 'You don't believe the truth'; **Gwra y grysi!** 'Believe it!' Cf. **krysi yn** §167(6).

(i)   **PLEGYA** 'please' uses either **dhe** or **gans** (§147) as its preposition: **Ny bleg an nowodhow dhymm** 'The news does not please me'; **mar pleg dhis/dhywgh** 'if it pleases you, please'. The verbal adjective **plegadow** (§79(4)) 'pleasing' is used to express general liking: **An boes ma yw plegadow dhyn** 'We like this food'.

(j)   **SKONYA** 'refuse' in the sense of forbidding someone to do something takes a direct object and denotes the forbidden action with **dhe**: **Ny'th skonyav dhe barkya ena** 'I don't forbid you to park here'. See also §126(1).

(k)   **SYNSYS** 'beholden', the past participle of the verb **synsi** 'hold', is followed by **dhe**. The source of the gratitude, the reason for it, is expressed through **a** 'from' or by the use of the present participle construction as in (d) above: **Synsys meur dhywgh yth on a'gas helder** 'We are much beholden to you for your hospitality'; **Synsys ens dhe bobel an eglos orth hy hoela dhedha** 'They were beholden to the people of the church for lending it to them'.

(16) The displaced verbal noun object of one of the auxiliary verbs may be syntactically connected to the verbal phase by **dhe**: **an hanafow a wrug Maria dhe wolghi** 'the cups which Mary washed'; **Kernewek ny wonn dhe gewsel** 'I don't know how to speak Cornish'; **moy kyn fynnes dhe gavoes** 'even though you should wish to have more', OM. 432. For a full discussion see §304(2).

(17) **Dhe** with a verbal noun is also used as the complement of the verb **bos** 'be', particularly when the passive aspect of the action is meant: **Yma ow gober dhe be** 'There are my wages to pay/to be paid'; **Nyns yns dhe drestya mes fals** 'They are not to be trusted but false', BM. 2045; **Nyns o hi dhe vlamya** 'She was not to be blamed'; **Yma ger dhe leverel yn kever henna** 'There is a word to be said/to say about that'.

(18) Nouns, adjectives and past participles are connected to verbal nouns by **dhe** when the meanings are linked. This translates the English 'to' with the infinitive: **Nyns eus ken dhe hwerthin** 'There is no reason to laugh';

§142   Prepositions

Diskwedh dhymm an fordh dhe holya! 'Show me the way to follow!' **gwiw dhe vos gweles** 'fit to be seen'; **Nyns en hardh dh'y lettya** 'We weren't bold (enough) to stop him'; **My ha'm gwreg ... bysi vydh dhe sostena** 'My wife and I ... will be occupied with getting sustenance', i.e. 'It will be hard for my wife and me to get sustenance', OM. 397-98; **Hemm yw es dhe wul** 'This is easy to do'; **parys dhe vos kwit** 'ready to go free'; **Hwi a veu gwrys dhe wortos** 'You were made to wait'.

Note that **kummyas** 'leave, permission' is usually followed by **a** 'of' (§126(8d)) but occasionally by **dhe**: **Skon ev a'n jevydh kummyas dhe lywya** 'Soon he will have permission to drive'.

(19) The infinitive construction, as it is often called, is formed by linking a noun or a pronoun to a verbal noun by the preposition **dhe**, the whole forming a noun phrase which may be treated in most respects as a simple noun (§334(3)): **rag own an dustunier dhe wirleverel** 'for fear (that) the witness (might) speak truthfully'; **pan glywis ty dhe seweni** 'when I heard (that) you (had) succeeded'.

The object of the verbal action in these constructions, when a pronoun, is expressed through the use of the possessive adjectives after **dhe** and before the verbal noun: **kyns my dhe weles an karr** 'before I saw the car' but **kyns my dh'y weles** 'before I saw it'.

(20) An exclamative use of **dhe** takes the forms **dhymm/dhymmo** 'to me', **dhis/dhiso** 'to you' which can be interpreted as 'I say!, then': **Ke dhymm dheves** 'Go away, I say!' **Taw dhymmo, Wella!** 'Be quiet then, Will!' **Kemmer e dhis!** 'Take it, then!' **Ressev i dhiso!** 'Take them, then!'

    For **diwar** see §162.
    For **diworth/dhiworth** see §153.

§142 **DRE/DER** 'through', the second form now adopted before vowels, though with **an** 'the' the contracted form **dre'n** may be used, mutates by softening. It has the spatial meaning 'through' extended to temporal relationships and then to abstract ideas. It thus comes to mean 'through the agency of, by means of'. The forms with the personal endings are as follows:

§142 Prepositions

1s.	**dredhov**	*through me*	1p.	**dredhon**	*through us*
2s.	**dredhos**	*through you*	2p.	**dredhowgh**	*through you*
3s.m.	**dredho**	*through him/it*	3p.	**dredha**	*through them*
3s.f.	**dredhi**	*through her/it*			

The meanings of **dre** are as follows:

(1) Spatial relationships when something passes through an existing opening: **An dowr a dhever der an tell** 'The water leaks through the holes'; **gorrys dredha (tell) rag aga lasya** 'put through holes to lash them', PD. 2574-75; **der an fenester** 'through the window'. Thence by making a way through something: **kentrow der an astell** 'nails through the plank'; **dre'n dowr** 'through the water'.

(2) Time: **dre dhydh** 'through the day, by day'; **dre nos** 'through the night, by night'.

(3) Figuratively: **Yma an loes der ow holonn** 'The pang is through my heart', PD. 1147; **dre hun, dre gosk** 'through sleep, in sleep'.

(4) Agency or means: **Dre gledha a vywo dre gledha a vydh ledhys** 'Who lives by the sword will be slain by the sword'; **Dre dha weres hemma a veu gwrys** 'Through your help this was done'; **Dre brevyans y tyskir** 'Through experience one learns'; **Ytho dre henna yth yw agas bos omma** 'So it is by means of that that you are here'; **gwrys dre jynnweyth** 'made by machinery'; **der an bellwolok** 'through (on) the television'; **der an pellgowser** 'by telephone'; **An chi yw toemmhes dre dredan** 'The house is heated by electricity'; **Dre dan y feu distruis** 'It was destroyed by fire'; **Dre liv an deves a veu beudhys** 'The sheep were drowned by a flood'; **dre wall (gwall** m. 'mischance') 'by accident'.

(5) In passive constructions with a past participle **dre** with a noun denoting an animate being implies that the person named is an intermediary in the carrying through of the action: **skoedhys der y vroder** 'supported by (the intervention of) his brother'; **Kusulys der an konsel o na ombrofya yn esel** 'He was advised (through the medium of the council) that he should not offer himself as a member'; **mayn dredhon a vydh kevys** 'a means will be found through us (with our aid)', BM. 1406; **Hemm a vydh gwrys dre Yowann** 'This will be done through John'. When the direct agent is to be named the preposition to be used is **gans** 'with' (§147(6)). Thus in contrast to the last example the statement **Hemm a vydh gwrys gans Yowann** is equivalent to the English 'This will be done by John' i.e. by him directly as the sole or immediate agent.

§144(3)   Prepositions

(6) Adverbially the form **dredhi** 'through it' (the circumstances (§71(3b)), is used to mean 'thereby': **Ev a dhehwelis tre, gallas y deylu heudhik dredhi** 'He returned home, his family were pleased thereby'.

§143 **DREFENN** (stress on the second syllable) 'because of, on account of' is used only with nouns, with verbal nouns and with the infinitive construction (§141(19)) where it may be regarded as a conjunction, followed in the negative by **na** 'not' (§346(2)): **drefenn downder an avon ena** 'because of the depth of the river there'; **drefenn assaya an apposyans a-varr** 'because of attempting the examination early'; **drefenn eva re** 'on account of drinking too much'; **Ny dheuthons drefenn aga bos skwith** 'They didn't come on account of their being tired'; **Drefenn an logos dhe dhensel an seghyer an ys o mostys** 'Because the mice (had) gnawed the sacks the wheat was spoilt'; **Pes da ens drefenn na fyllis an gwyns** 'They were pleased because the wind didn't fail'; **Drefenn mar veur yw an piwas, peub a stev** 'Because the prize is so great, everyone rushes'.

§144 **DRES** 'over, beyond' indicates movement across a thing to its other side or beyond. The forms with pronominal endings are as follows:

1s.	**dresov**	*over me*	1p.	**dreson**	*over us*
2s.	**dresos**	*over you*	2p.	**dresowgh**	*over you*
3s.m.	**dresto**	*over him/it*	3p.	**dresta**	*over them*
3s.f.	**dresti**	*over her/it*			

The meanings are:

(1) 'Over the top of, across, throughout': **Kemmer pows dresos!** 'Take a coat over you!' **Yma pons dres an gover** 'There is a bridge over the brook'; **Dell owgh penn dreson ni** 'As you are head over us'; **An ki a lammas dres an yet** 'The dog jumped over the gate'; **dres oll an veyn** 'across all the stones'; **dres keyn** 'across the back'; **Dres an mor di ev a dheuth** 'Across the sea he came there'; **Aswonnys yw dres oll Kernow** 'She is known throughout Cornwall'.

(2) 'To the other side of, on the other side of': **dres Karnbre** 'on the other side of Carn Brea'; **dres Tamer** 'on the other side of (the) Tamar'.

(3) Time: **Ganso dres an nos y hwoelya y dheuv** 'With him throughout the night there watched his son-in-law'; **pub seythun dres an vlydhen** 'every week throughout the year'.

§144(4) Prepositions

(4) Excess: **Ty re wrug dres y worhemmynn** 'You have exceeded his command'; **Yma gwydh hir ena dres oll gwydh an bys ma** 'There are tall trees there (tall) beyond any trees in (lit. 'of') this world'; **Ny yll bos splanna golow es henna dres an howl y honan** 'There cannot be a more splendid light than that other than the sun itself'; **dres hemma/henna** 'more than this/that, moreover'; **dres puptra** 'beyond everything'; **dres pub maner** 'exceedingly'; **dres eghenn/kinda** 'extraordinary', lit. 'beyond any sort'; **An kuntellyans o da dres eghenn** 'The meeting was extraordinarily good' (§267).

§145 **ER** 'by' does not cause mutation (though the Welsh *er* 'for' does). It is used only with nouns.

(1) The point of attachment or contact on the body: **Kemmerewgh e er an diwleuv!** 'Take him by the hands!' **My a'n kildenn er an treys** 'I will pull him back by the feet'; **Er an askell y'n towlsen** 'By the wing I would throw it'. See **erbynn** (§146) from **er** and **pynn** (**penn** 'head') 'against', lit. 'by the head, head-on'.

(2) Concern: **Lavar dhymm er kres ha kosoleth!** 'Tell me for the sake of peace and quiet!' **er jentylys** 'for politeness' sake'. Thus of a state of mind: **er ow gew** 'to my grief, worse luck for me'; **Go ni er bos dewolow** '(It's) our bad luck to be devils', RD. 301. Compare with **er** the Welsh *er* 'for', Middle Breton *er/her* 'because, for' and Cornish **herwydh** 'according to' (§149), **yn herwydh** 'nearby' (§171). Note also **erna(g)** conj. 'until' (**er** + **na** neg.part.). See §347(1).

§146 **ERBYNN** is formed from **er** 'by' (§145) and a mutated form of **penn** 'head' which in this expression is said to represent an old dative of the noun. The pronoun object is an infixed possessive adjective, as follows:

1s.	**er ow fynn**	*against me*	1p.	**er agan pynn**	*against us*
2s.	**er dha bynn**	*against you*	2p.	**er agas pynn**	*against you*
3s.m.	**er y bynn**	*against him/it*	3p.	**er aga fynn**	*against them*
3s.f.	**er hy fynn**	*against her/it*			

(1) The idea of encountering 'head-on', especially with **mos** 'go' and **dos** 'come': **Yth eth erbynn y goweth** 'He met his friend'; **Da vydh mos er hy fynn** 'It will be good to meet her'; **degys er y bynn** 'brought to (meet) him'.

Note that **metya** 'meet' is used with either **gans** or **orth**, depending on whether one overtakes the other person or meets face to face (§152(1)).

§147(2) Prepositions

(2) Attitude towards: **dell dhegoedh erbynn den wordhi** 'as is proper towards a distinguished man'; **Offens vydholl er dha bynn** '(No) offence at all to you'.

(3) Contrary action or attitude: **Yma meur a dus kuntellys er y bynn** 'There are many people gathered in opposition to him'; **Ny gewsydh er aga fynn** 'You say nothing against them'; **erbynn an lagha** 'against (the) law, illegal'; **erbynn ow difenn** 'in defiance of my prohibition'.

(4) A point in time as a limit in expressions such as 'by the time that, in readiness for': **erbynn hav** 'by summertime'; **erbynn bones henna gwrys** 'by the time that (was/is) done'; **Erbynn agan bos gansa, termyn vydh dhyn ni dhe goena** 'By the time we are with them, it will be time for us to have supper'; **Py le yw tewlys genowgh hwi bos erbynn nos?** 'Where do you plan to be by night(fall)?'

§147 GANS 'with'. The forms with pronominal endings are as follows:

1s.	**genev**	with me	1p.	**genen**	with us
2s.	**genes**	with you	2p.	**genowgh**	with you
3s.m.	**ganso**	with him/it	3p.	**gansa**	with them
3s.f.	**gensi**	with her/it			

Note that in the texts the form **gena'** = **genev** is found, as is more rarely **gene'ma** (§13, §64(3)).

The meanings of **gans**, all derived from the idea of being in company with, are as follows:

(1) 'In the presence of': **Yth esa an venyn gansa** 'The woman was with them'; **Ny vynnav triga genowgh** 'I will not live with you'; **Prag na dheuthons genes omma?** 'Why didn't they come here with you?' **My a gans ow thas** 'I go with my father'; **Ev a'th welas gans dha goweth** 'He saw you with your friend'. So the farewell salutation: **Dyw genes/genowgh** 'God with you! goodbye!'

Note also the phrase **gallas ganso** 'He's got it!, he's done for!' lit. 'It has gone with him'; **Gallas y wober ganso** 'He has got what he deserved', lit. 'His wage has gone with him'.

(2) Of articles which are with a person: **Yma lyver genev** 'I have a book with me'; **Y fydh tigenn gensi** 'She will have a bag with her'; **Gansa yth esa**

§147(2) Prepositions

ki 'There was a dog with them'; **Ni a dhug golow genen** 'We carried a light with us'.

(3) Accompanying circumstances: **Y teuth an spalyers gans pal ha pigell** 'The labourers came with spade and pick'; **Gans unn lev y tewissyn** 'We chose unanimously', lit. 'with one voice'; **Gans garm yeyn y koedhas hi** 'With a shrill cry she fell'; **gans gweres an dyskador** 'with the help of the teacher'; **gans meur a doeth** 'with much speed'; **gans nerth bras** 'with great strength'; **gans gwir** 'with truth, truthfully, rightly'; **Gans lavarow hepken y'n skoedhyas** 'They supported him with words only'; **gans kolonn vras** 'with great heart, heartily'; **gans golow** 'alight', lit. 'with light'; **gans tan** 'on fire', lit. 'with fire'. The polite enquiry, **fatla genes/genowgh?** 'How are you? may be classed here, see §77 and §260.

(4) The instrument or the means by which anything is done or the material which is employed: **Ev a'n igoras gans an keth alhwedh** 'He opened it with the same key'; **My a wolghas ow harr gans dowr yeyn** 'I washed my car with cold water'; **festys gans kentrow** 'fastened with nails'; **My a'n gwel gans ow dewlagas** 'I see it with my two eyes'; **Hi a's prenas gans hy gober** 'She bought it with her wages'. Thus with verbs of covering, hiding, clothing, etc.: **An leur o kudhys gans strel fethus** 'The floor was covered with a luxurious mat'; **An karregi ena yw kelys gans an mor** 'The rocks there are covered by the sea'; **Oll an fleghes hi a wiskas gans kwethow koth** 'All the children she dressed in old clothes'.

Note the word **pygans** m. 'wherewithal' in which **gans** is used as a suffix to the interrogative pronoun **py** 'what' (§74(1)).

(5) Feelings and opinions and so on are expressed by using certain adjectives and nouns in a construction with **gans**. The verb is a tense of **bos** 'be' which in the present and imperfect is the 'short' form (§255).

(a) The adjectives so used with a verbal noun as the subject are:-

DA 'good': **Da yw ganso triga omma** 'He likes living here', lit. 'Living here is good with him'.

DROG 'bad': **Drog vydh gensi gortos yndella** 'She will not like waiting like that', lit. 'Waiting ... will be bad with her'.

GWELL 'better': **Gwell o gans an den na studhya yn privedh** 'That person preferred to study in private', lit. 'Studying ... was better with ...'.

§147(6) Prepositions

POES 'heavy': **Y leveris y fia poes ganso gasa y dre** 'He said that he had been reluctant to leave home', lit. '... it had been heavy with him leaving ...'.

(b) The nouns are the subject of the sentence, the verb is **bos** 'be' in its short form where appropriate, and the verbal noun naming the action is often attached to the construction by the preposition **a** 'of' (§126(8d)).

BERN 'care, interest': **Nyns yw ganso bern dybri meur** or **Nyns yw bern ganso a dhybri meur** 'He does not care about eating a lot'.

EDREK 'regret': **Ny vydh edrek gansa a'y weres** 'They will not regret helping him'.

MALL 'haste, impatience': **Peub a woer bos mall gans an soedhek a worfenna y ober** 'Everyone knows that the official is impatient to finish his work'.

MARTH 'wonder': **Marth o gans an medhyk a'ga havoes yagh** 'The doctor wondered (was surprised) to find them well'.

METH 'shame': **Meth o ganso a leverel henna** 'He was ashamed of saying that'.

(c) The adverbial conjunction **fatell** 'how' has a similar construction except that the preposition is not used: **Fatell vydh ganso triga tramor?** 'How will he like living abroad?' lit. 'How will it be with him ...?'

(d) The verb **plegya** 'please' and its derivatives are used with either **dhe** 'to' (§141(15i)) or **gans**: **Bynner ny blegya y fara dhymm/genev** 'His behaviour never pleased me'.

(6) Human agency, the person with whom the direct and immediate responsibilty for the action lies, is denoted by **gans**; it is thus used with the past participle in the passive construction and translates the English 'by' in a similar usage (§245(3b)): **Y dowl a veu tewlys ganso** 'His plan was made by him'; **Gans y vamm y fia gwrys** 'By his mother it had been made'.

The preposition is also used with the impersonal of the verb: **Gansa y's gelwir Trewartha** 'By them it is called Trewartha', lit. 'By them there is a calling it Trewartha'.

119

§147(6) Prepositions

The use of **gans** to translate 'by' in this way is only occasionally extended to a non-human agency or cause: **Gans unn hwedhel re beun toellys** 'We have been deceived by a certain story'; **Lies toll gans an dreyn a veu tellys** 'Many holes were made by the thorns'. **Dre** (§142(4)) is the standard word with non-human causes of action and is commonly used of humans also when regard is had to the means through which something is done. Hence, **Hemm a veu gwrys ganso** 'This was done by him', i.e. either by him alone or directly by him, but **Hemm a veu gwrys dredho** 'This was done through him', i.e. he was the means or one of the means of its being done, not necessarily directly.

(7) **Gans** is used with the verbs **dyski** 'learn' and **klywes** 'hear' to signify the person with whom the action takes place, therefore the person from whom one learns or hears anything: **Yth esov ow tyski moy gans kowetha** 'I am learning more from (with) friends'; **Gans y das y tyskas Kernewek** 'He learnt Cornish from (with) his father'; **Genowgh teg yth ov dyskys** 'I have been well taught by (with) you'; **Re glywas gans ow mamm hi dhe vos genys yn Karesk** 'I have heard from (with) my mother (that) she was born in Exeter'; **Ni a glywas henna gans den skentel** 'We have heard that from (with) a learned person'.

(8) Other verbs which employ **gans** for particular meanings are: **akordya** 'agree': **Prag na akordyowgh genen?** 'Why don't you agree with us?' See also §152(4); **gul** 'do': **Ny wre hi ganso mann** 'She had nothing to do with him'; **kewsel** 'talk': **Ass wrons i kewsel an eyl gans hy ben!** 'How they do talk the one with the other!' **metya** 'meet': **Ny vetsyn gansa a-dhia goel Nadelik** 'We haven't met with them since Christmas time'. **Skornya** 'mock, make fun of' uses **gans** to denote the object of the action: **Na skorn genev!** 'Don't make fun of me!' **Gokki yw myns a skornyo ganso** 'Anyone who mocks him is foolish'.

(9) **Gans** is used with the demonstrative pronouns **hemma, henna** 'this', 'that' to mean 'moreover, herewith, besides this, as well as', etc.: **Gans hemma, pub huni eth** 'Moreover, everyone went'; **Gans henna, nyns eus boes y'n chi** 'Besides, there's no food in the house'.

§148 **HEB** 'without'. Mutation is confined to the softening of the initial consonant of **diwedh, dout, gorfenn, gow**; see below (2). The forms with pronominal endings are as follows:

1s.	**hebov**	*without me*	1p.	**hebon**	*without us*
2s.	**hebos**	*without you*	2p.	**hebowgh**	*without you*
3s.m.	**hebdho**	*without him/it*	3p.	**hebdha**	*without them*
3s.f.	**hebdhi**	*without her/it*			

§148(5)

The meanings of **heb** are as follows:

(1) The primary meaning of 'without': **Ny allav skrifa heb pluvenn** 'I cannot write without a pen'; **Hebos sy ny sped tra y'n chi ma** 'Without you nothing goes well in this house'; **gans kolonn dha, heb sorr** 'with good heart, without anger'; **heb na hirra lavarow** 'without any further words'.

(2) Idiomatic phrases in some of which **heb** is equivalent to the English 'un-, '-less': **heb bern (bern** 'care') 'willingly'; **heb danjer (danjer** 'objection, hesitation') 'without delay, demur'; **heb dhiwedh (diwedh** 'end') 'unending, endless'; **heb dhout (dout** 'doubt') 'doubtless(ly)'; **heb fall/falladow (fall/falladow** 'failure') 'without fail, doubtless': **Hemm yw marth, heb falladow** 'This is a wonder, undoubtedly'; **heb gil (gil** 'deceit') 'sincerely'; **heb joy** 'joyless'; **heb ken (ken** 'cause') 'without cause, groundless(ly)' (see also (6) below); **heb lett/lettya (lettya/lett** 'hinder/hindrance') 'freely'; **heb (neb) mar (mar** 'doubt') 'without any doubt, doubtless(ly)'; **heb namm (namm** 'defect') 'perfect(ly)'; **heb par/parow (par** 'equal') 'unequalled': **kaner heb par** 'a singer without equal, peerless'; **heb toell (toell** 'deceit') 'frankly'; **heb hwedhlow (hwedhel** 'story') 'in fact, without (telling) stories'; **heb worfenn (gorfenn** 'end') 'unlimited, limitless(ly)'; **heb wow (gow** 'lie') 'truly'; **heb ynni/ynniadow (ynni** v.n., **ynniadow** m. 'urge, urging') 'without urging, of one's own accord, freely'.

Such phrases serve as adjectives or adverbs, as indicated above: **ober heb dhiwedh** 'endless work'; **I a ober heb dhiwedh** 'They work endlessly'; **heb flows (flows** 'idle talk') 'sensibly'.

(3) After **bos** 'be' as the subject of a sentence to mean 'be without, not have': **Drog yw bos heb kowetha** 'It is bad to be without friends'; **Da vydh bos heb preder** 'It will be good not to have any worry'.

(4) **Heb** before a verbal noun makes a virtual negative of that noun: **heb hedhi** 'without stopping'; **Ny yll hi dos a-ji heb pe** 'She cannot come in without paying'; **heb y gampoella** 'without mentioning it'; **heb agan gweles** 'without seeing us'.

(5) Other meanings. 'Besides': **Yma lies omma hebov a woer an gwir** 'There are many here besides me who know the truth'. 'Not counting': **Yma trydhek esel devedhys heb an kaderyer** 'There are thirteen members present, not counting the chairman'. 'Before': **Gwayt na vydh pell heb dos dhyn!** 'Mind that it is not long before it comes to us!' BM. 3275.

§148(6) Prepositions

(6) **Hepken** adv. 'only' may be composed of **heb** and **ken** adj. 'other': **Ev a vyw orth dowr hepken** 'He lives on water only'. It should not be confused with **heb ken** 'without cause'; see (2) above.

§149 **HERWYDH** 'according to' is perhaps composed of **(h)er** (§145) and a mutated form of **gweyth** f. 'time, occasion'. It is used only with a noun and to denote abstract relationships. When a pronoun object occurs, **yn herwydh** is used in place of **herwydh**. The local sense 'in the company of, in the vicinity of' is confined to **yn herwydh** (§171).

Herwydh denotes abstract relationships and may be translated in several ways. 'According to': **Ni a wra breusi peub herwydh y ober** 'We shall judge everyone according to his work'; **herwydh skrifer an lyver** 'according to the writer of the book'. 'On the authority of': **herwydh an re a's tevo an maystri** 'on the authority of those who were in control'. 'In accordance with': **Hemm yw herwydh y nas** 'This is in accordance with his nature'.

§150 **KYNS/KYN** 'before, prior'. Of the two words, **kyns** is commoner in modern Cornish, **kyn** being confusable with **kyn** conj. 'though'. Both words are followed by a noun which is frequently a verbal noun: **kyns an kuntellyans** 'before the meeting'; **kyns an bennseythun** 'before the week-end'; **kyns penn tri dydh** 'before three days are up'; **kyns/kyn mos** 'before going'; **Kyns lamma, mir!** 'Before jumping, look!' Hence the meaning 'rather (than)': **Mernans kyns disenor** 'Death before dishonour'.

Kyns has a function as a comparative adjective (§82(4)): **yn prys kyns** 'at a former time'. With this comparative meaning it is followed by **es/ages** 'than' (§85): **kyns es henna**; 'before that, prior to that'; **kyns es koska** 'before sleeping'; **kyns es mora** 'before going to sea'. It is used with the infinitive construction; see §141(19): **kyns es i dhe dira** 'before they land/landed'. **Kyns** is linked to an inflected verb through the conjunction **dell** 'as' (§295); **kyns ages dell gemmersen an lyther** 'before we had received the letter'; **kyns es dell vo leverys** 'rather than it be said'.

The word **kyn** can be followed in similar circumstances by the inflected verb directly without the intervention of the verbal particle: **kyn ov loes** 'before I am grey'. This is a rarer construction, however. See also **nahen** (§83(7)).

§151 **MARNAS/MA'S** 'except', used in a negative context only with nouns and independent pronouns: **Kummyas a'th eus a skrifa war bub folenn marnas homma** 'You are allowed to write on every page but this one'; **An eseli a dhewisas marnas dew** 'The members voted except two'; **dhe beub oll**

§152(2)   Prepositions

marnas ev 'to everyone except him'; **Ny worthybis marnas Peder** 'No one answered except Peter'.

Marnas is used with the hour to denote minutes before the hour: **deg eur marnas ugens** 'twenty minutes to ten', lit. 'ten o'clock less twenty' (§112). It is also used in subtraction (§110(2)): **Onan warn ugens marnas tri a wra etek** 'Twenty-one less three makes eighteen'. For **marnas** as a conjunction see §286.

The form **ma's** is a contraction of **marnas** and is used similarly: **Ev a wre puptra ma's ober** 'He would do anything except work'; **Drog yw genev gul ma's da dhis** 'I am sorry to do anything but good to you, I wish only to do good to you'; **Ny vydh plegadow dhymm kewsel ma's Kernewek**; 'I like to speak nothing but Cornish'; **Ny vynnons ma's gul ges ahanas** 'They will only make fun of you'.

§152 **ORTH** 'at'. The fuller form **worth** occurs in the texts but **orth** is now regular in Modern Cornish. **Wor'** is used when the final -th is dropped; see below. The forms with pronominal endings are as follows:

1s.	**orthiv**	*at me*	1p.	**orthyn**	*at us*
2s.	**orthis**	*at you*	2p.	**orthowgh**	*at you*
3s.m.	**orto**	*at him/it*	3p.	**orta**	*at them*
3s.f.	**orti**	*at her/it*			

The primary meaning of **orth** is positional, being up close to, against, in contact with a thing.

(1) Positional 'at, against': **Yma hi a'y esedh orth an voes** 'She is seated at the table'; **orth an tan** 'at (by) the fire'; **Byttydh ny weresi orth an new** 'He would never help at the sink at all'; **yn-bann ughel orth skorrenn** 'high up against a branch', OM. 805; **Hi a bystigas hy throes orth men war an treth** 'She hurt her foot against a stone on the beach'; **Sett kador orth an daras!** 'Put a chair against the door!' **pan herdhyowgh orti hi** 'when you push against it'; **poesa orth** 'put one's weight against'; **skoedhya orth** 'lean against'; **Res yw dhodho kerdhes orth dew groch** 'He has to walk on two crutches'; **Pan gewsi orth y anow** 'when he had direct speech with him', lit. 'against his mouth'; **metya orth** 'meet with' (coming in the opposite direction) cf. §146(1).

(2) Temporal 'at': **orth an diwedh** 'at the end' and in combination **wor'tiwedh, wostiwedh, otiwedh** 'at last, finally'; **orth dalleth** 'at the beginning' with the combined form **wor'talleth** 'at first, initially'.

§152(3) Prepositions

(3) To denote a measure against which something is placed as a standard by which to judge: **Res yw ri piwas orth myns an pegh** 'It is necessary to make an award according to the measure of the offence', cf. MC. 117.5-6: **wor' troes-hys** 'by a foot length'; **orth niver** 'by/in number'; **orth koplow** 'by couples'; **orth bolonjedh, orth bodh, orth brys, orth desir** 'according to will, wish, desire'; **Bedhes gwrys orth y vrys!** 'Let it be done as he wishes!' **orth agan bodh** 'as we wish'; **I a welas orth y fas** 'They saw (judging by) his face'; **Ev a henwis an den orth y hanow** 'He called the man by his name'; **haval orth** (also **haval dhe**; see §141(9)) 'similar to, like': **Kernow yw haval orth Breten Vyghan** 'Cornwall is like Brittany'. Thus with expressions of buying and selling by measure or by quantity: **prena/gwertha orth an poes/kilo** 'buy/sell by the pound/kilo'. Note that price is denoted by **a** 'of' (§126(9)).

(4) The point of application of an action with a number of verbs and some nouns.

AKORDYA 'agree': **Na akordyas ev orth an vreus** 'He did not agree with the verdict'. See also §147(8).
AMBOSA v.n. 'promise, agree', **AMBOS** m. 'promise, agreement': **Gansa ambosow gwrys war anow orth estren a vydh bythkweth fast** 'With them agreements made verbally with strangers are always secure'.
ASPIA 'look out for, observe': **Aspiyn orth an geryow aga honan!** 'Let us observe the words themselves!'
BYWA 'live': **Hemm yw boes a yll den bywa orto** 'This is food which a man can live on'.
DERIVAS 'relate, tell': **Gwra derivas orth an medhyk fatell yw genes!** 'Tell the doctor how it is with you!' **Dhe** 'to' may also be used with **derivas**: **A dherivsys dhodho fatell o an dra?** 'Did you tell him how the matter was?'
DIFENN 'forbid': **Hemm yw difennys orth myns a grysso** 'This is forbidden to whomsoever may believe'.
GOSLOWES 'listen': **Yw goslowes orth ilow plegadow dhis?** 'Do you like listening to music?'
GOVYNN 'ask': **Govynn orthyn heb hokkya** 'Ask us without hesitation'; **My a wra govynn kummyas orth an perghenn** 'I shall ask permission from the owner'; **mar kovynnydh onan orth an den na** 'if you ask for one from that person'.
GUL 'make, do': **Pyth a vydh gwrys orth Davydh?** 'What will be done about David?' **Pyth yw an gusul wella dhe wul orth henna?** 'What's the best thing to do about that?'
GWERES 'help': **Hwans a'm beus a weres orth an hwel** 'I wish for help with the work'. **Gweres** is also used with the present participle construction (§243): **Ev a wra gweres dhis orth y wul** 'He is going to help you do it'.

124

§152(6) Prepositions

GWEYTHA 'work': **Menowgh y hweythons orth priweyth** 'Often they work at pottery'.
KEWSEL 'speak': **Pan gewsi ev orthiv y hwedhla** 'When he spoke to me he would tell stories', i.e. 'gossip'; (also used with **dhe** 'to').
KOELA 'trust': **mar mynnydh koela orthiv** 'if you will trust me'.
LEVEREL 'say': **Gwra dell leversys orthiv y hwres!** 'Do what you said to me you would do!'
MYNNES 'wish, be willing': **Ny vynnav orta bones na pell yn dises** 'I do not want them to be long in discomfort', cf. OM. 1431: **My a vynn orthowgh hedhi** 'I want you to stop'.
MIRES 'look': **I eth dhe vires orth an avon** 'They went to look at the river'.
NEGYS 'business': **Eus negys genes orth an skrifennyas?** 'Have you any business with the secretary?'
HWILAS 'look for, try': **Ny hwilsens mann orthiv vy** 'They had looked for nothing from me'.
HWITHRA 'examine, look closely at': **De y hwithras orto** 'Yesterday he looked closely at it'.

Note that the words **ambos, kewsel, negys** used with **gans** 'with' (§147) would imply co-operation or reciprocal action: **Yma ambos gwrys gansa** 'There is an agreement with them', that is to say, mutual agreement, a mutual promise: **An dyskador a gewsis gans an studhyer** 'The teacher talked with the student', both sides had something to say; **pan worfennsa y negys ganso** 'when he had finished his business with him', of mutual interest and with mutual involvement.

(5)   Attachment to anything and so found with the verbs **fasta/fastya/fasthe** 'fasten', **glena** 'stick', **kelmi** 'tie', **kentra** 'nail', **lasya** 'fix together', **latthya** 'latch'; **takkya** 'nail': **Hwi a yll y fasta orth an post ma** 'You can fasten it to this post'; **An stamp o glenys orth an maylyer** 'The stamp was stuck to the envelope'; **Kolm e orth an welenn!** 'Tie it to the stick!' **My a's kenter orth an prenn** 'I will nail it to the wood'; **Bedhens i tekkys orth an blynkenn!** 'Let them be nailed to the plank!'

(6)   Resistance and opposition: **Ny vatalyas orta** 'He did not fight against them'; **An bobel a omladha, an eyl orth y gila** 'The people were fighting, the one against the other'; **Parys yw an wlaskor dhe werrya orth pub eskar** 'The nation is ready to make war against every enemy'; **omma settya orth gwithyas** 'here resisting a policeman'; **Na sett orthyn, a vata!** 'Don't resist us, mate!' **perthi orth** 'hold out against, put up with'; **Ni dhe omdenna a via le poenvotter es perthi orta** 'Our withdrawing would be less bother than putting up with them'; **disputya orto** 'disputing with him'; **Nyns eus mann argya orti**

125

§152(6) Prepositions

'There's no arguing with her'. **Yowann a sevis orta** 'John stood (up) against them'.

Thus the expressions, **orth y eghenn** 'in spite of all he could do', lit. 'against his kind'; **yn despit orth** 'in spite of'; **yn despit orth dha dhens** 'in spite of you', lit. 'in spite of your teeth' (§170).

(7) Guarding against, preventing, with the verbs **gwitha** 'guard', **omwitha** 'guard oneself': **Hwath my a with orth henna** 'I will still guard against that'; **Ny with omdoemma orth anwoes** 'Keeping oneself warm is no protection against a cold'; **Dyw re wittho orth damaj!** 'May God guard (you) against harm!' **Bydh war! Omwith orth an gwyns yeyn!** 'Be careful! Protect yourself against the cold wind!' **Gwithys vydh an fleghes orth an kleves** 'The children will be protected against the disease'. With the verbal particle **na** 'not' and a tense of the subjunctive, such verbs denote that an attempt is made to prevent something: **Ni a with na enttro ev** 'We shall take care that he does not enter'; **Ny yllir gwitha na glappyo hi** 'One cannot ensure that she does not chatter'.

Absolute prevention is indicated by verbs like **lettya**, etc. (§126(1)). **Gwitha** and **omwitha** are also used with **rag** 'for' to mean 'protect from' (§154(4)).

(8) Feelings and emotions towards: **heweres orth ow theylu** 'helpful towards my family'; **hag ev yw marthys densa ... orth fleghes** 'and he is a marvellously good man ... towards children', BM. 40-41; **rag kerensa orthis** 'for love towards/for you'; **mar bytethus orth an voghosogyon** 'so compassionate towards the poor'; **Trest a'm beus bos akordys orth an re erell** 'I trust that I am in accord with the others'; **mar serrydh orth den** 'if you are angry with a person'; **sorr orth myns a'gan gasso** 'anger against anyone who may leave us'.

(9) Facial expressions, gestures directed at someone with verbs such as **deskerni** 'grin, snarl', **omgamma** 'make a wry face', **skrynkya** 'grimace', **hwerthin** 'laugh', **minhwerthin** 'smile': **Ev a omgammas orth y vamm** 'He made a wry face at his mother'; **Piw yw henna a vinhwarthas orthis?** 'Who is that who smiled at you?' **kronkya** 'strike' **Prag y kronkyas ev orthis?** 'Why did he strike at you?'

(10) The preposition **orth** in several forms combines with the verbal noun to make a phrase equivalent to a present participle. The normal form is **ow**, a reduced version of **orth** and it mutates by hardening (§25): **pan esen vy ow kerdhes** 'when I was walking'; **ow tybri (dybri)** 'eating'.

§154 Prepositions

Before vowels and **h-** the form is **owth**: **owth esedha nessa dhedhi** 'sitting nearest (next) to her'; **owth henwel hy fleghes** 'calling her children'.

When a possessive pronoun represents the object of the verbal noun the form used is **orth**: **orth agan shyndya** 'hurting us' (§243(I)).

§153 **DIWORTH/A-DHIWORTH/DHIWORTH** 'from'. All these forms have the same meaning and are used indifferently although **dhiworth** is most common in the texts. The pronominal endings are as for **orth** (§152), **diworthiv**, etc. **Diworth** denotes movement away from the position implied by **orth**. It therefore conveys more strongly than does **a** (§126(1),(2)) the sense of previous close proximity. The principal meanings are as follows:

(1) Movement away from a place: **diworth an voes** 'away from the table'; **a-dhiworth an dre gyllys** 'gone away from the town'; **Y sevis diworth y brys** 'He got up from his meal'; **Devedhys yw a-dhiworth Lyskerrys** 'He has come from Liskeard'; **Esedh diworth an fos!** 'Sit away from the wall!'

(2) Movement away from a person: **Ke a-dhiworta tamm byghan!** 'Go a little way away from them!' **Lavarow da a dheu a-dhiworto** 'Good words come from him'; **dannvenys a-dhiworth an skrifennyas** 'sent from the secretary'; **My a bys dhiworthis a wortos omma genen** 'I ask (from) you that you stay here with us' (**pysi** can also take the person asked as its direct object (§126(8c)); **Pandr'a wovynnydh sy a-dhiworthiv a'm ober?** 'What are you asking (of) me in respect of my work?' cf. §152(4); **Ev a'n jevydh sorr dhiworth y gowetha** 'His friends will be angry with him', lit. 'He will get anger from his friends'.

(3) With abstract nouns: **diworth an da** 'away from the good, bad'; **diworth an gwir** 'away from the truth, false'.

(4) Of time: **d'wor an nos** (accented on the last syllable) from **diworth an nos** 'at nightfall, by night'; **diworth an myttin** 'at daybreak, in the morning, a.m.'; **dhe dheg eur diworth an myttin** 'at ten o'clock in the morning, ten a.m.'; **dohajydh** from **diworth eghwa an jydh** 'in the afternoon, noon to sunset' (§258(2)).

§154 **RAG** 'for'. The forms with pronominal endings are as follows:

1s.	**ragov**	*for me*	1p.	**ragon**	*for us*
2s.	**ragos**	*for you*	2p.	**ragowgh**	*for you*
3s.m.	**ragdho**	*for him/it*	3p.	**ragdha**	*for them*
3s.f.	**rygdhi**	*for her/it*			

§154(1) Prepositions

(1) The primary meaning of **rag** is positional 'before, in front of' and it keeps this meaning when used as a prefix: **raglavar** 'foreword, preface'. It is rarely used independently with this simple meaning. In the expression **na ylli doen an grows rag dhodho** '(that) he was not able to carry the cross before him' it governs through the preposition **dhe** and has the local meaning. Similarly as an adverb in **Pysk ragov ny wra skeusi** 'A fish shall not escape from (lit. 'before') me'. This local, positional significance is now borne by the compounds **a-rag, derag, a-dherag, dherag**, for which see §155.

(2) The reason for an action or a state, whether that reason is regarded as a cause or as a purpose. The interrogative adverb **prag** is composed of **py** 'what' and **rag** used as a suffix (§74(16)).

(a) Cause: **Drog pes ov rag unn dra** 'I am displeased because of one thing'; **rag y wannder** 'because of his weakness'; **Nammna verwsyn rag yeynder** 'We almost died (because) of cold'; **Rag own y tewis vy** 'Out (because) of fear I was silent'; **Kasadow ova rag an pyth a leveri** 'He was hateful because of what he used to say'; **rakhemma, rakhenna** 'for this, for that (reason)'.

Hence the use of **rag** with the verbal noun or with the infinitive construction, **dhe** + verbal noun (§141(19)): **Serrys ens orto rag y vones maga tont** 'They were angry with him because of his being so impudent'; **Lowen ywa rag my dhe gewsel yn Kernewek** 'He is happy because I speak/spoke Cornish'.

Rag is occasionally used with expressions of gratitude: **dhiso y hwonn gras rag dha volonjedh da** 'I am grateful to you for your good wishes'. Cf. §126(8c) and §141(15(e)).

(b) Purpose: **Piw a wra estyllenn rag ow lyvrow?** 'Who is going to make a shelf for my books?'; **Omma yth on devedhys rag pysi dha gusul prest** 'We have come here to ask your advice straight away', BM. 2140-1; **Martesen y teuth ev rag kavoes arghans** 'Perhaps he came to get money'.

Rag is thus used with the verbal particle **may** 'that' to mean 'in order that': **rag may hylliv y weles** 'so that I may see him' (§349). With this meaning, **rag** and **dhe** overlap (§141(13)) but **rag** is understood as more distinctly implying purpose: **Y teuth dhe dhyski** 'He came to learn'; **Y teuth ev rag dyski** 'He came in order to learn'; **Y teuth rag may tyskka** 'He came in order that he might learn'.

(3) For the sake of: **oll ragdho ev** 'all for him'; **Ragon y fynna gowleverel** 'He was willing to lie on our behalf'; **pysi rag** 'pray on someone's behalf, for

§156 Prepositions

someone': **Pys ragov!** 'Pray for me!' **My a omgemmer ragowgh** 'I make myself responsible for you', BM. 1882; **Yth esen yn poenvos ragos** 'We were worried about you/ on your behalf'; **mos rag** 'vouch for': **My a ragdho** 'I vouch for him'.

(4) A barrier or protection before something, especially with the verbs **gwitha** 'guard', **omwitha**, 'guard oneself'; **kudha** 'hide', **omgudha** 'hide oneself', **lesta** 'prevent', **lettya** 'prevent', **omweres** (or in its shortened form **omeres** but both stressed on the first syllable) 'help oneself': **An fos a wra ow gwitha rag an gwyns** 'The wall will protect me from the wind'; **Gwith dha ji rag ladron, mar kyllydh!** 'Guard your house against thieves, if you can!' **Ny woer omwitha ragdho** 'He does not know how to protect himself from it'; **Omwithewgh rag megi!** 'Refrain from smoking!' **Ny's teves i omweres rag an kleves** 'They are helpless before the disease'; **Piw a yll omweres rag shyndya?** 'Who can protect himself from injury?' **An lowarth yw kudhys rag golok an dremenysi** 'The garden is hidden from the sight of passers-by'; **My a'th lett rag mos** 'I shall prevent you from going'; **Pyth a'n lest rag dyski Bretonek?** 'What prevents him from learning Breton?'

For **gwitha** and **omwitha** with **orth** see §152(7).

For **lettya** 'prevent' with **a** see §126(1).

(5) Time. **Rag** is used with a few words denoting an indefinite period of time as equivalent to the English 'for': **rag termyn** 'for a time'; **Gorta omma rag termyn!** 'Wait here for a time!' **rag nevra** 'for ever': **Yndella re bo rag nevra!** 'May it be so for ever!' (§113).

For **rag** used as a co-ordinating conjunction see §288.

§155 A-RAG/A-DHERAG/DERAG/DHERAG 'before, in front of' have personal endings as **rag**: **dhe wul defens a-rag tus** 'to make a defence in public', lit. 'before people'; **Sevyn a-rag an fenester!** 'Let's stand in front of the window!' **derag y gowetha** 'in front of his friends'; **An kaletter dheragon yw hemma** 'The difficulty before us is this'; **a'n gwelles jy a-dheragos** 'if you had seen him in front of you'.

A-rag is also used as an adjective (§78): **an lowarth a-rag** 'the front garden', and as an adverb: **ha bleujennow plynsys a-rag** 'and flowers planted in front'.

§156 RE/REN 'by' (in oaths). The form **re** softens a following consonant. It combines with the possessive adjectives as shown in §52 and contracts with **an**

§156 Prepositions

'the' to **re'n** 'by the!' (§50(2)). In other situations before vowels the form **ren** is used. This preposition is used only in oaths and is therefore seldom employed in modern conditions. Examples from the texts are: **Re Varia!** 'By Mary!' **Re Vighal** 'By (St) Michael!' and, with the omission of the preposition, **'Varia!**, **'Vighal!**; **Re Dhyw!** 'By God!' **Re'm lowta!** 'By my troth!' **Re'n Arloedh dhe'n bys a'm ros!** 'By the Lord who gave me to this world!' **Re'n enev eus y'm bodi!** 'By the soul which is in my body!' **Ren ow thas!** 'By my father!'

§157 **RYB** 'by, near to', in the form **rep**, may be used as a suffix to make nouns, masculine in gender: **morrep** (**mor** 'sea') 'seaside, shore'; **dorrep** (**dowr** 'water') 'waterside, strand'. The forms with pronominal endings are as follows:

1s.	**rybov**	*by me*	1p.	**rybon**	*by us*
2s.	**rybos**	*by you*	2p.	**rybowgh**	*by you*
3s.m.	**rybdho**	*by him/it*	3p.	**rybdha**	*by them*
3s.f.	**rybdhi**	*by her/it*			

Examples: **Gorrys veu ryb an wedrenn war an voes** 'It was put by the glass on the table'; **ryb y denewenn** 'by his side'; **Yma karrji rybdho** 'There is a garage beside it'.

§158 **SAW** 'except', etc. is followed by a noun or by an independent pronoun. In affirmative contexts it means 'in the absence of, without, save, except for': **Saw y ober, peub a fyll** 'Without his work, everyone fails'; **My re dheuth, saw gwell avis, rag godhvos ...** 'I have come, in the absence of better counsel, to know ...'; **Ni a aswonn oll an re omma saw ev** 'We know all the people here except him'; **saw dha revrons** 'saving your reverence'; **saw agas gras** 'saving your grace'. In negative contexts **saw** means 'only, none but': **Ny goskis saw unn lamm** 'I slept only a little'; **Ny henwis dhymm saw Peder** 'He named only Peter to me'; **Ny yll entra saw perghennow karr** 'None but car owners can enter'; **Nyns eus gwiw saw ty** 'There is no (one) worthy but you'.

Saw is used as a conjunction (§286).

§159 **TANN** 'by'. A rare word, perhaps a variant of **dann** 'under' and used only in oaths, in the phrase **tann ow fydh!** 'by my faith'.

§160 **TROHA(G)** 'towards' is composed of **tro** 'turn, circuit' and **ha(g)** 'and'. It adds a **-g** before a vowel unless, like **ha**, it combines with the following syllable (§50(2), §52). An alternative form, **troha ha(g)**, has a redundant **ha**. Pronoun objects are the independent forms.

§161(4) Prepositions

The meaning is 'towards, in the direction of' with an extension to a use with abstract ideas for which however **orth** (§152) is more usual: **Ni a alemma tro ha Lannwedhenek** 'We go from here towards Padstow'; **troha'm chi** 'towards my house'; **trohag ev** 'towards him/it'; **Edhomm a's ynnias troha toell** 'Need forced them towards deceit'.

§161 WAR 'on, on the top of, above, over the top of' mutates by softening. Cf. **gwartha** m. 'top'. The forms with pronominal endings are as follows:

1s.	**warnav**	*on me*	1p.	**warnan**	*on us*
2s.	**warnas**	*on you*	2p.	**warnowgh**	*on you*
3s.m.	**warnodho**	*on him/it*	3p.	**warnedha**	*on them*
3s.f.	**warnedhi**	*on her/it*			

The meanings of **war** are:

(1) Position on: **Yma goelann war doppynn an wern** 'There is a seagull on the top of the mast'; **My a vynn lesa dillas glan war an gweli** 'I will spread clean (bed)clothes on the bed'; **Gorr dha leuv war an toll!** 'Put your hand on the hole!' **war leur** 'on (the) floor'; **war fordh** 'on (the) road'; **war an ke** 'unclaimed', lit. 'on the hedge'.

(2) A point in time (rare): **war neb tro** 'on some occasion'; **ty re leveris war neb tro** 'you have said on some occasion'; **war Bask** 'at Easter'.

(3) Over, up against: **Warnodho yma men bras** 'There is a big stone over against it'; **war yew!** 'against the yoke!' a call to oxen to take up the strain but now used in a general sense to start an action going. In an abstract sense: **Na wrewgh drem warnav!** 'Make no lamentation over me!' **Gwith war an babi!** 'Look after the baby'.

Note the adverb **war-wartha** 'on (the) top' and the compound preposition and adverb **war-lergh** (§163).

(4) Advantage over, domination, hostility towards: **may kaffo ev gwayn warnodho dh'y fetha** 'so that he may get an advantage over him to beat him'; **An governans a'n jevydh maystri war an bobel bys vykken** 'The government will have power over the people always'; **Nyns eus acheson dhe wruthyl krodhvol na son warnas** 'There is no cause for grumbling nor clamour against you'; **Pana dra a ynniowgh hwi warnodho?** 'What do you urge against him?' MC. 99.1-2. **tyli dial war/gul dial war** 'take vengeance upon'.

§161(4)   Prepositions

So with exclamations: **A! Out warnas!** 'Ah! Out upon you!' **Deun warnedha!** 'Let's get at them!' **deghesi war** or **deghesi dhe** 'strike at'; **Deghesewgh warnedhi!** 'Strike at her!' BM. 3948; **yn despit war** 'in spite of' (§170).

(5) The ground on which something is done, the cause or basis of it: **Ny'm prev den war dhiekter** 'No one shall prove me of laziness', i.e. on the grounds of laziness; **Ev eth war edhomm gweles y deylu** 'He went on the grounds that he needed to see his family'.

(6) In the form **warn** this preposition is used to make the compound numerals from twenty-one to thirty-nine (§93(2), §101(4)): **deg warn ugens** 'thirty', lit. 'ten on twenty'.

(7) Direction: **rag y teu liv war an bys** 'for a flood will come upon the Earth'; **Da yw gansa gwandra war an menydhyow** 'They enjoy wandering on the mountains'; **war neb tu** 'in some direction, way'; **mar kallen y weles war neb tu** 'if I could see him in some way'. Cf. **war neb kor**, (11) below.

(8) Directing the attention on to something, inclining to: **poesa y benn warnans** 'leaning his head downwards'; **war-woeles** 'towards the bottom, downwards': **pan viras war-woeles** 'when he looked downwards'; **war-rag** 'forwards'; **war-dhelergh** 'backwards'; **war-vann** 'upwards'; **mires war** 'look upon'; **hwithra war** 'gaze upon'; **Unn prys y hwithris warnodho** 'On one occasion I gazed upon it'; **gwitha war** 'look after'; **mar mynnydh gwitha war ow thigenn** 'if you will look after my bag'. For adverbial uses see §259(2).

(9) Praying to someone for mercy or pity, usually with the verb **pysi** 'pray, ask': **Oll ni a bys war Dhyw mersi** 'We all pray to(wards) God (for) mercy'; **Arloedh, warnas tregeredh (y pysav)** 'Lord, to thee (for) pity (I pray)'.

Note that the direct object of the verb in these expressions is the thing asked for (§126(8c), §126(8e), §153(2)).

(10) The method by which something is done, the conditions according to which it is done: **Ny dheuth war an daras** 'He didn't come by way of the door'; **war anow** 'by (word of) mouth, orally'; **Yma war agan towl synsi kuntelles kyns pell** 'It is our intention to hold a meeting before long'; **war nebes lavarow, war verr lavarow** 'in a few words, in short'.

(11) The rate or standard according to which something is done. This yields a number of common adverbial expressions: **warbarth** (**parth** 'side') 'together'; **warbarth ha** 'together with, at the same time as' (§287); **A wel'ta ni devedhys**

§163(2)   Prepositions

warbarth ha'n kynsa galow? 'Do you see (that) we (have) come right at the first call?' **war gamm (kamm** 'pace') 'steadily'; **Hwyth war gamm!** 'Blow steadily!' **Gwask war gamm!** 'Strike steadily!' **A war dha gamm, ty Vighal!** 'Go steadily, Michael!' **war hast** 'hastily'; **war neb kor** 'in some way'; **Ny'n gwrussa den a-ji dhe unn seythun war neb kor** 'A person wouldn't do it in a week in any way' = 'in no way would ...'; **Gorfenn e war neb kor!** 'Finish it in some way!' **war nuk (nuk** 'notch') 'immediately'; **war skwych** 'with a jerk'; **war unn lamm** 'suddenly'.

(12) The thing of which we speak, the basis of conversation or thought: **Ty a gammdyb warnodho ev** 'You are mistaken about him'; **My a'm bo hwans kewsel war an negys na** 'I wanted to speak about that business'.

§162 **DIWAR** and **A-DHIWAR** 'off (the top of)' and 'from off (the top of)' respectively are constructed as **war** (§161) and imply an opposite set of meanings: **Ny'n drehev diwar y geyn** 'He will not lift it from off his back'; **Diwarnodho y teuth** 'It came from off it'; **An lyver a goedhas a-dhiwar an voes** 'The book fell from off the table'; **Re'th trehaffo a-dhiwar an leur!** 'May he raise you from off the ground!' (to a cripple), BM. 4227. Note also **diwar breder** 'after (taking) thought'.

§163 **WAR-LERGH** 'behind, after' is a compound preposition, made up of **war** (§161) and **lergh** 'trace'. It is used of space, time and abstract notions derived from these. The object, when a pronoun, is the possessive form (possessive adjective) and is put before the noun, thus:

1s.	**war ow lergh**	behind me	1p.	**war agan lergh**	behind us
2s.	**war dha lergh**	behind you	2p.	**war agas lergh**	behind you
3s.m.	**war y lergh**	behind him/it	3p.	**war aga lergh**	behind them
3s.f.	**war hy lergh**	behind her/it			

(1) Position 'behind, after' and usually with verbs of movement: **My a syw war-lergh dha garr** 'I will follow behind your car'; **Gwell yw mos war y lergh** 'It is better to go after him'; **War aga lergh fistenyn!** 'Let us hurry after them!'

Note that the idea of stationary position is denoted by **a-dryv** (§133).

(2) Time 'after' and generally used with a noun phrase of some sort, i.e. the verbal noun or the infinitive construction with **dhe** (§347(2)): **war-lergh henna** 'after that'; **war-lergh henna leverys** 'after that (having been) said'; **war-lergh koska mar boes** 'after sleeping so heavily'; **war-lergh dha vones dhe dre**

§163(2) Prepositions

'after your arrival home'; **war-lergh an den dhe wul y ober** 'after the man does/has done/had done his work'; **war-lergh ni dh'y weles** 'after we see/have seen/had seen him'.

(3) Following on, in accord with, according to: **I a wra oll war-lergh y lavarow** 'They do everything according to what he says'; **Bedhens rewlys war dha lergh!** 'Let them be ruled according to you!' (in accordance with your wishes); **war-lergh an skrifer na** 'according to that writer'; **Gwra war-lergh lavarow dha gerens** 'Do as your parents say!' Cf. **herwydh** (§149).

(4) Longing after: **Meur yw ow hireth war hy lergh** 'Great is my longing for her'; **Morethek yw hi war-lergh hy thre** 'She is longing for home'. So with **fienasow** m. 'grief', **hirethek** adj. 'yearning', **yeunadow** m., **yeunes** m. 'yearning', **yeuni** v.n. 'yearn', **trist** adj. 'sad': **Trist ywa war-lergh y yowynkneth** 'He has a sorrowful longing for his youth', lit. 'is sad after'.

§164 **WAR-TU HA(G)**. This expression is made up of **war** 'on' (§161) and **tu** m. 'side, direction' but without the expected mutation. It combines with a following syllable as does **ha(g)** 'and', the third element of the phrase (§50(2)) and (§52). A pronoun object has the independent form, **my, ty,** etc. The meaning is directional: **war-tu ha'y vamm** 'towards his mother'; **war-tu ha tre** (sometimes **war-tu tre**); **war-tu ha'n vorva** 'towards the shore'; **war-tu ha ty** 'towards you'; **war-tu hag i** 'towards them'; **war-tu ha'ga fenn** 'towards their heads'.

§165 **WAR-VES A** 'outwards from' refers to direction: **pan eth an kok war-ves a'n porth** 'when the fishing boat went outwards from the harbour'; **war-ves a'n botell fler, drog a fler** 'out from the bottle a smell, an evil (of a) smell'. Cf. §161(7), (8).

§166 **WOSA** 'after' is from **a-wosa** (§138) by the loss of initial **a**. This preposition is not used with personal pronouns as an object, **war-lergh** (§163) serving in its place. It denotes:

(1) Occurrence after a period of time or an event: **wosa seythun** 'after a week'; **wosa hemma/henna** 'after this/that'; **wosa mernans** 'after death'.

(2) With the verbal noun: **wosa dos** 'after coming'; **wosa mos** 'after going'; **wosa dybri koen** 'after eating supper'.

(3) In the infinitive construction (§141(19)): **wosa an vowes dhe wul hemma** 'after the girl does/did/had done this'; **wosa i dhe dhadhla unn lamm**

§167(3) Prepositions

'after they had held a discussion for a while'; **wosa hwi dh'y glywes** 'after you hear/heard/had heard him' (§347(2)).

§167 **YN** 'in' contracts with some possessive adjectives (§52) and with **an** 'the' to **y'n** 'in the' (§50(2)). The forms with pronominal endings are as follows:

1s.	**ynnov**	*in me*	1p.	**ynnon**	*in us*
2s.	**ynnos**	*in you*	2p.	**ynnowgh**	*in you*
3s.m.	**ynno**	*in him/it*	3p.	**ynna**	*in them*
3s.f.	**ynni**	*in her/it*			

The several meanings of **yn** are:

(1) Inside, in the interior of something: **An logel ynni an korf** 'the coffin (with) the body in it', RD. 2179-80; **yn ow roes** 'in my net'; **gorrys yn trog** 'placed in a chest'; **yn tre** 'at home'; **Piw eus yn tre?** 'Who is at home?' **yn chi** 'indoors, inside'; **Esowgh hwi yn chi?** 'Are you in?' The adverbs **a-bervedh**, **a-berth** 'inside' reinforce the preposition: **a'y esedh a-berth yn y jambour** 'seated in his bedroom'; **an prederow usi gwithys a-bervedh y'n golonn** 'the thoughts which are guarded within the heart'.

(2) With verbs of motion to mean 'into': **Prag na dheuthons i yn chi?** 'Why did they not come inside?' **ha'ga doen genev yn chi** 'and carry them with me into the house'; **Yn Kernow ... ty re dheuva** 'Into Cornwall, you have come,' BM. 622-23; **Ev a yn prison** 'He shall go (in)to prison'; **Yth eth yn y dhorn** 'It went into his hand'. The adverbs **a-bervedh** and **a-berth** are again used here: **Ke a-berth y'n krowji!** 'Go inside the shed!'

Adverbs formed with the implication of motion are: **yn-rag** 'forward'; **yn-bann** 'upwards'; **yn-nans** 'downwards' (§259(3)); cf. §161(8).

(3) At a place 'in': **yn pub le, yn pub plas** 'everywhere'; **yn ow nessa** 'nearest to me', BM. 1968; **yn lyver yma skrifys** 'in a book there is written'; **y'm diwleuv** 'in my hands' (also **ynter ow diwleuv** (§178(1))); **yn ughelder** 'in the height, on high'. **Yn** is used with **dalghenn** m. 'grip' and **dalghenna** v.n. 'grip'; **settya dalghenn ynno** 'get a hold on him'; **mar kavav dalghenn ynno** 'if I get hold of him'; **Dalghenn ynna!** 'Get a grip on them!' However the verb can be used directly: **My a'n dalghenn** 'I will seize him', PD.1131; **orth dha dhalghenna** 'seizing you', PD.1141. Adverbs are thus formed: **yn-mes** 'outside', **yn ogas** 'near', **yn pell** 'far off'; **naneyl ogas nag yn pell** 'neither near nor far', OM. 1141.

§167(3) Prepositions

Certain compound prepositions have **yn** as the first element: **yn-dann** 'below', **yn herwydh** 'nearby', **yn kyrghynn** 'around', **yn kever** 'about', **yn le** 'in place of', **yn mysk** 'in the midst of'. See the following sections.

(4) At a place 'on'; **yn tir hag yn mor** 'on land and sea', PD.392; **y'n treth** 'on the beach'; **y'n als** 'on the cliffs'; **Skrif ynno!** 'Write on it!' **Yesus y'n dor a skrifas** 'Jesus wrote on the ground', MC. 33.6; **y'n menydh** 'on the mountain'; **yn y dron** 'on his throne'; **y'n grows** 'on the cross' (the usual expression in the texts, **war** only being used when the cross was on the ground); **y'n kloghbrennyer** 'on the gallows', BM. 923; **y'n bys** 'on the earth', used to strengthen a negative to mean 'at all' (§266): **Ny wonn y'n bys** 'I don't know at all'; **y'n bys ma** 'on this earth'; **Yn sol!** 'On your feet!'

(5) Time in a less precise sense, so not with clock time or with dates for which see **dhe** (§141(12)): **y'n eur ma** 'now'; **y'n eur na** 'then'; **My a wodhvydh y'n eur na** 'I shall know then'; **skon y'n tor' ma** 'straight away'; **megys gans losow y'n tor' ma** 'nourished with vegetables now'; **y'n keth dydh na** 'on that same day'; **yn kettermyn** (**keth** 'same' + **termyn** 'time') 'at the same time'; **y'n termyn a dheu** 'in the time to come, in the future'; **naneyl yn nos nag yn jydh** 'neither by day nor by night'; **yn diwedh an bys** 'at the end of the world'; **y'n jydh diwettha a vis Meurth** 'on the last day of March'; **y'n tressa dydh** 'on the third day'; (also **dhe'n tressa dydh** (§141(12)); **y'n nos haneth** 'this evening'; **yn edhomm** 'at (a time of) need'; **y'n gwella prys** 'happily', ('on the best occasion'); **y'n gwettha prys** 'unhappily'. With a noun of time and a possessive adjective **yn** is equivalent to 'during': **yn ow oes/yn ow bywnans** 'during my lifetime, ever', etc. and with a negative context, 'never': **Moy poenvos ny'm darva yn ow oes** 'More trouble has never befallen me' (§258(8)); **hag yn y gows y'n fethyn** 'and in his talk we will overcome him', i.e. 'during his talk', RD. 251.

(6) With abstract nouns: **yn joy** 'in joy, joyfully'; **Kosk yn koseleth!** 'Sleep in peace!' **y'n keth galloes** 'in the same power'; **yn lavur hag yn anken** 'in toil and in misery'; **yn poynt da** 'in good health': **Esosta yn poynt da?** 'Are you well?' **Gyllys ov yn prederow** 'I am worried', lit. 'gone into worries', RD. 15; **yn kosk** 'asleep'; but note **difun** adj. 'awake' and **a-dhifun** adv. 'awake'; **krysi ynno** 'believe in him' (cf. §141(15g)); **yn peryll** 'at risk'; **Kemmer e yn ow feryll!** 'Take it at my risk!' i.e. 'I will take responsibility for it, accept the blame'.

(7) Manner: **yn neb maner** 'in some manner'; **yn pub maner** 'in every way'; **yn tenn** 'pulled out, stretched'; **lovanow an tylda yn tenn** 'the tent ropes taut'; **yn krog** 'tugged, hanged'; **pan esons i yn krog** 'since they are hanged',

§168(3) Prepositions

BM. 1264; **yn rew** 'in a row'; **Esedhewgh yn unn rew!** 'Sit in one row!' or 'in succession': **Red an henwyn yn unn rew!** 'Read the names one after another!' **yn unn golmenn** 'in a knot, knotted together'; **yndella** = **yn** + **dell** (**dell** 'way' in compounds) + **ma** 'in this way, thus'; **yn kettellma** = **yn** + **keth** + **dell** + **ma** 'in this same way'.

(8) As a particle, **yn** expresses the function which something has, an instrumental use (§47(4)): **yn prov** 'as a proof'; **yn tokyn len** 'as a true sign'; **yn attal** 'in repayment'; **yn ober** 'in fact'. For the use of **yn** as an adverb-forming particle see §92.

(9) An adverbial phrase which is sometimes called an adverbial present participle is formed by **yn unn** and a verbal noun. Softening of the initial consonant occurs after **yn unn**. It denotes the manner in which some action is carried out: **Gwann yw bys ma na yll ev gonis yn unn fistena** 'He is weak so that he cannot work quickly', lit. 'in a hurrying manner'; **yn unn oberi** 'in a practical manner'; **Yn unn sygera y kerdhi dhe skol** 'In a sluggish manner he would walk to school'; **yn unn dhidhana** 'amusingly'; **Hi a gewsi yn unn dhidhana a'y vyaj dhe Amerika** 'She spoke amusingly of her journey to America'. Compare the use of **yn-dann** (§168(3)) and contrast the function of the present participle construction with **ow** which is adjectival (§243(2)).

§168 **YN-DANN** 'under' softens the following consonant. The forms with pronominal endings are as follows:

1s.	**yn-dannov**	under me	1p.	**yn-dannon**	under us
2s.	**yn-dannos**	under you	2p.	**yn-dannowgh**	under you
3s.m.	**yn-danno**	under him/it	3p.	**yn-danna**	under them
3s.f.	**yn-danni**	under her/it			

The uses of **yn-dann** are:

(1) Position beneath anything: **yn-dann dha gasel** 'under your armpit'; **yn-dann y dhewdroes** 'under his feet'; **yn-dann an asow** 'under the ribs'; **My a's pe yn-dann onnenn** 'I will pay them under ash (birch or rod)', i.e. punish them.

(2) Abstract ideas: **Yn-dann ambos yth os** 'You are under a contract', PD.2259.; **yn-dann gel** (**kel** 'hiding') 'secretly'.

(3) Action going on at the same time as the main action. This is said to denote simultaneous, continuous action and is described as an adverbial present participle (§243(6)): **Skolkyewgh di yn-dann dava!** 'Creep up to the place,

§168(3) Prepositions

keeping in touch!' PD.1002; **Ny yllir kyni yn-dann hwerthin** 'One cannot mourn with laughter', lit. 'mourn under laughing'.

§169 **A-DHANN** 'from under' softens a following consonant and has pronominal endings as **yn-dann** (§168): **Tenn e yn-mes a-dhann an ven!** 'Pull it out from under the stone!' **Diskwedh i a-dhann dha glok!** 'Show them from under your cloak!'

§170 **YN DESPIT** 'in spite of' governs a following noun or pronoun object through the preposition **dhe** (§141) or more rarely **orth** (§152(6)) or **war** (§161(4)). The second element is found shortened to **spit**. The meaning is 'in spite of' in a defiant or an aggressive sense: **yn despit oll dh'y eghenn** 'in spite of all his effort'; **yn despit oll dh'aga eghenn** 'in spite of all they could do'; **yn despit dh'y das ha'y vamm** 'in spite of his father and his mother'. Expressions of defiance and challenge: **yn despit dh'y dhewlagas** 'in spite of his eyes'; **yn spit dha dhens/dhe'th tens/war dha dhens/orth dha dhens** 'in spite of your teeth'.

§171 **YN HERWYDH** (see also **herwydh** (§149)) 'nearby'. Pronoun objects are expressed by the possessive adjective before the second element, thus:

1s.	yn ow herwydh *or* y'm herwydh	*near me*	1p.	yn agan herwydh *or* y'gan herwydh	*near us*
2s.	yn dha herwydh *or* y'th herwydh	*near you*	2p.	yn agas herwydh *or* y'gas herwydh	*near you*
3s.m.	yn y herwydh	*near him/it*	3p.	yn aga herwydh *or* y'ga herwydh	*near them*
3s.f.	yn hy herwydh	*near her/it*			

The meaning is 'in the vicinity of, near': **yn herwydh Kammbronn** 'in the vicinity of Camborne'; **yn herwydh chi ow modrep** 'in the neighbourhood of my aunt's house'; **Yn dha herwydh yma hwel bal** 'Near you there is a mine'; **Y'ga herwydh yth esa penndra ena** 'There was a village in their neighbourhood there'.

§172 **YN KYRGHYNN** 'all around'. The noun **kyrghynn** occurring only in this context is said to mean 'the immediate surroundings'. Pronoun objects are put before the second element in the form of the possessive adjectives. Note **an kyrghynnedh** 'the environment'.

§174　　　　　　　　　　　　　　　　　　　　　　　　　　　　Prepositions

1s.	**yn ow hyrghynn** *or* **y'm kyrghynn**	*all around me*	1p.	**yn agan kyrghynn** *or* **y'gan kyrghynn**	*all around us*
2s.	**yn dha gyrghynn** *or* **y'th kyrghynn**	*all around you*	2p.	**yn agas kyrghynn** *or* **y'gas kyrghynn**	*all around you*
3s.m.	**yn y gyrghynn**	*all around him/it*	3p.	**yn aga hyrghynn** *or* **y'ga hyrghynn**	*all around them*
3s.f.	**yn hy hyrghynn**	*all around her/it*			

The meaning is 'all around, on all sides of' and particularly as applied to clothing or covering of some sort: **an bows usi y'th kyrghynn** 'the coat which is around you'; **Gwisk dha dhillas y'th kyrghynn!** 'Put your clothes around you!' **Mayl lystenn yn kyrghynn y gonna-bregh!** 'Wrap a bandage around his wrist!'

The more general meaning of 'around' is conveyed by **a-dro dhe** (§132).

§173 **YN KEVER** 'about'. The noun element **kever** is not known apart from this compound. It is said to mean 'direction, relationship' (cf. Breton *keñver* 'regard'). A pronoun object is the possessive adjective before the noun.

1s.	**yn ow hever** *or* **y'm kever**	*about me*	1p.	**yn agan kever** *or* **y'gan kever**	*about us*
2s.	**yn dha gever** *or* **y'th kever**	*about you*	2p.	**yn agas kever** *or* **y'gas kever**	*about you*
3s.m.	**yn y gever**	*about him/it*	3p.	**yn aga hever** *or* **y'ga hever**	*about them*
3s.f.	**yn hy hever**	*about her/it*			

The meanings are:

(1) Behaviour in respect of a person: **yn y gever dell veuv bad** 'as I was remiss in regard to him'; **Ev yw maw diek y'th kever** 'He is an idle lad where you are concerned'; **Drog yw genev bos re logh yn dha gever** 'I am sorry for being so lax towards you'. Cf. **orth** (§152(8)).

(2) With abstract ideas to mean 'concerning'. **Ny woer travydh yn kever an negys** 'He knows nothing concerning the message'; **yn kever an skrifenn ma** 'concerning this (piece) of writing'; **Deriv dhyn yn y gever!** 'Tell us about it!'

§174 **YN LE** 'in place (of)' is a compound with the noun **le** 'place'. Pronoun objects are expressed by the possessive pronoun before the noun.

§174 Prepositions

1s.	**yn ow le** *or* **y'm le**	*in my place*	1p.	**yn agan le** *or* **y'gan le**	*in our place*
2s.	**yn dha le** *or* **y'th le**	*in your place*	2p.	**yn agas le** *or* **y'gas le**	*in your place*
3s.m.	**yn y le**	*in his/its place*	3p.	**yn aga le** *or* **y'ga le**	*in their place*
3s.f.	**yn hy le**	*in her/its place*			

The meaning is the simple one of replacement: **Y teuth hy hwoer yn hy le** 'Her sister came in her place'; **yn le mos, gortos** 'in place of going, staying'; **Ny'gan beus travydh y'ga le** 'We have nothing in their place'.

§175 **YN-MES** A. The element **yn** may be omitted. This compound preposition, the government of which is that of **a** (§126), implies motion out of, position outside of: **Tamsyn, ke yn-mes a'm chi!** 'Tamsyn, go out of my house!' **Dew dhen yma a'ga esedh yn-mes anedhi** 'There are two persons sitting outside (of) it (the church)'; **Gyllys o mes a'y rewl** 'He was out of his mind', lit. 'gone out of his control'.

§176 **YN MYSK** can be shortened to **mysk** alone and is composed of **yn** with the noun **mysk** 'middle'.

It is used with a plural count noun or with mass nouns or with a possessive adjective before the second element to express the pronoun object, this possessive adjective being either the third singular or one of the plural forms.

1s.	-		1p.	**yn agan mysk** *or* **y'gan mysk**	*in the midst of us*
2s.	-		2p.	**yn agas mysk** *or* **y'gas mysk**	*in the midst of you*
3s.m.	**yn y vysk**	*in the midst of it*	3p.	**yn aga mysk** *or* **y'ga mysk**	*in the midst of them*
3s.f.	**yn hy mysk**	*in the midst of it*			

The meaning is 'in the midst of, amongst': **yn mysk oll dha gerens** 'amongst all your relations'; **yn mysk y gowetha** 'amongst his friends'; **yn mysk an soedhogyon** 'amongst the officials'; **den a vri yn mysk a'n aswonn** 'a man of reputation amongst those who know him'; **kosel yn mysk tervans meur** 'calm in the midst of great turmoil'; **yn mysk meur a dewolgow** 'in the midst of great darkness'; **Eus dallethoryon vydh y'gas mysk?** 'Are there any beginners at all amongst you?'

With a number, which may be arbitrary, **yn mysk** is used to denote excellence, outstandingness: **gwas pur uskis yn mysk naw** 'a very quick fellow', lit. 'a

§178 Prepositions

fellow very quick amongst nine'; **Sherewa yw yn mysk mil** 'He's a rascal in a thousand'.

§177 **YN OGAS** 'near to' forms an alternative construction to **ogas dhe** (§141(8)).

Pronoun objects are expressed by the possessive adjectives as follows:

1s.	**yn ow ogas** *or* **y'm ogas**	*near me*	1p.	**yn agan ogas** *or* **y'gan ogas**	*near us*
2s.	**yn dha ogas** *or* **y'th ogas**	*near you*	2p.	**yn agas ogas** *or* **y'gas ogas**	*near you*
3s.m.	**yn y ogas**	*near him/it*	3p.	**yn aga ogas** *or* **y'ga ogas**	*near them*
3s.f.	**yn hy ogas**	*near her/it*			

(1) Position: **Yma edhen yn dha ogas** 'There is a bird near you'; **mars eus lytherva yn y ogas** 'if there is a post office near it'. Compare also **yn ogas** as an adverb (§259(1)).

(2) Social relationships: **Nyns ova y'gas ogas** 'He wasn't near(ly) related to them'; **ogas dhe'n Dhuges yw hi** 'She is a near relative/a close friend of the Duchess'.

The superlative form **nessa** 'nearest' (§82(4)) is similarly used: **yn ow nessa** 'nearest to me', etc.: **My a woer bos an teylu Tommas ow triga yn y nessa** 'I know that the Thomas family is living nearest to him'; **Aga noy y'n Statow Unys yw y'ga nessa** 'Their nephew in the United States is most nearly (related) to them'.

Note that the short or the long form of the verb **bos** is used according to whether the relationship is physical or abstract.

§178 **YNTRA/YNTER** 'between'. The second form is the one now used regularly before vowels. The forms with pronominal endings are as follows:

1s.	**yntredhov**	*between me*	1p.	**yntredhon**	*between us*
2s.	**yntredhos**	*between you*	2p.	**yntredhowgh**	*between you*
3s.m.	**yntredho**	*between him/it*	3p.	**yntredha**	*between them*
3s.f.	**yntredhi**	*between her/it*			

The first and second persons of the singular, **yntredhov** and **yntredhos**, are less used than constructions consisting of the preposition with a following

§178 Prepositions

independent pronoun: **yntra my ha'n konsel** 'between me and the counsel' and not **yntredhov ha'n konsel**, but **yntredho ha'y gowetha** 'between him and his friends', PD. 1288. So **Yma an dra yntra my ha ty** 'The thing is between me and you' or **yntredhon** 'between us'.

The meanings are:

(1) A position between two objects or points, often expressed by the dual: **ynter y dhens ha'y daves** 'between his teeth and his tongue', OM. 826; **yntra dha dhiwleuv** 'between your (two) hands', 'in your hands'; **yntra diwleuv Dyw a-vann** 'between (in) the hands of God above'.

(2) A relationship made or broken between two objects or people: **Dibarth gwrav ynter an mor ha'n tiryow** 'I make a separation between the sea and the land(s)', OM. 25-26; **an akord gwrys yntredhov ha perghenn an chi** 'the agreement made between me and the owner of the house'.

(3) A position amongst a number of objects or people: **ynter an gwydh** 'between the trees'; **yntra ladron** 'between thieves'; **Hi a veu sevys yn-bann yntra benynes** 'She was lifted up among some women', MC. 172.2-3; **yntra y dhiwleuv** 'into his hands'.

(4) Division into parts (§110(4)

(a) Into two parts: **Vayl an Templa a skwardyas yntra dew** 'The veil of the Temple split into two'; **Omma kompes yntra dew my a'n tregh** 'Exactly here in two I cut it'.

(b) Into more than two parts: **Marth yw na skward ev yntra kans rann** 'It's a wonder it doesn't split into a hundred pieces'.

(c) Without a numerical element: **I a rannas yntredha oll an arghans** 'They divided all the money between them'; **mar mynnowgh ranna an termyn yntredhowgh** 'if you will divide the time between you'.

(d) With abstract qualities: **Ev a wra ranna an gwir yntredhon ni** 'He will divide the truth between us', i.e. judge between us.

❖ ❖ ❖ ❖ ❖

Verbs

§179 The forms of the verb Each verbal form is made up of two parts, the stem which carries the general meaning: e.g. **pren-** 'buy', and endings which indicate particular applications of the general meaning, as follows:

(1) **Person** There are 1st, 2nd and 3rd persons in the singular and plural and an impersonal 'open' reference, the English 'one does': **pren-ir** 'one buys, there is a buying'.

(2) **Tense** The tenses are:

Present/Future   Imperfect   Preterite   Pluperfect/Conditional

A present perfect is made by putting the verbal particle **re** before the preterite. The same particle confirms the pluperfect (§279).

(3) **Mood** There are three moods:

Indicative   Subjunctive   Imperative

All the persons and tenses are found in the indicative. All the persons of the present/future and the imperfect tenses are found in the subjunctive. The imperative has only a present/future tense and lacks a 1s. and the impersonal.

(4) Associated with the verb are a verbal noun (§233-§242), a present participle construction (§243) and a past participle (§244).

§180 The verbal suffixes of the indicative

	Pres./fut.	Preterite	Imperfect	Pluperfect
s. 1	-av	-is	-en (-yn)	-sen
s. 2	-ydh	-sys	-es (-ys)	-ses
s. 3	-	-as (-is)	-a (-i)	-sa
p. 1	-yn	-syn	-en (-yn)	-sen
p. 2	-owgh	-sowgh	-ewgh	-sewgh
p. 3	-ons	-sons	-ens	-sens
0	-ir	-as (-is)	-ys	-sys

Remarks on the verbal suffixes of the indicative.

§180(1)   Verbs

(1) The 3s. present/future consists of the stem only: **kara** v.n. 'love'; **kar** 'he/she loves'.

(2) In the preterite the 2s. and all the plural persons have an -s- before the pronominal ending proper.

(3) The 2s. endings **-ydh, -sys, -ses** may be modified before the reduced suffixed pronoun **-ta** (§64(3)).

(4) A number of verbs have 3s. preterite in **-is** instead of **-as**. These are:

(a) All verbs which have the verbal noun ending **-el** (§193).

(b) The following verbs:

aswonn	'know'	**gorhemmynn**	'command'
attylli	'repay'	**gorthybi**	'reply'
brewi	'break'	**hedhi**	'stop'
dagrewi	'weep'	**heveli**	'seem'
dedhewi	'promise'	**kemmynna**	'bequeath'
dehweles	'return'	**kentrewi**	'nail'
demmedhi	'marry'	**kreuni**	'accumulate'
derivas	'tell'	**krysi**	'believe'
diank	'escape'	**mollethi**	'curse'
dinewi	'pour'	**ombrederi**	'think'
dineythi	'give birth'	**omhweles**	'fall'
diskrysi	'disbelieve'	**prederi**	'think'
distrui	'destroy'	**pysi**	'pray'
domhwel	'overthrow'	**synsi**	'hold'
dybri	'eat'	**tevi**	'grow'
dynnerghi	'welcome'	**tybi** (§201)	'think'
erghi	'order'	**tyli**	'pay'
godhav (= **godhevel**)	'suffer'	**yeuni**	'yearn'

(5) The personal endings of the imperfect are similar to those of the pluperfect and the imperfect subjunctive.

Some verbs have -y-/-i- as the vowel of the singular persons and of the first person plural. These are:

(a) All verbs with the verbal noun suffix in **-el, -es** (except for **klywes** (§204) and **mynnes** (§226)), **-he** (§187) and **-i**.

§182 Verbs

(b) The following verbs:

amma	'kiss'	galloes (§227)	'be able'
aswonn	'know'	godhav	'suffer'
dalleth	'begin'	(= godhevel)	
dannvon	'send'	gonis	'work'
dervynn	'demand'	govynn	'ask'
dewis	'choose'	hembronk	'lead'
diberth	'part'	hwerthin	'laugh'
difenn	'forbid'	lavasos	'venture'
doen (§207)	'carry'	minhwerthin	'smile'
dyllo (§211)	'send out'	omladh	'fight'
folhwerthin	'giggle'		

(6) In the pluperfect a characteristic -s- precedes the pronominal endings proper. As noted above, the personal endings of the pluperfect are similar to those of the imperfect indicative and the imperfect subjunctive.

§181 **The verbal suffixes of the subjunctive**

	Pres./fut.	Imperfect
s. 1	-iv	-en
s. 2	-i	-es
s. 3	-o	-a
p. 1	-yn	-en
p. 2	-owgh	-ewgh
p. 3	-ons	-ens
0	-er	-ys

It will be noted that with the exception of the singular persons of the present/future, the personal endings are identical with those of the corresponding tenses of the indicative.

§182 **Modification of the stem in the subjunctive**

Hardening or doubling or both in the ending of the stem may occur in all persons of the present/future and the subjunctive.

These changes are as follows, the unmodified form being given first.

Verbs

b > pp	f > ff	kr > kkr	ndl > ntl	rg > rk	thl > tthl
bl > ppl	g > kk	l > ll	ndr > ntr	rj > rch	thr > tthr
br > ppr	gh > ggh	ld > lt	ng > nk	rv > rf	tl > ttl
ch > cch	gl > kkl	ldr > ltr	ngr > nkr	s > ss	v > ff
d > tt	gn > kkn	lv > lf	nj > nch	sh > ssh	vn > ffn
dh > tth	he > hah	m > mm	p > pp	sl > ssl	vr > ffr
dhl > tthl	j > cch	mbl > mpl	r > rr	sn > ssn	
dhr > tthr	k > kk	mbr > mpr	rd > rt	sw > ssw	
dhw > tthw	kl > kkl	n > nn	rdr > rtr	t > tt	
dr > ttr	kn > kkn	nd > nt	rdh > rth	th > tth	

The ending of the stem may be a single consonant, a doubled consonant or a cluster. The change is due to the influence of an **-h-** which in a former state of the language occurred in the subjunctive (LP §203). The **-y-** of a verbal noun ending such as **poenya** does not affect the change. Nor is there any change in verbs which end in **-ia** such as **afia**.

§183 **The verbal suffixes of the imperative** There is only one tense, the present/future, in this mood.

2s. -   3s. -es   1p. -yn   2p. -ewgh   3p. -ens

Remarks on the verbal suffixes of the imperative:

(1) There is no 1s. form of the imperative. The phrases **gas vy dhe ...** in the singular and **gesewgh vy dhe ...** in the plural 'allow me to ...' with a verbal noun supply the want: **Gas vy dhe goska!** 'Let me sleep!' (§66(3c)).

(2) The 2s. is the stem itself: **Pren!** 'Buy!' This form always displays the original stem vowel: **Son!** 'Sound!' but verbal noun **seni** 'sound(ing)' (§14).

(3) The 3s. in Modern Cornish has restored the use of the forms in **-es**. The 3p. in **-ens** had taken its place in many instances.

§184 **The several classes of verbs may be conveniently listed as follows**:

Type examples

(1) Regular verbs: **PRENA** (§185), **AFIA** (§186)

(2) Verbs with verbal nouns ending in **-he**: **BERRHE** (§187)

(3) Verbs with verbal nouns in -ya: **POENYA** (§188)

(4) Verbs with vowel affection: **TAVA** (§189), **IGERI** (§190), **ERGHI** (§191)

(5) Verbs with a vowel added in the stem: **GELWEL** (§193), **HWITHRA** (§194), **GWYSTLA** (§195)

(6) Verbs with a consonant omitted in the stem: **LESTA** (§196)

(7) Irregular verbs with distinctive verbal endings: **BOS** (§197), **Y'M BEUS** (§198), **PIW** (§199), **GODHVOS** (§200), **TYLI** (§201), **KLYWES** (§204), **MOS** (§205), **DOS** (§206), **GUL** (§225), **GALLOES** (§227), **DOEN** (§207), **RI** (§208), **DRI** (§209), **TI** (§210), **DYLLO** (§211)

(8) Defective verbs which are restricted to a few persons or tenses: **HWARVOS** (§202), **DARVOS** (§203) and others, described in (§213-§224).

REGULAR VERBS

§185 **PRENA** 'buy'. The paradigm of the regular verb. For the meanings and uses of the tenses of the indicative see §228. For the uses of the subjunctive see §229.

In the paradigms of the verbs '0' stands for the impersonal.

	Indicative				*Imperative*
	Pres./fut.	*Preterite*	*Imperfect*	*Pluperfect*	
s.1	prenav	prenis	prenen	prensen	-
s.2	prenydh	prensys	prenes	prenses	pren
s.3	pren	prenas	prena	prensa	prenes
p.1	prenyn	prensyn	prenen	prensen	prenyn
p.2	prenowgh	prensowgh	prenewgh	prensewgh	prenewgh
p.3	prenons	prensons	prenens	prensens	prenens
0	prenir	prenas	prenys	prensys	-

	Subjunctive		
	Pres./fut.	*Imperfect*	*Verbal noun*
s.1	prenniv	prennen	prena
s.2	prenni	prennes	
s.3	prenno	prenna	*Present participle construction*
p.1	prennyn	prennen	ow prena
p.2	prennowgh	prennewgh	
p.3	prennons	prennens	*Past participle*
0	prenner	prennys	prenys

§186 AFIA 'affirm'.

(1) Verbs with the stem ending in -ia are quite regular. The -i- remains in all parts of the verb.

(2) Paradigm of the verb **afia** 'affirm':

	Indicative				*Imperative*
	Pres./fut.	*Preterite*	*Imperfect*	*Pluperfect*	
s.1	afiav	afiis	afien	afisen	-
s.2	afiydh	afisys	afies	afises	afi
s.3	afi	afias	afia	afisa	afies
p.1	afiyn	afisyn	afien	afisen	afiyn
p.2	afiowgh	afisowgh	afiewgh	afisewgh	afiewgh
p.3	afions	afisons	afiens	afisens	afiens
0	afiir	afias	afiys	afisys	-

	Subjunctive		*Verbal noun*
	Pres./fut.	*Imperfect*	
s.1	afiiv	afien	afia
s.2	afii	afies	
s.3	afio	afia	*Present participle construction*
p.1	afiyn	afien	owth afia
p.2	afiowgh	afiewgh	
p.3	afions	afiens	*Past participle*
0	afier	afiys	afiys

(3) Other verbs with -i- as the last letter of the stem and conjugated as **afia** are as follows:

aspia	'observe'	**gwrias**	'sew'
aswia	'make a gap'	**kenkia**	'contend'
chastia	'chastise'	**kontradia**	'contradict'
dasknias	'chew the cud'	**kovia**	'cherish'
defia	'defy'	**kria**	'cry'
dustunia	'testify'	**knias**	'gnaw'
fia	'flee'	**kywnia**	'grow mossy'
gia	'spear'	**lia**	'take an oath'
golia	'wound'	**provia**	'provide'
gowlia	'swear falsely'	**sakrifia**	'sacrifice'
gryghias	'neigh'	**sevia**	'pick strawberries'
gwari	'play'	**sia**	'buzz'
gwia	'weave'	**ti**	'roof'
gwrias	'sew'	**ynnia**	'urge'

§187(3e) Verbs

Some of these verbs have the verbal noun ending -as. **Gwari** 'play' has no verbal noun ending. **Sevia** 'pick strawberries' is only used as a verbal noun (§234) and **ti** '(make a) roof' is both the verbal noun and the stem although the associated noun is **to** m. 'roof' cf. §210.

§187 **BERRHE** 'shorten'

(1) Verbs ending in **-he** are derived from adjectives and have a conjugation which is regular but slightly different from that of **prena**.

(2) Paradigm of the verb:

	Indicative				*Imperative*
	Pres./fut.	*Preterite*	*Imperfect*	*Pluperfect*	
s.1	berrhav	berrhis	berrhyn	berrhasen	-
s.2	berrhydh	berrhasys	berrhys	berrhases	berrha
s.3	berrha	berrhas	berrhi	berrhasa	berrhes
p.1	berrhyn	berrhasyn	berrhyn	berrhasen	berrhyn
p.2	berrhowgh	berrhasowgh	berrhewgh	berrhasewgh	berrhewgh
p.3	berrhons	berrhasons	berrhens	berrhasens	berrhens
0	berrhir	berrhas	berrhys	berrhasys	-

	Subjunctive		*Verbal noun*
	Pres./fut.	*Imperfect*	berrhe
s.1	berrhahiv	berrhahen	
s.2	berrhahi	berrhahes	
s.3	berrhaho	berrhaha	*Present participle construction*
p.1	berrhahyn	berrhahen	ow perrhe
p.2	berrhahowgh	berrhahewgh	
p.3	berrhahons	berrhahens	*Past participle*
0	berrhaher	berrhahys	berrhes

(3) **Remarks on the form of the verb**

(a) The 3s. pres./fut. ends in **-a** and is not the stem alone as is usual.

(b) Forms of the verbal endings which have an inserted **-s-** (2s. and all p.) have an **-a-** added before the **-s-**.

(c) Subjunctive forms retain the extra syllable **-ah-**.

(d) The past participle always adds **-es** to the stem.

(e) Stress is throughout on the syllable commencing with the first **-h-**: **berr`hav** 'I shorten' (§9(13)).

§188 POENYA 'run with effort'

(1) Verbs with the verbal noun ending in -ya. The -y- is a semi-vowel (§4).

(2) Paradigm of the verb:

	Indicative Pres./fut.	Preterite	Imperfect	Pluperfect	**Imperative**
s.1	poenyav	poenis	poenyen	poensen	-
s.2	poenydh	poensys	poenyes	poenses	poen
s.3	poen	poenyas	poenya	poensa	poenyes
p.1	poenyn	poensyn	poenyen	poensen	poenyn
p.2	poenyowgh	poensowgh	poenyewgh	poensewgh	poenyewgh
p.3	poenyons	poensons	poenyens	poensens	poenyens
0	poenir	poenyas	poenys	poensys	-

	Subjunctive Pres./fut.	Imperfect	**Verbal noun**
s.1	poenniv	poennyen	poenya
s.2	poenni	poennyes	
s.3	poennyo	poennya	**Present participle construction**
p.1	poennyn	poennyen	ow poenya
p.2	poennyowgh	poennyewgh	
p.3	poennyons	poennyens	**Past participle**
0	poennyer	poennys	poenys/poenyes

(3) Remarks on the form of the verb:

The -y- of the verbal noun ending is retained in all parts of the verb except when another -y-, an -i- or an -s- occurs in the ending or when there is no verbal suffix, as in the 3s. pres./fut. and the 2s. imperv.

Note however that when a pronoun which is a vowel stands as object after the 2s.imperv., the -y- is retained and the verb and the pronoun are said as a whole: **redy e!** 'read it!' as though it were **redye!**; **holy i** 'follow them'; as **holyi** (§66(5).

VERBS WITH VOWEL AFFECTION

Vowel changes may take place in the penultimate syllable of the verb forms due to the nature of the vowel in the final syllable (§14, §15).

§189 TAVA 'touch'

(1) Paradigm of the verb:

	Indicative				*Imperative*
	Pres./fut.	*Preterite*	*Imperfect*	*Pluperfect*	
s.1	tavav	tevis	taven	tavsen	-
s.2	tevydh	tevsys	taves	tavses	tav
s.3	tav	tavas	tava	tavsa	taves
p.1	tevyn	tevsyn	taven	tavsen	tevyn
p.2	tevowgh	tevsowgh	tavewgh	tavsewgh	tevewgh
p.3	tavons	tavsons	tavens	tavsens	tavens
0	tevir	tavas	tevys	tevsys	-

	Subjunctive			
	Pres./fut.	*Imperfect*	*Verbal noun*	
s.1	tyffiv	taffen	tava	
s.2	tyffi	taffes		
s.3	taffo	taffa	*Present participle construction*	
p.1	tyffyn	taffen	ow tava	
p.2	tyffowgh	taffewgh		
p.3	taffons	taffens	*Past participle*	
0	taffer	tyffys	tevys	

(2) Verbs of the type **TAVA** with the verbal noun ending -a- which have an -a- as the last vowel of the stem change this to -e-, less often to -y- when the vowel of the verb ending is -i-, -y-, or -owgh (this last by analogy). In the present/future of the subjunctive the vowel is regularly narrowed further to -y- (enhanced affection). The stem vowel also changes before -ewgh- of the 2s. imperative.

(3) The verb **amma** 'kiss' changes the -a- to -y-: **ammav** 'I kiss', **ymmydh** 'you kiss', as does **ranna** 'divide': **rynnys** 'divded'.

(4) These remarks also apply to verbs with verbal nouns in -ya (§188) (and those where three consonants follow -a- in the stem e.g. **tardra** 'drill' > **terdrys** 'drilled' but not where the -a- is the first element of a diphthong e.g. **amaya** 'dismay' > **amayys** 'dismayed'). Many of these are borrowings from English: **kachya** 'catch'; **kampya** 'camp'; **shakya** 'shake'; **talkya** 'talk'. So **shekyowgh** 'you shake'; **kechys** 'caught'; **kempis** 'I camped', etc. The stem vowel remains unchanged if the past participle is formed with the suffix -**yes**: **parkyes** (§244(2)).

(5) The verb **bryjyon** 'boil': stem **bros**- changes -o- into -y- in the same

§189(5)   Verbs

circumstances: Pres./fut. indic. **brojyav, bryjydh, bros, bryjyn, bryjyowgh, brojyons**, etc.

(6) In the verb **pregowtha** 'preach' the alternation is between the diphthongs -ow- in the unaffected forms and -ew- in the affected forms: **pregowthav** 'I preach', **pregewthydh** 'you preach', etc. Past participle **pregewthys** 'preached'.

(7) With -o- changed to -e- in the same circumstances as the vowel change in **tava**: **dannvon** 'send'; **daskorr** 'yield'; Hence **dannvonav** 'I send', **dannvenydh** 'you send'; **daskorrav** 'I yield'; **daskerydh** 'you yield'.

§190 **IGERI** 'open'

(1) Paradigm of the verb:

	Indicative				*Imperative*
	Pres./fut.	*Preterite*	*Imperfect*	*Pluperfect*	
s.1	igorav	igeris	igeryn	igorsen	-
s.2	igerydh	igersys	igerys	igorses	igor
s.3	iger	igoras	igeri	igorsa	igeres
p.1	igeryn	igersyn	igeryn	igorsen	igeryn
p.2	igerowgh	igersowgh	igerewgh	igorsewgh	igerewgh
p.3	igerons	igorsons	igerens	igorsens	igerens
0	igerir	igoras	igerys	igorsys	-

	Subjunctive		
	Pres./fut.	*Imperfect*	*Verbal noun*
s.1	igerriv	igorren	igeri
s.2	igerri	igorres	
s.3	igorro	igorra	*Present participle construction*
p.1	igerryn	igorren	owth igeri
p.2	igerrowgh	igorrewgh	
p.3	igorrons	igorrens	*Past participle*
0	igorrer	igerrys	igerys

(2) Verbs of the type **IGERI** retain the original stem vowel, -a- or -o-, in the following tenses:

Indicative			*Subjunctive*	
Present/future	1s.		Present/future	3s. and 3p.
Preterite	3s. and 3p.		Imperfect	all persons
Pluperfect	all persons		*Imperative*	2s.

§191(1) Verbs

In all other persons the stem vowel is changed to -e-.

(3) Like **IGERI** with the original stem vowel -o- are:

ankevi	(ankov)	'forget'	megi	(mog)	'smoke'
dasseni	(dasson)	'resound'	pedri	(poder)	'rot'
dasserghi	(dassorgh)	'arise'	perthi	(porth)	'bear'
dedhwi	(dodhw-)	'lay eggs'	previ	(prov)	'prove'
goderri	(godorr)	'interrupt'	renki	(ronk)	'snore'
kelli	(koll)	'lose'	seni	(son)	'sound'
kelmi	(kolm)	'knot'	serri	(sorr)	'be/make angry'
keski	(kosk)	'admonish'			
kregi	(krog)	'hang'	telli	(toll)	'make holes'
lenki	(lonk)	'swallow'	terri	(torr)	'break'
leski	(losk)	'burn'	treghi	(trogh)	'cut'

(4) Like **IGERI** but with original stem vowel -a- are:

dalleth	(dallath)	'begin'	minhwerthin	(minhwarth)	'smile'
diberth	(dibarth)	'part'	peski	(pask)	'fatten'
hwerthin	(hwarth)	'laugh'			

(5) Other points with respect to these verbs are: **dedhwi (dodhw-)** 'lay eggs' adds a vowel of accommodation in certain parts of the verb: 1s. pres./fut. **dodhwav**, 3s. pres./fut. **dedhow**, 3s. pret. **dodhwas**, 3p. pret. **dodhwsons** or **dowdhsons**, 3s. pres./fut. subj. **dodhwo**. Cf. §193.

§191 ERGHI 'order'

(1) Paradigm of the verb:

	Indicative				*Imperative*
	Pres./fut.	*Preterite*	*Imperfect*	*Pluperfect*	
s.1	arghav	erghis	erghyn	arghsen	-
s.2	erghydh	erghsys	erghys	arghses	argh
s.3	ergh	erghis	erghi	arghsa	erghes
p.1	erghyn	erghsyn	erghyn	arghsen	erghyn
p.2	erghowgh	erghsowgh	erghewgh	arghsewgh	erghewgh
p.3	erghons	arghsons	erghens	arghsens	erghens
0	erghir	erghis	erghys	erghsys	-

§191(1)   Verbs

	Subjunctive		
	Pres./fut.	*Imperfect*	*Verbal noun*
s.1	ergghiv	argghen	erghi
s.2	ergghi	argghes	
s.3	arggho	arggha	*Present participle construction*
p.1	ergghyn	argghen	owth erghi
p.2	ergghowgh	argghewgh	
p.3	argghons	argghens	*Past participle*
0	erggher	erghhys	erghys

(2) Verbs of the type **ERGHI** undergo vowel affection exactly as does **igeri** (§190) with the addition of the 3s. preterite which, ending in **-is** (§180(4)) also has a vowel change.

These include verbs with verbal nouns ending in **-el**, **-wel** (§193) and a few others which are listed below.

The original stem vowel, **-a-** or **-o**, is retained in certain tenses as follows.

Indicative   *Subjunctive*
Present/future   1s.   Present/future   3s. and 3p.
Preterite   3p. only   Imperfect   all persons
Pluperfect   all persons   *Imperative*   2s.

Conjugated like **ERGHI** are the following verbs:

(3)   Stem vowel **-a-**:

densel	(dans)	'bite'	**lemmel**	(lamm)	'jump'
diank	(diank)	'escape'	**leverel**	(lavar)	'say'
drehevel	(drehav)	'build'	**sevel**	(sav)	'stand'
dynnerghi	(dynnargh)	'welcome'	**terlemmel**	(terlamm)	'frisk'
fyllel	(fall)	'fail'	**tewel**	(taw)	'be quiet'
godhevel	(godhav)	'suffer'	**tyli** and	(tal)	'pay'
gweskel	(gwask)	'strike'	**attyli**	(attal)	'repay'
heveli	(haval)	'seem'		(see §201)	

(4)   Stem vowel **-o-**:

dagrewi	(dagrow)	'shed tears'	**kewsel**	(kows)	'speak'
dedhewi	(dedhow)	'promise'	**kynyewel**	(kynyow)	'dine'
dinewi	(dinow)	'pour'	**mollethi**	(molloth)	'curse'
kentrewi	(kentrow)	'nail'			

§193(1) Verbs

(5) Other changes affecting these verbs are:

dinewi has 3s. pres./fut. **dinwa**;
drehevel has 3s. pres./fut. **drehav, dreha** or **derav**, and 2s. imperv. **drehav** or **dreva**, 3s. pret. **drehevis** or **derevis**;
dybri (deber) 'eat' is described under §194;
godhevel has an alternative verbal noun, **godhav**;
gweskel has 3s. pres./fut. **gwysk** (§192), past participle **gwyskys** and undergoes loss of the **-k-** in some parts of the verb as described in §196;
tyli and **attyli** are treated as irregular verbs (§201).

(6) The small group of verbs with -w- and the verbal noun ending in -el and included in this group is described below (§193).

§192 A few verbs narrow the vowel in the 3s. pres./fut. also.

		3s. pres./fut	stem for rest of conjugation	
eva	'drink'	yv	ev	
galloes	'be able'	gyll	gall/gyll	(§227)
gedya	'guide'	gyd	ged	
gweskel	'strike'	gwysk	gwask/gwesk	(§191)
kavoes	'find'	kyv	kav/kev	(§189)
kelli	'lose'	kyll	koll/kell	(§190)
pobas	'bake'	peb	pob/peb	
tevi	'grow'	tyv	tev	

VERBS WITH AN ADDED VOWEL

Some verbs break up a group of consonants by adding a vowel when necessary.

§193 **GELWEL** 'call'

(1) Paradigm of the verb:

	Indicative *Pres./fut.*	*Preterite*	*Imperfect*	*Pluperfect*
s.1	galwav	gelwis	gelwyn	galwsen *or* gawlsen
s.2	gelwydh	gelwsys	gelwys	galwses *or* gawlses
s.3	gelow	gelwis	gelwi	galwsa *or* gawlsa
p.1	gelwyn	gelwsyn *or* gewlsen	gelwyn	galwsen *or* gawlsen
p.2	gelwowgh	gelwsowgh *or* gelwsowgh	gelwewgh	galwsewgh *or* gawlsewgh
p.3	gelwons	galwsons *or* gawlsons	gelwens	galwsens *or* gawlsens
0	gelwir	gelwis	gelwys	galwsys *or* gawlsys

155

§193(1)   Verbs

	Imperative	Subjunctive		
		Pres./fut.	Imperfect	Verbal noun
s.1	-	gelwiv	galwen	gelwel
s.2	galw	gelwi	galwes	
s.3	gelwes	galwo	galwa	*Present participle construction*
p.1	gelwyn	gelwyn	galwen	ow kelwel
p.2	gelwewgh	gelwowgh	galwewgh	
p.3	gelwens	galwons	galwens	*Past participle*
0	-	galwer	gelwys	gelwys

(2) Verbs of the type **GELWEL** 'call' are conjugated as **erghi** (§191). They have the following characteristics:

(a) The stem ends in **-l, -n,** or **-r** followed by **-w-** to which the verbal ending **-el** is affixed: **gelw-el** 'call'.

(b) The original stem vowel is **-a-**: **galw**.

(c) In the 3s. pres./fut. an **-o-** is put before the **-w-**: **gelow** 'he calls' (§17(4)).

(d) In the 2s. of the imperative no vowel is added and the **-w-** is silent unless a vowel follows in the next word: **Galw!** 'Call!' [gal] but **Galw y vamm!** [galwI vamm] 'Call his mother!'

(e) When the verbal ending starts with an **-s-**, the **-w-** is silent: **gelwsys** [gelsIs] 'you called'.

(f) However in those parts of the verb in which the original stem vowel **-a-** is retained and the verbal ending starts with an **-s-** the **-w-** may be left silent, as stated above, or be transferred to the previous syllable to form a diphthong: **galwsons** [galsons] or **gawlsons** 'they called'.

(3) The verbs in this group are:

gelwel	(galw)	'call'	**merwel**	(marw)	'die'
henwel	(hanw)	'name'	**selwel**	(salw)	'save'
lenwel	(lanw)	'fill'			

(4) For **dedhwi** 'lay eggs', which also adds **-o-** in certain parts of the verb, see §190(5).

§194 HWITHRA 'examine'

(1) Paradigm of the verb:

§194(5) Verbs

	Indicative				Imperative
	Pres./fut.	Preterite	Imperfect	Pluperfect	
s.1	hwithrav	hwithris	hwithren	hwith'sen	-
s.2	hwithrydh	hwith'sys	hwithres	hwith'ses	hwither
s.3	hwither	hwithras	hwithra	hwith'sa	hwithres
p.1	hwithryn	hwith'syn	hwithren	hwith'sen	hwithryn
p.2	hwithrowgh	hwith'sowgh	hwithrewgh	hwith'sewgh	hwithrewgh
p.3	hwithrons	hwith'sons	hwithrens	hwith'sens	hwithrens
0	hwithrir	hwithras	hwithrys	hwith'sys	-

	Subjunctive		Verbal noun
	Pres./fut.	Imperfect	
s.1	hwitthriv	hwitthren	hwithra
s.2	hwitthri	hwitthres	
s.3	hwitthro	hwitthra	**Present participle construction**
p.1	hwitthryn	hwitthren	ow hwithra
p.2	hwitthrowgh	hwitthrewgh	
p.3	hwitthrons	hwitthrens	**Past participle**
0	hwitthrer	hwitthrys	hwithrys

(2) The verb has the following characteristics:

(a) The stem ends in two consonant sounds, the second of which is -l-, -m-, -n-, or -r-.

(b) In the 3s. pres./fut. and the 2s. imperv. a vowel is introduced to aid pronunciation. **Hi a hwither** 'She examines'; **Hwither!** 'Examine!'

(c) The inserted vowel is usually -e-, sometimes -o- or -y-.

(d) When the verbal ending starts with an -s- the final consonant of the stem may drop out and shortening, shown by an apostrophe, take place: **hwith'sa** for **hwithrsa** 'he had examined'.

(3) The verb **delivra** 'deliver' changes -vr- into -rv- in the cases described under (1) above: **delivrav** 'I deliver'; **delirv** 'he/she delivers', **deliver! delirvsyn** 'we delivered'; **delirvsa** 'he/she had delivered, etc.

(4) In the subjunctive tenses it is the consonant before the liquid or nasal -l-, -r-, -m-, -n- which undergoes hardening or doubling (§182): **mettro ev (medra)** 'he may notice'; **lattren ni (ladra)** 'we might steal'.

(5) Verbs like **hwithra**. The form with the inserted vowel is shown in paretheses.

§194(5a) Verbs

(a)　With -e-:

dybri	(deber)	'eat'	meythrin	(meyther)	'nurse'
fagla	(fagel)	'flame'	pedri	(peder)	'rot'
gwedhra	(gwedher)	'wither'	pobla	(pobel)	'populate'
hwedhla	(hwedhel)	'tell tales'	ravna	(raven)	'plunder'
hwyrni	(hwyren)	'buzz'	sotla	(sotel)	'use artifice'
ladra	(lader)	'steal'	sugna	(sugen)	'suck'
lymna	(lymen)	'paint'	trobla	(trobel)	'trouble'
medra	(meder)	'aim, notice'			

(b)　With -o-:

resna	(reson)	'reason'	sokra	(soker)	'help'

(c)　With -y-:

fekla	(fekyl)	'flatter'	takla	(tekyl)	'furnish'

§195 GWYSTLA 'pledge'

(1)　Paradigm of the verb:

	Indicative				*Imperative*
	Pres./fut.	*Preterite*	*Imperfect*	*Pluperfect*	
s.1	gwystlav	gwystlis	gwystlen	gwystelsen	-
s.2	gwystlydh	gwystelsys	gwystles	gwystelses	gwystel
s.3	gwystel	gwystlas	gwystla	gwystelsa	gwystles
p.1	gwystlyn	gwystelsyn	gwystlen	gwystelsen	gwystlyn
p.2	gwystlowgh	gwystelsowgh	gwystlewgh	gwystelsewgh	gwystlewgh
p.3	gwystlons	gwystelsons	gwystlens	gwystelsens	gwystlens
0	gwystlir	gwystlas	gwystlys	gwystelsys	-

	Subjunctive			
	Pres./fut.	*Imperfect*	*Verbal noun*	
s.1	gwystliv	gwystlen	gwystla	
s.2	gwystli	gwystles		
s.3	gwystlo	gwystla	*Present participle construction*	
p.1	gwystlyn	gwystlen	ow kwystla	
p.2	gwystlowgh	gwystlewgh		
p.3	gwystlons	gwystlens	*Past participle*	
0	gwystler	gwystlys	gwystlys	

(2)　This and similar verbs have the following characteristics:

§196(1) Verbs

(a) The final consonant is -l-, -m-, -n- or -r- and this is preceded by two adjacent consonant sounds.

(b) In the 3s. pres./fut. and 2s. imperv. an -e- is put before the final consonant: **gwystel** 'he/she pledges, pledge!'

(c) When the verbal ending starts with an -s-, the same vowel is put before the final consonant of the stem and the verb remains uncontracted, in contrast to the usage described in §194: **gwystelsyn** 'we pledged'.

(d) In this group of verbs modification of the subjunctive ending takes place only with the endings:

-ndl- > -ntl-;   -ldr- > -ltr-;   -rdr- > -rtr-.

(3) Like **gwystla** are the following verbs. The added vowel is -e-.

dampnya	(dampen)	'condemn'	moldra	(molder)	'murder'
entra	(enter)	'enter'	restra	(rester)	'tidy'
gustla	(gustel)	'riot'	sklandra	(sklander)	'slander'
gwandra	(gwander)	'wander'	sompna	(sompen)	'summon'
handla	(handel)	'handle'	tardra	(tarder)	'bore hole'
hwystra	(hwyster)	'whisper'	tempra	(temper)	'tame'
kentra	(kenter)	'nail'	terlentri	(terlenter)	'shine'

VERBS WITH CONSONANT OMITTED

§196 **LESTA** 'prevent'. A verbal stem may end in an -s- followed by another consonant. When the verbal ending starts with an -s- also, this second consonant may be passed over in speech. This is optionally shown in writing by the omission of the consonant and its replacement by an apostrophe.

(1) Paradigm of the verb:

	Indicative				*Imperative*
	Pres./fut.	*Preterite*	*Imperfect*	*Pluperfect*	
s.1	lestav	lestis	lesten	les'sen	-
s.2	lestydh	les'sys	lestes	les'ses	lest
s.3	lest	lestas	lesta	les'sa	lestes
p.1	lestyn	les'syn	lesten	les'sen	lestyn
p.2	lestowgh	les'sowgh	lestewgh	les'sewgh	lestewgh
p.3	lestons	les'sons	lestens	les'sens	lestens
0	lestir	lestas	lestys	les'sys	-

§196(1)   Verbs

| | Subjunctive | |
	Pres./fut.	Imperfect	Verbal noun
s.1	lesttiv	lestten	lesta
s.2	lestti	lesttes	
s.3	lestto	lestta	*Present participle construction*
p.1	lesttyn	lestten	ow lesta
p.2	lesttowgh	lesttewgh	
p.3	lesttons	lesttens	*Past participle*
0	lestter	lesttys	lestys

(2) Verbs which are conjugated like **lesta**:

bostya	'boast'	mostya	'soil'
diwiska	'undress'	ostya	'lodge'
dyski	'learn, teach'	peski	'graze'
gweskel	'strike'	raska	'plane'
gwiska	'dress'	restya	'rest'
kestya	'trick'	rostya	'roast'
koska	'sleep'	tergoska	'doze'
leski	'burn'	trestya	'trust'

IRREGULAR VERBS

Irregular verbs have forms which differ more or less from those given for **prena** in §185. Foremost among these irregular verbs is **bos** 'be' (§197) with its derivative **y'm beus** 'have' (§198).

Other verbs use parts of **bos** to form endings in certain tenses and so may be considered irregular. These are:

darvos	'happen'	§203
dos	'come'	§206
godhvos	'know'	§200
hwarvos	'happen'	§202
klywes	'hear'	§204
mos	'go'	§205
piw	'own'	§199
tyli	'owe'	§201

Besides these there is a group of verbs with anomalous endings in some tenses:

doen	'carry'	§207
dri	'bring'	§209
dyllo	'send out'	§211

§197(1) Verbs

gul	'do, make'	§225
ri	'give'	§208
ti	'swear'	§210

There are a few verbs with other minor irregularities which are mentioned in the appropriate sections below.

The two regular verbs **galloes** (§227) and **mynnes** (§226) are given in full after **gul** because of their association with that verb as auxiliaries.

§197 BOS/BONES 'be'

(1) Paradigm of the verb:

	Indicative				*Imperative*
	Present, short form	*Present, long form*	*Preterite*	*Future*	
s.1	ov	esov	beuv	bydhav	-
s.2	os	esos	beus	bydhydh	bydh
s.3	yw	usi/yma/eus	beu	bydh	bedhes
p.1	on	eson	beun	bydhyn	bedhen
p.2	owgh	esowgh	bewgh	bydhowgh	bedhewgh
p.3	yns	ymons/esons	bons	bydhons	bedhens
0	or	eder	beus	bydher	-

	Indicative			
	Imperfect, short form	*Imperfect, long form*	*Habitual imperfect*	*Pluperfect*
s.1	en	esen	bedhen	bien
s.2	es	eses	bedhes	bies
s.3	o	esa	bedha	bia
p.1	en	esen	bedhen	bien
p.2	ewgh	esewgh	bedhewgh	biewgh
p.3	ens	esens	bedhens	biens
0	os	eses	bedhes	bies

	Subjunctive		
	Pres./fut.	*Imperfect*	***Verbal noun***
s.1	biv	ben	bos *or* bones
s.2	bi	bes	
s.3	bo	be	***Present participle construction***
p.1	byn	ben	ow pos *or* ow pones
p.2	bowgh	bewgh	
p.3	bons	bens	***Past participle***
0	ber	bes	bedhys *but only used in compounds as* -vedhys

§197(2)   Verbs

(2)   Remarks on the form of the verb:

(a)   The verb **bos** differs from the schemes of the regular verb in that it has a true future tense which also serves as an habitual present. In the present and imperfect tenses there is a short and a long form. Additionally there is an habitual imperfect. Of the two forms of the verbal noun, **bos** is the more frequently used and the same remark applies to the present participle construction.

(b)   Present indicative, long form. This is basically the prefixing of the syllable **es-** to the short form. **Yma** and **ymons**, 3s. and 3p. respectively, are forms of unknown origin. **Eus** has a special function as an indefinite 'there is'.

(c)   Imperfect. Similarly the short and long forms of the ordinary imperfect differ in the addition of the syllable **es-** in the latter form. The 3s. of the long form **esa** has **-a** as the second vowel and not **-o** owing to loss of stress.

(d)   The impersonal is not used in all the compounds of **bos**.

(e)   The perfective particle, **re** (§179(2)), is put before the preterite to form a present perfect and optionally before the pluperfect (§228(5)) but the initial **b-** of the verb does not undergo the expected mutation: **re beu** 'have been'; **re bia** 'had been'.

(f)   The 3s. future in **-vydh** is added to the 3s. pres./fut. of some common verbs to form a distinct future: **karvydh (kara)** 'will love'; **gwelvydh (gweles)** 'will see'; **prenvydh (prena)** 'will buy'.

For the use of the various tenses and forms of **bos** see §331 to §333.

§198 **Y'M BEUS** 'have'

(1)   The paradigm of the verb:

	Indicative			
	Present	*Future*	*Preterite*	*Pluperfect*
s.1	y'm beus	y'm bydh	y'm beu	y'm bia
s.2	y'th eus	y'fydh	y'feu	y'fia
s.3m.	y'n jeves	y'n jevydh	y'n jeva	y'n jevia
s.3f.	y's teves	y's tevydh	y's teva	y's tevia
p.1	y'gan beus	y'gan bydh	y'gan beu	y'gan bia
p.2	y'gas beus	y'gas bydh	y'gas beu	y'gas bia
p.3	y's teves	y's tevydh	y's teva	y's tevia

§198(2g)   Verbs

	Indicative		*Subjunctive*	
	Imperfect	*Habitual imperfect*	*Pres./fut.*	*Imperfect*
s.1	y'm bo	y'm bedha	y'm bo	y'm be
s.2	y'th o	y'fedha	y'fo	y'fe
s.3m.	y'n jevo	y'n jevedha	y'n jeffo	y'n jeffa
s.3f.	y's tevo	y's tevedha	y's teffo	y's teffa
p.1	y'gan bo	y'gan bedha	y'gan bo	y'gan be
p.2	y'gas bo	y'gas bedha	y'gas bo	y'gas be
p.3	y's tevo	y's tevedha	y's teffo	y's teffa

(2) Remarks on the forms of the verb:

(a) The 3s. forms of **bos** are used with an infixed pronoun having dative meaning (§65(7a)) to give a compound 'there is to me', etc. The compound is treated as though it were a transitive verb with the meaning 'have'.

(b) The tenses of **bos** so used are: simple present, **eus**; simple imperfect, **o**; future, **bydh**; habitual imperfect, **bedha**; preterite, **beu**, pluperfect, **bia**; present/future subjunctive, **bo**; imperfect subjunctive, **be**. The imperative is not used. There are no impersonal forms. There is no verbal noun and therefore no present participle construction. **Kavoes** 'get' or a similar verb is used to supply the deficiency. In the paradigm of the verb the particle **y** has been chosen to support the infixed pronoun.

(c) 1s. The present and the simple imperfect of the indicative and of the subjunctive have a **b-** prefixed to the verb, perhaps by analogy with the 'b' tenses of the base verb **bos.**

(d) 2s. The infixed pronoun **'th** is only expressed in the present and the simple imperfect. It is omitted in all other tenses but the mutation of **b-** to **f-** is retained (§65(2)).

(e) 1p. and 2p. The present and the simple imperfect of the indicative and of the subjunctive moods also have a prefixed **b-**. Alternative forms of the infixed pronouns are **'an** or **'n** and **'as** or **a's** (§65(3)).

(f) 3s.m. The verb has the prefix **je-**. A **-b-** belonging to the verb becomes **-v-** which is hardened to **-ff-** in the subjunctive.

(g) 3s.f. and 3p. These forms are identical. The verbal prefix is **te-**. A **-b-** commencing the verb becomes **-v-** which is hardened in the subjunctive to **-ff-**.

§198(2h)   Verbs

(h) The origin of these prefixes, **je-** and **te-**, is that they apparently represent original **de-** which became nasalized to **j-** after the masculine pronoun **'n** and **te-** after the feminine pronoun **'s** by unvoicing of the **d-**. See §20(2).

For the uses of **y'm beus** see §250.

§199 PIW 'have, possess, own, win'

(1) The paradigm of the verb:

	Indicative			
	Present	*Future*	*Preterite*	*Pluperfect*
s.1	piwov	piwvydhav	piwev	piwvien
s.2	piwos	piwvydhydh	piwes	piwvies
s.3.	piw	piwvydh	piwva	piwvia
p.1	piwon	piwvydhyn	piwven	piwvien
p.2	piwowgh	piwvydhowgh	piwvewgh	piwviewgh
p.3	piwyns	piwvydhons	piwvons	piwviens
	piwor			

	Indicative		*Subjunctive*	
	Imperfect	*Habitual impferfect*	*Pres./fut.*	*Imperfect*
s.1	piwen	piwvedhen	piwviv	piwven
s.2	piwes	piwvedhes	piwvi	piwves
s.3	piwo	piwvedha	piwvo	piwva
p.1	piwen	piwvedhen	piwvyn	piwven
p.2	piwewgh	piwvedhewgh	piwvowgh	piwvewgh
p.3	piwens	piwvedhens	piwvons	piwvens
	piwer	piwvedhes	piwver	piwves

(2) Remarks on the form of the verb:

(a) Although originally made up of an interrogative pronoun and **yw**, the 3s. present tense of **bos** 'be', a complete verb system has been developed by the addition of other persons and tenses of **bos**. There is no verbal noun and so no present participle construction.

(b) The form **piw** under which the verb is quoted is the 3s. present. The past participle would be **piwvedhys** 'owned'. In the 1s. and 2s. of the preterite the forms in -e- are used, the stress having moved to the first syllable. The 3p. present is also found as the forms **piwons**.

(c) This verb is less used than the several other ways of expressing possession, for which see §249-§256.

§201(1) Verbs
§200 GODHVOS 'know, know how to, understand'

(1) Paradigm of the verb:

	Indicative				
	Pres./fut.	*Preterite*	*Imperfect*	*Pluperfect*	*Future*
s.1	gonn	godhvev	godhyen	godhvien	godhvydhav
s.2	godhes	godhves	godhyes	godhvies	godhvydhydh
s.3	goer	godhva	godhya	godhvia	godhvydh
p.1	godhon	godhven	godhyen	godhvien	godhvydhyn
p.2	godhowgh	godhvewgh	godhyewgh	godhviewgh	godhvydhowgh
p.3	godhons	godhvons	godhyens	godhviens	godhvydhons
0	godhor	godhves	godhyes	godhvies	godhvydher

	Subjunctive		*Imperative*	
	Pres./fut.	*Imperfect*		*Verbal noun*
s.1	godhviv	godhven	-	godhvos
s.2	godhvi	godhves	godhvydh	
s.3	godhvo	godhve	godhvydhes	*Present participle construction*
p.1	godhvyn	godhven	godhvydhyn	ow kodhvos
p.2	godhvowgh	godhvewgh	godhvydhewgh	
p.3	godhvons	godhvens	godhvydhens	*Past participle*
0	godher	godhves	-	godhvedhys

(2) Remarks on the form of the verb:

(a) The habitual imperfect is not used.

(b) Endings are those of **bos** except in the present and the imperfect indicative.

(c) In the tenses of the indicative and the imperative a -**b**- becomes -**v**-. The sequence -**dhv**- tends to become in speech -**vv**- or even -**ff**-.

(d) In the 3s. preterite the reduction of **beu** is found as -**va**.

(e) The 2s. pres./fut. may contract to **gosta** (§64(3)).

For the use of **godhvos** as an auxiliary see §308.

§201 **TYLI** 'pay, owe, be worth'

(1) Paradigm of the verb:

§201(1) Verbs

	Indicative Pres./fut.	Preterite	Imperfect	Pluperfect	Future
s.1	talav	tylis	telen	talvien	talvydhav
s.2	tylydh	tylsys	teles	talvies	talvydhydh
s.3	tal	tylis	tela	talvia	talvydh
p.1	tylyn	tylsyn	telen	talvien	talvydhyn
p.2	tylowgh	tylsowgh	telewgh	talviewgh	talvydhowgh
p.3	talons	talsons	telens	talviens	talvydhons
0	tylir	tylys	teles	talvies	talvydher

	Subjunctive Pres./fut.	Imperfect	Imperative	
				Verbal noun
s.1	tylliv	tallfen	-	tyli
s.2	tylli	tallfes	tal	
s.3	tallo	tallfa	teles	Present participle construction
p.1	tyllyn	tallfen	telen	ow tyli
p.2	tyllowgh	tallfewgh	telewgh	
p.3	tallons	tallfens	telens	Past participle
0	taller	tallfes	-	tylys

(2) Remarks on the forms of the verb:

(a) An alternative verbal noun, **talvos**, with past participle **talvedhys**, sometimes contracted to **talvys**, is used with the meaning 'to value, price' but the conjugated parts of the verb are as those for **tyli**.

(b) Endings from **bos** are found in the future, the pluperfect and the imperfect subjunctive.

(c) **Tyli** undergoes vowel changes in the stem (§191(3)).

(d) **Attyli** 'repay' is conjugated in the same way as **tyli**.

For the use of **tyli** to mean 'duty, obligation'; see §248(5).

§202 **HWARVOS** 'happen, befall'

Hwarvos is found only in the 3s. using those tenses of **bos** which begin with a **b-**.

(1) Paradigm of the verb:

	Indicative Present	Future	Preterite	Pluperfect
s3	hwer	hwyrvydh	hwarva	hwarvia

§204(1) Verbs

	Subjunctive Pres./fut.	Imperfect	Verbal noun	Present participle	Past participle
s3	hwarvo	hwarva	hwarvos	ow hwarvos	hwarvedhys

(2) Remarks on the forms of the verb:

(a) The ending of the preterite is -**va**, see **godhvos** §200.
(b) **Hwarvos** is used either with the preposition **dhe** (§141(6)) or with an infixed pronoun having dative meaning (§65(7c)).
(c) Several alternative forms are made by analogy with the regular verb.

Preterite	Pluperfect	Past participle
hwyris	hwarvsa	hwyrvys

Thus the passage in RD. 1190, **Ev a leveris oll anodho dell hwyris** 'He told us all that occurred regarding him' has this alternative preterite and not, as formerly believed, an otherwise unattested impersonal form of the imperfect indicative.

§203 **DARVOS** 'happen' is a compound of an intensive prefix **dar-** and **bos**. Like **hwarvos** it is restricted to those tenses of **bos** which begin with a **b-** and then only in the preterite and past participle

Preterite	Past participle
darva	darvedhys

§204 **KLYWES** 'hear, feel, sense'

(1) Paradigm of the verb:

	Indicative Pres./fut.	Preterite	Imperfect	Pluperfect	Imperative
s.1	klywav	klywis	klywen	klywsen	-
s.2	klywydh	klywsys	klywes	klywses	klyw
s.3	klyw	klywas	klywo	klywsa	klywes
p.1	klywyn	klywsyn	klywen	klywsen	klywyn
p.2	klywowgh	klywsowgh	klywewgh	klywsewgh	klywewgh
p.3	klywons	klywsons	klywens	klywsens	klywens
0	klywir	klywas	klywes	klywsys	-

§204(1)   Verbs

	Subjunctive		
	Pres./fut.	*Imperfect*	*Verbal noun*
s.1	klywviv	klywven	klywes
s.2	klywvi	klywves	
s.3	klywvo	klywva	*Present participle construction*
p.1	klywvyn	klywven	ow klywes
p.2	klywvowgh	klywvewgh	
p.3	klywvons	klywvens	*Past participle*
0	klywver	klywves	klywys

(2) Remarks on the forms of the verb:

(a) The verbal noun was formerly **klywvos** (**klyw** + **bos**).

(b) The imperfect indicative, the pres./fut. subjunctive and the imperfect subjunctive have endings from **bos** 'be'.

(c) A 3s. future is formed by the addition of **-vydh** (**bydh**) to the stem: **klywvydh** (§197(2f)).

(d) **Omglywes** 'perceive onself to be' is similarly conjugated.

§205 MOS/MONES 'go'

(1) Paradigm of the verb:

	Indicative				
	Pres./fut.	*Preterite*	*Imperfect*	*Perfect*	*Pluperfect*
s.1	av	yth	en	galsov	gylsen
s.2	edh	ythys	es	galsos	gylses
s.3	a	eth	e	gallas	galsa
p.1	en	ethen	en	galson	gylsen
p.2	ewgh	ethewgh	ewgh	galsowgh	gylsewgh
p.3	ons	ethons	ens	galsons	gylsens
0	er	es	es/os	-	-

	Subjunctive		*Imperative*	
	Pres./fut.	*Imperfect*		*Verbal noun*
s.1	ylliv	ellen	-	mos *or* mones
s.2	ylli	elles	ke *or* a	
s.3	ello	ella	es	*Present participle construction*
p.1	yllyn	ellen	deun	ow mos *or* ow mones
p.2	yllowgh	ellewgh	kewgh *or* ewgh	
p.3	ellons	ellens	ens	*Past participle*
0	eller	elles		gyllys

§205(2h) Verbs

(2) Remarks on the forms of the verb:

(a) There are distinct forms for the present, perfect and the pluperfect. It has been suggested (LP. §460d, CEMN. p.207) that these are from a stem **gal/gyl** with the present and imperfect tenses of **bos** suffixed to the stem, either the short form giving **gal(s)ov**, the -s- representing the usual preterite -s- etc. or the long form giving **gal(e)sov**, etc.

The meaning is literally 'I am/was gone, etc. Hence these forms are not accompanied by verbal particles, express only positive statements and can be placed anywhere in the sentence e.g. **Gallas dhe Loundres** 'He has gone to London'. They particularly indicate a change of condition, 'becoming': **Gallas klav** 'He has fallen ill', lit. 'gone ill'; **Gallas y wober ganso** 'He has got what he deserves', lit. 'His reward has gone with him'.

(b) The same stem as that mentioned in (a) provides the past participle, **gyllys** 'gone' with the addition of the regular past participle ending **-ys** in place of **-vedhys** (§197(1)) which might have been expected from what has been said above.

(c) A present perfect is also formed in the usual way with the addition of the verbal particle **res** (§279(2)) to the preterite when actual movement is meant: **Ev res eth dhe Bennsans** 'He has gone to Penzance'.

(d) In the imperative another root supplies **ke/kewgh**. The singular **a** is found in the texts with plural use (MC. 99.6, RD. 2464, BM. 2022) The 2s. **deun** is borrowed from the verb **dos** 'come' (§206).

(e) The subjunctive in **-ll-** is from another root.

(f) Contractions with suffixed pronouns are as follows: 1s.pres./fut. **a'ma** (**av ma**) 'I go', 1s. preterite **yth'a** (**yth ma**) 'I went', 2s. pres./fut. **e'ta** (**edh ta**) 'you go' (§64(3)).

(g) Of the two forms of the verbal noun, **mos** and **mones,** **mos** is the more commonly used but the mutated form **vones** is usefully distinguished from **vos** (**bos**).

(h) The expression **mos ha bos** 'go and be' is equivalent to the English 'become': **Yth ethen ha bos aga howetha** 'We became their friends'. Only the first verb is conjugated. See §206(2g) for a similar usage with **dos** 'come'.

§206 DOS 'come'

(1) Paradigm of the verb:

	Indicative Pres./fut.	Preterite	Imperfect	Perfect	Pluperfect
s.1	dov	deuth	den	deuvev	dothyen
s.2	deudh	deuthys	des	deuves	dothyes
s.3	deu	deuth	do	deuva	dothya
p.1	deun	deuthen	den	deuven	dothyen
p.2	dewgh	deuthewgh	dewgh	deuvewgh	dothyewgh
p.3	dons	deuthons	dens	deuvons	dothyens
0	deer	deuthes	des	deuves	dothyes

	Subjunctive Pres./fut.	Imperfect	**Imperative**	
s.1	dyffiv	deffen	-	**Verbal noun**
s.2	dyffi	deffes	deus	dos *or* dones
s.3	deffo	deffa	des	
p.1	dyffyn	deffen	deun	**Present participle construction**
p.2	dyffowgh	deffewgh	dewgh	ow tos *or* ow tones
p.3	deffons	deffens	dens	**Past participle**
0	deffer	deffes		devedhys

(2) Remarks on the forms of the verb:

(a) The special present perfect tense is made up of a stem, **deu**, to which is attached the preterite of **bos** in its mutated and lightened form, **vev** for **veuv**, **ves** for **veus**, **va** for **veu**, etc.

This tense is used both in the affirmative and the interrogative without verbal particles: **Lemmyn deuva ken termyn** 'Now another time has come' **Deuvons?** 'Have they come?' The perfective particle **re** (§279) can be used but is not necessary for the perfect sense: **Ni re dheuva** or **Deuven** 'We have come'.

(b) In the negative all the particles are used: **Ny dheuvons** 'They have not come'; **Prag na dheuva an lyther?** 'Why has the letter not come?' **Skrif hanow keniver na dheuva** 'Write the name of any who have not come.

(c) The pluperfect ending is in -**ye**-.

(d) The form of the verbal noun most used is **dos**, hence the commonest present participle construction is **ow tos**.

§207(2c) Verbs

(e) The past participle employs the form derived from **bos** (§197(1)) added to the stem, thus **devedhys** (de + bedhys).

(f) Contractions with the suffixed pronouns are: 2s. pres./fut. **deu'ta** (**deudh + ta**), 2s. pret. **deuth'ta** (**deuthys + ta**), (§64(3)).

(g) The phrase **dos ha ...** followed by a verbal noun has the meaning 'happen to ...'; **mar teu ev ha gul yndella** 'if he happens to to so'. Cf. §205(2h)

§207 **DOEN** 'carry'

(1) Paradigm of the verb:

	Indicative				*Imperative*
	Pres./fut.	*Preterite*	*Imperfect*	*Pluperfect*	
s.1	degav	dug	degyn	degsen	-
s.2	degedh	duges	degys	degses	dog
s.3	deg	dug	degi	degsa	deges
p.1	degon	dugon	degyn	degsen	degyn
p.2	degowgh	dugowgh	degewgh	degsewgh	degewgh
p.3	degons	dugons	degens	degsens	degens
0	degir	dug	degys	degsys	-

	Subjunctive	
	Pres./fut.	*Imperfect*
s.1	dykkiv	dekken
s.2	dykki	dekkes
s.3	dokko	dekka
p.1	dykkyn	dekken
p.2	dykkowgh	dekkewgh
p.3	dokkons	dekkens
0	dokker	dekkys

Verbal noun
doen *or* degi

Present participle construction
ow toen *or* ow tegi

Past participle
degys

(2) Remarks on the forms of the verb:

(a) The 1s. and the 3s. preterite resemble the corresponding forms of the verb **gul** 'do, make' (§225) in ending in **-g** and in having no personal endings (LP. §460d).

(b) A derived verbal noun **degi** is formed from the past participle **degys**.

(c) The reflexive prefix **om-** with verb **doen** gives **omdhoen** which being stressed on the first syllable `omdhoen gives 'bear a child' and on the second syllable **om`dhoen** 'behave' §9(12), (§232). The conjugation in each case is as for **doen**.

171

§208 RI 'give'

(1) Paradigm of the verb:

	Indicative Pres./fut.	Preterite	Imperfect	Pluperfect	**Imperative**
s.1	rov	res	ren	rosen	-
s.2	redh	resys	res	roses	ro *or* roy
s.3	re	ros	ri	rosa	res
p.1	ren	resen	ren	rosen	ren
p.2	rowgh	resowgh	rewgh	rosewgh	rewgh
p.3	rons	rosons	rens	rosens	rens
0	rer	ros	res	rosys	-

	Subjunctive Pres./fut.	Imperfect	
s.1	rylliv	rollen	**Verbal noun**
s.2	rylli	rolles	ri
s.3	rollo	rolla	**Present participle construction**
p.1	ryllyn	rollen	ow ri
p.2	ryllowgh	rollewgh	
p.3	rollons	rollens	**Past participle**
0	roller	rollys	res

(2) Remarks on the forms of the verb:

(a) In the imperative the form **ro** is used before a consonant. **Ro dhymm dha dhorn!** 'Give me your hand!' The form **roy** is used before vowels: **Roy y dhymm!** 'Give it to me!' **Roy** is also used as an optative, equivalent to **Re rollo!** 'May he give!': **Roy lowena dhis!** 'May he grant you happiness!' which could be equally **Re rollo lowena dhis!** Note the noun **ro** m. 'gift', p. **rohow**.

(b) The subjunctive forms in -ll- are comparable with similar forms in **mos** (§205). See also LP. §453(d).

§209 DRI 'bring'

(1) Paradigm of the verb:

§210(1)   Verbs

	Indicative				*Imperative*
	Pres./fut.	Preterite	Imperfect	Pluperfect	
s.1	drov	dres	dren	drosen	-
s.2	dredh	dresys	dres	droses	dro/doro/doroy
s.3	dre	dros	dri	drosa	dres
p.1	dren	dresen	dren	drosen	dren
p.2	drowgh	dresowgh	drewgh	drosewgh	drewgh
p.3	drons	drosons	drens	drosens	drens
0	drer	dros	dres	drosys	-

	Subjunctive		*Verbal noun*
	Pres./fut.	Imperfect	
s.1	drylliv	drollen	dri
s.2	drylli	drolles	
s.3	drollo	drolla	***Present participle construction***
p.1	dryllyn	drollen	ow tri
p.2	dryllowgh	drollewgh	
p.3	drollons	drollens	***Past participle***
0	droller	drollys	dres

(2) Remarks on the forms of the verb:

(a) This verb is made up of the prefix **d(o)** and **ri** (§208) hence the personal endings are virtually the same.

(b) In the 3s. pres./fut. **dre** is used. Other forms found, **doro** and **dro**, are influenced by the 2s. imperative.

(c) The usage in the 2s. imperative is similar to that found with **ri** in that **doro** is used before consonants and **doroy** before vowels, this latter form also being used as an optative: **Doro dhe'n chi an pyth yw gwrys seulabrys!** 'Bring to the house that which is already done!' **Doroy an boes!** 'Bring the food!' **Doroy dha wrians sewena!** 'May your action bring success!'

§210 TI 'swear'

(1) Paradigm of the verb:

	Indicative				*Imperative*
	Pres./fut.	Preterite	Imperfect	Pluperfect	
s.1	tov	tes	ten	tosen	-
s.2	tedh	tesys	tes	toses	to
s.3	te	tos	te	tosa	tes
p.1	ten	tesen	ten	tosen	ten
p.2	towgh	tesowgh	tewgh	tosewgh	tewgh
p.3	tons	tosons	tens	tosens	tens
0	ter	tos	tes	tosys	-

§210(1)   Verbs

	Subjunctive Pres./fut.	Imperfect
s.1	tylliv	tollen
s.2	tylli	tolles
s.3	tollo	tolla
p.1	tyllyn	tollen
p.2	tyllowgh	tollewgh
p.3	tollons	tollens
0	toller	tollys

Verbal noun
ti

Present participle construction
ow ti

Past participle
tes

(2) Remarks on the forms of the verb:

(a) Endings are as for **ri** above (§208).

(b) It may be noted that there is coincidence of form between certain parts of **ti** and certain parts of **tyli** 'pay' (§201), e.g. the 1s., 1p., 2s. and 2p. present subjunctive.

(c) The verb **ti** 'roof' is regular in its conjugation: **tiav** 'I roof', **tiydh** 'you roof', **tias** 'he/she roofed' etc. (§186(3)).

§211 **DYLLO** 'send out, issue, publish'

(1) Paradigm of the verb:

	Indicative Pres./fut.	Preterite	Imperfect	Pluperfect	**Imperative**
s.1	dyllav	delles	dyllyn	dyllsen	-
s.2	dyllydh	dellesys	dyllys	dyllses	dyllo
s.3	dyllo	dellos	dylli	dyllsa	dylles
p.1	dyllyn	dellesyn	dyllyn	dyllsen	dyllyn
p.2	dyllowgh	dellesowgh	dyllewgh	dyllsewgh	dyllewgh
p.3	dyllons	dellesons	dyllens	dyllsens	dyllens
0	dyllir	dellos	dyllys	dyllsys	-

	Subjunctive Pres./fut.	Imperfect
s.1	dylliv	dellen
s.2	dylli	delles
s.3	dello	della
p.1	dyllyn	dellen
p.2	dyllowgh	dellewgh
p.3	dellons	dellens
0	dyller	dellys

Verbal noun
dyllo

Present participle construction
ow tyllo

Past participle
dyllys

§212 Minor irregularities are found in the 3s. pres./fut. of a few common verbs, otherwise regular.

dinewi	'pour'	**dinwa** (§191(4))
diskwedhes	'show'	**diskwa** *for* **diskwedh**
drehevel	'build'	**drehav/dreha/derev** (§191(3))
gortos	'await'	**gorta**
hwilas	'look for, try'	**hwila**

DEFECTIVE VERBS

Defective verbs are those which are restricted to a few tenses or persons. **Hwarvos** and **darvos** have been described in §202 and §203 respectively.

§213 **BERN** 'it concerns, it matters' is found only in the 3s. pres./fut. Cf. **bern** m. 'care, concern': **heb bern** 'without minding'. For constructions with **bern** see §246(1).

§214 **DARWAR!** 'be forewarned!, be careful!' is used in the imperative only: **Darwar na vi toellys!** 'Be careful that you be not deceived!' The plural is **darwaryewgh!** See also **war** §224.

§215 **DEGOEDH/KOEDH** 'be due, suitable, fitting', lit. 'it falls', is the stem of the verb **koedha** 'fall' with 3s. endings from **bos**.

	Indicative				*Imperative*
	Pres./fut.	*Preterite*	*Imperfect*	*Pluperfect*	
s.3	degoedh *or* koedh	degoedhva *or* koedhva	degoedho *or* koedho	degoedhvia *or* koedhvia	*not found*

	Subjunctive	
	Pres./fut.	*Imperfect*
s.3	degoedhvo *or* koedhvo	degoedhva *or* koedhva

For constructions see §248(1).

§216 **DELLEDH** 'it behoves, it is proper' is the 3s. pres./fut., the only form. For constructions see §248(2))

§217 **DEUR** 'it matters, concerns, is of real interest'. The 3s. pres./fut. is the only form in use. For constructions see §246(3).

§218 **HWELES** 'turn' is only found in compounds: **dehweles** 'return, come back, repent'; **omhweles** 'fall over, overthrow'; **domhwel** (**de** + **om** + **hweles**) 'upset, ruin, overthrow'.

§219 **MEDHES** 'say, speak' is the verbal noun. The inflected forms are those of the present tense and these are preceded by the word **yn** which has no significance for the meaning. Thus:

    1s. **yn-medhav (vy)**   3s. **yn-medh (ev/hi)**   3p. **yn-medhons (i)**

A suffixed pronoun or noun suject follows. These forms are used without change in past narration to mean 'I said', 'he/she said', 'they said'. For construction and examples see §336(5a).

The stem is used in compounds: **konvedhes** 'understand'.

§220 **PARGH/PARAGH** 'endure, put up with, hold out, last' has only this, the verbal noun, which is constructed with an auxiliary verb, **mynnes** or **galloes**: **Na fella ny vynnav paragh henna** 'No longer will I put up with that'; **Mar kyll'ta paragh bys yn a-vorow** 'If you can hold out until tomorrow'.

§221 **RES** 'it is necessary' is the 3s. pres./fut. and the only part of the verb found. **Henna a res** 'That is necessary'. More frequently **res** is treated as an adjective with a part of **bos** and **dhe** (§141(5)). For constructions with **res** in both usages see §247.

§222 **SKILA** 'causes' is usually a noun with the meaning 'cause' but is used as verb in the 3s. pres./fut. only: **Natur (a) skila oll y (= arloedh da) sojetys dhe vos grevys** 'Nature causes all his (a good lord's) subjects to be grieved'; **Henna a skila an dowr dhe vryjyon** 'That causes the water to boil'. Cf. **gul dhe** §141(7).

§223 **TANN! TANNEWGH!** 'take! hold!' 2s. and 2p. only of the imperative: **Tann, syns e!** 'Take, hold it!' **Tannewgh te kyns mos!** 'Take tea before going!'

§224 **WAR!** 'take care!' is employed only in this, the 2s. and 2p. of the imperative: **War y'n gwryllowgh yn ta!** 'Take care that you do it well!' The 2p. is **waryewgh!** See also **darwar** §214.

§225(2d)   Verbs

THE AUXILIARY VERBS

The verbs **gul** 'do, make', (§225, §305), **mynnes** 'wish, be willing' (§226, §306) and **galloes** 'be able' (§227, §307) are used with verbal nouns as auxiliary verbs. Less often used in this way is **godhvos** 'know how to' (§200, §308).

§225 **GUL** 'do, make' ('shall, did' as auxiliary verb)

(1) Paradigm of the verb:

	Indicative				*Imperative*
	Pres./fut.	*Preterite*	*Imperfect*	*Pluperfect*	
s.1	gwrav	gwrug	gwren	gwrussen	-
s.2	gwredh	gwrussys	gwres	gwrusses	gwra
s.3	gwra	gwrug	gwre	gwrussa	gwres
p.1	gwren	gwrussyn	gwren	gwrussen	gwren
p.2	gwrewgh	gwrussowgh	gwrewgh	gwrussewgh	gwrewgh
p.3	gwrons	gwrussons	gwrens	gwrussens	gwrens
0	gwrer	gwrug	gwres	gwrussys	-

	Subjunctive		
	Pres./fut.	*Imperfect*	*Verbal noun*
s.1	gwrylliv	gwrellen	gul/gwruthyl/gruthyl/guthyl
s.2	gwrylli	gwrelles	
s.3	gwrello	gwrella	*Present participle construction*
p.1	gwryllyn	gwrellen	ow kul, ow kwruthyl, ow kruthyl, ow kuthyl
p.2	gwryllowgh	gwrellewgh	
p.3	gwrellons	gwrellens	*Past participle*
0	gwreller	gwrellys	gwrys

(2) Remarks on the forms of the verb:

(a) Of the several forms of the verbal noun **gul** is the most commonly used. The same applies to the present participle construction.

(b) The 1s. and 3s. preterite in -g with no personal ending are comparable with the corresponding forms of **doen** 'carry' (§207).

(c) Forms in the subjunctive with -ll- are analogous to the similar forms of **mos** 'go' (§205) and **ri** 'give' (§208).

(d) Contractions with the suffixed pronouns are: 1s. pres./fut. **gwra'ma** (**gwrav** + **ma**), 1s. pret. **gwrug'a** (**gwrug** + **ma**), 2s. pres./fut. **gwre'ta** (**gwredh**

§225(2d) Verbs

+ **ta**) 2s. pret. **gwruss'ta** (**gwrussys** + **ta**) and with the same contracted form, 2s. plup. **gwruss'ta** (**gwrusses** + **ta**) (§64(3)).

(e) **Omwul** 'make onself out to be' is similarly conjugated.

For the use of **gul** as an auxiliary see §304.

§226 **MYNNES** 'be willing'

(1) Paradigm of the verb:

	Indicative				*Imperative*
	Pres./fut.	*Preterite*	*Imperfect*	*Pluperfect*	
s.1	mynnav	mynnis	mynnen	mynnsen	*not used* -
s.2	mynnydh	mynnsys	mynnes	mynnses	
s.3	mynn	mynnas	mynna	mynnsa	
p.1	mynnyn	mynnsyn	mynnen	mynnsen	
p.2	mynnowgh	mynnsowgh	mynnewgh	mynnsewgh	
p.3	mynnons	mynnsons	mynnens	mynnsens	
0	mynnir	mynnas	mynnys	mynnsys	-

	Subjunctive		
	Pres./fut.	*Imperfect*	*Verbal noun*
s.1	mynniv	mynnen	mynnes
s.2	mynni	mynnes	
s.3	mynno	mynna	*Present participle construction*
p.1	mynnyn	mynnen	*not used*
p.2	mynnowgh	mynnewgh	
p.3	mynnons	mynnens	*Past participle*
0	mynner	mynnys	*not used*

(2) Remarks on the forms of the verb:

(a) **Mynnes** is regular in its conjugation except that the imperative, the present participle construction and the past participle are not used.

(b) Contractions with suffixed pronouns are confined to the 2s. pres./fut. **mynn'ta** (**mynnydh** + **ta**), 2s. pret. **mynns'ta** (**mynnsys** + **ta**) and 2s. plup. **mynns'ta** (**mynnses** + **ta**) with similar form (§64(3)).

For the use of **mynnes** as an auxiliary see §306.

§227 **GALLOES** 'be able'

(1) Paradigm of the verb:

§228(1)   Verbs

	Indicative				*Imperative*
	Pres./fut.	*Preterite*	*Imperfect*	*Pluperfect*	
s.1	gallav	gyllis	gyllyn	gallsen	*not used*
s.2	gyllydh	gyllsys	gyllys	gallses	
s.3	gyll	gallas	gylli	gallsa	
p.1	gyllyn	gyllsyn	gyllyn	gallsen	
p.2	gyllowgh	gyllsowgh	gyllewgh	gallsewgh	
p.3	gyllons	gallsons	gyllens	gallsens	
0	gyllir	gallas	gyllys	gallses/gallser	-

	Subjunctive		
	Pres./fut.	*Imperfect*	*Verbal noun*
s.1	gylliv	gallen	galloes
s.2	gylli	galles	
s.3	gallo	galla	*Present participle construction*
p.1	gyllyn	gallen	*not used*
p.2	gyllowgh	gallewgh	
p.3	gallons	gallens	*Past participle*
0	galler	galles	*not used*

(2) Remarks on the forms of the verb:

(a) **Galloes** is regular in its conjugation except that the imperative, the present participle construction and the past participle are not used.

(b) The imperfect indicative has the **-y-/-i-** form (§180(5)).

(c) The pluperfect in its conditional use (§228(6)) has a distinct impersonal form **gallser**.

(d) The 2s. contracts as follows: pres./fut. **gyll'ta** (**gyllydh** + **ta**); pret. **gylls'ta** (**gyllsys** + **ta**); plup. **gall'sta** (**gallses** + **ta**) (§64(3)).

THE USES OF THE TENSES

§228 **The indicative mood** states facts or enquires about them without implying any opinion or judgement on the part of the speaker.

(1) **Present/future** This tense indicates unrestricted, indefinite time and duration in the present or the future: **y prenav** 'I buy/shall buy'.

An habitual action: **Y skrif ev pub Sadorn** 'He writes every Saturday'.

A continuing state: **Ny wodhons an yeth** 'They don't know the language'.

§228(1)
A simple future: **My a dhe Garesk a-vorow** 'I go to Exeter tomorrow'.

The use of this tense does not imply that the action is taking place at the time of speaking. It may or may not be so. By contrast the present participle construction can only be translated by the English continuing present: **Yth esov vy owth oberi** 'I am working' (§243(3)).

A narrative present tense may be used of events in past time to give a sense of immediacy or urgency: **My a elwis war an keth hemma, prest y teu dhymm hag y'm dynnergh** 'I called to the same (man), straight away he comes and greets me'.

(2) **Preterite** This tense denotes that which is done and complete at some past time and is the normal tense of narrative when successive events are desribed: **Ev a venegas aga bos skwith hag yth ethons dhe bowes** 'He mentioned that they were tired and they went to rest'; **Ny glywsyn an pyth a leveris kyn harmas** 'We didn't hear what he said although he shouted'.

(3) **Present perfect** This is a tense which is formed by prefixing the perfect particle **re** (§279) to the tenses of the preterite. It indicates action completed from the point of view of present time: **Ev re gewsis** 'He has spoken'; **An rewler re'gas gwelas** 'The manager has seen you'; **Lies daras re igorsons** 'Many doors they have opened'; **Re re dhiskryssys** 'You have been too unbelieving'; **Ple res eth ev?** 'Where has he gone?' **Nyns eus denvydh omma, dell re welsowgh** 'There is no one here, as you have seen'.

There is no negative or direct interrogative in this tense.

The verbs **mos** (§205) and **dos** (§206) have an independent perfect tense.

(4) **Imperfect** This tense denotes a state or an action of undefined duration, habitual, repeated or continuous action in the past.

Habitual state: **Ny wodhyens piw a'n lad'sa** 'They didn't know who has stolen it'; **Boghosek ens pup-prys** 'They were always poor'.

Habitual action: **Hi a esedha war an gador na orth an tan** 'She used to sit on that chair at the fire'; **An ydhyn a nija yn troyow ughel a-ugh an garrek** 'The birds would fly in circles high above the rock'.

Repeated action: **Y gi a entra dhe'n skiber hag a hartha bys pan dewlis vy gwelenn ragdho** 'His dog kept coming into the barn and barking until I threw a

§229 Verbs

stick for him'.

Continuous or near continuous state or action: **De my a'm bo drokpenn** 'Yesterday I had a headache'; **Jori a lanhi an karr our ha hanter** 'George was cleaning the car for an hour and a half'.

Originally an optative expressing a wish, the imperfect often keeps this element of meaning (Cf. WG. p.315): **An lowarther a leski an del marow war dansys** 'The gardener would burn the dead leaves on a bonfire'. If used with inanimate subjects it thus personalises them: **An gwyns a dhigempenna hy gols** 'The wind would untidy her hair' (as though it meant to).

Action which is future to some action or state in the past, the 'future in the past': **An traytour a gewsis ... dhe'n tressa dydh y sevi** 'The traitor said ... (that) on the third day he would rise'; **pan welas na ylli gweres an den ow peudhi** 'when he saw that he would not be able to help the drowning man'; **Ni a wodhya y tifunen kyns an bora** 'We knew (that) we would wake up before the dawn'. It is the habitual imperfect tense of **bos** which is used in this way: **An benynes re ambossa y fedhens ena a dermyn** 'The women had promised (that) they would be there on time' (§333(1b)).

(5) **Pluperfect** This tense denotes a state or an action already finished or completed from the point of view of some time in the past: **Kettell dhothya dh'y ugensves bloedh, y hasas y dre** 'As soon as he had come to his twentieth year, he left his home'; **Ny gowldhrehavsens an chi erbynn an jydh ambosys** 'They had not completely built the house by the date agreed'.

With this sense only the perfective particle **re** may optionally be put before the verb: **Ev re dhianksa kyns hanternos** 'He had escaped before midnight'. The conditions for the use of **re** with the pluperfect are the same as those which limit its use with the preterite, see above (3) and §279.

(6) **Conditional** This is not a separate tense but a specialised use of the pluperfect. Arising from the idea of a completed action is a secondary one which regards the action as though it were as good as completed, provided that some condition be fulfilled. Hence the meaning to be attributed to this tense in the main clause of a conditional construction, equivalent to the English 'would': **A kalla, y tempersa an gwyns** 'If he were able to, he would tame the wind'; **Mara'th fe an huni gwynn, da via homma genev** 'If you had the white one, that would be fine with me'. For conditional clauses, see §344.

§229 **The subjunctive mood** introduces into the statement a judgement or

§229 Verbs

opinion as to the truth, probability or possibility of the action taking place.

(1) The present/future is used after **re** (§279) to express a wish or a hope, an optative use. As such it forms an independent sentence, a principal clause, the only occurrence of the subjunctive in an independent sentence. The negative is **bynner re** 'never may': **Lowen re bi!** 'May you be happy!' **Re'th serffyo!** 'May it be of use to you!' **Re sewennowgh orth y wul!** 'May you succeed in doing it!' **Lowender re'gas bo!** 'May you have happiness!' **Bynner re hwarvo!** 'May it never happen!' **Bynner re fallons a'ga forpos!** 'May they not fail in their purpose!' In common greetings the syllable **dur** is a contraction of **Dyw roy** or **Dyw re** (§208(2a), §352(8)): **durnostadhis** (**Dyw roy nos dha dhis**) 'May God grant you a good night!' **Dursoenno!** (**Dyw re soenno**) 'May God bless!'

(2) Relative sentences with an indefinite subject or object use the subjunctive to express that indefiniteness (§340(8)(9)): **awos travydh a hwarvo** 'in spite of anything which may happen'; **poll mayth effo den** 'a pool from which a (some) man may (perhaps) drink'; **Go-ev na'n gwrella** 'A pity for he (= anyone) who might not have done it'.

(3) Clauses which stand as the objects of verbs the meanings of which imply the use of the will in some degree, use a tense of the subjunctive to convey the idea that the speaker is aware that the action may or may not be in fact carried out. The conjunctions are **may(th)** in the affirmative and **na(g)** in the negative.

Examples of such verbs follow:

(a) Wishing, wanting (**mynnes, mynnes orth**): **My a vynn may fo dyllys an towlennow** 'I wish (that) the programmes may be issued'; **An dyskador a vynnas orth an studhyoryon na dreylyens an kows** 'The teacher wanted the students not to translate the speech'.

(b) Desiring (**hwans a'n jeves, yeuni**, etc.): **Hwans a'gan beus ma'n rylli dhedha** 'We want you to give it to them'; **Meur y yeuni Margh may tehwella tre** 'Mark yearned greatly that he might return home'.

(c) Hoping (**gwaytya**): **An rann vrassa ahanan a wayt may fo an gewer syggha y'n seythun a dheu** 'Most of us hope that the weather may be drier next week'.

(d) Asking (**pysi**): **Y'th pysav na enttri** 'I ask you not to enter'.

§229(5) Verbs

(e) Ordering (**gorhemmynn, erghi, kommondya**, usually with **dhe** and the person), telling someone to (**leverel dhe**): **A's gorhemmynnes mayth hokkyons** 'Let him order them to delay!' **Gans henna an gwithyas a erghis dhyn mayth hetthen toeth da** 'With that the policemen ordered us to stop straight away'; **pan lavarav dhodho na dheffo** 'when I tell him that he should not come'.

(f) Forbidding, preventing (**difenn, lettya, gwitha**): **oll an re na orth y dhifenn na saffo** 'all of them forbidding him to stand'; **Gwithewgh na yffowgh re!** 'Take care that you do not drink too much!'

(g) Advising (**kusulya**): **Na drest neb a'th kusul may kammwrylli!** 'Don't trust anyone who advises you to do wrong!'

(h) Causing, bringing about (**gul dhe, grontya, ordena, dyghtya**): **mar kwredh dhe'n eseli may pessyons ow klappya pella** 'if you get the members to carry on talking longer'; **Gront dhedhi mayth ello yn kosoleth** 'Grant her that she may go in peace!' **Piw re ordenas ma's gwellewgh?** 'Who arranged that you might see them?' **mar tyghtyav may trollo an lyvrow yn y garr** 'if I arrange that he should bring the books in his car'.

(i) Taking care, ensuring (**gwaytya**, etc.): **kyn hwaytyn may fo prennys an daras** 'though we take care that the door be locked'; **Gwaytyn na fistennyn re!** 'Let's make sure that we don't hurry too much!'

This use of **may** and the subjunctive overlaps its use to express purpose. See §349.

(4) The occurrence of the subjunctive also introduces the idea of uncertainty or contingency into dependent questions after interrogative adverbs: **Ny ylli dismygi p'eur y'n gwella** 'He could not find out when he might see him' as contrasted with **Ny ylli dismygi p'eur y'n gweli** (imperf.indic.) 'He could not find out when he would see him', the first construction implying that it was possible in the judgement of the speaker that the meeting might not take place. See §322, §327.

(5) As described in the last paragraph, for most expressions in which a subjunctive is used there is a choice of an alternative construction if no judgement is implied as to the probability or possibility of the action: **Argh dhodho may fo furra nessa!** 'Tell him that he should be more careful next time!' as against **Argh dhodho bos furra nessa!** 'Tell him to be more careful next time!'

§229(6) Verbs

(6) Adverbial clauses in which an element of uncertainty or indefiniteness is implied similarly use the subjunctive. Such clauses are:

Causal clauses (§346)
Comparative clauses (§348)
Concessive clauses (§345)

Conditional clauses (§344)
Final clauses (§349)
Temporal clauses (§347)

§230 **The uses of the imperative** The imperative mood expresses direct command: **Sav!** 'Stand!' pl. **Sevewgh!** Cornish distinguishes between address to a single person and address to a group (§71(1)). For the pronoun subject or object see §66. As stated in §183(1) there is no 1s. form and the imperative of **gasa** 'allow' is used in a circumlocution: **Gas vy dhe entra!** 'Let me come in!' **Gesewgh vy dhe vos efanna** 'Let me be more explicit!' The 1p., 3s. and 3p. are translated by a similar English phrase, 'Let ...!': **Hwithryn!** 'Let's look!' **Redyes hi yn ughel!** 'Let her read out loud!' **Lowenhens i!** 'Let them rejoice!'

The negative particle is **na(g)** (§276(1)): **Na boen!** 'Don't run!' **Na vedhen diek!** 'Let's not be lazy!'

§231 **The impersonal** The tenses of the indicative and the subjunctive moods have an impersonal form (denoted by 0 in the paradigms of the verbs). It indicates that the action of the verb occurs without specifying any subject. It is active in meaning, hence used freely in intransitive verbs, though it is often translated by the English passive or by 'one': **Y hwrer tros** 'There is a noise being made', lit. 'There is a making a noise'; **Y kerdhir** 'One walks, there is walking'; **Gwayt na skonnyer!** 'Mind there be no refusing!' The involvement of an agent can be shown by the use of **gans** (§147(6)): **Y redir ganso** 'There is a reading (done) by him'; **rag may ewnir gansa** 'so that there may be a correction done by them'.

The above remarks apply to those verbs which govern two direct objects (§305(7)): **An Tas a'n nev y'm gelwir** 'The Father of heaven I am called', lit. 'There is a calling me Father of heaven'; **Y'n ordenir Bardh Meur a Gernow** 'He is appointed Grand Bard of Cornwall', lit. 'There is an appointing him ...'. The preposition **gans** can be added as above to indicate an agent: **Mester genowgh y'm gelwir** 'I am called master by you', lit. 'There is a calling me master by you', PD.873.

§232 **Reflexive and reciprocal verbs** The prefix **om-** gives a verb a reflexive sense, turning the idea of the action back to the subject (§273).

Examples:

§232   Verbs

Gul 'make', **omwul**; make oneself (out to be), pretend (to be)': **Ny omwra lywyer da** 'He doesn't pretend to be a good driver'.
Klywes 'sense', **omglywes** 'sense oneself to be, feel': **Yth omglywav yagh** 'I feel well'.
Kregi 'hang', **omgregi** 'hang oneself'.
Previ 'prove', **ombrevi** 'prove oneself'.
In some cases the prefix **om-** gives a reciprocal meaning to the verb.
Examples:

kuntell 'gather', **omguntell** 'gather with others, meet'.
kusulya 'advise', **omgusulya** 'consult with one another'.
sywya 'follow', **omsywya** 'follow one another, result'.
tewlel 'throw', **omdewlel** 'wrestle (with one another)'.

With either of the above senses a change of stress and a consequent loss of the verbal noun ending may accompany change of meaning.

Examples:

dadhla 'argue', **`omdhal** 'quarrel'.
doen 'bear', **`omdhoen** 'bear a child', **om`dhoen** 'bear, carry oneself, behave'.
gweres 'help', **`omweres** 'take care of oneself, manage'; **om`weres** 'help one another'.
ladha 'kill', **om`ladha** 'kill oneself'; **`omladh** 'kill one another, fight'.
perthi (stem **porth**) 'support', **`omborth** 'balance' (stem of the verb **omberthi**, or noun).

The verb **govynn** 'ask' normally governs through **orth** (§152(4)), this preposition translating the English 'of': **Ev a wovynnas orth y wreg** 'He asked (of) his wife'. The verb can however be made reflexive by the addition of the prefix **om-** to give the meaning 'ask oneself, wonder': **Yn fenowgh yth omwovynnav mars yw gwir** 'I often wonder (= ask myself) if it is true'.
Further examples of reflexive, reciprocal verbs are as follows:

Reflexive

ombareusi	(pareusi)	'prepare oneself'
ombrederi	(prederi)	'think to oneself, ponder'
omdenna	(tenna)	'withdraw, retreat'
omdhiskwedhes	(diskwedhes)	'show oneself'
omgudha	(kudha)	'hide oneself'
omri	(ri)	'give oneself up, surrender'
omwiska	(gwiska)	'dress oneself'

185

§232
Reciprocal

omgana	(kana)	'sing to one another, in concert or harmony'
omgnoukya	(knoukya)	'hit one another'

THE VERBAL NOUN - FORM

§233 The form of the verbal noun The verbal noun is in most cases formed from a stem by the addition of a suffix. These suffixes are as follows, listed approximately in order of frequency. Section references give information about conjugation, etc.

(1) **-A**: **kromma** 'bend'; **mora** 'go to sea'; **sygha** 'dry out' (§185). Verbs with **-i-** as the last letter of the stem are to be included here: **aswia** 'make a gap' (§186). Some of these verbs are formed directly from nouns by the addition of the verbal suffix: **lytherenna (lytherenn** 'letter of the alphabet') 'spell'; **perghenna (perghenn** 'owner') 'own'; **prenna (prenn** 'log') 'bar a door by putting a log of wood across it'.

(2) **-YA**: **mellya** 'interfere'; **plegya** 'bend' (§188). This is the form used for almost all borrowings and neologisms: **fyttya** 'make ready'; **konkludya** 'finish an argument'; **kampya** 'camp'.

(3) **-I**: **dyski** 'learn, teach'; **tryghi** 'conquer'; **kentrewi** 'fasten with nails'; **dagrewi** 'shed tears'. These last two are from the plurals of **kentrow** 'nails' and **dagrow** 'tears' respectively (§180(5a)). This ending is added to adjectives in **-k** to form a verb, the **-k** becoming **-g**: **mosegi (mosek)** 'stink'; **muskegi (muskok)** 'rave'; **plosegi (plos)** 'get dirty'.

(4) **-IA/-IAS**: **golia** 'wound'; **knias** 'gnaw'. The **-i-** is a part of the stem and acts as a syllable in all parts of the verb (§186).

(5) **-HE**: verbs with this ending are formed from adjectives. The stress in all parts of the verb is on the syllable commencing with **-he**: **duhe (du)** 'blacken'; **ledanhe (ledan)** 'widen' §180(5a), §187).

(6) **-EL**: **drehevel** 'raise'; **sevel** 'stand' (§191); **gelwel** 'call'; **henwel** 'name' (§193, 180(4a)(5a)).

(7) **-ES**: **kemmeres** 'take'; **konvedhes** 'understand'; **mires** 'look'; **mynnes** 'wish' (§180(5a), §226).

§232(13)   Verbs

(8)   -AS: **hwilas** 'seek, try'; **palas** 'dig'; **pedrevanas** 'creep on all fours'. Some verbs with -i- as the last element of the stem are included here: **gwrias** 'sew' (§186).

Of the twelve hundred or so verbs recorded in current dictionaries the forms in -a and -ya account for about two thirds in equal proportions. Those ending in -i number about two hundred. The forms in -**he**, -**el**, -**es** and -**as** have a few dozen examples each. Other, less common, verbal endings are as follows.

(9)   -OES: **galloes** 'be able' (§227); **kavoes** 'get'.

(10)   -OS: **desevos** 'suppose'; **gortos** 'await', **lavasos** 'venture'.

(11)   -YLLI implies a repeated action: **kryghylli** 'jolt, rattle'.

(12)   Certain verbs have verbal noun endings peculiar to themselves. The stem is given in parentheses.

-ETH: **marghogeth** 'ride' (**marghog-**).
-YON: **bryjyon** 'boil' (**bryj-**). See §189(5).
-IN: **hwerthin** 'laugh' (**hwerth-**), **minhwerthin** 'smile'; **meythrin** 'rear'. See §190(4).
-EK: **resek** 'run' (**res**). Note however that in BM. 2263 the verbal noun is used as the stem: **Y woes a resek dhe'n leur** 'His blood shall run to the ground'. The derivative **daromres** 'frequent' has lost the verbal noun ending.
-O: **dyllo** 'issue' (**dyll-**). See §211.

(13)   Some verbal stems serve as verbal nouns without any addition:

arvedh	'affront'	**gormel**	'praise'
arveth	'hire'	**gromyal**	'growl'
astell	'discontinue'	**gwari**	'play'
aswonn	'know'	**gweres**	'help'
daffar	'provide'	**hepkorr**	'renounce'
dalleth	'begin'	**hembronk(ya)**	'lead'
dannvon	'send'	**hunros(a)**	'dream'
daskorr	'give back'	**kanmel**	'praise highly'
dendil	'earn'	**kemmynn(a)**	'bequeath'
dervynn	'demand'	**kuntell**	'gather'
dewis	'choose'	**kynnik**	'offer'
diank	'escape'	**meythrin**	'rear'
diberth	'part'	**omdhal**	'quarrel'

§232(13) Verbs

difenn	'forbid'	**omguntell**	'gather together'
difres	'relieve'	**omwen**	'wriggle'
dolos	'pretend'	**pe**	'pay'
dyerbynn(a)	'meet'	**powes**	'rest'
godhav	'endure'	**pregowth**	'preach' (§189(6))
(also **godhevel**)		**sommys**	'flit'
godros	'menace'	**tynkyal**	'tinkle'
gorhemmynn	'order'	**yes**	'confess'

A few of the above verbs have an alternative with an affixed verbal noun ending as shown.

(14) The verb **gonis** v.n. 'work' has the stem **gonedh-** in all parts, 1s.p./f. **gonedhav**, 2s.p./f. **gonedhydh**, 3s.imperf. **gonedhi** (§180(5b)), 3s.pret. **gonedhas**, etc. except the 3s.pres./fut. and the 2s.imperv. which are both **gonis** 'he/she/it works', 'work!' So also **kammwonis** 'blunder'.

(15) A few verbal nouns are not obviously similar to the associated finite verb: **mones/mos** 'go' (§205); **gul** 'do, make' (§225); **doen** 'carry' (§207).

§234 There is a class of verbal nouns, used only as such, with no associated finite verb, derived from names of natural beings or substances and with the meanings of hunting, gathering, seeking, etc. They can be conjugated using an auxiliary verb: **Ev a wre pyskessa pub dydh** 'He would go fishing every day'.

(1)   With final **-a**:

benyna	(**benyn** 'woman')	'consort with women'
krampoetha	(**krampoeth** 'pancakes')	'beg for pancakes'
mela	(**mel** 'honey')	'collect honey'
mesa	(**mes** 'acorns')	'gather acorns'
meskla	(**meskel** 'mussels')	'look for mussels'
sevia	(**sevi** 'strawberries')	'gather strawberries'
ydhna	(**ydhyn** 'birds')	'go fowling'

(2)   With doubling of the final consonant of the plural or collective noun and the addition of **–a**:

devessa	(**deves** 'sheep')	'round up sheep'
gwibessa	(**gwibes** 'gnats')	'chase gnats', ('waste time')
hwilessa	(**hwiles** 'beetles')	'look for beetles'
keunyssa	(**keunys** 'firewood')	'gather firewood'

§235(6) Verbs

kevelekka	(kevelek 'woodcock')	'hunt woodcock'
koninessa	(konines 'rabbits')	'hunt rabbits'
kregynna	(kregyn 'shells')	'look for shells'
legessa	(logos 'mice')	'hunt mice'
melhwessa	(melhwes 'snails')	'look for snails'
pryvessa	(pryves 'vermin')	'hunt vermin'
pyskessa	(puskes 'fish')	'go fishing'

THE VERBAL NOUN - SYNTAX

§235 General

(1) The verbal noun names the action and no more. Ideas of time, connection with a subject or an object, the active or the passive aspect of the action, can only be supplied by the context: **Ev a wra gorfenna an oberenn** 'He will finish the job' (active); **An oberenn a dal hy gorfenna** 'The job should be completed', lit. 'The job owes its being completed' (passive).

(2) The verbal noun may take a definite article: **Pandra yw an fyski ha'n terlemmel?** 'What's the hurry and the frisking about?' BM. 2099.

(3) The verbal noun is masculine in gender with no plural form: **An dadhla o hir ha nyns o ev plegadow dhymm** 'The discussion was long and I did not like it'.

(4) The verbal noun can be accompanied by an adjective which may be translated adverbially: **kerdhes skav** 'nimble walking, walking nimbly'; **klappya medhow** 'drunken talk(ing), talking drunkenly'; **koska hweg** 'sweet sleep(ing)' or 'sleeping sweetly'.

(5) Certain adjectives precede the verbal noun and are joined to it as a compound, softening the initial consonant of the verbal noun: (§61(1g), §83(4c)): **kammwul** (**kamm** + **gul**) 'wrongdo'; **hirleverel** 'speak at length'; **brasleverel** 'talk big, boast'; **kollenki** (**kowal** + **lenki**) 'swallow completely' (§268).

The adjective in these cases is treated as an integral part of the stem **Hi a debeldhyghtya an ki** 'She ill-treated the dog' (**tebel** + **dyghtya**).

(6) The verbal noun may be governed by a preposition: **dre weres** 'by helping'; **rag leverel** 'in order to say'; **heb hedhi** 'without stopping'.

§236 **The verbal noun as subject of a sentence** A verbal noun can stand as the subject of a sentence: **Neuvya a vydh pup-prys gwell es beudhi** 'Floating is always better than sinking'; **Nyns eus triga ganso na fella** 'There is no living with him any longer'; **Ny bleg gensi goelya** 'She doesn't like sailing', lit. 'Sailing doesn't please her'.

§237 Common nouns and adjectives are thus used in idioms with a verbal noun as subject. The verb is a tense of **bos** 'be'.

(1) With **dhe** 'to' (§141(5)).

BYSI 'important': **Bysi vydh dhe fleghes gwari** 'Playing is important for children'.
GWELL 'better': **Gwell yw dhymm powes** 'Resting is better for me' = 'It is better for me to rest'.
RES 'necessary': **Res o dhe'n marner mos** 'The sailor had to go'. Cf. §221, §247.

(2) With **gans** 'with'. See §147(5) for a full list of the adjectives and nouns used. Examples: **Da yw ganso delinya** 'He likes to draw', lit. 'Drawing is good with him'; **Poes o gans an kaderyer dewis** 'The chairman was reluctant to vote'; **Marth o gans pub huni godhvos henna** 'Everyone was surprised to know that'.

§238 **The verbal noun as the direct object of a finite verb**

(1) With auxiliary verbs. The verbs **gul** 'make, do' (§225), **mynnes** 'be willing'(§226), **galloes** 'be able' (§227) and, to a lesser extent, **godhvos** 'know how to, be able' (§200) are frequently used with a verbal noun to make a compound verbal construction.

Because they contribute to the total meaning, these verbs are called auxiliaries in this connection. See also §304: **Pan wrussyn govynn orti, ny vynnas hi gorthybi** 'When we asked her, she was not willing to answer'; **Keniver a allo igeri an gyst na a yll kavoes an pyth usi ynni** 'Anyone who can open this box can have what is inside it'; **Gwynn aga bys myns a woer omweres** 'Lucky for them who know how to help themselves'.

(2) With other verbs. **Ny gar an kog sawra an boes** 'The cook does not like tasting the food'; **Gas klappya dha flows** 'Give over chattering your nonsense!' **Kyn porthav bos neghys, nyns yw honna da genev** 'Though I put up with being denied, I am not content with it'.

(3) The verbal phrase **y'm beus** (§198, §250) may have a verbal noun as its effective object to express capability, probability, especially in the negative: **Hi a's teves kewsel da** 'She can speak well'; **Mar ny'th eus koska, red!** 'If you can't sleep, read!' Since the verbal noun is in these cases the grammatical subject of the verb **eus** 'there is', etc., these sentences are literally 'She, there is good speaking to her' and 'If there is no sleeping to you'.

§239 The verbal noun as the complement of BOS 'be'

(1) The complement of **bos** 'be' is often a verbal noun, sometimes with its associated object: **Aga soedh a vedha gwitha an morrep** 'Their task used to be guarding the seaboard'; **A nyns yw agan lowender aga degemmeres yn hegar?** 'Isn't it our happiness to receive them hospitably?' It will be noted that the English translation is either the gerund in '-ing', as in the first example, or the infinitive with the preposition 'to', as in the second example. Cf. §141(18).

(2) Preceded by the preposition **dhe** 'to' the verbal noun may render an English passive: **An gegin yw dhe gempenna** 'The kitchen is to be cleaned'; **Nyns yns i dhe weres** 'They are not to be helped'; **Yth o an kig dhe dhybri** 'The meat was to be eaten'; **Henn yw dhe leverel** 'That is to say (be said)' (§141(17)).

§240 The subject and object of the verbal noun

(1) Verbal nouns associated with transitive verbs. The subject in these cases is represented by a noun or by an independent pronoun connected to the verbal noun by the preposition **dhe** 'to', the 'infinitive' construction (§141(19)), whilst the object is represented by a noun in the possessive construction (§55) after the verbal noun or by a possessive adjective (§51) before it: **An tiek dhe brena deves a bris isel o towl mas** 'The farmer's buying sheep at a low price was a good plan', lit. 'the farmer to buy sheep'; **Ni a wodhya an re na dhe gemmynna oll aga arghans dhe'n eglos** 'We knew that those (people) bequeathed all their money to the church', lit. 'those (people) to bequeath'; **A allav vy dha weres war neb kor?** 'Can I help you in some way?' lit. 'Can I your helping ...?'

(2) Verbal nouns associated with intransitive verbs. The subject is usually expressed by the construction with **dhe** mentioned in (1) above: **an vowes dhe resek pell** 'the girl's running far'; **hi dhe resek** 'her running'; **honna dhe resek** 'that (female's) running'. So with **bos** 'be': **hy thas dhe vos klav** 'her father's being ill'; **ev dhe vos klav** 'his being ill'; **henna dhe vos klav** 'that (man's) being ill'.

§240(2) Verbs

Alternatively the subject of a verbal noun associated with an intransitive verb may be represented by a noun in the possessive construction or by a possessive adjective. Cf. (1): **resek an vowes** 'the girl's running'; **hy resek** 'her running'.

(3) When the subject or object of the verbal action in any of these expressions is a noun, it can be emphasised by being put earlier in the sentence. Its place is then taken by the corresponding pronoun or possessive adjective: **My a woer an tiek dhe brena leughi** 'I know (that) the farmer buys/bought calves', etc., becoming **An tiek, my a woer ev dhe brena leughi** '(As to) the farmer, I know (that) he ...'. Similarly **wosa prena leughi** 'after buying calves' becomes **leughi wosa aga frena** '(as to) calves after buying them'.

All the phrases described in §240 are then used as units in larger constructions. See Sentences, §334-§337.

(4) Abstract nouns, as distinct from verbal nouns proper, when associated with transitive verbs, are used with a following noun in the possessive construction or with a possessive adjective and this may represent either the subject or the object (§56(1)(2)): **kerensa gwreg** 'a wife's love' or 'love of a wife'. The ambiguity can be removed either by the context or by the use of a preposition to denote the object of the action: **rag dha gerensa** 'for love of you', MC. 139.5; **y gerensa orti** 'his love towards her' (§152(8)); **gwrians den** 'a person's creation/the creation of a person' but **gwrians gans den** 'creation by a person'; **liwyans flogh** 'a child's picture', **liwyans a flogh** 'a picture of a child' (§57), **liwyans gans flogh** 'a picture by a child' (§147(6)).

(5) **Dyski** v.n. has, like the Welsh and Breton cognates *dysgu*, *deskiñ*, the dual meanings of 'learn' and 'teach': **dyski Kernewek** 'learning Cornish/teaching Cornish'. When there is a need to distinguish, constructions with prepositions can be used: **dyski Kernewek gans Mtr Thomas** 'learning Cornish with (= from) Mr Thomas' (§147(7)); **dyski Kernewek dhe fleghes** 'teaching Cornish to children'.

§241 **The verbal noun used in place of a finite verb** Statements linked by a co-ordinating conjunction and having the same grammatical subject may have a finite verb in the first statement and verbal nouns in subsequent statements: **Ev a esedhas ha kemmeres an lyther ha'y lenna** 'He sat down and took the letter and read it aloud'; **Ny'n klywis na'y weles** 'I neither heard nor saw it'; **Derives dhyn ha leverel ple fynn ev mos!** 'Let him report to us and say where he will go!' **Pren e ha'y witha!** 'Buy it and look after it!' **Ev a gerdhi dh'y soedhva po lywya y garr** 'He would walk to his office or drive his car'. If however each separate act is to be emphasised or if there is a change of tense to be indicated

§243(2) Verbs

or if the subject changes, then each verb is inflected and is preceded by the appropriate verbal particle: **Y teuth tre hag yth omwiskas yn y dhillas gwella hag yth eth yn-mes arta** 'He came home and he dressed himself in his best clothes and he went out again'; **Ni a woslow orth an radyo po a red** 'We listen to the radio or we read'; **Kevyn esedhva ha dybryn agan kroust!** 'Let's find a place to sit and let's eat our picnic!' **Ty re ros dhodho an jekkenn hag y'fydh an akwityans** 'You have given him the money and will get the receipt'; **An fleghes a omladhas ha ny's kessydhyas hi** 'The children fought together and she did not punish them'.

§242 The negative of the verbal noun can be expressed in various ways, most directly by using the preposition **heb** 'without': **heb koska** 'without sleeping'; **Hedh ena heb mos na fella!** 'Stop there without going any further!' (§148(4)). Alternatively, and less directly, a circumlocution can be used, a finite verb after the verbal particle **na** 'not' (§276): **An medhyk a woer na goskav meur** 'The doctor knows (that) I don't sleep much', being equivalent more or less to **An medhyk a woer ow bos heb koska meur**; or by certain verbs followed by **rag** and the verbal noun: **My a'th lest rag mos** 'I shall stop you (from) going'; **Ny woer ev omwitha rag trebuchya** 'He doesn't know how to stop himself from falling' (§154(4)).

THE PRESENT PARTICIPLE CONSTRUCTION

§243 **The form of the present participle construction** The verbal noun is used in several constructions which are equivalent to the English present participle in '-ing'.

(1) With the preposition **orth** 'at' (§152(10)) which in this usage takes one of a number of forms: **ow** before a consonant with hardening in certain cases (§25); **owth** before a vowel or h- and **orth** before a possessive adjective denoting the direct object of the verbal action (§240(1)): **ow leverel** 'saying', lit. 'at the act of saying'; **ow tybri (dybri)** 'eating'; **owth eva** 'drinking'; **owth hanasa** 'sighing'; **orth agan gweles** 'seeing us', lit. 'at our seeing'.

(2) This construction is adjectival, in an attributive or a predicative use:

Attributive **An skrifer a dhegeas an lyver ow leverel, 'Gorfennys!'** 'The writer closed the book, saying, "Finished!"'; **An bagas a dheuth orth den owth hembronk ki** 'The group met a man leading a dog'; **Yn fenowgh i a viri an howl ow sedhi** 'They would often observe the setting sun'; **'An Howl Ow Sevel'** 'The Rising Sun' as the name of a public-house.

§243(2) Verbs

Predicative As a predicate, the complement of **bos** 'be', the present participle construction is accompanied by the long form of the tense if the tense is the present or the simple imperfect (§332(3c)): **Mir! Yma tus ow tos** 'Look! There are people coming'; **Dowr a vydh ow sygera der an to** 'Water will be seeping through the roof'; **Genen yth esens ow klappya** 'With us they were talking'; **Ow broder re beu ow vyajya tramor** 'My brother has been travelling overseas'; **Ow tadhla i re bia** 'Holding a discussion they had been'.

(3) The present participle denotes contemporary action: **Y'n varghas ma y pren ow gwreg hy losow** 'In this market my wife buys her vegetables' (but is not necessarily doing so now as I speak); **Y'n varghas ma yma ow gwreg ow prena hy losow** 'In this market my wife is buying her vegetables' (now, as I speak). This construction therefore easily translates the English 'continuous' tenses. See also clauses of attendant circumstances (§351).

(4) If the object of the verbal action is a noun it regularly follows the verbal noun in the present participle construction but if it is placed earlier in the sentence for emphasis, a referring possessive adjective accompanies the verbal noun: **an mebyl pan esen ni orth aga harga y'n kert** '(as to) the furniture when we were loading it in the cart'.

(5) The phrase **yn unn** 'in a' precedes a verbal noun which undergoes mutation by softening and with it forms an adverbial expression to be translated by English adverbs in '-ly', 'at a', 'in a', and so on: **A-hys an kay y kerdhas yn unn sygera** 'He walked along the quay sluggishly'; **Yn unn hwerthin y kewsens a-dro dhodho** 'They would speak about him laughingly'; **Prest y hworthybis yn unn guhudha** 'Immediately he answered accusingly'; **Ev a dheuth yn unn boenya** 'He came at a run'; **Dybri ni a wrug yn unn fyski** 'We ate in a hurry' (§167(9)).

(6) The preposition **yn-dann** 'under' (§168(3)) followed by a verbal noun denotes action going on at the same time as another action. It can be translated by the English 'all the time', 'at the same time', etc.: **Ev a glappya yn-dann dhybri** 'He would chatter, eating all the time'; **Esedhyn ni a-ragdho yn-dann dewel kettell vo du an gan!** 'Let us sit in front of him, at the same time remaining quiet until the song be finished!' **Toellores o hi yn-dann omwul lelgowethes** 'She was a deceiver while making herself out (to be) a true friend'.

THE PAST PARTICIPLE

§244 The form of the past participle

(1) The past participle is usually formed by the addition of the syllable -ys to the verbal stem (§79(8)): **kemmerys (kemmer-es)** 'taken'; **gweresys (gweres)** 'helped'. A stem vowel -a- changes by vowel affection to -e-, less often to -y- (§14): **gesys (gas-a)** 'left'; **kerys (kar-a)** 'loved'; **henwys (henw-el)** 'named'; **rynnys (rann-a)** 'divided'; **ymmys (amm-a)** 'kissed'.

(2) Verbs with verbal nouns ending in -ya (§188) have the past participle in -yes or -ys: **redyes**, or **redys**, this last form being preferred in modern Cornish. It should be noted that vowel affection takes place only in the second version of the participle: **skwardyes (skwardya)** 'torn' but **skwerdys**; **gwastyes (gwastya)** 'laid waste' but **gwestys**; **parkyes (parkya)** 'parked' (of a car) with **perkys**.

(3) Verbs with verbal nouns ending in -he (§187) add -s to make the past participle: **berrhes (berrhe)** 'shortened'; **duhes (duhe)** 'blackened'.

(4) Irregular are the following:

***bedhys (bos)** 'been' which is found only in its mutated form in compounds such as **godhvedhys (godhvos)** 'known'; **devedhys (dos)** 'come'.

degys	(doen §207)	'brought'	**gyllys**	(mos §205)	'gone'
dres	(dri §209)	'brought'	**res**	(ri §208)	'given'
gwrys	(gul §225)	'done, made'			

Note also **deges (degea)** 'closed'; **kes (ke)** 'hedged'; **marow** 'dead' which serves as a past participle to **merwel** 'die'; **parys** 'prepared' from which the verb **para** seems to have been formed as though **parys** were its past participle; **pareusi** 'prepare food, cook' has the participle **pareusys** 'prepared'; **pes (pe)** 'paid, requited' and so **pes da** 'requited well, pleased'; **drog pes** 'ill-pleased'. **Igor** is the simple adjective 'open' and **igerys** the past participle means 'opened'.

§245 The syntax of the past participle

(1) A past participle is an adjective denoting a state or condition resulting from completed action. It has a passive sense when derived from a transitive verb and an active sense when derived from an intransitive verb.

§245(1a)   Verbs

(a)   From transitive verbs: **breusys (breusi)** 'judged'; **gweskys (gweskel)** 'struck'; **kelmys (kelmi)** 'tied'; **koselhes (koselhe)** 'subdued'; **skoellys (skoellya)** 'wasted, scattered'; **synsys (synsi)** 'seized'.

(b)   From intransitive verbs: **fiys (fia)** 'having fled'; **gwiskys (gwiska)** 'having put on clothes, dressed'; **gyllys (mos)** 'gone'; **hwarvedhys (hwarvos)** 'occurred, having happened'; **koedhys (koedha)** 'fallen'; **neuvys (neuvya)** 'afloat'.

(2)   The past participle may accompany its noun directly as attributive adjective, following the rules for mutation: **margh temprys** 'a broken-in horse'; **mamm gerys** 'a beloved mother'; **an daras deges** 'the closed door'; **an fenester dheges** 'the closed window'; **mowesi klav** 'sick girls'; **mebyon glav** 'sick boys'.

(3)   On the other hand, the past participle may be the complement of a tense of **bos** 'be' and therefore predicative.

(a)   With the imperfect tense the participle denotes a continuing state and is descriptive: **Shyndys en** 'I was hurt', i.e. that was the condition I was in. **I o gyllys** 'They were gone away, absent'; **An bara o treghys** 'The bread was cut' (a state).

(b)   Used with the preterite tense, which presents the action at the moment it happens, the past participle provides a true passive construction: **An bara a veu treghys hware** 'The bread was cut straight away' (an action took place). The agent of the action is signified by **gans** 'with' with a noun or a pronoun (§147(6)): **An wydhenn a veu plensys gans an vyghternes** 'The tree was planted by the queen'; **Gans an bellenn y feuv shyndys** 'By the ball I was injured'. Other prepositional relationships are retained: **My a gampoellas dhodho an nowodhow** 'I mentioned the news to him' becomes in the passive **Dhodho y feu kampoellys an nowodhow genev** 'The news was mentioned to him by me'.

(4)   Used with tenses of **bos** other than the imperfect or the preterite, the past participle may be either a descriptive adjective or help form a passive tense as above. The particular meaning of the verb and the context will determine which sense is to be taken.

(a)   **Descriptive** **Serrys ywa orthis** 'He is angry at you'; **Kuntellys i re bia lies mis** 'They had been gathered together (for) many months'; **Kows rag may fo kryjyans dhis!** 'Speak so that you may be believed!' **Ass yw hi aswonnys** y'n dre! 'How well-known she is in the town!'

(b) **Predicative Gwelys vydhav gans an medhyk a-vorow** 'I shall be seen by the doctor tomorrow'; **Hy jynn-radyo re bia ledrys** 'Her radio had been stolen'; **A-dhistowgh ev a wodhva y fia toellys** 'Straight away he knew that he had been deceived'.

(5) The comparative and superlative forms of past participles are made by using **moy** 'more' and **(an) moyha** '(the) most' as adverbs: **Henn o moy berrhes es hemma** 'That (one) was more abbreviated than this (one)'; **Piw yw an moyha kerys?** 'Who is the most loved?' **Le** 'less' and **(an) lyha** '(the) least' are similarly used: **le usys** 'less used'; **an lyha usys** 'the least used'.

(6) Like other adjectives past participles can be used with the adverb forming particle **yn** (§92): **yn koedhys** 'in a fallen state'; **yn pusornys** (**pusornas** v.n. 'bundle together') 'in a bundled-up condition'; **yn tuhes** 'in a blackened state'; **yn hwiys** (**gwia** v.n. 'weave') 'in a tangled state'.

(7) The English direct object with a past participle in agreement is rendered in Cornish by the verbal noun with either a dependent noun or a possessive adjective. Such expressions occur after verbs of seeing, hearing, etc.: **Ny welas hi gul priweyth** 'She has not seen pottery made', lit. 'the making of pottery'; **Ple klywsys jy gelwel Yowann ow howeth?** 'Where did you hear John called my friend?' lit. 'the calling John my friend'; **My a glywas kana kan** 'I heard a song sung', lit. 'the singing of a song'.

IMPORTANCE, NECESSITY, DUTY

§246 **Importance** That something is or is not of importance is expressed in the following ways.

(1) **BERN** vb. (§213) has a subject but no indirect object: **Henna a vern meur** 'That matters a lot'. In the negative: **Travydh ny vern** 'It doesn't matter at all'; **Ny vern leverel dhis** 'There's no harm in telling you'. As an exclamation, **Ny vern!** 'It doesn't matter!'

(2) **BYSI** adj. 'busy' is used in sentences with the special meaning of 'important'. The thing or action which is important is expressed by a noun or by a verbal noun or by a noun phrase. The person to whom the action is important is introduced by the preposition **dhe** 'to': **Bysi vydh dhedhi mos dhe'n dre a-vorow** 'It is important that she goes to town tomorrow'; **Bysi yw dhymm**

§246(2) Verbs

hwithra an mater dour 'It is important that I examine the matter carefully'. It may be noted that English uses a 'dummy' subject, 'it', in these and similar expressions but that this does not appear in the Cornish.

(3) **DEUR** vb. 'it concerns, is of interest' (§217). An infixed pronoun represents the indirect object 'to me', etc. (§65(7b)). The object of the concern follows the preposition **a** 'of' (§126(8)): **Klyw! mara'th teur** 'Hear! if it interests you'; **Ev a lever y'n deur a henna** 'He says that that interests him'; **Anodho travydh ny'm deur** 'I am not interested in it at all'; **A weles an chi ny'gan deur mann** 'We don't mind the house being seen'.

(4) **FORS** m. 'power, force' is used with the negative of several verbs to indicate that something is of little importance or interest. With **gul** 'do, make': **Fors ny wra ev a gerdhes** 'He doesn't care for walking'. With **ri** 'give': **A dhybri a-ves fors ny rov** 'I don't go much on eating outside'. As exclamations: **Na fors!** and **Nyns eus fors!** 'Never mind!' 'It doesn't matter!' In conjunction with the word **res** 'necessary' (§237(1)), **fors** makes phrases which can be followed by clauses introduced by interrogative words: **pandra, pyth** 'what'; **ple, py** 'where'; **fatell** 'how'; **prag** 'why'; **piw** 'who': **Ny res dhedha fors pandr'a wra hi** 'It is of no concern to them what she does'; **Ny res dhe nebonan fors fatell verwis** 'It matters to no one how he died'.

(5) The negatives of **synsi** 'hold', **ri** 'give', **settya** 'value' may have a noun associated with them to show the level of contempt, etc.: **Ny synsav ahanas favenn goeg** 'I esteem you (no more than) an empty bean'; **Ny rov gwelenn gala anodho** 'I don't give a straw for him'; **A lavarow aga thas ny settyens demma** 'For the words of their father they cared not a half-penny'. With **gul** 'do, make' the noun of measure is **bri** 'value' mutated to **vri** (§23(3d)): **A ny wre'ta vri a'ga nivera?** 'Don't you consider that counting them is of any importance?' (§126(9)).

§247 **Necessity**

RES is an adjective, 'necessary' or, more rarely, a defective verb, 'is necessary' (§221). The thing or action which is necessary is expressed by a verbal noun or by a noun phrase. The person on whom the obligation falls is indicated by **dhe** 'to' (§141(5)).

(1) As an adjective: **Res yw dybri** 'Eating is necessary, One must eat'; **Res o ni dhe hwithra an ken** 'We had to look for the cause'; **Res yw dhodho bos war** 'He has to be careful'; **Res vydh dhe'n fleghes omwolghi kyns dybri** 'The children must wash themselves before eating'.

§248(5d) Verbs

(2) As a verb: **Hemma a res** 'This is necessary'; **Gwrewgh dell res!** 'Do as is necessary!' **mar dha dell res** 'as good as need be'; **Ny res henna** 'That is not necessary'; **Dhymm y res** 'I must'.

§248 **Duty** What ought to be done is expressed in a number of ways.

(1) **DEGOEDH/KOEDH** (§215) is probably connected to the full verb **koedha** 'fall' with the special meaning 'it falls to'. The construction makes the action which is due, the subject and the person on whom it devolves, the indirect object through **dhe** 'to' (§141(5)): **Y tegoedh dhodho gul gwell** 'He should do better', lit. 'Doing better falls to him'; **Y koedh dhedhi gwitha an arghans** 'She must look after the money'; **Mar tegoedhva dhyn y nagha, y'n gwrussen** 'If it were right for us to deny it, we would have done it'.

(2) **DELLEDH** vb. (§216) 'it is right, proper, it behoves'. The subject is a noun phrase and there is no indirect object: **Y telledh aga bos warbarth** 'It is right (that) they should be together'; **Y telledh ni dhe berthi kov a'n re dremenys** 'It is proper (that) we should remember those (who have) passed on'.

(3) **DESEDH** is the 3s.p./f. of **desedha** 'seat, set in place, fit, suit', etc.: **Kows par dell dhesedh dhe geniver a grys ynno!** 'Speak as befits all those who believe in him!'

(4) **DEVAR** m. 'duty, what is due, incumbent': **Ow devar a vydh gortos** 'My duty will be to remain'.

(5) **TYLI** vb. (§201) 'pay, be worth', etc. The several meanings and constructions associated with **tyli** are as follows.

(a) The simple meaning of paying: **Ev a dylis dhyn an jekkenn** 'He paid me the cheque'; **Ev a'n dylis dhodho dre jekkenn** 'He paid it to him by cheque'.

(b) Something worth doing, which would repay the person doing it: **An ober na a dal y wul** 'That work is worth doing'; **Ny dal an jynn y wertha** 'The machine is not worth selling'.

(c) A moral debt which one owes ('ought' is the old past tense of the English 'owe'); **My a dal y weres** 'I ought to help him'; **Y tylydh dos dh'agan skoedhya** 'You ought to come and help us'.

(d) The pluperfect/conditional **talvia**, etc. means 'ought to have, would have been worth': **My a dalvia mos yn-mes** or **Y talvien mos yn-mes** 'I ought to

§248(5d) Verbs

have gone out'; **An lyver ma a dalvia y studhya** 'This book would have been worth studying'.

(e)　The phrase **durdalla dhywgh (hwi)!** is a contraction of **Dyw re dhallo dhywgh (hwi)/dhiso (jy)!** 'May God repay you!' (§229(1)).

(f)　The English 'pay for' is translated by **prena** 'buy, pay for': **Piw a vynn prena an diwes?** 'Who will pay for the drink?' as compared with **Piw a vynn tyli an reken?** 'Who will pay the bill?'

POSSESSION

§249 Possession is expressed either from the point of view of the possessor or from the point of view of the thing possessed. Thus the subject of the sentence names either the possessor or the possessed, e.g. English 'Mr Fraser owns the house' or 'The house is Mr Fraser's'.

In Cornish the possessor is named as the subject of one of the verbs **y'm beus** 'have', **perghenna** 'own', **kemmeres** 'receive', **kavoes** 'get, have'. The thing possessed is the subject of the verb **bos** 'be' and there are two constructions, depending on whether the subject is definite or indefinite (§253).

§250 **Y'M BEUS** As explained in §198, the verbal element here is a tense of **bos** 'be' in the 3s. An infixed pronoun as indirect object (§65(7a)) denotes the owner, the meaning being 'there is to me', etc. The resulting phrases have however come to be regarded as parts of a transitive verb 'have'.

(1)　If the subject or the object in an affirmative statement comes first, the verbal particle used is **a** or **re**. Otherwise it is **y**; see Verbal Particles: **An ser prenn a'n jeva y wober** 'The carpenter had his wage'; **Hi a's teves naswydh** 'She has a needle'; **An fleghes re's teva rohow** 'The children have had presents'; **Kummyas a'm bydh skon** 'I shall have permission soon'; **Oll an galloes re'gan bia kyns an prys na** 'We had had all the power before that time'; **Anodho y'fedha marth** 'You used to wonder at it'.

(2)　It should be noted that when an independent subject, noun or pronoun, comes before the verbal part of the phrase, there is agreement in person and number: **Ni a'gan bo skath** 'We had a boat'; **An keun a's tevydh an eskern** 'The dogs will have the bones' and examples in (1).

(3)　A pronoun object is expressed by the appropriate suffixed form after the

200

§252(1) Verbs

phrase: **My a'm bydh ev/hi/i** 'I shall have it/them'. The shorter form of **ev, e** is also used (§64(1)): **Ty a'fydh e** 'You shall have it'.

(4) The negative particle is **ny**: **Ny'th o karr y'n dydhyow na** 'You didn't have a car in those days'.

(5) Subordinate sentences are introduced by **y, ma(y), na**. Relative sentences are introduced by **a, re, na**. See under verbal particles, §274-§281.

(6) The present/future subjunctive is used after **re** to denote a wish (§229(1)): **Sewena re'gas bo!** 'May you have success!' This is the usual way of expressing the optative of 'have'.

(7) The commonest meaning of **y'm beus** is that of getting, receiving but it is used alongside **yma genev, yma dhymm** with the simple meaning 'have' and in this sense it is used with abstract nouns of emotion: **Edhomm i a's teves** 'They have need' (§255).

(8) With a verbal noun as object **y'm beus** means 'have the power to, be able to', especially in the negative: **Ny's teves an edhen na nija** 'That bird cannot fly', lit. 'has not flying' (§238(3)).

(9) **Y'm beus** is not used in direct questions with the interrogative particle **a** but it may be preceded by interrogative words: **piw** 'who', **pyth** 'what', **p'eur** 'when' etc.: **Piw a'n jevydh an piwas?** 'Who will have the prize?' **Pyth a'th o?** 'What did you have?' **P'eur y'm bydh derivas?** 'When will I have the report?' The phrase is also used in indirect questions, especially with a noun preceded by **pan, pana** 'what' (§74(2),(3)): **Diskwedhewgh dhymm pana acheson a'gas beus!** 'Show me what reason you have!' **Lavar dhodho p'eur y'fydh an gorthyp!** 'Tell him when you will have the answer!'

§251 **KAVOES** 'have, get'; **KEMMERES** 'get, receive'; **PERGHENNA** 'own' are inflected and constructed normally and they supply verbal nouns and participles with the sense of possession: **Ny berghennens travydh** 'They owned nothing'; **My a wra kavoes an lyver** 'I shall get/have the book'; **ow kavoes, ow kemmeres, ow perghenna** 'having'; **kevys, kemmerys, perghennys** 'owned, received, got'.

§252 **PIW** (§199) 'have, own' is constructed in one of two ways.

(1) The subject is connected to the 3s. of the verb by the particle **a**, the object being a noun following the verb: **Ty a biw ow herensa bys vykken** 'You have

§252(1)

my love for ever' or an infixed pronoun: **My a's piw** 'I have it, I own it'.

(2) The noun object is joined to the verb by the particle **a** and the verb is inflected to show the subject: **hag oll an tir a biwvi** 'and all the land (which) you may have'.

§253 **Constructions with BOS** 'be' are used to direct attention to the thing possessed. They are of two kinds, depending on whether the noun involved is indefinite or definite.

(1) **Indefinite** All tenses of **bos** are used and in the present and the simple imperfect these are in the long form (§197(2b,2c)). The prepositions **dhe** 'to' and **gans** 'with' are used to indicate the possessor, **dhe** standing for general ownership and **gans** being used when the meaning is that the thing possessed is actually with or near its owner.

(a) With **dhe**: **Yma ki dhodho** 'He owns a dog'; **Yth esa flogh dhedhi** 'She had a child'; **Dhe'n kaderyer y fydh galloes lowr** 'The chairman will have enough power'; **Y'n eur na y feu chi bras dhodho** 'At that time he had a large house' (at a defined time); **Dhedha y fia termyn may hallens powes** 'They had time in which they might rest'.

(b) With **gans**: **Yma ki ganso** 'There is a dog with him'; **Yth esa flogh gensi** 'There was a child with her'; **Prest y hwelis y feu kollell lymm gans an kiger** 'Straight away I saw that the butcher had a sharp knife'; **Y fedha modrep goth gansa pup-prys** 'They always had an elderly aunt with them'.

(c) In interrogative and negative sentences the present tense form is **eus**: **Eus ki dhodho?** 'Has he a dog?' **Eus ki ganso?** 'Has he a dog with him?' **Esa gwreg dhodho?** 'Did he have a wife?' **Esa benyn ganso?** 'Did he have a woman with him?' **A veu karr dhodho pan y'n gwelsys?** 'Did he have a car when you saw him?' (at a defined time); **Ny veu koweth ganso** 'There wasn't a companion with him'.

(d) In subordinate sentences after the conjunctions **pan** 'when', **a-ban** 'since', **mars** 'if', **kynth** 'though', **dell** 'as' and the verbal particle **nans** 'now', the form **eus** is used: **pan eus ki dhodho** 'since he has a dog'; **Nans eus skath dhodho** 'Now he has a boat'. **Eus** is also used in relative sentences: **Skrifys yw yn lyver eus ganso** 'It is written in a book which he has'.

(e) The preposition **dhe** may express social relationships: **Yma myrgh dhyn** 'We have a daughter'.

§255 Verbs

(2) **Definite** A definite noun or pronoun denoting the thing possessed is the subject of **bos** and the possessor is again denoted by **dhe** or **gans**. However the short forms of the verb are used in the present and the imperfect with **dhe** because the sense is adjectival, equivalent to the English possessive ending '-s' or the possessive pronoun 'mine', etc.

(a) With **dhe**: **Dhe biw yw an ki?** 'Whose is the dog?' and the answer **Dhe Lorna yw** 'It's Lorna's' or **Dhedhi yw ev** 'It's hers'; **Dhe biw o an ki?** 'Whose was the dog?' with the answer **Dhe Lorna ova** 'It was Lorna's' or **Dhedhi ova** 'It was hers'. With other tenses: **Dhedhi y fia lies blydhen** 'It had been hers (for) many years'; **Dhe Lorna y feu** 'It was Lorna's' (at a defined time).

(b) With **gans** the sense is local and so the long forms of the verb **bos** are used in the present and the simple imperfect: **Gans piw usi an ki?** 'Who's the dog with?' **Gans Lorna ymava** 'It's with Lorna'. **Gans piw esa an ki?** 'Who was dog with?' **Gans Lorna yth esa** 'It was with Lorna'. Other tenses are as above (1): **Gans Lorna y fydh/feu/fia** 'It will be/was/had been with Lorna'.

§254 Possessive pronouns as such do not occur in Cornish so that there are no equivalents to the English 'mine', 'his', etc. The constructions used are derived from those described above: **chi dhymm** 'a house of mine' = **chi a biwav** 'a house which I own' = **chi eus dhymm** 'a house which I have'; **Sur ov y ladras ev pluvenn dhymm** 'I'm sure (that) he stole a pen of mine'. In the same way the English 'whose?' is translated by **dhe biw?** 'to whom?' **Piw a biw?** 'Who owns?': **Dhe biw yw an karr ma?** 'Who owns this car' = 'Whose is this car?' **Piw a biw an bows na?** 'Who owns that coat?'

Reference should also be made to the appositional genitive construction (§55). Cf. also §343(1).

§255 Nouns of sensation or emotion may be included in such constructions. The verb is either **y'm beus** (§250) with the person affected named as subject or a tense of **bos** (§197) (long form in the present and the simple imperfect) with the person affected indicated by the preposition **dhe** 'to' (§141(4)). The nouns are:

debron	'itch, urge'	hireth	'longing'	meth	'shame'
dout	'fear'	hwans	'desire'	nown	'hunger'
dughan	'grief'	lust	'lust'	own	'fear'
edhomm	'need'	mall	'eagerness'	sians	'fancy, whim'
edrek	'regret'	marth	'wonder'	syghes	'thirst'
ewl	'craving'				

203

§255 Verbs

The cause or the object of the sensation or the emotion is expressed most usually by a verbal noun. The nouns **edrek, marth, meth** are linked to this verbal noun by the preposition **a** 'of': **Yma dhymm marth a'y wul henna** 'I wonder at his doing that'.

The remainder of the abstract nouns govern either directly through the genitive construction or through the preposition **a**: **Ev a'n jevo own koedha** or **Ev a'n jevo own a goedha** 'He had a fear of falling'/'He was afraid of falling'.

These same words are used occasionally with the preposition **awos** 'because of' when the cause of the emotion is to be indicated (§139(6)): **Ny's teves meth awos gul henna** 'She is not ashamed of doing that' (something past = 'of having done that') and **Ny's teves meth awos gul henna** 'She is not ashamed of doing that' (something past = 'of having done that') and **Ny's teves meth a wul henna** 'She is not ashamed of doing that (action completed).

For the nouns **edrek, mall, marth** and **meth** there is an alternative construction using **gans** and a tense of **bos** (short forms in the present and simple imperfect). **Marth o gans an medhyk a'm gweles yagh** 'The doctor was surprised to see me well' (§147(5)); **Y hwoer a's teves edrek a'y sorr** or **Yma edrek dh'y hwoer a'y sorr** 'His sister regrets her anger'; **My a'm beu mall dybri/mall a dhybri ow hoen** or **Y feu mall genev a dhybri ow hoen** 'I was eager to eat my supper'; **Ni a'gan bo marth a glywes an nowodhow** or **Marth o genen a glywes an nowodhow** 'We wondered to hear the news'; **Yth esa syghes dhe'n vowes** 'The girl was thirsty'; **mara'th eus hwans mos/a vos** 'if you want to go'.

The cause of the sensation or emotion can of course be described by an infinitive construction or by a complete sentence: **Marth a'm bo an chi dhe vos mar goth/pan welis an chi koth** 'I wondered that the house was so old/when I saw the old house'.

§256 **PERTHI** 'carry, bear, endure', etc. takes certain abstract nouns as objects with the meaning 'have, be affected by'. The nouns are:

ahwer	'distress'	**dout**	'fear'	**meth**	'shame'
avi	'ill-will'	**kov**	'remembrance'	**own**	'fear'
danjer	'hesitation'				

Examples: **Na borth ahwer!** 'Don't be upset!' **Peub ahanan a berth kov a henna** 'Every one of us remembers that'. See also §255.

❖ ❖ ❖ ❖ ❖

ADVERBIALS

§257 Adverbial expressions consist of single words, phrases or complete sentences: **Ena/y'n eur na/pan dheuth tre/ y terivis dhyn an hwedhel** 'Then/at that time/when he came home/ he told us the story'.

(1) Single word adverbs are sometimes compounds or contractions of phrases: **byttegyns** 'nevertheless' is from **bydh dhe gyns** 'ever/never the sooner'.

(2) A preposition and its noun or pronoun form an adverbial phrase and many such phrases have become permanent expressions: **a-dermyn** 'in time'; **war gamm** 'steadily'; **dredhi** 'thereby'.

The prepositions which are so used are: **a** 'from, at' (§126); **bys** 'until' (§140); **dhe** 'to, at' (of time) (§141); **war** 'in the direction of' (§161); **wor'** (for **worth**) 'at' (§152); **yn** 'at' (place or time) (§167). The two words are written separately, hyphenated or united as one word: **yn tien** 'completely'; **war-vann** 'up'; **wor'tiwedh** 'finally'. Some forms are used both as prepositions and as adverbs without change: **a-rag an chi** 'in front of the house'; **Esedh a-rag**! 'Sit in front!' See also §78.

(3) Adjectives can, as mentioned in §91, be used as adverbs without addition or change: **Garma a wrug ev garow** 'He shouted rough(ly)'. On the other hand the adverb-forming particle **yn** (causing mixed mutation, §26) may precede the adjective: **yn harow (garow)** 'roughly'; **yn fen (men)** 'strongly'.

Sentences with adverbial force which form part of another sentence are described in the sections dealing with subordinate sentences (§344 - §351).

(4) An adverb can come almost anywhere in a sentence, not however between a verbal particle and its verb or between other words which are closely connected syntactically. The choice is a matter of emphasis and style.

No list of adverbs can be complete. A selection of the most important of them is given in the sections which follow. They are grouped by class and sub-class according to meaning as far as possible: time (§258), place (§259), manner (§260), equative and comparative (§261), additive (§262), concessive and conditional (§263), causal (§264), affirmative (§265), negative (§266), degree (§267).

§258 Time

(1) Time at which - general

p'eur	'when?' *interr. with verbs* (§74(15))	y'n tor' ma	'at this time'
		y'n tor' na	'at that time'
		neb eur	'at some/any time'
y'n eur ma	'now'		
y'n eur na	'then'	a'n eyl torn	'at the one time'
lemmyn	'now'	a-ji dhe our	'within an hour'
ena	'then'		

(2) Time at which - particular

nosweyth	'in the night'	dy' Gwener dhe nos	'Friday night'
diwor' an nos/ d'wor' an nos	'by night'	an Gwener	'on Friday(s)'
dygynsete	'the day before yesterday'	dohajydh (diworth ewha an jydh)	'afternoon'
de	'yesterday'		
nyhewer	'last night'	androweyth	'in the afternoon'
yn nyhewer gorthugher	'yesterday evening'	gorthugher	'this (coming or present) evening'
diworth an myttin	'in the morning'	haneth y'n nos	'tonight'
		haneth (dhe nos)	'in this coming night'
hedhyw	'today'		
diworth an jydh	'today, in the day'	ternos vyttin	'tomorrow morning'
y'n jydh hedhyw	'today, in the day' *(pres./fut)*	a-vorow	'tomorrow'
hedhyw y'n jydh	'in this/that day' *(pres. or past)*	trenja	'the day after tomorrow'
hedhyw vyttin	'this morning'	warlyna	'last year'
Dy' Gwener vyttin	'Friday morning' *(and other days similarly)*	hevlyna	'this year'
		y'n vlydhen a dheu	'next year'

(3) Simultaneous time

kettell (§347)	'as soon as' *with verb*	war henna	'thereupon'
		war-not	'simultaneously'
kettoeth (ha)	'as quickly (as)'	yn kettermyn (ha)	'at the same time (as)'
war hemma	'hereupon'		

§258(7) Adverbials

(4) Time at which - former time

wostalleth	'at first'	a-gynsow	'lately'
kyns	'formerly'	a-dhiwedhes	'lately'
a-varr	'early'	nammnygen	'just now'
a-brys	'early, in time'	degynsow	'recently'
a-dermyn	'in time'	seulabrys	'formerly'
nowydh	'newly, just'	seuladhydh	'long since'

(5) Time at which - immediate future

distowgh	'immediately'	a-boynt	'promptly'
a-dhistowgh	'immediately'	desempis	'immediately'
dihwans	'quickly, eagerly'	a-dhesempis	'immediately'
a-dhihwans	'quickly, eagerly'	sket	'straightaway'
war nuk	'quickly, by return'	skon	'quickly'
prest	'quickly, at once'	yn skon	'quickly'
hware	'at once, soon'	uskis	'quickly'

(6) Time at which - later time

wor'tiwedh	'finally'	dhe-hys	'at length'
wostiwedh	'finally'	war-lergh	'afterwards'
gordhiwedh	'finally'	a-wosa	'afterwards'
ottiwedh	'finally'	a'y wosa	'after that'

(7) Time - how often

peskweyth*	'how often'	menowgh	'often'
py lies gweyth*	'how often'	yn fenowgh	'often'
py lies treveth*	'how often'	nameur	'often' *With*
py lies termyn*	'how often'	(§83(7))	*neg.* 'seldom'
pup-prys	'always'	treweythyow	'sometimes'
pub eur	'every hour, always'	anvenowgh	'infrequently'
pub dydh	'every day, always'	nammenowgh	'seldom'
pub mis	'every month'	boghesvenowgh	'seldom'
pub Sadorn	'every Saturday'	bynner	'never' *Used*
	(and other days similarly)	(§229(1))	*with* re *and optative*
pub blydhen	'every year'	wor'talleth ha	'first and last,
lies torn	'often'	wor'tiwedh	ever'

*these are both interr. and dem.

§258(7)   Adverbials

Those adverbs with the meaning 'ever', when used in conjunction with a negative, expressed or implied, have the meaning 'never'.

(8) Time - how long

pes termyn	'how long' *rel., interr. and dem.*	**bydh moy**	'any more' *(no mutation)*
pygemmys termyn	'how long' *rel., interr. and dem.*	**bythkweyth**	'ever'
		byttydh	'any day, ever'
ogas ha blydhen/ dydh/our, etc.	'almost a year/ day/ an hour'	**(bydh yn dydh, bydh dydh)**	
pell	'for a long time'	**bys pan** (§347)	'until'
hirneth f.	'(for) a long time'	**trank heb worfenn**	'without end, for ever'
bys omma	'up to now'	**a'y oes**	'ever' *(past)*
seulabrys	'for a while past'	**yn y oes**	'ever' *(past)*
seuladhydh	'for a long time past'	**bys nevra**	'for ever'
		bynari	'for ever'
hwath	'still yet'	**bys vynari**	'for ever'
nevra	'ever, always'	**bys vynytha**	'for ever'
nevr'	*before vowels*	**bys vykken**	'evermore'
jammes	'ever'	**byttiwedh**	'to the end'
bydh	'ever'	**bykken**	'ever'

bydh causes mutation of the following word in a compound as follows: **b-**, **g-**, **gw-**, **m-** are softened; **k-**, **p-** unchanged; **d-** usually becomes **t-**; **-dh** + **t-** becomes **-tt-**.

§259 Place

(1) Place at which

ple(th)	these are all the	**a-bell**	'far off'
py(th)	interrogative	**yn pell**	'far off'
py plas	'where' *described*	**a'n eyl tu**	'aside, away'
py tyller	*in* §74(12), (14)	**dhe wari**	'away, free'
py kost	*and* §75	**a-ji**	'within'
yn neb tu	'some-/anywhere'	**a-bervedh**	'in the interior'
pub plas	'everywhere'	**yn chi**	'at home, in'
pub tu	'on all sides'	**tre**	'at home'
a-dro	'round about'	**yn tre**	'at home, indoors'
a-derdro	'around'	**a-dre**	'away from home'
a bub tu	'on every side of'	**y'n dre**	'in town'

§259(2)   Adverbials

a-denewenn	'aside, to one side'	a-ves	'outside'
a'n eyl tu	'aside, away'	a-rag	'in front'
a-dheghow	'on the right'	a-dryv	'behind'
a-dheghowbarth	'on the right, southwards'	a-dhelergh	'behind'
		war-tu delergh	'aft, at the back'
a-gledh	'on the left'	a-ugh	'above'
a-gledhbarth	'on the left, northwards'	a-vann	'above'
		a-wartha	'above, on top'
omma	'here'	a-barth a-wartha	'on the upper side'
ogas	'near at hand'		
ogas omma	'near here'	a-woeles	'below, at the bottom'
yn ow ogas	'near me', etc.		
yn ogas	'nearby, close at hand'	a-barth a-woeles	'on the lower side'
yn-nes	'closer, nearer'	a-is	'lower, below'
ena	'there'	war an leur	'on the ground'
eno, enos	'over there', (distant but visible)	hons	'yonder, in the distance' *(not necessarily visible)*
		yn-hons	
yn-hons dhe	'on the far side of'		

(2) Place - posture

a-worwedh   'in a lying position, lying down'
a-sav   'in a standing position, standing up'
a-esedh   'in a sitting position, sitting down'

These three expressions can have a possessive adjective after the preposition **a**: **Mir orth an gath na a'y esedh war an to!** 'Look at that cat sitting on the roof there!' **Yma hi a'y worwedh lemmyn** 'It's lying down now' (§126(4)).

a-dreus   'athwart, across, contrariwise'
kewsel a-dreus   'to contradict'

The following expressions are used when the direction of looking, pointing, etc. is to be emphasised:

war-vann	'upwards'	war-rag	'forwards'
war-wartha	'upwards'	war-dhelergh	'backwards'
war-nans	'downwards'	war-ves	'outwards'
war-woeles	'downwards'	war-bervedh	'inwards'
war-leur	'downwards'	war-ji	'homewards'
war-tu	'towards'		

§259(3)
(3)   Place - motion implied

Adverbials

a by le, a-ble (§74(13))	'whence, from what place' *interr.*	hys-ha-hys war fordh	'from end to end' 'on the way'
alemma	'from this place, hence'	pell	'for a long distance'
ahanan	'away, off, hence'	yn-bann	'upwards'
dhe-ves	'off, away'	dhe-wartha	'to the top'
yn kerdh (kerdh 'walk')	'away, off'	dhe-woeles yn-nans	'to the bottom' 'downwards'
yn kyrgh (kyrgh 'way')	'away, off'	dhe'n leur	'downwards, to the ground'
alena	'from that place, thence'	yn leur	'downwards, to the ground'
a-dhia	'from yonder'	a-dhiwar-leur	'from off the
a-dhihons	'from yonder'		ground'
a-dhihons dhe	'from the far side of'	tre	'homewards, back'
bys omma	'up to here, hither'	dhe-dre	'homewards, back'
di/dhi	'thither'	tu ha tre	'homewards'
bys di/bys ti	'right up to'	dhe'n dre	'to (the) town'
ogas ti/ ogasti/ogatti	'near to, thereabouts'	tu ha'n dre dhe-denewenn	'townwards' 'to the side'
byttiwedh	'to the very end'	yn-rag	'forwards'

As will be seen from the above lists, **war** generally denotes stationary position or direction of inclination, looking, whereas **yn** indicates static position or movement 'in, into'.

§260 Manner

fatell	'how' *interr.* before verbs, §77	a-dhifun yn kosk	'awake' 'asleep'
fatla	'how' *(independent form)*	a-droes tys-ha-tas	'on foot' 'tit for tat, blow for blow'
Dienkys ywa, ny wonn fatla	'He has escaped, I don't know how'	warbarth	'together'
yndella	'so, thus'	dibarow	'separately'
yndellma	'in this way'	dhe wari	'freely, at liberty'
y'n tor' ma/na	'in this/that way'	dison	'without more
yn kettellma	'just like this'		ado, forthwith'
yn kettella	'in that same way'	dihwans	'eagerly'
par	'as, so'		

§262   Adverbials

kepar	'like, as' *followed by* **ha** *or by* **dell** *and verb* (§287)	toeth bras, toeth da, toeth men, totta	'rapidly'
par dell	'just as' *followed by verb*	war hast	'hurriedly'
		uskis	'quickly'
avel	'as, like' (§84)	hwymm- hwamm	'capriciously, slapdash'
mar	'so, such' (§84)	semli, yn semli	'becomingly'
war neb kor	'somehow, in some way'	treus	'perversely'
y'n keth maner ma/na	'in this/that same manner'	war gamm	'steadily'
		dour	'scrupulously'
konter, kontrari	'contrary, opposite'	diblans	'distinctly'
ken	'otherwise'	preshyous	'precisely'
poken	'or else'	stark	'fixedly'
a-wel	'in the sight of'	y'n gwella prys	'luckily'
a-les	'openly'	y'n gwettha prys	'unluckily'
yn priva, yn privedh	'privately'	yn ober	'in fact'
		speshyal	'especially'

§261 Equative and comparative

kemmys 'as, so much as, so great, so many as'. The comparison is expressed through **ha(g)** 'and' (§287). This word is also used as a pronoun and as an adjective (§72(2)).

For adverbial numbers with **kemmys** as the second part of the compound see §121(3).

kekemmys	is used in the same way as **kemmys** but has slightly more force.
kehys	'of the same length'. The comparison is expressed through **ha(g)** (§287).
avel	'as, like'. Used with nouns and pronouns (§84).
es/ages	'than'. Used with nouns and pronouns (§84).

§262 Additive

yn ta, maga ta	'as well as'	ynwedh	'also, furthermore'
moy yn ta	'yet more'	keffrys, kekeffrys	'also, moreover, too'

§263 Concessive and conditional

a'y wosa	'nevertheless, notwithstanding'	na hwath (na = neb)	'yet, all the same, notwithstanding'
byttele (bydh+ dhe + le)	'nevertheless, 'any the less'	hogen martesen	'still, yet' 'perhaps'
byttegyns (bydh + dhe + kyns)	'nevertheless'	byttiwettha	'nevertheless'

§264 Causal

dredhi	'thereby'. *3s.f.* of **dre** 'through' (§142(6)).
prag	'why' interr. followed by a verb (§74(16)).
praga	'why' is used in situations other than before a verb. No mutation: **Gyllys yw ev, ny wonn praga** 'He's gone, I don't know why'.

§265 Affirmative

sertan	'certainly'	re Synt Devri	'by Saint Surely' *(ironic)*
devri (de + bri)	'indeed'		
yn tevri	'certainly'	redi, yredi	'readily'
dhe-wir, yn hwir (gwir *adj.*)	'truly'	sur, yn sur, yn surredi	'surely, readily'
pur wir yn ta	'right truly'		
porres (pur + res)	'urgently, absolutely'		

Some of these adverbs of affirmation are used as the equivalent of **ya** 'yes', not as the reply to a direct question requiring information but in agreement, assent, acknowledgement (§352(1)).

§266 **Negative** The adverbials given here are not in themselves negative but they are frequently used with a negative expressed or implied in the context by way of reinforcement or emphasis. Some of these have already been mentioned in the sections above.

Banna 'a drop' accompanies expressions of seeing, hearing, knowing, saying, etc. to mean 'at all', usually in the negative sense: **Ny gewsons banna** 'They didn't speak at all'.

Bydh '(not) ever, (not) any'. Softens **b-, g-, gw-, m-** (except in **bydh moy**,

§266 Adverbials

bythkweth); k-, p- unchanged, d- becomes t-: **Bydh na vynnav y wul** 'I will never do it, I won't do it at all'.

Bydh moy '(not) any more, (not) yet': **Nyns yw kevys bydh moy** 'It is not found any more'.

Bydh onan '(not) any one': **ma na vo bydh onan gesys dhe goll** 'that not one be allowed (to go) to waste'.

Bydh well '(not) any better': **Bydh well ny ylli hi gul** 'She could not do any better'.

Kammenn, kammenn vydh. Kammenn 'a step', and so 'at all'. Before a following **n-** it is found as **kamm**. It reinforces the negative sense of a preceding **ny, nyns** 'not': **Ny welis kammenn** 'I didn't see at all'; **Nyns eth kammenn** 'He didn't go at all'. On the other hand it can introduce a negative clause with the particle **na: Kammenn/kamm na allav assentya** 'In no way can I agree'; **Kamm na ylli y doella** 'in no way could he deceive him'.

Mann 'nothing' is used like **kammenn** in emphasising a preceding negative: **Ny'm deur mann** 'It concerns me not at all'. For the use of **mann** as meaning 'zero, nought' see §94.

Nameur (= **neb meur** 'any much') is used with a negative to mean '(not) much at all, (not) anything at all': **Ny'm aswonn nameur a dus** 'Not many people know me'; **Nameur ny yll y grysi** 'He can scarcely believe it'; **Ny'n jeves nameur a furneth** 'He is not very wise', lit. 'He has not much at all of wisdom'.

Namoy (= **neb moy**) '(not) any more, (not) again': **Na wra namoy!** 'Don't do any more!' **Ny's gwelydh namoy** 'You will see her no more'. With a noun between the two elements: **Na gows na ger moy!** (= **neb ger moy**) 'Don't say any more!'

Nes is the irregular comparative of **ogas** 'near' (§82(4)) with the literal meaning 'nearer' but it is used as a reinforcement of a negative to mean 'at all, any more': **Na dav vy nes!** 'Do not touch me at all!' It is found with repeated negatives: **Ny vynnsen mos di, na vynnsen nes** 'I would not want to go there, I really wouldn't'; **Ny vedhav kewsel dhodho, na vedhav nes** 'I don't dare speak to him, I don't at all'; **Ny'n aswonn, na wra nes** 'He doesn't know him, he doesn't at all'.

§266 Adverbials

Tamm (vydh) 'a bit' reinforces a negative: **Ny wrug an vowes dybri tamm** 'The girl did not eat at all'.

Toch (vydh) 'a touch, a moment': **Ny gosk ev toch vydh** 'He doesn't sleep at all'.

Unnweyth 'once' (§121): **Ny esedhsyn unnweyth** 'We didn't sit once/at all'.

Vydh is a derivative of **bydh**; it usually follows its verb, noun or adjective and means 'any, whatever, at all, ever, never', etc. It is extensively used with a noun to give it an indefinite sense: **Nyns eus tamm vydh a vara** 'There isn't a single scrap of bread'; **Ny wonn travydh** 'I don't know anything at all'.

Y'n bys '(not) at all', lit. 'in the world'. A general reinforcement of a negative. **Nyns esa blas y'n bys y bar** 'There was no flavour in the world like it', i.e. no flavour at all like it. This phrase is also used in affirmative sentences with an equative meaning: **kepar y'n bys ha hemma** 'exactly like this'; **kepar y'n bys dell gerowgh** 'just as you like'. (§287).

§267 Degree

Boghes 'slightly, little, un-, in-' softens **b-, g-, gw-, m-** of the following adjective or adverbs. The sounds of **k-, p-, t-** are unchanged. Additionally in compounds where it can be regarded as a prefix **d-** is hardened to **t-**: **boghes venowgh** 'not often'; **boghes veur** 'not much'; **boghes kemmyn** 'uncommon'. **Boghes** also functions as an adjective before a noun which is singular. Mutation is confined to the softening of **b-, g-, gw-, m-**: **boghes vara** 'not much bread'.

Dres eghenn. Eghenn 'sort, any sort', so **dres eghenn** 'beyond anything, extraordinary, extraordinarily': **Ev a'n jeves nerth dres eghenn** 'He has extraordinary strength'; **Fur o hi dres eghenn** 'She was extraordinarily wise'.

Euthek from **euth** m. 'horror, terror' with the meaning 'frightfully' has an emphasising function with a following adjective: **euthek garow** 'terribly rough'.

Fest/fast 'firmly, very, right' can precede or follow the word it qualifies: **fest lowen** 'very happy'; **fest yn ta** 'very well'; **wor'tiwedh fest** 'right at the end'.

Glan 'quite, utterly, completely', lit. 'clean': **gyllys glan** 'gone completely', **yn glan** 'cleanly, wholly' (§92).

§267 Adverbials

Hanter 'half': **Nyns o hanter da rygdhi** 'It wasn't half good (enough) for her' (§109(1)).

Kyns oll 'especially', lit. 'before all': **Na grys dhodho, kyns oll mara'n te** 'Do not believe him, even if he swears (to) it'.

Kowal 'completely, fully, wholly'. For its use as a prefix in the forms **kowl/kol** see §268. **Ev a'th trest kowal** 'He trusts you completely'. **Kowal** can also be used as an adjective: **Hemm yw agan pyth kowal** 'This is our whole wealth'.

Le 'less' and **(an) lyha** 'the least' (§82(4)) are used with adjectives to denote an inferior degree of a quality: **le aswonnys** 'less known'; **an lyha aswonnys anedha** 'the least known of them'; **Sowsnek yw le usys ages Kernewek yntredhon** 'English is less used than Cornish amongst us'; **Hy gour o an lyha heweres orti** 'Her husband was the least helpful to her'.

Lowr 'enough' precedes or follows its adjective, verb, adverb: **lowr brav/ brav lowr** 'fine enough'; **Lowr y hwoer ev** 'He knows well enough'; **Ni a yll lowr y leverel** 'We may as well say it'; **lowr uskis/ uskis lowr** 'rapidly enough'. **Lowr** is also used as an adjective (§83(6b)).

Marthys 'marvellously, suprisingly, much': **marthys krev** 'wonderfully strong'; **marthys yn fras** 'marvellously greatly'; **marthys kerys** 'much loved'.

Moy 'more' (§82(4)): **mara'n toelles moy** 'if you were to deceive him more'; **Na gosk moy!** 'Don't sleep (any) more!' Cf. **namoy, bydh moy** (§266), **(an) moyha** 'the most' (§82(4)): **myns a garro an moyha** 'whoever loves the most'. These words **moy, moyha** may be used to form the comparative and superlative of adjectives instead of the inflected forms (§82) and are always so used with longer adjectives and with past participles: **moy hir** 'longer' in place of **hirra**; **an moyha down** 'the deepest' in place of **an downna**; **moy kasadow** 'more hated'; **moy skwerdys** 'more torn'; **an moyha gormelys** 'the most praised' (§245(5)).

Meur 'much, greatly', etc.: **shyndys meur** 'gravely injured'; **An ys re devis meur** 'The corn has grown a lot'.

Nammna(g) 'almost, nearly, all but' (**namm** 'fault' + **na** 'that not') is used directly before an inflected verb and takes **-g** before those forms of **bos** 'be' and **mos** 'go' which begin with a vowel. **Nammna verwis** 'He nearly died'; **Nammnag ethons yn-mes a'ga rewl** 'They almost lost control of themselves'.

§267 Adverbials

Nebes 'slightly, little': **Ev a sevis y benn nebes** 'He lifted his head slightly'; **Nebes lent ywa** 'He is a little slow'. **Nebes** is also used independently as an adjective or as a noun: **Nebes moy, ass ywa meur! nebes le, ass ywa nebes!** 'A little more, how much it is; a little less, how little it is!' See also §72(6).

Ogas 'nearly, almost' precedes an adjective without causing mutation: **ogas marow** 'almost dead'; **ogas gyllys** 'almost gone'. With a noun the form is **ogas ha**: **ogas ha mildir** 'almost a mile' (§287).

Ogas di/ ogasti/ ogatti 'near to it, almost': **Hi yw dewdhek bloedh ogatti** 'She's almost twelve years old'; **Gorfennys ow ober ogasti** 'My work (is) nearly finished'. Cf. **di** (§259(3)).

Pes interr. adv. 'how much' (§76).

Poran (pur + ewn) 'exactly, just right': **Deg eur poran yw hi** 'It's ten o'clock exactly'; **My a'n gwerthas a ugens peuns poran** 'I sold it for twenty pounds exactly'; **Ke yn-rag poran!** 'Go straight forward!' **poran dell wre an re goth** 'just as the old folk used to do'.

Pur is the adjective **pur** 'pure' used adverbially. It softens the following consonant: **pur gales** 'very hard'; **pur wir** 'very truly'.

Pygemmys interr. adv. 'how much': **pygemmys hys?** 'how long?; **pygemmys les?** 'how wide?' **pygemmys downder?** 'how deep?' **pygemmys ughelder?** 'how high?' **pygemmys hirder?** 'how tall?' etc. See §74(8).

Re 'too, excessively' softens a following consonant and is used before an adjective, adverb or verb: **Ny yllir bos re war** 'One cannot be too careful'; **Re nebes, re helergh** 'Too little, too late'; **Ny allav re y wordhya** 'I cannot praise him too much'; **Na gosk re!** 'Don't sleep too much!' **Re** may be regarded as a noun, 'too much, an excess of (a)': **Re a unn dra ny dal mann** 'Too much of one thing is worthless'; **Na dheber re kyns neuvya!** 'Do not eat too much before swimming!'

(Saw) unnsel 'only, but only': **Ny welas travydh, saw unnsel y vab a'n gwelas** 'He saw nothing, only his son saw it'; **Ny garav saw unnsel ti** 'I love only you'.

Skant 'scarcely, hardly' is sometimes used with an affirmative statement, sometimes with a negative statement: **Skant y hallas kerdhes** or **Skant ny allas kerdhes** 'He could scarcely walk'.

§267 Adverbials

Skantlowr 'scarcely, hardly' is used without a negative: **Skantlowr y klywsyn ni unn ger** 'We hardly heard one word'.

Teg 'quite', lit. 'lovely, fair': **sewyes pur deg** 'completely cured'; **Yth yw teg lowr dhe weles** 'It is quite (easy) to see'. The form with **yn** is also used: **hanter kans chi yn teg** 'a complete half-hundred houses, quite fifty houses'.

❖ ❖ ❖ ❖ ❖

PREFIXES

Prefixes are adverbial in nature, modifying the verbs, verbal nouns, adjectives or adverbs to which they refer. They are here grouped approximately according to the type of modification they produce. Most are active in modern Cornish in the formation of new words.

§268 **Intensive**

ARGH- 'chief' does not cause mutation: **arghdrewydh** 'archdruid'; **arghel** 'archangel' (**el** 'angel').

DE- 'very' is followed by soft mutation. Before vowels it becomes **dy**: **degemmeres** 'receive' (**kemmeres** 'take'); **dehelghya** 'chase along' (**helghya** 'hunt'); **dewana** 'penetrate' (**gwana** 'stab'); **dyerbynna** 'meet' (**erbynn** prep. 'against'); **dyegrys** 'shaken, shocked' (cf. W. *egryn* n. 'trembling'). The prefix is reduced to **d-** in **domhwel** 'upset' (**de** + **omhweles** 'fall down') and in combination with an old prefix **ann-** 'in' gives **dannvon** 'send' (**de** + **ann** + **mones** 'go' in the form **mon**); **dynnerghi** 'welcome' (**dy** + **ann** + **erghi** ('bid, call for').

DRE- 'thoroughly' does not cause mutation: **drehedhes** (**hedhes** 'reach'); **dremas** 'thoroughly good (man)' (**mas** 'good').

GOR- 'completely' softens **b-, d-, g-, m-**, aspirates **k-, p-**: **gorowra** 'gild over' (**owra** 'gild'); **gordhiwedh** 'conclusion' (**diwedh** 'end'); **gorwitha** 'mind' (**gwitha** 'keep'); **gorhemmynn** 'command' (**kemmynn** 'commend'); **gorfenna** 'complete' (**penn** 'end').

Examples of non-mutation are: **gormel** 'praise' (cf. W. *moli* 'praise'); **gorgul** 'do strictly' (**gul** 'do').

KOWL-/KOL- 'completely' is followed by the soft mutation: **kowlwul** (**gul** 'do, make') 'finish doing or making'; **kollenki** (**lenki** 'swallow') 'swallow completely, gulp'. The independent adverbial form is **kowal** 'complete(ly)' (§267).

POR- (perhaps for **pur** adj. 'pure', cf. §267) is found only in **porres** 'very necessary' (**res** 'necessary'); **poran** 'exactly' (**ewn** 'right').

TRE- is a rare prefix occurring perhaps in **trethes** 'extreme heat' (**tes** 'heat') where there is apparent spirant mutation.

UGH- 'high': **ughhewoel** 'wide-awake' (**hewoel** 'vigilant'). The meaning 'high' is usually supplied by **ughel** adj. used as a prefix: **ugheldir** 'highland' (**tir** 'land').

§269 **Negative and privative**

AN- 'without, un-, dis-' causes soft mutation of **b-, g-, gw-, m-**. It becomes **av-** before **l-**: **anvlas** 'tastelessness' (**blas** 'taste'); **anvodh** 'unwillingness' (**bodh** 'will'); **ankov** 'forgetfulness' (**kov** 'memory') and **ankevi** vn. 'forget'; **anwoes** 'chill' (**goes** 'blood'); **anwiw** 'unfit' (**gwiw** 'fit'); **anvab** 'childless' (**mab** 'child, son'); **avlavar** 'dumb' (**lavar** 'speech').

BOGHES- 'slightly'. Mutations: **b-, g-, gw-, m-** are softened; **k-, p-, t-** are unchanged while **d-** is hardened to **t-**: **boghestiblans** 'not very distinct' (**diblans** 'distinct'). For **boghes** as a separate adverb see §267.

DI- 'not, without' causes soft mutation: **dinatur** 'unnatural' (**natur** 'nature'); **diliw** 'colourless' (**liw** 'colour'); **dialar** 'without grief' (**galar** 'grief'); **dibenn** 'headless' (**penn** 'head'); **diveth** 'shameless' (**meth** 'shame'); **digreft** 'inexpert' (**kreft** 'craft'). Words derived from **hun** m. 'sleep' change the **h-** to **f-**: **difun** 'awake'; **difunedh** 'sleeplessness'.

DIS- 'not' hardens **g-** to **k-** and so **gw-** to **kw-** although in some cases **gu-** and **go-** have soft mutation to **wu-, wo-**: **disenor** 'dishonour' (**enor** 'honour'); **diskressys** 'disgraced' (**gras** 'grace'); **disprevi** 'disprove' (**previ** 'prove'); **diswul** 'undo' (**gul** 'do').

ES- is a rare form found only perhaps in **eskar** 'enemy' (**kar** 'friend'), pl. **eskerens**.

GO- 'decreasing, rather, slightly, somewhat, sub-' causes soft mutation in most cases but **k-** is sometimes aspirated: **gobrena** 'hire' (**prena** 'buy'); **goderri** 'interrupt' (**terri** 'break'); **godrev** 'small farm' (**trev** 'settlement'); **goheles** 'shun' (**keles** 'hide').

MYS- 'mis-' does not cause mutation: **myskemmeres** 'mistake' (**kemmeres** 'take') and is found in English borrowings: **mystrest** 'mistrust' (**trest** 'trust').

SKYLL- 'not very, decreasing, mini-' is a very rare prefix which causes soft mutation: **skyllwynn** 'whitish' (**gwynn** 'white').

§270 Repetitive

AS- 're-, back, again' softens b-, g-, gw-, m-. There is no mutation of k-, p-, t-. A d- becomes t- which may change the prefix as- to at-: aswels 'new growth of grass' (gwels 'grass'); aswonn 'know, recognise' (gonn 1s. of godhvos 'know'); astiveri 'pour back, make up' (diveri 'pour'); attelinya 'redraw' (delinya 'draw'); attyli 'pay back' (tyli 'pay').

DAS- 're-, back, again' is a stronger form of as- above, with the same mutations: dasleverel 'repeat' (leverel 'say'); dasvywa 'revive' (bywa 'live'); daswul 'do again' (gul 'do, make'); dastrehevel 'rebuild' (drehevel 'build'); dastewynnya 'reflect' (dewynnya 'shine').

TER- indicates repeated, intermittent or feeble action. It causes soft mutation: tergoska 'doze' (koska 'sleep'); terlemmel 'jump about, frisk' (lemmel 'jump'); ternija 'flutter' (nija 'fly').

§271 Associative

KE- (also kem-, ken-, kev-, ky-) 'together, with' causes occasional soft mutation: kehaval 'similar' (haval 'like'); kemmys 'so much' (my(n)s 'amount'); kendevryon 'meeting of waters' (devryon 'waters'); kevarwoedha 'direct' (arwoedha 'make a sign'); kyhwedhel 'tidings' (hwedhel 'story').

KES- 'together, joint, co-' softens b-, g-, gw-, m- but does not affect k-, p- or t-. An initial d- becomes t- which may change the preceding -s to give -tt-: kesvywa 'live together' (bywa 'live'); kesstrivya 'compete' (strivya 'strive'); keskewsel 'converse' (kewsel 'talk'); kesskrifa 'correspond' (skrifa 'write'); kesreynya 'co-reign' (reynya 'reign').

KOM-/KON- 'with' is found chiefly in English borrowings with these prefixes: komparya 'compare'; kontrolya 'order about'; konvedhes 'understand' (medhes 'say, speak' (§219)); kompleth 'complex' (pleth 'fold'); kompoester 'evenness' (poester 'weight').

§272 Positional and temporal

AR-/DAR- 'fore-, pre-' causes soft mutation: arvor 'coast' (mor 'sea'); arwystel 'pledge' (gwystel 'pledge'); darbari 'prepare' (par-ys 'prepared'); dargan 'forecast' (kan 'song, incantation'); darwar 'be forewarned' (war 'careful') (§214).

§273 Prefixes

GORTH- 'against' is followed by the soft mutation with the usual restriction after -th, i.e. **k-**, **p-**, **t-** are not affected: **gorthenep** 'reverse side' (**enep** 'side'); **gorthvil** 'venomous, hostile creature' (**mil** 'animal'); **gorthybi** 'reply' (cf. W. *eb* 'says, said').

IS- 'below, under': **islonk** 'abyss' (**lonk** 'swallowing'); **iskessedhek** 'sub-committee' (**kessedhek** 'committee').

KYN(S)- 'before': **kynweres** 'first-aid' (**gweres** 'aid'); **kynyav** 'autumn' (**gwav** 'winter').

RAG-/RAK- 'before, preceding' causes soft mutation: **ragdas** 'forefather' (**tas** 'father'); **ragbrena** 'subscribe' (**prena** 'buy'); **ragvreus** 'prejudice' (**breus** 'judgement'); **rager** 'foreword' (**ger** 'word'); **ragworra** 'prefix,' (**gorra** 'put'); **ragwel** 'foresight' (**gwel** 'sight'). Before initial **h-** the form **rak** is used: **rakhanow** 'pronoun' (**hanow** 'name') (§154).

TRE-/TER- 'over, beyond': **trenja** 'the day after tomorrow' (= **tre an jydh**); **ternos** 'overnight, the next day' (**nos** 'night').

TREUS- 'across, athwart': **treusprenn** 'crossbeam' (**prenn** 'log'); **treuslytherenna** 'transliterate' (**lytherenna** 'spell').

YN- 'in' causes no mutation: **ynkleudhyas** 'bury' (**kleudhya** 'dig a ditch') (§167).

§273 **Miscellaneous**

HE- 'easily, readily, -able' produces soft mutation: **hebleth** 'pliable' (**pleth** 'flexible'); **hedrogh** 'sliceable' (**trogh** 'cut'); **hegar** 'amiable' (**kar** 'friend'); **hedorr** 'fragile' (**torr** 'break').

KORR- 'micro-, dwarf' causes soft mutation: **korrdonn** (**tonn** 'wave') 'microwave'; **korrgi** (**ki** 'dog') 'little dog'.

LES- 'half-, step-, substitute, vice-' softens **b-**, **g-**, **gw-**, **m-** but **k-**, **p-**, **t-** are unchanged. A **d-** becomes **t-**: **leshanow** 'nickname' (**hanow** 'name'); **leslywydh** 'vice-president' (**lywydh** 'president'); **lesvab** 'stepson' (**mab** 'son'); **lestas** 'stepfather' (**tas** 'father').

OM- 'self, one another' causes soft mutation: **omri** 'give oneself, surrender' (**ri** 'give'); **omjersya** 'be at ease' (**chersya** 'put at ease'); **omweres** 'take care of

§273　　　　　　　　　　　　　　　　　　　　　　　　　　　　　Prefixes

oneself' (**gweres** 'help'); **omwethhe** 'deteriorate' (**gwethhe** 'make worse'); **omdewlel** 'throw one another, wrestle' (**tewlel** 'throw'). See also reflexive and reciprocal verbs, §232.

❖ ❖ ❖ ❖ ❖

§274(5)

VERBAL PARTICLES

Finite verbs, with a few exceptions which will be mentioned, are preceded by one of the verbal particles. These words have an important part to play in the structure of the sentence. The particle **y** is affirmative, **ny** and **na** are negative. The particles **re** and **nans** define the completeness and the time of the action respectively and **ass** adds exclamatory force to the verb.

§274 **Y** causes the fifth state, the 'mixed' mutation (§26), and adds -**th** before all vowels and **h**- but not of course the radical **hw**- or when the mutated form is itself an **h**- or **hw**-: **Y hyll (gyll) ev mos** 'He can go'. In both forms the vowel has an obscure sound like the 'e' in English 'the'.

(1) The particle is used in affirmative sentences and introduces the verb when this stands at the head of the sentence though it is usually preceded in this position by an adverbial expression:

Y hwelav sterenn a-vann 'I see a star above'; **A-woeles an vre yth esa koes** 'At the bottom of the hill there was a wood'; **Dell os an skrifennyas y hwredh an ober** 'As you are the secretary, you do the work'.

It is unilateral in that it does not link parts of the sentence as does, for example **a** (§278).

(2) The particle is always omitted in replies which repeat the verb of the question: **A vynn'ta gweres? Mynnav!** 'Will you help? I will!' **A welsowgh perghenn an gwerthji? Gwelsyn!** 'Did you see the owner of the shop? We saw' (= 'we did'); **A dybowgh hwi bos an gewer toemm lowr?** 'Do you think (that) the weather is warm enough?' **Tybyn!** 'We think!' (= 'we do!').

(3) There is no particle before the positive forms of the imperative: **Ke!** 'Go!' **Bydh furra nessa!** 'Be wiser next (time)!' However an infixed pronoun object may be supported by the particle **a** (§66(3c)).

(4) Tenses and persons of the subjunctive used after a comparative adjective with an equative sense are deemed to be without a particle: **Gorfenn e skonna gylli!** 'Finish it as soon as you can!' (§348(5)).

(5) The particle **y(th)** can, exceptionally, be omitted in normal sentences: **Synsav an morthol** 'I'll hold the hammer'; **Kachyav y benn** 'I'll hold his head'; **Par dell wonn lavarav dhis** 'As I can I will tell you', MC. 8.2; **Gonn**

§274(5)   Verbal Particles

meur ras 'Many thanks'; **Aswonnav gras dhis** 'Thank you', in place of **Y synsav ..., Y kachyav ...**, etc. The verb is most often in the 1s. as in the examples and the usage is confined to poetry or to familiar phrases as above.

(6)   **Prag** 'why' is followed by **y** in affirmative sentences: **Prag y treylyons i?** 'Why do they turn?' (§74(16)). The negative is **na**; see below.

(7)   Certain other interrogative adverbs are followed by **y** to introduce the question. They are **py plas, py tyller, py kost**, all meaning 'where' (§74(14)); **peskweyth** 'how often' and **pestermyn** 'how long' (§76): **Py plas y fydhydh wosa unnek eur?** 'Where will you be after eleven o'clock?' **Pestermyn y teu hi omma?** 'How often does she come here?'

(8)   The particle is assumed to combine with certain other interrogative adverbs and subordinating conjunctions as follows.

a.   **Kyn** 'though' (§293) adds the **-th** before all vowels and initial **h-**. **Kynth ov skwith, yth av** 'Though I am tired, I shall go'; **Kynth holyas an fordh, ev a omgollas** 'Though he followed the road, he lost himself'.

b.   **May** 'that, when, where' (§291) contains the particle **y** and therefore adds **-th** before all vowels and initial **h-**; **Gortewgh poran y'n le mayth esowgh!** 'Stay exactly where you are!' **Ti a hwither an bleujennow rag mayth helwi pubonan anedha** 'You examine the flowers so that you may name every one of them'.

c.   **Ple** and **py** 'where' (§74(12)) and (§75) add **-th** before initial vowels in the verbs **bos** 'be' and **mos** 'go' only. Mutation is as for **y**: **Ple fiens i?** 'Where had they been?' **Pyth esos jy?** 'Where are you?' Note that **a ble** 'from where, whence' (§74(13)) is anomalous in that it does not add **-th** in these circumstances although it causes mixed mutation **A ble tons i?** 'Where do they come from?'

(9)   After certain subordinating conjunctions and adverbs the particle **y** is introduced to support an infixed pronoun. Such are: **kyn** 'though'; **pan** 'when'; **a-ban** 'since'; **kettell** 'as soon as'; **fatell** 'how'; **dell** 'as'. See the chapter on conjunctions. The same usage applies after the interrogative adverb **p'eur** 'when' in the same circumstances: **kyn y's gwelav** 'though I see them'; **a-ban y'gan pysis a wul hemma** 'since he asked us to do this'; **Ny wonn p'eur y's dyerbynnav i** 'I do not know when I shall meet them'.

(10)   A subordinate noun clause may be introduced by the particle **y** (§334(1)).

Gwir yw y kowssa dhedha 'It is true (that) he had spoken to them'. In this situation the particle translates the English 'that' and may be regarded as a conjunction (§291): **rag own yth omdhisaffes** 'for fear that you might stumble/lest you stumble', MC. 14.5.

§275 **NY(NS)** 'not' is the general negative particle in principal clauses. It causes soft mutation and adds **-ns** before vowels in **bos** 'be' and **mos** 'go': **Ny woer konvedhes** 'He doesn't understand'; **Nyns yw hemma re dhrog** 'This is not too bad'; **Nyns av** 'I do not go'. **Ny(ns)** must directly precede its verb except that an infixed pronoun may come between **ny** and the inflected verb: **Ny'gan gweresas** 'He did not help us'.

§276 **NA(G)** 'not' is a negative particle which adds **-g** before vowels in **bos** 'be' and **mos** 'go'. It has the following uses.

(1) As the negative particle before the imperative: **Na esedh!** 'Don't sit down!' **Na serryn!** 'Let's not get cross!'

(2) In negative replies to questions when the verb of the previous utterance is repeated (§321). **A wodhes ta kewsel Kernewek?** 'Can you speak Cornish?' **Na wonn!** 'I cannot!' **Osta lowen?** 'Are you happy?' **Nag ov!** 'I am not!'

(3 Agreement with a negative command is expressed by the use of the appropriate form of the verb with **na**: **Na sevewgh yn-bann!** 'Do not stand up!' **Na sevyn!** or **Na wren!** 'We won't!'

(4) Reinforcement of a negative assertion also uses **na** with the repeated verb: **Ny vynnav mos - na vynnav!** 'I will not go - I won't!'

(5) As the negative subordinating conjunction 'that not', the negative of **y** (§291): **Y hwodhir nag o gwir** 'One knows (that) it was not true', and following certain other conjunctions to make a negative. These are: **a-ban** 'since', **pan** 'when' (§347), **kyn** 'though' (§345), **ma(y)** '(so) that' (§349), **drefenn** 'because', **rag** 'because' (§346), **prag** 'why' (§74(16)). **Kamm(enn)** 'at all, in no way' is also followed by **na** when it introduces a statement: **Kammenn na devons i y'n dor na** 'They do not grow at all in that ground' (§260).

(6) As the negative relative particle. Like the relative particle **a** (§278) it may represent either the subject or the object of the sentence and be used either with an antecedent, which is more usual, or as a pronoun. It is to be translated in this latter case by 'he/she who ... not, that which ... not': **Golow na dhewynnas pell**

§276(6)   Verbal Particles

'a light which did not shine far'; **Na'n jeves hwans a vos, triges tre!** '(He) who does not wish to go, let him stay at home!'

Note that this word is not to be confused with the co ordinating conjunction **na(g)** 'nor': **Golow nag esa nag y'n nor nag y'n ebrenn** 'a light that (never) was on land or in the sky' (§284).

§277 **A** is the interrogative particle which is placed directly before the verb and usually at the head of the sentence. It causes soft mutation: **A dybowgh hwi yndella?** 'Do you think so?' This interrogative is not used before parts of **bos** 'be' and **mos** 'go' which have an initial vowel: **Yw hi glyb?** 'Is it (the weather) wet?' **Ythys ty di?** 'Did you go there?' In negative questions **a ny** is employed: **A ny droghsens an prenn?** 'Had they not cut the wood?' For the use of **a** in questions see §320.

§278 **A**, the relative particle, causes soft mutation. It is used either as the subject or as the object of a relative sentence, usually with an antecedent but sometimes standing as a pronoun, cf. **na** §276(6). It comes immediately before the verb except that an infixed pronoun may intervene: **An venyn a'th weres yw klav** 'The woman who helps you is ill'.

(1)   It serves as the subject of a relative sentence: **Hemm yw an arwoedh a dhiskwedh an le** 'This is the sign which shows the place'; **Y karav henna a sev war an estyllenn** 'I like that (one) which stands on the shelf'.

(a)   If there is an antecedent it need not come immediately before the particle: **Hemm yw an chi, koth ha hanter koedhys kynth yw, a vydh gwerthys a-dhistowgh** 'This is the house, old and half fallen (down) though it is, which will be sold straight away'.

(b)   The particle occasionally stands by itself without an antecedent: **A'n gwra an gwella, ev a'n jevydh an piwas** '(He) who does it the best, he will have the reward'; **A hokyas a gollas an lanwes** 'The one who delayed missed the tide'. Thus the particle is translated, as in these examples, by 'he who, she who, the one who, that which', etc.

(c)   The particle is not used before parts of **bos** 'be' and **mos** 'go' which begin with a vowel: **Ottomma an del yw dhe dhybri** 'Here are the leaves which are to be eaten'; **Ni a aswonn myns eth di** 'We know those who went there'.

(d)   The particle is occasionally left out before other words in the texts: **Ty allsa (ty a allsa)** 'You could'. This is purely poetic licence.

(e) If the perfective particle **re** (§279) introduces the verb, the relative particle is left out: **Homm yw an vaghteth re wolghas an lestri** 'This is the maid who has washed the dishes'.

(2) The particle **a** may represent the object of the relative sentence: **Kemmer an lyver a dhewissys!** 'Take the book which you chose!'

(a) There is usually an antecedent but this need not come directly before the particle: **Gwelewgh an kommolennow du pan sedh an howl kogh a omles y'n ebrenn avel diwaskell brini kowrek** 'See the black clouds when the red sun sinks, which spread in the sky like the wings of giant crows'.

(b) The particle can stand by itself without an antecedent and mean 'he whom, she whom, that which', etc.: **My a woer a hwilowgh hwi** 'I know whom you seek'.

(c) Thus **a** is used as an introductory particle when an infixed pronoun comes before the imperative: **A'n kaves!** 'Let him have it!' (§66(3c)).

(d) This relative particle acts as the verbal particle in nominal sentences and connects the subject or the object to the verb (§303): **Peub a armas** 'Everyone shouted'; **Keun a welsons** 'Dogs they saw'.

§279 **RE** is the perfective participle, marking the completion of an act in relation to a particular time. It immediately precedes the verb, except that an infixed pronoun may come between the particle and the verb: **An tiek re vagas an deves** 'The farmer has reared the sheep'; **An tiek re's magas** 'The farmer has reared them'. **Re** softens the following consonant: **Pub huni re gewsis** 'Everyone has spoken'.

(1) The preterite, pluperfect and present/future subjunctive of **bos** 'be' are exceptions to the rule in that no mutation of the initial **b-** of these tenses takes place (§333(1d,e)): **Ev re beu**; **Ev re bia**; **Re bo!** 'He has been'; 'He had been'; 'May he be!'

(2) The particle takes the form **res** before the preterite of **mos** 'go': **Ev res eth** 'He has gone' (§205(2c)).

(3) It precedes the preterite to make a present perfect tense equivalent to the English 'I have', etc.: **An dus re worfennas an hwel** 'The people have finished the work' (§228(3)). For present perfect tenses of **mos** 'go' and **dos** 'come' without the use of **re** see §205(2a) and §206(2a).

§279(4)   Verbal Particles

(4) The particle can optionally be used with the pluperfect to distinguish the indicative from the conditional use of the same form (§228(5)(6)): **Ni a rossa war an woen** 'We had wandered on the down' or, under certain circumstances, 'We would wander on the down', whereas **Ni re rossa war an woen** can only have the pluperfect sense.

(5) The particle **re** joins the subject to a following verb (§303(1)): **Hi re gewsis** 'She had spoken'; **Dha lyther re dheuth** 'Your letter has come'; **My re'gas gweresas** 'I have helped you'; **An vamm re gempennsa an gweliow** 'Mother had tidied the beds'. This is the commonest construction with **re**.

(6) The particle joins a direct object, when this is a noun, to a following verb (§303(2)): **Lies daras re igorsons** 'Many doors they have opened'; **Meneges henna re wrussta** 'You had mentioned that'.

(7) The perfective particle sometimes precedes a personal tense of the verb when some part of the sentence which is neither subject nor object comes first: **Maria, re beuv re logh** 'Mary, I have been too remiss', BM. 3798; **Bythkweth re beu us genowgh** 'Always you have had a custom', PD. 2034; **Re re dhiskryssys** 'Overmuch you have disbelieved', RD. 1040; **Poes re dewlsowgh agas klun** 'Too heavily you have you thrown your hip(s) (on the ground)' i.e. 'You have slept too heavily', RD. 523.

(8) In comparative clauses (§348) **dell** 'as' can be followed by **re**: **Nyns eus denvydh omma dell re welsys** 'There is no one here as you have seen'. **Re** is not used after the conjunctions **kyn** 'though', **mar** 'if', **a** 'if', **may** 'that'.

(9) **Re** is used after the interrogative adverbs **ple** 'where', **p'eur** 'when', **prag** 'why' (§74(12)(15)(16)) in direct and indirect questions: **Ple res ethons?** 'Where have they gone?' **Ny wonn ple res ethons** 'I don't know where they have gone'. The particle is not used in direct questions except as described here or in negative tenses of the indicative. The English equivalent to **A dewlsowgh hwi hemma?** is either 'Did you plan this?' or 'Have you planned this?' and to **Ny glywis** either 'I didn't hear' or 'I have not heard'.

(10) **Re** is used to introduce a dependent clause in indirect speech (§334(1)): **Dhymm y teriv re's degemmeras i** 'He tells me that he has received them'.

(11) A relative sentence can be introduced by **re** without the relative particle **a** (§340(4)): **Diskwedh dhodho an hwedhel re skrifsys!** 'Show him the story which you have written!' **Yth esa ev ow kewsel a-dro dhe'n towl re bia deneghys seulabrys** 'He was talking about the plan which had already been rejected'.

§281   Verbal Particles

Re is not admitted in negative relatives as explained above (9).

(12) The same particle **re** is used with the present/future tense of the subjunctive in an optative sense to express a wish: **Re sewenno!** 'May he succeed!' **Lowena re'th fo!** 'May you have happiness!' For the optative of **ri** 'give' see §208 and of **dri** 'bring' see §209.

(13) A negative wish is expressed by **bynner** (= **bydh yn eur**) before **re** and the present/future subjunctive: **bynner re'th fo banna kosk!** 'May you never have a wink of sleep!' **Bynner re sewennons y'ga thowl!** 'May they never succeed in their plan!' (§229(1)).

§280 **NANS** is only used before parts of the verb **bos** 'be'. It marks the nearer limit of a period of time and so may be translated 'now, at this time, then, at that time'. The word **lemmyn** 'now' can be used with it: **Nans yw (lemmyn) deg mynysenn my re beu orth dha wortos** 'I have been waiting for you for ten minutes', lit. 'It is now ten minutes I have been ...'; **My a wrug y weles nans yw (lemmyn) unn mis** 'I saw him one month ago', lit. 'I saw him now it is one month'; **Nans o diw vlydhen ev re bia ow triga tramor** 'At that time he had been living abroad for two years'; **Y kowssen dhodho nans o hanter our** 'I had spoken to him half an hour before (that time)'. Simple duration of time requires no particle or preposition; see (§113) and (§154(5)).

§281 **ASSA** is an exclamatory particle usually expressing admiration or wonder. It causes soft mutation and drops the final -**a** before initial vowels of **bos** 'be' and before **w** of the mutated forms of **gul** 'do, make'. This particle is most often found with the verbs **bos, gul,** and **galloes** 'be able': **Assa veuv gokki!** 'How foolish I was!' lit. 'How I was foolish!' **Assa veu henna mater tykkli!** 'What a delicate matter that was!' **Ass osta fur!** 'How wise you are!' **Ass wrons i garma!** 'How they do cry out!' **Ass wrussowgh hwi plynchya!** 'How you flinched!' **Assa ylli ev resek!** 'How he used to be able to run!'

❖ ❖ ❖ ❖ ❖

CONJUNCTIONS

Conjunctions are co-ordinative or subordinative. A few are used in both roles.

CO-ORDINATING CONJUNCTIONS

§282 Co-ordinating conjunctions link items of speech which have the same status and function. These items may be whole sentences, phrases, nouns, verbs, adjectives or adverbs: **Hware y teuth an lader hag ev a dorras an fenester** 'Immediately the thief came and he broke the window'; **Nyns esa y'n amari mes warnodho** 'It wasn't in the cupboard but on it'; **lyvrow po paperyow po daffar skrifa** 'books or papers or writing materials'; **Nag omma nag ena y hyllir aga havoes** 'Neither here nor there are they to be found'.

The items need not be in the same form so long as they have the same function: **Po yn-hons po yn neb le a vydh dewisys ragos y trigydh** 'Either over there or in some place which will be chosen for you you will stay', where each alternative is an adverbial expression.

§283 **Additive**

HA 'and' adds **-g** before all vowels. It may be omitted in a series of similar words: **den bras ha krev** 'a big and strong man' or **den bras, krev** 'a big, strong man'.

As a correlative the conjunction is repeated, **ha ... ha** 'both ... and ..., ... as well as': **ha dydh ha nos** 'both day and night'; **hys-ha-hys** 'end to end'; **dorn ha dorn** 'hand in hand'.

For **mos ha** 'become' see §205(2h) and for **dos ha** 'happen to' see §206(2g).

For **ha** with possessive adjectives see §52; with the definite article see §50(2).

For **ha** within comparisons see §287 and, describing attendant circumstances §300.

§284 **Separative**

NA 'nor' adds **-g** before all vowels. There is no mutation after this word. It is used with a negative, expressed or implied: **Nyns o da na drog** 'It was neither

§286 Conjunctions

good nor bad'; **Ny bowessyn na gosksyn** 'We didn't rest nor did we sleep'. Correlatives are not confined to two terms: **Ny'm beus na delinyans na skeusenn na deskrifans anodho** 'I haven't a drawing, or a photograph or a description of it'.

Naneyl may take the place of the first **na** when the reference is to two terms only: **Ny ros dhyn naneyl boes na diwes** 'He gave us neither food nor drink'.

For **na** with possessive adjectives see §52 and for **na** with the definite article see §50(2).

§285 Alternative

PO/BO/PY 'or'. The form **po** is the one most used in modern Cornish: **A vynnta gul devnydh a'n bal po a'n bigell?** 'Do you want to use the spade or the hoe?' **Yw hi Frynkes po Almanes?** 'Is she a Frenchwoman or a German woman?'

As correlatives repeated before each of the terms **po ... po ...** 'either ... or ..., whether ... or ...': **po war dharas po war fenester** 'by way of a door or by way of a window'; **Po lamma po koedha hi a wra** 'Either jump or fall she will'. The usage can be extended to more than two terms: **po men po brykk po legh** 'stone or brick or slate'.

Po is probably a form of the 3s.pres./fut. subj. of **bos** 'be' with the meaning 'be it'.

POKEN/BOKEN 'or else' (**po** + **ken**) 'other'; see §83(5b): **Deus omma poken yth av** 'Come here or else I'm going'. **Poken** etc. may serve as the first term of a series of correlatives: **Poken dre nerth po dre sotelneth** 'either by force or by craftiness'.

NA, §284, see above, is found rarely in affirmative sentences with the meaning 'or': **Gul pysadow my a vynn kyns eva na dybri meur** 'I will pray rather than drink or eat much'; **Emperour na myghtern gwlas na sodon kyn fo mar vras a yll aga removya** 'Emperor or king of a country or sultan, though he be (ever) so great, will be able to remove them', OM. 2055-57. These expressions seem to imply some act of denial or negation.

§286 Adversative

MARNAS/MA'S 'unless, except, only' is used with a subject preceding the 3s. verb: **marnas ty a'n gwra** 'unless you do it'; **Re vyghan o dhe weles marnas**

an ki a'n kavas 'It was too small to see but the dog found it'.

If an adverbial phrase intervenes, the verb is inflected and preceded by **y**: **marnas gans an bal y pelowgh an dor** 'unless with a spade you dig the ground'; **marnas dhe well y'm gorthybowgh** 'unless you answer me better', RD. 47.

Marnas is also used as a preposition (§151).

MES 'but': **Mes nyns owgh oll da na hweg** 'But you are not all good or sweet', MC. 47.4.; **Ev a's gelwis mes ny'n klywas hi** 'He called her but she did not hear him'.

SAW 'save, unless, except, only': **Ny'n lettyas saw unn lamm** 'I stopped him for only a moment'; **Dha lev a glywav saw dha fas ny welav** 'I hear your voice but I don't see your face'. This word is also used as a preposition (§158).

§287 Comparative

HA(G) 'and'. The conjunction **ha** 'and' (§283) joins two ideas to indicate their equality in some respect. The first element of the comparison often contains a demonstrative word, e.g. **keth** 'same'. The following list contains the chief comparative expressions.

AN KETH ... HA 'the same ... as' (§83(5c)): **an keth lyver ha'n huni a redsys** 'the same book as the one you read'.

KEFFRYS/KEKEFFRYS HA 'as well as, also': **keffrys gwer ha benynes ha fleghes** 'men as well as women and children'.

KEHYS HA 'the same length as': **An astell ma yw kehys ha honna** 'This plank is the same length as that (one)'.

KEMMYS/KEKEMMYS HA 'as much as, as many as' (§72(2)): **Ny welis bykken kemmys ha'n re usi omma** 'I have never seen as many as these which are here'.

KENIVER HA 'as many as, the same number as': **Yma an darasow keniver ha'n fenestri** 'There are as many doors as (there are) windows'.

KEPAR HA 'the same kind as': **Neuvya i a wre kepar ha puskes** 'They swam just like fish'.

KETTOETH HA 'as soon as, as quick as': **kettoeth ha'n gorhemmynn** 'on the order'; **kettoeth ha'n ger** 'on the word, straight away'.

MAR ... HA 'so ... as, as ... as': **Ober yw mar es hag i dh'y worfenna kyns penn our** 'Work easy (enough) for them to finish before the end of an hour'. This construction allows a phrase to be used as the second element of the comparison (cf. §84).

MIR HA 'see how! see the degree to which!': **Mir ha krev yw an gordenn!** 'See how strong the cord is!'

OGAS HA 'nearly' is used with a noun: **ogas ha blydhen** 'nearly a year'; **ogas ha droglamm** 'nearly an accident'. Cf. §267 under **ogas**.

OTT(A) HA 'see how!': **Ott ha tewl yw an nos!** 'See how dark the night is!' cf. §67.

WARBARTH HA 'together with': **skoellya an babi warbarth ha dowr an bath** 'throwing the baby away with the bath water'.

If a verbal phrase is to follow one of these comparative expressions, the connection is made through the subordinating conjunction **dell** with or without the **ha**: **Mar kertthes kemmys (ha) dell gerdhav** 'If you were to walk as much as I walk'; **Ott ha dell res hi!** 'See how she runs!' (§348).

§288 Causal

RAG 'for' (§154): **Y sygeras y'n pras rag an gewer o splann** 'He loitered in the field for the weather was fine'. The negative is **rag ny(ns): Gwell via dhis mos dhe-dre rag nyns eus prow dhis ow kortos ena** 'It would be better for you to go home for there is no advantage to you (in) waiting there'.

Rag is also used as a subordinating conjunction and the negative is then **rag na(g)** (§294).

§289 Consequential

YTHO 'then, in that case, so, in consequence': **An gador ma yw terrys ytho y fydh res kavoes onan arall** 'This chair is broken so it will be necessary to get another'.

This word is frequently used to introduce an independent sentence and at the same time to refer to a previous statement: **My yw skwith. Ytho esedh!** 'I am tired. In that case, sit down!' **Rag** is less frequently used in this way. The stress in **ytho** is on the last syllable so that the first syllable tends to be lost in speech and the word said as **'tho**.

SUBORDINATING CONJUNCTIONS

§290 Subordinating conjunctions introduce sentences which have the status of nouns, adjectives or adverbs within another sentence (§334-§350). Some subordinating conjunctions are conjunctions proper, others are verbal particles acting as conjunctions. These two classes are marked (v) in the lists below.

These conjunctions and verbal particles used as conjunctions are followed immediately by a finite verb. Only a negative particle or an infixed pronoun can come between such conjunctions and the verb: **mar kwra** 'if he does'; **mar ny wra** 'if he does not'; **mar y'n gwra** 'if he does it'; **mar ny'n gwra** 'if he does not do it'.

Those conjunctions which end in a consonant require the particle **y** (§274(8)) before the infixed pronoun to facilitate pronunciation: **pan welav** 'when I see'; **pan y'gas gwelav** 'when I see you'; **pan na welav** 'when I do not see'; **pan ny'gas gwelav** 'when I do not see you'.

A few prepositions governing noun phrases may conveniently be considered here. They are marked (n).

§291 **General**

Y (v) (§274) causes mixed mutation. The clause which it introduces may be the subject or the object of the verb of the principal sentence or the complement of **bos** 'be' in the principal sentence: **Gwir yw y fydh kuntelles an Yow ma** 'It is true that there will be a meeting this Thursday' (subject); **Peub a wodhya y fia ev toellys** 'Everyone knew that he had been cheated' (object); **An gwiryonedh o y feu ev an toeller** 'The truth was that he was the cheater' (complement).

NA (v) 'not' (§276) is followed by soft mutation. It is the negative equivalent of **y**: **Gwir yw na vydh kuntelles an Yow ma** 'It is true that there will not be a meeting this Thursday'.

MAY (v) 'that'. This conjunction is made up of a relative particle **ma** which has the general meaning 'where, whereby' and the verbal particle **y** as above. It is therefore followed by the mixed mutation and adds **-th** before a vowel or **-h** as **y** does (§274). It becomes **ma** before the **n-** of negative particles and before infixed pronouns. The negative of **may** is therefore **ma na** 'that not': **ma na vo galar yntredhowgh hwi** 'that there be no grief between you'; **ma'gas lett a redya** 'that he prevents you from reading'. This conjunction introduces a noun clause as the direct object of certain verbs (§336(3)) but is more usually found with oblique relative sentences (§342) from which are derived adverbial uses.

§292 Conditional

A (v) 'if' causes fourth state mutation (hardening). The negative is **na** 'if … were not'.

MAR/MARA/MARS/MARAS (v) 'if' is followed by fourth state mutation (hardening). The forms in **-s** are used before vowels. The negative is **mar ny** 'if not' or **na** 'were not'.

For the use of these conjunctions in conditional sentences and indirect questions see §322 and §344(5).

§293 Concessive

KYN (v) 'though, although, even though' (§274(8a)). This conjunction causes mixed mutation and adds **-th** before all vowels and **h-**. Before an infixed pronoun the particle **y** is regularly inserted for ease of pronunciation to give **kyn y'n** etc.: **kyn y'n aswonnydh** 'though you know him'.

Before other vowels and **h-** the form is **kynth: kynth aswonnons an fordh** 'although they know the way'; **kynth hol ev dha gusul** 'although he follows your advice'.

With the 3s. and 3p. forms of **y'm beus** 'have' (§198) however the infixed pronoun and therefore the particle **y** may be omitted: **kyn jeves, kyn teves** 'though he/it has, though she/it has, though they have'; **kyn jeffo, kyn teffo** 'though he/it may have', 'though she/it may have, though they may have'; **kyn jeffa, kyn teffa** 'though he/it might have, though she/it might have, though they might have'. The negative of **kyn** is **kyn na** 'though … not': **Kyn na woer kewsel Bretonek, hegar orth an yeth yw yn sur** 'Though he does not know how to speak Breton he is certainly sympathetic to the language'.

Concessive clauses are described in §345.

§294 Causal

A-BAN (v) 'since, because' (**a** + **pan** 'when') causes second state mutation (softening). The particle **y** is added before infixed pronouns as described in §274(7). The negative is **a-ban na** 'since ... not': **I a dheuth a-ban y's tevo hwans a omlowenhe** 'They came because they wanted to enjoy themselves'; **Ny evons i a-ban nag eus syghes dhedha** 'They are not drinking because they are not thirsty'.

AWOS (n) 'because' is a preposition which, followed by a verbal noun or by the infinitive construction with **dhe**, introduces causal clauses (§139(5)). There is no negative. It also less commonly means 'in spite of' (§139(9)): **Nyns av yn-mes awos bos an gewer hager** 'I'm not going out because the weather is foul'.

DREFENN (n) 'because' (§143) is also a preposition whch is followed by a verbal noun or by the infinitive construction, that is, a verbal noun preceded by **dhe** 'to' (§141(19)): **Na gemmer an towell ma drefenn y vos glyb!** 'Don't take this towel because it is damp!' The negative is **drefenn na** 'because ... not': **My a vynn pesya ow kul hemma drefenn nag ov skwith** 'I will carry on doing this because I am not tired'.

PAN (v) 'since' causes soft mutation. The primary meaning is 'when' (§295) but there is a derived causal meaning. The particle **y** is added to accommodate an infixed pronoun. The negative is **pan na** (v): **Nyns ethons i a-dhistowgh pan esens ow pywa a-bell** 'They didn't go immediately because they were living at a distance'; **Ny yll Peder mos pan nag yw koth lowr** 'Peter cannot go because he is not old enough'.

RAG (n) 'because' is a preposition and is followed either by a verbal noun or by the infinitive construction with **dhe** (§141(19)). A negative is made by adding **na**, **rag na** (v): **Ny balas y'n lowarth rag bos an dor re gales** 'He did not dig in the garden because the ground was too hard'; **Ass o glyb an dillas rag na's torras hi a dermyn** 'How wet the clothes were because she did not pick them (in) in time'.

Rag is also used as a co-ordinating conjunction with a negative **rag ny** (§288).

For causal clauses see §346.

§295 **Temporal**

A-BAN (v) 'since', see §294 above, used in a temporal sense: **A-ban goedhas ny'n jevydh ev na fella resek yn es** 'Since he fell, he can no longer run easily'.

BYS PAN (v) 'until when' is made up of the preposition **bys** 'until' and **pan** 'when'. The negative is **bys pan na**: **Garm bys pan y'th klywo!** 'Shout until he hears you!' **Mr Penngelli a oberi bys pan na'n jevo an nerth dhe besya** 'Mr Pengelly worked until he had not the strength to continue'.

ERNA (v) 'until' causes soft mutation and adds -g before vowels in **bos** 'be' and **mos** 'go'. It is not used in the negative: **Esedhyn omma war amal an als erna sedh an howl!** 'Let us sit here on the edge of the cliff until the sun sets!'

HEDRA (v) 'while, as long as' is followed by soft mutation but is used only before **bywa** 'live' and those tenses of **bos** 'be' which start with **b-**. This restriction is made up for by the use of **ha** 'and' describing attendant circumstances (§351). There is no negative: **Ny'n ankovav hedra vywiv** 'I shall not forget it as long as I live'; **Hedra vons hwath ow pleujyowa ny's torrav** 'While they are still flowering I shall not pick them'.

KYN (v) or (n) 'before': **kyn os re goth** 'before you are too old'.

KYNS/KYNS ES (n) 'before' is a preposition which introduces a noun phrase consisting of a verbal noun or of the infinitive construction (§141(19)). It adds **dell** 'as' to connect it with a verb: **kyns ev dhe dhifuna/kyns es ev dhe dhifuna** 'before he wakes/awoke', etc. lit. 'before he to awake'; **kyns es dell dhifun** 'before he awakes'; **kyns es dell dhifunas** 'before he awoke'.

KETTELL (v) 'as soon as' (**keth + dell**) is followed by soft mutation and accommodates an infixed pronoun by adding **y**: **Deber hi kettell vo hi pebys!** 'Eat it as soon as it is cooked!' **kettell y'n degemmeris** 'as soon as I received it'. There is no negative.

MAY (v) See §291 above. If preceded by an expression of time this particle can be translated as 'when': **y'n jydh may feu hi genys** 'on the day when she was born' (§347(1)).

PAN (v). See §294 above. The negative is **pan na** (v) 'when ... not': **Pan wrussens i gorfenna, i o lowen fest** 'When they had finished, they were very happy'; **Nyns eus kosk pan nag eus kosoleth** 'There is no sleep when there is no quiet'.

§295   Conjunctions

WAR-LERGH (n) 'after' is a preposition (§163(2)) which is followed by a verbal noun or by the infinitive construction (§141(19)): **War-lergh an edhen dhe derri an vleujenn, hi a's tewlis war an dor** 'After the bird had picked the blossom, it threw it on the ground'.

WOSA (n) 'after' is a preposition (§166(2)(3)) which introduces temporal expresssions made up of a verbal noun or of the infinitive construction (§141(19)): **Na dreyl wosa dalleth war an hyns!** 'Don't turn after starting on the way!' **Wosa an tri anedha dhe vyskemmeres an fordh ny's gwelsyn kyns hwegh eur, soweth!** 'After the three of them had mistaken the road we did not see them before six o'clock, unfortunately!'

For temporal clauses see §347.

§296 **Local**

MAY (v). See §291 above. When preceded by an expression of place this particle can be translated by 'where' or by various prepositional phrases, 'on which, to which', etc. according to the context. A preposition with its object may be used to define the relationship more closely: **An tyller may tyv an dherwenn goth yw an tyller may feu gwrys an kevambos** 'The place where the old oak grows is the place where the agreement was made'; **Diskwedh dhyn an men may ma an alhwedh yn-danno!** 'Show us the stone where/under which the key is!'

§297 **Comparative**

DELL (v) 'as' causes soft mutation and takes an added **y** to accommodate an infixed pronoun. **Dell** can be followed by the perfective particle **re** (§279): **Gwra dell vynnowgh!** 'Do as you will!' **Ny yll hi gul dell re ambosas hi** 'She cannot do as she promised'. More forceful versions are: **par dell, kepar ha dell** 'just as'.

KEPAR HA PAN (v) 'just as though' is used as **pan** (§274): **An maw a gramblas yn bann kepar ha pan ve sim** 'The boy scrambled up just as though he were a monkey'.

For comparative clauses see §348.

§298 **Final**

MAY (v) 'in order to'. See §291 above. **Rag may** is more precise: **An kaderyer a bonkyas war an voes rag may tallettha an kuntelles** 'The chairman banged on the table in order that the meeting might begin'. The negative is **ma na**: **Ni a with a yer a-ji krow nosweyth ma na's synsso an lowarn** 'We keep the hens in a shed at night so that the fox may not get them'. For final clauses see §349.

§299 **Consecutive**

MAY (v) 'that, so that, as a result'. See §291 above. With this meaning **may** is reinforced by adding **bys** 'until' (§140), **bys may: Ev a asas fenester an gegin yn igor bys mayth entras lader** 'He left the kitchen window open so that a thief got in'.

For consecutive clauses see §350.

§300 **Attendant circumstances**

HA(G) (n) (§283) introduces a phrase which describes the circumstances in which the principal action takes place: **Toeth da an vamm a gempennas an chambour ha'n tas ow koska orth an tan** 'Straight away mother tidied the bedroom while father was sleeping by the fire' (lit. 'and father sleeping ...'); **Pub huni a halya orth an lovan ha'n kapten ow karma, 'Tennewgh warbarth!'** 'Everyone hauled on the rope while the captain shouted, "Pull together!"' **Ha'n gath gyllys, y hyll an logos gwari** 'While the cat's away, the mice can play'.

For clauses of attendant circumstances see §351.

❖ ❖ ❖ ❖ ❖

SENTENCES

SENTENCE STRUCTURE

§301 **General** Sentences in Cornish are formed in one of two ways. In the first, the verbal phrase, consisting of a verbal particle, the verb and any associated adverbs, are put at the head of the sentence. These are called 'verbal sentences'.

In the second type of sentence a noun phrase consisting of a noun or pronominal, representing either the subject or the object, is put before the verb and linked to it by the particle **a** (§278) which is relative in origin, or by the particle **re** (§279) which is perfective. Sentences of this sort are called 'nominal sentences'.

These two types of construction are variously named elsewhere. The verbal sentence is called the inflected conjugation (Norris), the personal conjugation (Nance), the personal tense (Smith). The nominal sentence is called the impersonal conjugation (Norris, Nance), the impersonal tense (Smith), the emphasising relative or the relative circumlocution (Lewis and Pedersen). Since however the term 'impersonal' is also generally used for the neutral form of the verb, e.g. **gwelir** 'one sees' (§231) and since also the contrast is not strictly one of conjugation or of tense, the nomenclature 'verbal sentence' and 'nominal sentence' is used in this book.

VERBAL SENTENCES

§302 **Verbal sentences**, those giving precedence to the verb, have the following characteristics.

(1) The verb is preceded by a verbal particle. Affirmative sentences employ the particle **y** (§274): **Y hwolghas y dhewlagas gans y dhiwleuv** 'He washed his eyes with his hands'; **Yth eth dhe-dre** 'He went home'. An adverbial usually comes before the verb and its particle, whether relating to the whole sentence or to the verbal phrase alone: **Prest y sevis yn-bann** 'At once he got up'; **Sur y fynna ev mos** 'Surely he was wanting to go'. See (7) below.

The particle is rarely omitted: **Rov dhis ow ro** 'I give you my gift'; **Lemmyn hanwav an flogh ma** 'Now I name this child' in place of the regular **Y rov dhis ...; Lemmyn yth hanwav ...** Cf. §274(5).

240

§302(5) Sentences

Negative sentences are introduced by **ny** (§275) or by **na** (§276): **Ny balas ev y'n lowarth** 'He did not dig in the garden'; **Gwayt na fylli!** 'Mind you don't fail!' An adverbial can come before the particle: **Yn fenowgh ny gosk an kothwas moy es our** 'Often the old chap does not sleep more than an hour'.

Direct questions are introduced by the interrogative particle **a** (§277) or by adverbial interrogative words: **A gerowgh hwi an keth venyn?** 'Do you love the same woman?' **Ple trigsens i bys y'n eur na?** 'Where had they lived until that time?' See further the sections on questions, §320 and §330.

(2) The verb is inflected to show person, number, tense and mood: **A-dhiwar an leur y sevsyn** 'Up from the ground we rose', 1p. preterite and indicative being shown by the ending **-syn**.

(3) The subject of the sentence is shown by this verbal ending and is rendered in English by an appropriate pronoun: **I a wodhya y kowssen** 'They knew that I had spoken'; **Leversys** 'You said!' in answer to a question. The verbal ending may be reinforced by a suffixed pronoun (§64): **Y klywas ev** 'He heard'; **Y kerdhsyn ni** 'We walked'. The suffixed pronoun is necessarily used when a distinction has to be made between male and female: **Gans lavar hegar dhe beub yth hasas** 'With a kind word to all he/she left' being ambiguous. The suffixed pronoun is also usefully added in questions: **A wodhowgh hwi konvedhes?** 'Do you understand?'

(4) Alternatively the subject of the verb can be a separate noun or noun phrase in apposition to the subject implied in the verbal ending. This noun or noun phrase follows the verb, which remains singular even when the subject is plural: **Y resas fenten dowr** 'A spring of water gushed out'; **Ternos y sordyas an vresel** 'Next day the war broke out'. With plural subject: **Hware y poenyas an fleghes** 'Straight away the children ran hard'.

(5) If the verb has a direct object it can be a noun or a noun phrase. It usually follows the verb, coming after the subject if this is separately expressed: **Dhymm yth ystynnas y leuv** 'To me he extended his hand'; **Ny gar an ki palas y'n dor** 'The dog is not fond of digging in the ground', where the whole phrase, **palas y'n dor** is the object of the verb.

The direct object can also take the form of an infixed pronoun (§65) and it comes between the particle and the verb: **War an voes y'n gorras ev** 'On the table he put it'; **Wosa henna y'gan gweresas ow klanhe an karr** 'After that he helped us clean the car'.

(6) An anticipatory noun subject may be put before the verb and its particle in apposition to the subject implied in the verbal ending: **Y wordhya y telledh dhis** 'Praising him is proper or you', OM. 1775.

The same process can be applied to a noun object: **Ha'm bennath y rov dhis** 'And my blessing I give to you'. When a noun object is thus transposed an infixed pronoun is usually inserted to refer back to the object: **Ha'n loer y's gwelav** 'And the moon I see her' (§65(5)).

The purpose of this construction is to place emphasis on the subject or object and it is appropriate to a poetic or rhetorical style.

(7) Adverbial expressions occur anywhere in the sentence except between the particle and its verb or between the parts of other close syntactic groupings such as the article and its noun: **Distowgh y harmas** 'At once he called out'; **Y teuthons omma** 'They came here'; **Dre unn skochfordh y poenyas (hi)** 'Through a certain short cut she ran', MC. 164.5. See above, (1).

(8) Sentences which serve as subordinate clauses and which are introduced by the conjunctions described in §290 to §299, being there marked (v), are always verbal sentences.

NOMINAL SENTENCES

§303 **Nominal sentences**, those giving prominence to the subject or to the object, are relative in origin and arose as follows. When the subject or the object was to be emphasised it was made the complement of a sentence after a tense of **bos** 'be' §331(1) and the remainder of the statement followed as a relative sentence: **Yth yw my a dheber bara** 'It is I who eat bread'; **Yth yw bara a dhebrav** 'It is bread which I eat'. The introductory phrase then fell away to leave **My a dheber bara** and **Bara a dhebrav** respectively. These two statements may be taken to be replies to the implied questions, **Piw a dheber bara?** 'Who eats bread?' and **Pandr'a dhybrydh?** 'What do you eat?' respectively.

The form with the subject before the verb as in the first example lost its emphasising character in Cornish and became the normal type of affirmative statement (§309).

Nominal sentences have the following characteristics:

§303(5) Sentences

(1) When the subject comes first in the form of a noun or a pronominal, it is linked to the verb by the relative particles **a** or **re** as explained above: **An howl a splann** 'The sun shines'; **Ev a lever yndella** 'He says so'. Since the grammatical subject of the sentence is in fact the particle **a**, the verb agrees with it and so remains 3s. whatever the number and person of the logical subject: **My a dyb** 'I think'; **An ydhyn a gana hweg** 'The birds sang sweetly'; **Hwi a woer oll an dra** 'You know it all'.

If the perfective particle **re** (§279) is used before the verb, the particle **a** is omitted: **An flogh re dorras klegh an eos y'n gelli** 'The child has picked harebells in the wood'.

(2) The direct object of the verb can similarly be placed before it and joined to it by the relative particle **a**: **Henna a gasav** 'That I hate'; **Kowl a brensons** 'Cabbage they bought'. The particle **a** is now the grammatical object of the sentence and so in this case the verb is inflected to show the person and number of the subject: **An daras a igorav pan vo edhomm** 'The door I open when there is a need'.

When the perfective particle **re** is put before the verb, the particle **a** is omitted as above (1): **Pronter minrew re welis a-bervedh an eglos** 'A grey-bearded parson I have seen in the church'.

When an interrogative pronoun stands as object to the verb, a question results: **Pandr'a dorras ev, ytho?** 'What did he break, then?' (§320-§321).

(3) The direct object is either a noun which follows the verb: **Spavenn a holyas an hager awel** 'A calm followed the storm', or an infixed pronoun which comes betweeen particle **a** and the verb: **Ena ni a's syghas** 'Then we dried them'.

(4) Ambiguity can arise when both the subject and the object of the verb are nouns: **An ki a shyndyas an fleghes** may be either 'The dog hurt the children', which would be the more normal interpretation, or, more rarely, 'The children hurt the dog'. In most cases the context of the utterance will decide the matter but an alternative construction is possible: **An fleghes a veu shyndys gans an ki** 'The children were injured by the dog' or **An ki a veu shyndys gans an fleghes** 'The dog was injured by the children'.

(5) The remarks made above about the position of adverbial phrases apply in nominal sentences also: **Ganso hi a driga**; **Hi ganso a driga**; **Hi a driga ganso** 'She used to live with him', with varying emphasis on the several elements of the sentence.

COMPOUND CONSTRUCTIONS

§304 **Auxiliary verbs**

The verbs **gul** 'do, make' (§225), **mynnes** 'be willing' (§226), **galloes** 'be able' (§227) and, to a lesser extent, **godhvos** 'know how to, understand' (§200) are used with a verbal noun as a direct object (§238). Employed in this way they are conveniently known as auxiliary verbs because they help with the formation of the verbal phrase. Either of the constructions described in §302 and §303 can be used.

Verbal sentence: **Pub dydh y hwrav mos di** 'Every day I shall go there'.

Nominal sentence: **My a wra mos di pub dydh**, with approximately the same meaning but with a variation in emphasis according to which part of the sentence is said first.

(1) The verbal noun may itself have an object: **My a yll nivera an bleujennow** 'I can count the (individual) flowers'. If this object is a pronoun it is represented by a possessive adjective with the verbal noun: **My a yll aga nivera** 'I can count them', lit. 'I can their counting'; **Ow hommendya dhedha a wrug ev** 'He introduced me to them', lit. 'My introducing to them he did'.

This possessive adjective representing the direct object of the verbal noun is sometimes inserted redundantly to connect with a noun or pronoun object already placed first for emphasis: **An lovan my a yll hy therghi** '(As to) the rope I can coil it'. The possessive adjective need not be used in this case: **An lovan my a yll terghi** is adequate but less precise. So **Hemma ty a vynn y witha** or **Hemma ty a vynn gwitha** '(As to) this you will look after it'. Cf. §65(5).

(2) The object of a verbal noun which is itself the direct object of one of the verbs **gul, mynnes, galloes, godhvos** may be put before the verb and linked to it by the particle **a** and thus come to stand as the direct object of that verb. The verbal noun being displaced in this way is connected to the verbal phrase in one of two ways:

(a) The first method is to put the preposition **dhe** 'to' before the verbal noun (§141(16)): **An gwel diworth an leur gwrav dhe dreghi** 'The stems from the ground I shall cut' (**gwrav** for **a wrav**), OM. 1987-88; **dydh a vynn dhe dhewis** 'a date he will choose'. The construction is found in relative sentences:

244

§305(4) Sentences

Dog alena an tri gwel a wrug Moyses dhe blansa! 'Take from there the three stems which Moses planted!', OM. 1945-46; **Meur ras a'n gweres a vynnowgh dhe wul dhymmo** 'Thank you for the help which you wish to give me'; **Yw hemma an gwella a yllons dhe wul?** 'Is this the best they can do?' **chyf weythoryon oll a'n wlas a wodhor dhe dhismygi** 'all the chief workmen of the land that one may think of', OM. 2331-32.

Questions commonly have this form: **Pandra a vynn'ta dhe wul?** 'What do you want to do?' **Py tesenn a yll hi dhe bobas?** 'What cake can she make?'

(b) The second method is to put the appropriate possessive adjective before the verbal noun: **Pana ji a wrug ev y dhrehevel?** 'What house did he build?' lit. What house did he its building?' **Py yeth a woer hi hy hewsel gwella?** 'Which language does she speak best?' **Piw a vynnons i y dhewis?** 'Whom will they choose?'

(c) If, in affirmative statements, this transference of object does not occur, then the particle is **y**: **Dydh y fynn ev dewis** 'A date he will choose', emphasising the term **dydh**.

§305 **GUL** used as an auxiliary defines the tense, person and mood of the verbal phrase and thus provides the grammatical framework which the verbal noun completes by naming the action.

(1) Since the present/future of **gul**, which is **gwra** 'does, will do', is thus separately stated, the compound construction comes to denote a simple future: **Ni a wra mos dhe Bennsans** 'We shall go to Penzance'; **An dowr a wra kudha an garrek kyns pell** 'The water is going to cover the rock before long'.

(2) The same consideration applies to the imperfect when it means 'the future in the past' in indirect speech (§228(4)): A-**dhistowgh y leveris ev y hwre doen an begh** 'At once he said (that) he would carry the load'.

(3) In replies to questions, instead of repeating the verb used in a previous utterance, the appropriate part of **gul** can be used: **Ke dhe dhegea an fenester!** 'Go and shut the window!' **Gwrav!** 'I shall do (so)!' **A gewsis ev yndella?** 'Did he speak so?' **Gwrug!** 'He did!' in place of the alternative answers **Av!** 'I go!' and **Kewsis!** 'He spoke (so)!' (§321).

(4) **Gul** and a verbal noun are used to form an imperative: **Gwra esedha!** 'Do sit down!' **Na wrewgh ow gasa!** 'Do not leave me!' **Gwres ev y denna yn-mes a'n dowr!** 'Let him pull him out of the water!'

§305(5)   Sentences

(5) In final clauses which state the purpose of the action, **gul** is followed by **may** 'that' and a tense of the subjunctive: **Ni a wra may fo gwell** 'We shall bring it about that it be better'.

(6) **Gul** is, of course, used as a verb in its own right: **gul da/drog** 'do good/evil'; **gul negys** 'do an errand/business'; **gul son** 'make a sound'; **gul tra** 'make/ create something'; **gul les** 'cause benefit'; **gul dughan** 'cause grief'; **gul prov** 'prove'; **gul dhe nebonan gul neppyth** 'cause/make someone do something' (§141(7)); **gul vri** 'hold in esteem' (§23(3d)).

(7) The verb **gul** may take two direct objects: **gul kledha sogh** 'make a sword (into) a ploughshare'; **My a'n gwra ow howeth** 'I will make him my friend'.

So with other verbs with the general sense of making something into something else. Such are **ordena** 'appoint'; **sakra** 'consecrate, ordain'; **henwel** 'name'; **gelwel** 'name' (§231).

§306 **MYNNES** (§226) implies a willingness, a wish, an intention to do something; cf. **mynnes** *m.* 'a wish, will, purpose, intention, desire'. It is therefore only applicable to sentient beings or to personalised objects: **Mamm a vynn pobas tesenn** 'Mother will bake a cake'; **Myns a vynno y weres, y'n gwres!** 'Whoever wishes to help him, let him do it!' **A vynn'ta kavoes sugra?** 'Will you have sugar?' **Ev a leveris y fynna an gwyns distrui an chi yn tien** 'He said that the wind would destroy the house entirely' (implying a degree of intention on the part of the wind).

(1) The same variety of constructions is found in verbal or nominal sentences, and the same combinations of word order are found with **mynnes** as with **gul**: **Hi a vynn kempenna hy chambour kyns gasa an chi** 'She will tidy her bedroom before leaving the house'; **Gul war dha lergh my a vynn** 'I wish to follow you in what you do'; **Lemmyn y fynnons skoedhya ken bagas** 'Now they will support another party'; **Skrifa a vynna y das dhodho** 'His father would write to him'. See further the sections on word order, (§309-§319).

(2) The direct object of **mynnes** may be the infinitive construction with **dhe** and a verbal noun (§141(19)): **My a vynn hi dhe dhos** 'I wish her to come'; **Piw a vynn my dh'y weres?** 'Who wishes me to help him?' If the verb **bos** is the direct object of **mynnes** it may also have its subject represented by a dependent noun or pronoun: **Ev a vynnas bos an kuntelles synsys** 'He wished the meeting to be held'; **Toeth da y fynnsyn y vos gwrys** 'Straightaway we wished it to be done' (§336(1)).

(3) Alternatively the conjunction **may** 'that' and a tense of the subjunctive can be used in a final clause: **Hi a vynn may fo ev brewys** 'She wants it to be broken into pieces'; **Prest y fynna may hwrella da** 'He was always intending that he should do good' (§336(3)).

(4) With the preposition **orth** to mark the indirect object, **mynnes** translates the English 'want someone to ...': **Pub huni a vynn orti gortos** 'Everyone wants her to stay'. Again the direct object can be represented by a tense of the subjunctive after **may** 'that': **Pub huni a vynn may hworto** (§152(4)).

(5) The contrast between the simple and the intended future is seen in the following examples: **Ternos yth a ev tramor** and **Ternos y hwra ev mos tramor** 'Tomorrow he goes abroad', both meaning only that the event is going to happen, whereas **Ternos y fynn ev mos tramor** indicates an intention or a willingness to do so on the part of the person spoken of.

§307 **GALLOES** (§227). The ability, the power to do anything, the existence of circumstances which allow the act to take place, are all expressed by **galloes**; cf. **galloes** m. 'power, ability, control, might': **I a allsa gweles an tour alena** 'They would be able to see the tower from there'; **Hemma a yll bos** 'This can be, is possible'; **Y hyllir dismygi** 'It can be imagined'.

(1) The variety of constructions is also found with either the verbal or the nominal type of sentence are used with **galloes** also: **Heb gow vydh y hallav leverel henna** 'Without any lie I can say that'; **An ki ma a yll omwitha** 'This dog can look after itself'; **Bythkweth ny yllens i ervira** 'They were never able to decide'; **Ty a allas eva an koffi na** 'You were able to drink that coffee'; **Klywes a allsons** 'They could (were able to) hear'; **Lies gwydhenn a yllyn aga homptya** 'Many trees we can count'. See further the sections on word order, (§309-§319).

(2) Phrases with **galloes** in a relative sentence can be regarded as equivalent to the English adjectives in -able, -ible, etc. The generalised sense of these words is provided in one of two ways:

(a) By the use of the impersonal form of the verb: **hwedhel a yllir y grysi** 'a credible story'; **studh a yllir y berthi** 'an endurable state'; **tros a yllir y glywes** 'an audible sound'. If the noun which is to be qualified in this way is governed by a verbal noun and a preposition, e.g. **krysi dhe** 'believe', **trestya yn** 'trust in', etc., then the conjunction **may** is used in place of the particle **a**: **gour may hyllir krysi dhodho** 'a credible man'; **kowetha may hyllir trestya ynna** 'trustworthy friends'; **fos a yllir tremena dredhi** 'a penetrable wall' (§342(2)).

(b) The second way of stating the general nature of the quality concerned is to use a 3s. tense of **galloes** with the verbal noun **bos** 'be' and an appropriate past participle: **dowr a yll bos evys** 'drinkable, potable water'; **arwoedh a yll bos gwelys** 'a visible sign'.

Negatives of these expressions are formed by using **na** or **ma na** before the verb: **gwriow na yllons bos gwelys** 'invisible stitching'; **Koes ma na yllir tremena dredho** 'an impenetrable wood'. See also adjectives in -**adow** (§79(4)) and the prefix **he-** (§273).

§308 **GODHVOS** (§200) is used in the particular sense of knowing how to, of being mentally able to do something: **Konnyk ywa, ev a woer ewna y garr** 'He is clever, he knows how to mend his car', whereas **Ev a yll ewna y garr** would mean not only that he knew how to do so but also that circumstances were favourable to his doing so. **Konvedhes an yeth a wodhyens** 'They understood the language'.

WORD ORDER

The choice of construction and of word order is not arbitrary. Both arise from the circumstances of the utterance, the context in which the utterance is placed and the need to indicate changing points of interest. In describing the various types of word order the elements **an diogyon** 'the farmers' as subject, a verbal particle **gwerth** 'sell' as verb and **leth** 'milk' as object are used to form model sentences.

Affirmative statements

§309 The normal form of affirmative statement in principal sentences is the nominal sentence (§303) with the following patterns:

(1) Noun subject and noun object:
An diogyon a werth leth   'The farmers sell milk'

(2) Noun subject and pronoun object:
An diogyon a'n gwerth   'The farmers sell it'

(3) Pronoun subject and noun object:
I a werth leth   'They sell milk'

(4) Pronoun subject and pronoun object:
I a'n gwerth   'They sell it'

§313 Sentences

The verb may be in any tense but in the 3s. of that tense.

(5) **I a werthi leth** 'They used to sell milk'

The perfective particle **re** (§279) may be used in place of the particle **a**:

(6) **An diogyon re werthas leth** 'The farmers have sold milk'

§310 If the noun object is to be emphasised one of the following nominal patterns may be used:

(1) **Leth an diogyon a werth** 'Milk the farmers sell'

(2) **Leth a werth an diogyon** 'Milk the farmers sell'

(3) **Leth a werthons** 'Milk they sell'

§311 If an adverbial phrase is to be emphasised, the above forms are used with the adverbial expression first:

(1) **Pub dydh an diogyon a werth leth** 'Every day the farmers sell milk'

§312 If the whole verbal phrase with its adverbial element is to be emphasised, a verbal sentence (§302) may be used.

(1) **Pub dydh y hwerth an diogyon leth** 'Every day the farmers sell milk'

(2) **Pub dydh y hwerthons leth** 'Every day they sell milk'

(3) **Pub dydh y'n gwerth an diogyon** 'Every day the farmers sell it'

(4) **Pub dydh y'n gwerthons** 'Every day they sell it'

§313 Affirmative subordinate sentences are always verbal (§302):

(1) **Gwir yw y hwerth an diogyon leth** 'It is true (that) the farmers sell milk'

(2) **Gwir yw y'n gwerth an diogyon** 'It is true (that) the farmers sell it'

(3) **Gwir yw y hwerthons leth** 'It is true (that) they sell milk'

(4) **Gwir yw y'n gwerthons** 'It is true (that) they sell it'.

See further the chapter on subordinate sentences.

Negative statements

§314 The verb is made negative by putting **ny(ns)** (§275) or in certain circumstances **na(g)** (§276) before it. Negative sentences, whether principal or subordinate, are always verbal sentences and their syntax is described in §302.

(1) **Ny werth an diogyon leth** — 'The farmers do not sell milk'

(2) **Ny'n gwerth an diogyon** — 'The farmers do not sell it'

(3) **Ny werthons leth** — 'They do not sell milk'

(4) **Ny'n gwerthons** — 'They do not sell it'

(5) **Gwir yw na werth an diogyon leth** — 'It is true (that) the farmers do not sell milk'

(6) **Gwir yw na'n gwerth an diogyon** — 'It is true (that) the farmers do not sell it'

(7) **Gwir yw na werthons leth** — 'It is true (that) they do not sell milk'

(8) **Gwir yw na'n gwerthons** — 'It is true (that) they do not sell it'

§315 Into the affirmative and negative statements described in sections §309-§314 one or another of the auxiliary verbs may be introduced to add the ideas of simple futurity (**gul**), volition (**mynnes**) and ability (**galloes**). The auxiliary becomes the main verb and the accompanying verbal noun is its direct object. The several variations of word order follow those described above.

The verbal noun itself may have an object and if this is a pronoun it is represented by a possessive adjective before the verbal noun. See also the sections on auxiliary verbs, §304-§308.

Examples:

(1) **An diogyon a vynn gwertha leth** — 'The farmers will sell milk'

(2) **An diogyon a vynn y wertha** — 'The farmers will sell it'

(3) **Ny vynn an diogyon gwertha leth** — 'The farmers will not sell milk'

(4) **Ny vynn an diogyon y wertha** — 'The farmers will not sell it'

§316 A noun or an independent pronominal can be put before the verbal phrase as an anticipatory subject and is picked up by the verbal ending:

(1) **An spiser ny'n gwerth**   'The grocer he doesn't sell it'

(2) **Ev ny werth leth**   'He, he does not sell milk'

(3) **An diogyon ny werthons leth**   'The farmers they do not sell milk'

(4) **I ny werthons leth**   'They, they do not sell milk'

Note that the verb agrees in number with the plural anticipatory subject.

§317 A noun object may be emphasised by being placed before the particle at the head of the sentence:

(1) **Leth ny werth an diogyon**   'The farmers do not sell milk'

(2) **Leth ny werthons**   'They do not sell milk'

This second form can be ambiguous, e.g. **An fleghes ny welsons** may be either 'They did not see the children', the subject being the pronoun implicit in the verbal ending, or '(As to) the children, they did not see'. Cf. §316(1).

§318 The patterns of word order using auxiliary verbs which are described in the above sections are those used in normal speech and writing, but other combinations using the two variables separateness and precedence can be used to give shades of emphasis, variations of style in rhetorical or poetical contexts. The emphasis is on those parts of the statement which come first.

(1) Examples of positive statements.   Emphasis on:

   Gwertha leth a vynn an diogyon   'selling milk, will'
   Gwertha leth a vynnons   'selling milk'
   Y wertha a vynnons   'selling it'
   Gwertha leth an diogyon a vynn   'selling milk, the farmers'
   Y wertha an diogyon a vynn   'selling it, the farmers'
   Y wertha i a vynn   'selling it, they'
   Pub dydh y fynn an diogyon gwertha leth 'every day, will'
   Pub dydh y fynnons gwertha leth   'every day, they will'
   Pub dydh y fynnons y wertha   'every day, they will'

§318(2)   Sentences

(2) Examples of negative statements.   Emphasis on:

Gwertha leth ny vynn an diogyon   'selling milk'
Y wertha ny vynn an diogyon   'selling it'
Y wertha ny vynnons   'selling it'
Gwertha leth an diogyon ny vynnons   'selling milk'
Y wertha i ny vynnons   'selling it'
An diogyon ny vynnons gwertha leth   'the farmers'

§319 Although all the examples of normal and less usual word orders given above use a transitive verb, **gwertha**, the same principles apply when an intransitive verb occurs.

(1) Normal orders are:

An benynes a gan   'The women sing'
I a gan   'They sing'
Yn hweg y kan an benynes   'Sweetly the women sing'
Yn hweg y kanons (i)   'Sweetly they sing'
Ny gan an benynes   'The women do not sing'
Ny ganons (i)   'They do not sing'

(2) With an auxiliary:

An benynes a yll kana   'The women can sing'
I a yll kana   'They can sing'
Yn hweg y hyll an benynes kana   'Sweetly the women can sing'

Yn hweg y hyllons (i) kana   'Sweetly they can sing'
Ny yll an benynes kana   'The women cannot sing'
Ny yllons (i) kana   'They cannot sing'

(3) Other possible orders.   Emphasising:

An benynes i a gan   'The women'
An benynes yn hweg a gan   'The women, sweetly'
An benynes ny ganons (i)   'The women'
Kana a yll an benynes   'Sing'
Kana ny yll an benynes   'Sing'
Kana ny yllons (i)   'Sing'

QUESTIONS AND ANSWERS

Questions are introduced by the interrogative particle **a** (§277) or by an interrogative pronominal or adverb. These interrogative words are linked to the remainder of the sentence in various ways as explained below.

§320 The interrogative **a** and its negative **a ny(ns)** are both followed directly by an inflected verb in a verbal sentence: **A goenowgh hwi?** 'Do you take a late dinner?' **A ny skubsa hi an leur?** 'Had she not swept the floor?' **A nyns a ev dhe Bennsans?** 'Isn't he going to Penzance?'

(1) The subject follows the verb as a noun or a suffixed pronoun (§64): **A red an den na?** 'Does that person read?' **A dhesevsons i yndella?** 'Did they suppose so?' If the noun subject is plural, the verb remains in the singular: **A woer an wesyon nag yw gwir?** 'Do the fellows know that it is not true?'

(2) The object, when a noun, comes after the verb and after the suffixed subject: **A werths'ta dha ji hwath?** 'Have you sold your house yet?' **A berghenna Mtr Leti an gwerthji na?** 'Did Mr Laity own that shop?' So in compound constructions with an auxiliary verb: **A ny vynnons i gweres aga broder?** 'Aren't they willing to help their brother?'

(3) A pronoun object is either an infixed pronoun: **A's terrsons i** 'Have they broken it?' or, in the case of the compound construction, a possessive adjective: **A yllons i hy ewna?** 'Can they mend it?'

(4) The interrogative particle is omitted before initial vowels in forms of **bos** 'be' and **mos** 'go': **Osta lowen?** 'Are you happy?' **Eth an dus di?** 'Did the people go there?

(5) The particle is also left out after an interjection, though the mutation which would follow it remains: **P'yw! Grys ev henna?** 'What! Does he believe that?' **Pla! Ny's gwelsys?** 'What a nuisance! Didn't you see her?'

(6) A noun object may precede the verbal phrase, especially if it is a verbal noun in the compound construction: **Kommol a wel'ta?** 'Do you see clouds?' **Krysi dhedhi a ny wre'ta?** 'Don't you believe her?' In these cases an interjection can precede without the omission of the particle **a** mentioned in (5) above: **Dar! Krysi dhedhi a wre'ta?** 'What! Do you believe her?;' **Ty wokki! Krysi dhedhi a ny wre'ta?** 'Stupid! Won't you believe her?'

§321
Sentences

§321 Answers to questions introduced by **a**, **a ny(ns)** repeat the verb of the question in the appropriate person, without a particle if affirmative: **A wodhesta an fordh?** 'Do you know the road?' **Gonn!** 'Yes!' lit. 'I know!' **A redyas Jowann an lyther?** 'Did John read the letter?' **Redyas!** 'Yes!' lit. 'He read!'

Negative replies repeat the verb in an appropriate person with **na** (§276(2)) put before it: **A gowssons i dhis?** 'Did they speak to you?', **Na gowssons!** 'They did not!' lit. 'They spoke not!'

A form of **gul** 'do, make' may be used in place of the particular verb (§305(3)): **A gavas dha gowethes hy hath?** 'Did your friend find her cat?' may be answered either as above or by **Gwrug!** '(She) did!' or **Na wrug!** 'She did not!'

§322 Indirect questions are introduced by **mar** 'if', **mar ny(ns)** 'if not', in place of **a**: **Govynn orto mars yw homma an fordh dhe Logh** 'Ask him if this is the way to Looe'; **Gyllys yw Myrna dhe weles mar kyll hi kavoes boesti** 'Myrna has gone to see if she can find a restaurant'; **Lavar dhymm mar ny wodhesta konvedhes an lyver ma** 'Tell me if you cannot understand this book' (§344(5)).

§323 **FATELL** 'how' (§77) is followed by an inflected verb in a verbal sentence and is used in direct and in indirect questions: **Fatell vydh hi ganso?** 'How will it be with him?' **Fatell yll henna bos?** 'How can that be?' **Ny wodhon fatell vydh hi ganso** 'We do not know how it will be with him'; **Deriv dhodho fatell a puptra omma!** 'Tell him how everything goes here'. A negative question is either simple or in the form of a relative clause, in both cases with **na(g)** as the particle: **Hemma a dhiskwedh fatell na yllir koela orta** 'This shows how one cannot trust them; **Fatell yw hi na dheuth hi tre a-dermyn?** 'How is it that she did not come home on time?'

A reply to a question introduced by **fatell** takes the form of an adverbial phrase, whether incorporated into a sentence or not: **Fatell a ev dhe Garesk?** 'How is he going to Exeter?' **Yn y garr yth a di** 'In his car he will go there' or merely **Yn y garr** 'In his car'.

§324 **PRAG** 'why' (§74(16)), **PY KOST, PY LE, PY PLAS, PY TYLLER**, 'where' (§74(14)), **PESKWEYTH** 'how often', **PES TERMYN** 'how long' (§76), all interrogative adverbs, are followed by a verbal sentence which starts with the particle **y**. These adverbs are used in both direct and indirect questions: **Prag y fynnons i gortos?** 'Why will they wait?; **Py kost y trig hi lemmyn?** 'Where does she live now?' **Peskweyth y'n jevydh prys boes?** 'How often

§326 does he have a meal?' **Leverewgh dhedha py le yth oberowgh!** 'Tell them where you work!'

Prag when negative is followed by **na**: **Prag na vynnewgh kammenn gwari peldroes?** 'Why would you not play football at all?'

§325 When replying to **prag**, **prag na** a causal clause is appropriate (§346): **Prag y hwyster ev?** 'Why does he whisper?' **Awos bos anwoes warnodho (y hwyster)** 'Because he has a cold (he whispers)'; **Prag na dheber hi meur?** 'Why doesn't she eat much?' **Drefenn bos dhedhi hwans a omvoenhe (ny dheber hi meur)** 'Because she wants to be slim (she doesn't eat much)'.

Replies to questions with **py kost**, etc. supply the information asked for in place of the interrogative word, the remainder of the sentence, if uttered, being unchanged: **Py tyller y fydh synsys an kuntellyans?** 'Where will the meeting be held?' **Yn Ponsmeur (y fydh synsys an kuntellyans)** 'In Grampound (the meeting will be held)'; **Peskweyth y hwolghons an garth?** 'How often do they wash the yard?' **Diwweyth y'n jydh (y hwolghons an garth)** 'Twice a day (they wash the yard)'.

§326 **PLE** 'where' (§74(12)), **A BLE** 'whence, from where' (§74(13)), **PY** 'where' (§75), **P'EUR** 'when' (§74(15)), are all followed directly by an inflected verb in a verbal sentence without the intervention of a particle. They cause fifth state mutation which perhaps is a sign that **y** (§274) has dropped away here: **Ple fydh an nosweyth lowen?** 'Where will the 'Nosweyth lowen' be?' **Pyth ethons i?** 'Where did they go?' **A ble'feu an bysow brav na?** '(From) where did you get that fine ring?' **P'eur hassons i an chi?** 'When did they leave the house?' Negative questions are introduced directly by **ny(ns)**: **Ple ny yllyn ni esedha?** 'Where can we not sit?' A relative form can be used: **Py le yn bys eus ma nag ethons?** 'Where in the world have they not been?' **P'eur yw ma na vydh igor an gwithti?** 'When is it that the museum is not open?' These questions are answered by replacing the interrogative word with the information asked for, followed by a verbal sentence introduced by **y** if a full statement is required. Thus alernative replies to the above questions might be: **Yn hel an dre (y fydh an nosweyth lowen)** 'In the town hall (the 'Nosweyth lowen' will be)'; **Dhe Vosvenegh (yth ethons)** 'To Bodmin (they went)'; **A-dhiworth ow mamm wynn (y'm beu ev)** 'From my grandmother (I had it)'; **Nyhewer (y hassons an chi)** 'Last night (they left the house)';

In the negative form: **Y'n rew a-rag (ny yllowgh esedha)** 'In the front row (you cannot sit')'; **Dhe'n Statow Unys (nyns ethons)** 'To the United States (they have not been)'; **An Yow (yw ma na vydh igor an gwithti)** 'On

§326 Sentences

Thursday (it is that the museum is not open)'.

§327 **PIW** 'who' (§73(1)), **PANDRA** 'what' (§74(4)), **PY RE** 'which ones' (§74(6)), **PY SEUL** (§74(10)), **PYGEMMYS** 'how much, how many'(§74(8)), **PY LIES** 'how much, how many'(§74(9)), **PYTH** 'what' (§74(5)), **PY SORT, PY KINDA, PY EGHENN, PY PAR** 'what kind of' (§74(11)), are all constructed with the particle **a** linking them to the verb. In this position they stand as either the subject or the object of a nominal sentence. The question can be direct or indirect:

Subject: **Piw a wra pareusi an te?** 'Who is going to get the tea ready?' **Py lies a vynn omdenna?** 'How many wish to withdraw?' **Py eghenn a byw y'n gwylvos?** 'What species lives in the desert?' **Ny wonn piw yns** 'I do not know who they are'.

Object: **Pandr'a wrug ev dhodho?** 'What did he do to it?' **Py re a dorrsons i?** 'Which ones did they break?' **Pygemmys a ros dhis?** 'How much did he give you?' **Sur y hwoer hi pyth a yll hi y wul** 'Of course she knows what she can do'.

A negative question is direct or relative using **ny(ns)** or **na(g)** respectively: **Piw ny gerdh pub dydh?** 'Who does not walk every day?' **Piw yw na gerdh pub dydh?** 'Who is it who does not walk every day?' **Py lies anedha ny vynnons mos?** 'How many of them do not wish to go?' **Py eghenn a viles ny's tevydh edhomm a eva?** 'What kind of animals have no need to drink?' **Py eghenn a viles eus na's tevydh edhomm a eva?** 'What kind of animals are there which have no need to drink?'

Answers to this type of question replace the interrogative word with the information asked for, the remainder of the sentence, if it is to be repeated, remaining unchanged: **Piw yw ev?** 'Who is he?' **Skrifennyas an Konsel (yw ev)** 'The Secretary of the Council (he is)'; **Pandr'a wel'ta?** 'What do you see?' **Tewlder (a welav) a bub tu hepken** 'Darkness (I see) on every side, nothing else'; **Pygemmys a brensons i?** 'How much did they buy?' **Tri hanspoes (a brensons)** 'Three hundredweight (they bought)'; **Pandra ny ('n) (g)welas ev?** 'What did he not see?' **An grows y'n gorflann ny(s) (g)welas** 'The cross in the churchyard (he did not see)'; **Piw y'ga mysk eus ma nag yw da gansa gweres?** 'Who amongst them are there who is not glad to help?' lit. 'that it is not good with them helping'.

§328 **PY, PAN, PANA,** 'what' (§74(1),(2),(3)), **PYNEYL** 'which of two' (§74(7)), **PES** 'how much (§76), dependent interrogatives, function as

§330   Sentences

adjectives and the type of construction used in the question will depend on the status of the noun which they accompany. Usually this noun will be a subject or an object and the sentence will be a nominal one, the particle **a** being used: **Pyneyl chi yw gwell gensi?** 'Which house (of two) does she prefer?' **Pana desenn a gerydh jy?** 'Which cake do you like?' **Pes termyn a'th eus?** 'How much time have you got?'

In other cases the noun will be part of an adverbial construction: **Py gwerthji y prenas hi an krys ynno?** 'In which shop did she buy the shirt?' **Py mis y fydh dha benn-bloedh?** '(In) which month will your birthday be?' **Pana bons y hyllir treusi an avon warnodho?** 'Which bridge can one cross the river on?'

Negative questions take the following forms:

Direct: **Py lyver nyns yw ev dhe redya?** 'Which book is not to be read?' **Pana gusul ny bleg dhodho?** 'What advice does not please him?'

or relative: **Py lyver yw nag yw dhe redya?** and **Pana gusul yw na bleg dhodho?**

Replies to the questions introduced by these words replace the interrogative with the information asked for: **An huni ughella (yw gwell gensi)** 'The higher one (she prefers)'; **Yn Marks ha Spencer (y'n prenas)** 'In Marks and Spencer (she bought it)'.

§329 As with affirmative and negative sentences, questions may have the compound construction with an auxiliary verb and a verbal noun: **A vynn ev eva banna korev?** 'Will he drink a drop of beer?' **A vynn ev y eva** 'Will he drink it?' **Eva banna korev a vynn ev?** 'Drink a drop of beer, will he?' **Eva a vynn ev banna korev?** 'Drink will he a drop of beer?' etc.

Answers will repeat the auxiliary verb in the appropriate person: **Mynn!** 'He will!' **Na vynn!** 'He will not!'

§330 Oblique questions are those in which the noun or the pronoun which names the topic is neither subject nor object to the verb but stands in some other relationship to it, often defined by a preposition: 'by whom', 'by what', 'to whom', 'to what', etc. Some examples have been given above.

The interrogative word begins the sentence and is followed later in the sentence by the appropriate preposition referring back to the interrogative word. The verb is preceded by the particle **y**: **Py lyver y fynnowgh hwi redya anodho?**

§330 Sentences

'What book do you wish to read from?' **Piw y feu hemma gwrys ganso?** 'By whom was this done?' **Pandra y hyll hi gorra an seth warnodho?** 'What can she put the jar on?' **Piw y sev orto?** 'Whom does he oppose?'

For variation of style or of emphasis the preposition can be placed after the interrogative word: **Piw ganso y feu hemma gwrys?** 'By whom was this done?' **Pandra warnodho y hyll hi gorra an seth?** 'What can she put the jar on?' **Py lyver anodho y fynnowgh hwi redya?** 'What book do you wish to read from?' **Piw orto y sev ev?** 'Whom does he oppose?' Indirect questions of this nature have the same form: **Diskwedh dhymm pyneyl kyst yma an euryor ynni!** 'Show me which box the watch is in!' **Leveres piw ganso y feu gwyskys!** 'Let him say by whom he was struck!' cf. PD. 1373.

This construction is analogous to that with **prag** = **py** + **rag** 'what for' and a following verb introduced by **y** (§74(16)) and (§324).

Note that the interrogative pronoun **piw** may be governed directly by **gans** and by **dhe**: **Gans piw y feu hemma gwrys?** 'By whom was this done?' **Dhe biw yw an lyver ma?** 'Whose is this book?' (§254).

THE VERB *BOS* IN SENTENCES

The forms of **bos** (§197) fall into three categories. They are: the simple present and the simple imperfect (short forms); the positional of the simple present and of the simple imperfect (long forms); the future/habitual present, habitual imperfect, preterite, pluperfect, present subjunctive and imperfect subjunctive (**b-** tenses).

These tenses are now described separately in respect of (1) forms and uses, (2) type of subject, (3) type of complement, (4) construction and word order, (5) negative forms, (6) interrogative forms.

§331 **The simple present and the simple imperfect**

(1) All forms start with a vowel and are monosyllables.

	1s.	2s.	3s.	1p.	2p.	3p.	0
Present	ov	os	yw	on	owgh	yns	or
Imperfect	en	es	o	en	ewgh	ens	os

§331(4ai) Sentences

The person and the number are indicated by the unique form of the verb, augmented as required by a suffixed pronoun: **ov vy** 'I am'; **ova** 'he was'. These short forms are used as a link between the subject and that part of the sentence which completes the statement about the subject (the complement). The simple present refers only to present time and the simple imperfect refers to a continuing, indefinite state in the past.

(2) The subject may be contained in the verb, rendered by a pronoun in English, and augmented as stated above by a suffixed pronoun: **yth yns i** 'they are'.

The subject may be an independent pronominal or a noun: **Hemm o gwir** 'This was true'; **Ty yw an gwella** 'You are the best'; **Noeth yw an skorrenn** 'Bare is the branch'.

A noun phrase can serve as the subject, in which case the corresponding English phrase often has a dummy subject 'it', the real subject occurring later in the sentence: **Res yw bones war** 'It is necessary to be careful'; **Godhvedhys o bos y vlew loes kyns y vos ugens bloedh** 'It was known that his hair was grey before he was twenty years old'.

(3) The complement of the sentence is a noun: **My yw Mighal** 'I am Michael';

a pronominal: **An kaletter o hemma** 'The difficulty was this'; **My ywa** 'It is I'; a noun phrase or clause: **Y ewnter o penn an teylu** 'His uncle was head of the family'; **An ken o y vos heb chi** 'The cause was his being without a house';

an adjective or a past participle: **Diek yns** 'Lazy they are'; **Kudhys ens gans kweth lyb** 'Covered they were with a wet cloth'. This last example shows that the complement may be split.

For past participles with the long forms of **bos** see §332(3d,e).

(4) The construction of the sentence follows either the verbal or the nominal pattern (§302) and (§303). These are now separately described.

(a) **The verbal sentence**

(i) The verb is inflected to show the person and number of the subject. An independent pronoun or a noun may follow the verb in apposition to the subject indicated by the verbal ending. However the verb remains singular with a plural

§331(4ai)   Sentences

noun subject: **Noeth o an skorrennow** 'Bare were the branches'.

(ii)   The particle **yth** is used only in the following cases:

when the verb starts the sentence: **Yth yw ow morthol** 'It is my hammer'; **Yth or skwith** 'One is tired'. An adverb or a prepositional phrase stands at the head of the sentence: **Byttegyns yth en vy pes da** 'Nevertheless I was satisfied'; **Gans lies yth o ev kerys** 'By many he was loved';

when the complement or some part of it is to be emphasised: **Pith yth ens i** 'Stingy they were'; **Y hwans yth ywa** 'His wish it is'. The normal unemphatic forms of these sentences would be: **Pith ens i** and **Y hwans ywa**;

when a noun or a pronoun acts as an anticipatory subject, the true subject being indicated in the verbal ending: **An hwedhel yth yw gokkineth hepken** '(As to) the story, it is foolishness (and) nothing else'; **My yth ov heb towlow vydh** 'I, I've got no plans at all';

when the complement is derived from a verb which governs two direct objects (§305(7)), these being placed on either side of the verb: **Kaderyer yth yw gwrys** 'He is made chairman'; **Kerensa yth ov gelwys** 'Kerensa I am called'.

(iii)   The word order in these verbal sentences is as follows:

Adverbial	particle	verb	(subject)	complement

Pup-prys yth os karadow dhyn 'Always you are dear to us'.

Complement	(particle)	verb	(subject)

Gwrys gans ow diwleuv evy (yth) o (ev): 'Made with my own hands it was'; **Euthek yw bos y'n chi na nosweyth** 'Frightful is it to be in that house at night-time'; **Byghan yw an fenestri** 'Small are the windows'; **Soudoryon yns** 'Soldiers they are'.

Complement 1	(particle)	verb	(subject)	complement 2

Synsys meur (yth) on dhis 'Very beholden we are to you'; **Dhywgh hwi yth on synsys** 'To you we are beholden'.

Emphasis is on the first element of the sentence and the use of the particle **yth** is optional (see ii above).

§331(5) Sentences

(b) **The nominal sentence**

(i) In the nominal sentence the subject must be a separate noun or pronoun and must come at some point before the verb which is always 3s. whatever the person and number of the subject.

The particle **a** is not used (§303(1)). Thus:

An gour }		'The man is/was	}
An benynes }		'The women are/were	}
My }		'I am/was	}
Ty }		'You are/were	}
Ev }	yw/o lowen	'He/it is/was	} happy'
Hi }		'She/it is/was	}
Ni }		'We are/were	}
Hwi }		'You are/were	}
I }		'They are/were	}

(ii) The construction requires that the subject shall come before the verb but the complement, whether in one part or more, can come anywhere in the sentence:

Subject	verb	complement

(the usual order): **An lestri yw ploes** 'The dishes are dirty'.

Subject	complement	verb

Y skoedh kamm yw 'His shoulder crooked is'.

Complement	subject	verb

(emphasising the complement or that part of it which is put first): **Lel gowetha hwi yw** 'Loyal friends you are'; **Omma my yw devedhys** 'Here I have come'.

(5) Negative forms. The negative particle is **nyns** and the sentence is necessarily a verbal sentence (§302). The word order is regularly the following:

Particle	verb	(subject)	complement

Nyns ewgh hwi sotel lowr 'You were not subtle enough'; **Nyns o an daras deges** 'The door was not shut'.

§331(5) Sentences

The verb remains singular with a plural noun subject:

Nyns yw an eseli unnver ganso 'The members are not in agreement with him'.

The subject, noun or pronoun, can precede the verb, anticipating the subject implied in the verbal ending. In this case a plural noun is followed by a plural verb: **An spiser nyns yw diek** 'The grocer, he's not lazy'; **Plenkys an leur nyns yns (i) leven** '(As to) the floorboards, they are not smooth'; **Ty nyns osta gwiw dhe vos dewisys** 'You, you are not worth choosing'.

The complement can be put before the verb for special effect or for emphasis: **Melyn nyns o an pann** 'Yellow the cloth wasn't'. In the case of a longer complement it can be split: **Omma nyns ywa trigys** 'He is not resident here'.

(6) Questions do not require the interrogative particle **a** (§277). The verb comes first and is followed by subject and complement or complement and subject according to the emphasis, the information which is sought. A singular verb accompanies a plural noun subject: **Osta prederys?** 'Are you worried?' **Yw puptra parys?** 'Is everything ready?' **O an gusul na fur?** 'Was that advice wise?' **Fur o an gusul na?** 'Was that advice wise?' **Yw an moesow kempenn?** 'Are the tables tidy?' **Yw my a hwilowgh hwi?** 'Is it I whom you seek?' **Yw ty a'n gwrug?** 'Is it you who did it?' **O i a'n gwitha?** 'Was it they who looked after it?'

Replies are in the appropriate verbal form. The negative particle is **nag**: **Osta prederys?** 'Are you worried?' **Ov!** 'I am!' or **Nag ov!** 'I am not!' **Yw an moesow kempenn?** 'Are the tables tidy?' **Yns!** 'They are!' or **Nag yns!** 'They are not!'

Negative questions are introduced by **a nyns**: **A nyns ens i diwysyk?** 'Were they not hard working?' **Ens!** 'They were!' or **Nag ens!** 'They were not!'

§332 The long forms of **bos** are confined to a simple present and a simple imperfect.

(1) The verbal forms resemble the corresponding short forms with the addition of the syllable **es-**.

	1s.	2s.	3s.	1p.	2p.	3p.	0
Present	esov	esos	usi/yma	eson	esowgh	esons/ymons	eder
Imperfect	esen	eses	esa	esen	esewgh	esens	eses

262

§332(3e) Sentences

The unique form **eus** has the meaning 'there is, there are'; see below (5) and (6).

In affirmative sentences **yma** has replaced **usi** and **eus** and similarly **ymons** is used in place of **esons**. In negative, interrogative and subordinate sentences **usi**, **eus** and **esons** remain (§197(2)).

The general meaning of these forms is that something exists: **Yma tros** 'There is a noise'. This is the substantive use of 'is', that something has existence and is contrasted with its use as a copula which joins two elements of the statement as having some sort of equivalence: **An tros na yw re ughel** 'That noise is too loud'.

(2) The subject of the verb is shown by its unique form: **Esos** 'You are', reinforced if required by a suffixed pronoun: **Yma ev** 'He is'. The subject can be a noun: **Yma an golow a-ughon** 'The light is above us'. The verb remains singular with a plural noun: **Yma bleujennow ena** 'There are flowers there'; **Ymons ow pleujyowa yn helergh** 'They are flowering late'.

The plural subject may precede **ymons** and **esens** in anticipation but the grammatical subject remains the pronoun implied in the verb: **An warioryon ymons (i) ow sevel stag** '(As to) the players, they are standing still'; **An rohow yth esens (i) a-dro dhe'n sybwydhenn Nadelik** 'The presents, they were around the Christmas tree'.

(3) The complement consists of those words or phrases which add information about the condition of the subject.

(a) Place (adverb of place): **Ymons i omma** 'They are here'; (prepositional phrase) **Yth esov yn ow chi ow honan** 'I am in my own house'.

(b) Position (adverbial phrase): **Yth esa hi a'y esedh** 'She was sitting down'; **A-dreus an kleudh yma** 'Across the ditch it is'.

(c) What the subject is doing (present participle construction), (§243): **Yth eson ni ow kwaytya** 'We are waiting'; **Ow kewsel yth eder** 'There is (someone) speaking' or 'They are saying' (impersonal), OM. 2794.

(d) What has been done to the subject, its state as a result of some action (past participle) (§245): **Yma chi flamm nowydh drehevys ryb an fordh veur** 'There is a brand new house built next to the main road'.

§332(3e)   Sentences

(e) Past participles are thus used with both the short forms and the long forms of **bos** (§331(3)). The following considerations apply:

i. If the subject is an indefinite noun or pronoun and the complement consists of the past participle only, the long form of **bos** (**yma, eus, esa**) is used: **Yma boes parys** 'There is food prepared'; **Yma re gwrys** 'There are some done'; **Eus tra varthys hwarvedhys?** 'Has something marvellous happened?' **Nyns esa nebonan gyllys y'n eur na** 'No one had gone at that time'.

ii. If the subject is definite, the verb is a short form of **bos**: **An boes yw parys** 'The food is prepared'; **Henna yw gwrys** 'That is done'; **Oll an hwel yw diswrys** 'All the work is undone'; **Nyns en ni gyllys y'n eur na** 'We had not gone at that time'.

iii. If however the definite subject is followed by a complement which consists of a past participle together with an expression of place or posture, the speaker uses either the short form or the long form of **bos** to emphasis the adjectival or the local aspect of the statement, as the following pairs of examples show:

Trigys on a-berth y'n fosow 'We are settled within the walls'; **Yth eson ni omma warbarth kuntellys** 'We are gathered here together'.

Gwithys yns a-ji dhe glos 'They are protected within an enclosure'; **Y'n dor ymons oll gwreydhys** 'In the earth they are completely rooted'. **Osta devedhys a-ji dhe'n yet?** 'Are you (= have you) arrived inside the gate?' **Ple'th esosta gyllys?** 'Where are you (= have you) gone?' **Ughel yth os esedhys** 'You are seated on high'; **Yth esos war ow hador esedhys** 'You are seated on my chair'; **Nyns yw ev hwath tremenys alemma** 'He is (= has) not yet passed on from here'; **Yma ev devedhys omma dhe'n dre** 'He is (= has) come here to town'.

(4) The long forms of **bos** are used in verbal sentences only. The verb is therefore always preceded by the particle **yth** with the exception of 3s. **yma** and 3p. **ymons**. This is probably because the initial **y-** of the verb has become identified with the particle **y**.

The order of words is normally:

Particle	verb	subject	complement

Yth esov y'n lowarth 'I am in the garden'; **Yma an maw ena** 'The boy is there'; **Yth esa an vergh y'n peurla** 'The horses were in the pasture'.

§332(6) Sentences

This order may be varied to make some part of the sentence more prominent:

Complement	particle	verb	subject

Ryb y denewenn yth esen ni 'By his side we were'.

Particle	verb	complement	subject

Yth esa ganso sommenn vras a arghans 'He had with him a large sum of money'.

Subject	complement	particle	verb

Gwelenn-vaner war benn an menydh yma 'A flagpole on the top of the hill there is'.

(5) Negative sentences are introduced by the particle **nyns**: **Nyns esowgh hwi owth oberi meur** 'You are not working much'. The forms **yma** and **ymons** are not used in negative sentences. **Yma** is replaced by **usi** when the subject is definite and by **eus** when the subject is indefinite. **Ymons** is similarly replaced by **esons** in negative statements and in this case the subject is necessarily defined: **Nyns usi an lytherwas ow tos** 'The postman is not coming'; **Nyns eus lyther ragos** 'There is no letter for you'; **Nyns esons i owth omdhoen orto yn fas** 'They are not behaving well towards him'.

The subject follows the verb as in these examples, the verb remaining singular with a plural noun subject: **Nyns usi an fergh war an voes** 'The forks are not on the table'; **Nyns eus fronnow** 'There are no brakes'.

The subject may precede the verb for emphasis in the usual way (§331(5)): **Alhwedh an daras a-rag nyns usi yn y doll** 'The front door key, it isn't in its (key) hole'; **An gorholyon nyns esens ow mora** '(As to) the ships, they were not putting to sea'; **Ni nyns eson yn y glas** 'We, we aren't in his class'.

(6) Questions do not require the use of the particle **a**: **Esowgh hwi omma pub dydh?** 'Are you here every day?' **Esa dargan dha?** 'Was there a good (weather) forecast?'

In place of **yma**, **usi** is used with definite, **eus** with indefinite subjects: **Usi an gyst yn-dann an gweli?** 'Is the box under the bed?' **Usi hi ow kul gwell?** 'Is she doing better?' **Eus dowr toemm?** 'Is there (any) hot water?'

§332(6) Sentences

A noun subject follows the verb and the verb remains singular even with a plural noun: **Usi an benynes y'n keth tyller?** 'Are the women in the same place?' **Eus fleghes ow kwari y'n garth gwari?** 'Are there (any) children playing in the playground?'

A suffixed pronoun is usually put in apposition to the subject implied by the verbal ending: **Esowgh hwi ow hwilas gul ges anodho?** 'Are you trying to make fun of him?' **Esens i a'ga sav?** 'Were they standing up?'

An anticipatory subject may precede the verb, a plural verb following a plural subject: **Dha gentrevek usi ev ow kesoberi genes?** 'Your neighbour, is he co-operating with you?' **An re goth esons i ow powes hwath?** 'The old people, are they still resting?'

Negative questions are introduced by **a nyns**: **A nyns esens i a-bervedh y'n diwotti?** 'Weren't they inside the pub?' **A nyns eus bleus lowr rag pobas tesenn?** 'Is there not enough flour to bake a cake?'

The complement usually follows the verb and subject as in the examples above but it may precede the verb for special effect or for emphasis: **Ow kul glaw usi hi?** Raining is it?' **Yn-mes a'th weli esosta?** 'Out of your bed are you?'

Replies to questions repeat the verb, using the appropriate form and person. The negative particle is **nag**: **Esowgh hwi yn poynt da?** 'Are you well?' **Eson!** 'We are!' or **Nag eson!** 'We are not!' **Esens i a-dermyn?** 'Were they on time?' **Esens!** 'They were!' or **Nag esens!** 'They were not!'

(7) The rule that **yma** is used in all principal, affirmative sentences, while in negative, interrogative and subordinate sentences **usi** is regularly used with a definite subject and **eus** with an indefinite subject, is adhered to in modern Cornish. In the list of interrogative words which follows some anomalous cases are noted.

PLE(TH) 'where' (§74(12)) combines with **yma** and **ymons** to give **ple'ma** and **ple'mons**: **Ple'ma'n nessa karrji?** 'Where is the next garage?' **Ple'mons i ow kavoes aga boes?** 'Where are they getting their food?'

PY(TH) 'where' (§75) also combines with **yma**, **ymons** and gives **py'ma**, **py'mons**: **Py'ma'n wolghva?** 'Where is the bathroom?' **Py'mons i lemmyn?** 'Where are they now?' Note that **PLE(TH)** is generally used in modern Cornish.

§332(7)

The expressions **py kost, py plas, py tyller** are followed by **yma, ymons** in full: **Py tyller yma Mtr Leskrow?** 'Where is Mr Lescrow?' (§74(14)).

Other persons and tenses are regular: **Ple'th esowgh hwi ow triga?** 'Where are you living?' **Pyth esa ev y'n eur na?** 'Where was he at that time?' **Lavar dhymm, mar pleg, py tyller yth esov vy ow mos dhe goska!** 'Tell me, please, where I am going to sleep!'

PANDRA 'what' (§74(4)) is followed by **eus**: **Ny wonn pandra eus dhe leverel** 'I don't know what there is to say'; **Pandra eus y'n amari?** 'What is in the cupboard?'

PAN, PANA 'what' (§74(2)(3)) with a noun can be followed by either **yma** or by **eus**: **Pan prow yma/eus a hemma?** 'What advantage is there from this?' **Pana lytherenn yma/eus skrifys yn-danno?** 'What letter is written beneath it?'

PRAG 'why' (§74(16)) is regular with all long forms, being followed by **yma, ymons** and the other inflected persons: **Prag yma an losow ow merwel?** 'Why are the plants dying?' **Prag ymons i ow tos ha bos krin?** 'Why are they becoming dry?' **Prag yth esowgh hwi tre mar a-varr?** 'Why are you home so soon?'

FATELL 'how' (§77) is regularly followed by **eus/usi**: **Fatell eus dowr war an leur?** 'How is there water on the floor?' **Fatell usi an ober ow mos?** 'How is the work going?' Note the expression **Fatell esowgh hwi?** where **ow mos** 'going on' or a similar phrase must be understood. See BM. 4310.

MAY(TH) 'that, where, when', both of these last in a relative sense (§291), is followed by **yma, ymons** shortened to **ma, mons** to give **may ma** and **may mons** respectively, the y- of the verb being dropped, probably because of its being identified with the particle **y**. Other forms are regular: **Tellek yns may ma an dowr ow sygera yn-mes anedha** 'They are full of holes so that the water is leaking from them'; **Aga gorra a wrug ev yn-dann alhwedh may mons yn le salow** 'He put them under key so that they are in a safe place'; **Ke war-nans dhe blen an dre may ma lies gwerthji fethus!** 'Go down to the town square where there are many fine shops!' **Hemm yw penn-bloedh y enesigeth may ma solempnyta meur sevys** 'This is the anniversary of his birth when there is a great ceremony held'; **Hemm yw an ken mayth esov vy omma** 'This is the reason for which I am here'; **Bras o an poenvos mayth eses ta ynno** 'Great was the trouble which you were in'; **Magoryow koedhys lemmyn yth yw an kastylli mayth esa myghternedh ow reynya pell** 'Fallen ruins now are the castles where kings ruled long'.

§332(7) Sentences

Negative expressions use the particle **na(g)** to give **ma nag usi, ma nag eus, ma nag esons**: **ma nag usi an men warnodho** 'so that the stone is not on it'; **Tre ma nag eus diwotti** 'A town where there is no public house'; **Gesys ynmes ens bys ma nag esons dhe gavoes na fella** 'They were left outside so that they are not to be found any longer'. The adverbial particles **nans** 'now' (§280), **ass!** 'how!' (§281), and **nammna(g)** 'almost' (§267) are regularly construed with **usi/eus**: **Nans usi an re na genen** 'Now there are those with us; **Ass eus nebes gwiw lowr dh'y gemmeres!** 'How few there are fit to receive it!'

DELL 'as' is normally followed by **usi/eus** but exceptionally **yma** is found: **dell yma skrifys** 'as it is written'; **dell (y)ma gwelhevin an pow** 'as are the chief people of the country', BM. 2797. In the texts there are cases of **eus** used in place of **yma** in principal, affirmative statements when the subject is indefinite: **Keudh eus y'm kolonn** 'There is sorrow in my heart'.

§333 The forms of **bos** in b- are set out in full in §197(1). The 3s. of each tense is repeated here for reference.

Hab. pres./fut.	Hab. imperf.	Pret.	Plup./cond.	Imperv.	Pres./fut. sub.	Imperf. sub.
bydh	bedha	beu	bia	bydh	bo	be

(1) Remarks on the tenses:

(a) The habitual present/future is most often used as a simple future: **Ni a vydh diwedhes** 'We shall be late' but it also serves in certain contexts as an habitual present: **'Lagasek' ev a vydh henwys gans y gowetha** 'He is called "big eyes" by his friends'.

(b) The habitual imperfect denotes an action continued or repeated in the past: **Naw blydhen y fedhen ni kesskriforyon** '(For) nine years we were regular correspondents'.

This tense is used in indirect statements (§336(4)) to indicate the 'future in the past': **Y ambos o y fedha yn Kernow erbynn Nadelik** 'His promise was that he would be in Cornwall by Christmas.'

(c) The preterite indicates an action or a state at a more or less definite time in the past. As such it serves with a past participle as complement to form a passive construction (§245(3b)): **Rynnys veu an desenn yntra hwegh rann** 'The cake was divided into six pieces': **Gwelys vons gans pub huni** 'They were seen by everyone'; **Ni a veu anniys** 'We were vexed'.

(d) The present perfect is formed by putting the perfective particle **re** (§279) before the preterite. The usual mutation of **b-** to **v-** does not take place (although examples are found in the texts): **Ow broder re beu y'n dre nammnygen** 'My brother has been in town recently'; **An skrifennyades re beu ow jynnskrifa an derivas** 'The secretary has been typing the report.'

(e) The pluperfect/conditional. As a simple pluperfect this tense denotes an action or state completed, viewed from a point in past time. With this meaning the particle **re** can be used without mutation: **Menegys hemma a via** 'This had been mentioned'; **An glaw re bia ow koedha hirneth** 'The rain had been falling (for) a long time' The particle **re** is not used when the meaning is conditional (§228(6)): **Da via y weles arta** 'It would be good to see him again'.

(2) The subject may be indicated by the verbal ending: **Y fydhons lowen** 'They will be happy', and the verbal ending can be reinforced by the suffixed pronouns: **Ny vydhav vy bysi wosa li** 'I will not be busy after lunch'. A separate noun or noun clause can be used as subject: **An loer a vydh leun** 'The moon will be full'; **Ty a veu klywys** 'You were heard'; **Nevra ny vedha es y gonvedhes** 'It was never easy to understand him', lit. 'His understanding was never easy'; **Poes via ganso omdenna a'n para** 'He would be reluctant to withdraw from the team.'

(3) The complement of the **b-** forms of **bos** may be of any kind: noun, noun clause, pronoun, adjective, past participle, present participle construction, adverb, prepositional phrase: **Henna a vydh an diwedh** 'That will be the end'; **Y lavar a vedha a'y oes y tehwelli neb prys** 'His saying was always that he would return some time'; **An toeller a veu ty** 'The cheat was you'; **Y vamm a veu trist** 'His mother was sad'; **Terrys veu an hanaf** 'Broken was the cup'; **Gensi y fydh yndella pup-prys** 'It is so with her always'; **I a via orth ow heski mayth astelliv** 'They would be exhorting me to give up'; **Ni re bia re dont** 'We had been too insolent'; **Y'n nos i a veu genev** 'In the night they had been with me'; **My a vydh yn-mes alemma rag** 'I shall be outside from now on.'

(4) Construction. The **b-** tenses of **bos** are used in both verbal and nominal sentences.

(a) In verbal sentences the verb is inflected to show the number and person of the subject. The verb remains singular with a plural noun subject: **Skon y fydh an hwedhlow oll ankevys** 'Soon the stories will be completely forgotten.'

A plural subject, whether noun or pronoun, can precede a plural verb in anticipation of the person implied by the verbal ending: **An dhewisoryon y fiens toellys** '(As to) the voters they had been deceived'; **Hwi y fydhowgh gweresys kyns pell** 'You, you will be helped before long.'

The particle **y** is used when the verb begins the sentence, a less usual order, or if it is preceded by an adverb or by a prepositional phrase: **Y fydh an gusul wella** 'It will be the best plan'; **Yn Pow Sows y fedhens i trigys** 'In England they used to be settled'; **Gans bilienn y feu shyndys** 'With a stone he was injured'; **Menowgh y fien ni kusulys gensi** 'We had often been advised by her.'

The particle is also retained when an anticipatory subject precedes as in the examples above.

The particle is used if the complement or a part of it is emphasised and precedes the verb: **Ow howeth y fydh ev** 'My companion he will be'; **Skwerdys y feu an gweth** 'Torn was the garment'; **Diwysek y fiens i** 'Industrious they had been.'

This **y** is not used if less emphasis on the complement is required but in this case the **b-** of the verb is softened to **v-**.

Thus the above examples would become: **Ow howeth vydh ev**; **Skwerdys veu an gweth**; **Diwysek viens i** (§331(4a,ii)).

(b) Nominal sentences are regular. The subject, noun or pronominal, must come at some point before the verb and is joined to it by the particle **a**. The complement usually comes after the verb: **I a veu re ger** 'They were too dear'.

Other types of word order in nominal sentences are used:

Complement	subject	particle	verb

Hir ha garow an fordh a vydh 'Long and hard the road will be.'

Subject	complement	particle	verb

An kelorn gorlenwys a dhowr a veu 'The bucket overfilled with water was'.

Nominal sentences are more common as principal affirmative sentences than are verbal sentences (§309).

(5) The negative of the verb is regular, the negative particle being **ny**,

§333(6) Sentences

replaced by **na** in replies to direct questions (see below (6)) and in most subordinate sentences: **Ny vien sowdhenys a honna** 'I would not be surprised at that'; **Gwayt na vi re helergh!** 'Mind you're not too late!'

The order of words in negative sentences is also regular and is usually:

Particle	verb	subject	complement

Ny veu an gwas lettys a vos dhe wari 'The fellow was not prevented from going free'.

The complement is sometimes put before the subject for emphasis:

Particle	verb	complement	subject

Ny via re dhrog an tybyans na 'It would not be too bad, that idea'.

Similarly an anticipatory subject can be put first:

Subject	particle	verb	complement

My ny vydhav ena 'I will not be there'.

(6) Questions are introduced by the interrogative particle **a**: **A vydhydh jy ow triga ganso?** 'Will you be living with him?' **A ny** is used for negative questions: **A ny vedha ev klav pup-prys?** 'Wasn't he always ill?' Replies are constructed in the usual way by repeating the verb of the question in an appropriate person: **A vewgh hwi gwelys?** 'Were you seen?' **Beun!** 'We were!' or **Na veun!** 'We were not!' **A ny via gwell?** 'Wouldn't it be better?' **Bia!** 'It would!' or **Na via!** 'It would not!'

Questions with other interrogative words are regularly constructed (§320-§330): **Ple fydh hi?** 'Where will she be?' **Fatell vons i?** 'How were they?' **P'eur fydh an ordenor a-ji?** 'When will the organiser be in?' **Pyth a veu kewsys yntredha?** 'What was said between them?' **Piw a vydh hy gweresores?** 'Who will be her assistant?'

❖❖❖❖❖

SUBORDINATE SENTENCES

A sentence may be included or 'embedded' in another sentence with the role of noun, adjective or adverb within that sentence. It is then known as a noun clause, an adjectival clause or an adverbial clause.

NOUN CLAUSES

§334 A sentence which is to act as a noun within another sentence may be left as it is or changed in form.

(1) A verbal sentence is left unchanged with the particles **y, na** or **re** introducing the verb: **Y kanas an edhen** 'The bird sang', **My a woer y kanas an edhen** 'I know that the bird sang' where the embedded sentence is the object of **My a woer**; **Ny neuvya hi mar bell** 'She did not swim so far', **Gwir yw na neuvya hi mar bell** 'It is true that she used not to swim so far' in which the embedded sentence is the subject; **Fest yn fenowgh y leverir re lad'sa an bows dhiworth an gwerthji mayth oberi hi** 'It is very often said that she had stolen the dress from the shop where she worked'.

All **b-** tenses of **bos** 'be' within a verbal sentence are so treated: **Da o ganso y fiens i kowsoryon a Gernewek** 'He was pleased that they had been speakers of Cornish' (subject); **Lavar na vydhydh helergh!** 'Say that you won't be late!' (object).

(2) A verbal sentence in which the verb is **bos** 'be', the simple present or the simple imperfect in either the short or the long form, is changed as follows:

(a) The finite verb is replaced by the verbal noun **bos**.

(b) This verbal noun is put into a possessive construction with either a following noun or a possessive adjective to represent the subject. Examples are:

Yth ov	I am	
Yth esov	I am	all become
Yth en	I was	**ow bos**
Yth esen	I was	

Yth os	you are	
Yth esos	you are	all become
Yth es	you were	**dha vos**
Yth eses	you were	

Yth yw ev/hi	*he/she/it is*	
Yma ev/hi	*he/she/it is*	all become
Yth o ev/hi	*he/she/it was*	**y vos/hy bos**
Yth esa ev/hi	*he/she/it was*	

Yth yw an den	*the man is*	
Yma an den	*the man is*	all become
Yth o an den	*the man was*	**bos an den**
Yth esa an den	*the man was*	

Yth on	*we are*	
Yth eson	*we are*	all become
Yth en	*we were*	**agan bos**
Yth esen	*we were*	

Yth owgh	*you are*	
Yth esowgh	*you are*	all become
Yth ewgh	*you were*	**agas bos**
Yth esewgh	*you were*	

Yth yns	*they are*	
Yth esons	*they are*	all become
Yth ens	*they were*	**aga bos**
Yth esens	*they were*	

The idea of time is lost and can only be inferred from the context: **Y hwodhor bos pub ger gow** 'It is known that every word is/was a lie'; **Gwir yw y vos klav de** 'It is true that he was ill yesterday'.

The noun phrase representing the subject should come immediately after the verbal noun **bos** (§55). If for emphasis it is put earlier in the sentence, its place is taken by a possessive adjective with the verbal noun. Thus variants of the example given above would be: **Pub ger y hwodhor y vos gow** and **Y hwodhor pub ger y vos gow**.

(3) A nominal sentence embedded in another is changed into the infinitive construction which is thus described:

(a) The noun or pronoun subject remains unchanged.

(b) The particle **a** is replaced by the preposition **dhe** 'to'.

(c) The finite verb in the 3s. is replaced by the verbal noun of that verb.

§334(3d) Subordinate Sentences

(d) A direct object, if a noun, remains.

(e) A direct object, if a pronoun, is replaced by the corresponding possessive adjective.

Examples:

An wydhenn a bodras 'The tree rotted', **wosa an wydhenn dhe bedri** 'after the rotting of the tree'; **I yw agan meni** 'They are our people', **Sur ov i dhe vos agan meni** 'I am sure that they are/were our people'; **An governans a voghhas an toll** 'The government increased the tax'; **I a sorras drefenn an governans dhe voghhe an toll** 'They were angry because the government increased the tax'; **Ev a'n gorfennas** 'He finished it', **Ni a grys ev dh'y worfenna** 'We believe that he finished it'.

In this case too, a noun or pronoun can be put earlier in the sentence and a referring possessive adjective be put in the subordinate phrase: **An toll/ev drefenn an governans dh'y voghhe a sorras lies** 'The tax/it because the government increased it, angered many'.

The construction here described is used with all indicative tenses of all verbs with the exception of the positional (long) forms of **bos** which are not used in nominal sentences (§303).

As nominal sentences are more common in principal affirmative statements (§309), the infinitive form given above is correspondingly more common in such statements than the construction with **y** described in (1) above.

(4) Negative sentences are always verbal sentences (§302(1)) and so remain unchanged when incorporated into another sentence, but the particle **ny** becomes **na** and **nyns** becomes **nag**: **Ny dheuth ev** 'He did not come', **Ni a leveris na dheuth** 'We said that he did not come'; **Nyns eus amanenn** 'There is no butter', **Osta sur nag eus amanenn?** 'Are you sure that there is no butter?' **Nyns av** 'I shall not go', **Yth hevel nag av** 'It seems that I shall not go'.

(5) Questions which are embedded in another sentence are known as indirect questions and are dealt with in §344(5)(6).

§335 The noun clause as subject

A noun clause is found as the subject of statements when the mere existence of a fact, its truth, necessity, propriety, is asserted.

§336(3) Subordinate Sentences

In English these statements often have a dummy subject, 'it', the actual subject, being introduced by 'that': **yth hevel ...** 'It seems that ...'; **Y hyll bos ...** 'It is possible that ...'; **Gwir yw ...** 'It is true that ...'; **Res yw ...** 'It is necessary that ...'; **Bysi yw ...** 'It is important that...'; **Da/drog/gwell yw ...** 'It is good/bad/better that ...'; **Y koedh ..., Y tegoedh ...** 'It is suitable that...'; **Y tesedh ...** 'It is seemly that ...' **Ny vern ...** 'It does not matter that ...'; **Meur dhe les yw ...** 'It is very useful that ...'; etc.

In Cornish however this dummy subject is not supplied, the subject being the noun clause itself directly: **Sur y hyll bos y tigolmas an skath** 'Surely (it) is possible that he untied the boat'; **Res yw hy bos ganso** 'She must be with him', lit. Her being with him is necessary'; **Gwell o gansa i dhe vos aga honan** 'They preferred to be on their own'; **Y koedh ni dhe wul ken** 'We must do otherwise'; **Meur dhe les y feu na dheuthons a-varr** 'It was very useful that they did not come early'.

A noun clause may also stand as the subject of the passive construction (§245(3b)) of a verb of saying, thinking, knowing, hearing, etc.: **Derivys yw an gannas dhe assoylya an kas hware** '(It) is reported that the representative resolved the matter straight away'; **Godhvedhys veu na vynna gwertha y ji** '(It) was known that he would not sell his house'. Cf. §337.

§336 **The noun clause as object**

(1) A noun clause serves as the object of an expression of knowing, thinking, believing, saying, promising, threatening, swearing, seeing, hearing, seeming, hoping, feeling, doubting, etc.: **Lavar dhedha y fydhav gansa kyns na pell!** 'Tell them that I will be with them before long!' **Godhvedhewgh y's bydh selwyans!** 'Know that you will have salvation!' RD. 1574; **Ena y tannvonsons bos an tokynyow ow tos** 'Then they sent (to say that) the tickets were coming'; **A grysydh jy bos an hwel ma dhe dyli y wul?** 'Do you believe that this work is worth doing?' **Lemmyn y hwaytir na vydh an hav ma re doemm** 'Now one hopes that this summer will not be too warm'.

(2) When several dependent clauses are used as objects of the same verb and linked by conjunctions, the construction can be varied for stylistic purposes: **Ni a woer ev dhe vos an gwella ha'y vos gwiw** 'We know that it is the best and that it is suitable'; **Kampoellys veu y tothya seulabrys hag ev dhe wodhvos an kas** 'It was mentioned that he had already come and that he knew the situation'.

(3) A noun clause with its verb in the subjunctive follows the verbal particle

§336(3)   Subordinate Sentences

may 'that' (§291) as the object of expressions in which the exercise of the will is given prominence (§229(3)): **Gwra dhodho may tawo!** 'Make him be quiet!' lit. 'Do to him that he may be quiet!' **Hwans a's tevo ma'n gwella** 'She had a desire that she might see him'; **Ni a vynn may hwellhaho** 'We wish that he may get better'. The negative is **na**: **Yma debron dhe'n venyn na dheppro re** 'The woman has an urge not to eat too much'.

(4) This noun clause as object is often described as indirect statement: **Peder a gar lowartha** 'Peter loves gardening', **Ev a lever Peder dhe gara lowartha** 'He says that Peter loves/loved gardening'. However, direct statement in place of the indirect constructions described above is not uncommon and consists of a principal sentence with a supporting assertion, often introduced by the conjunction **dell** 'as': **Gonn lowr ty yw trist** 'I know (well) enough you are sad' in place of **Gonn lowr ty dhe vos trist**; **Nyns eus banna leth dhe bareusi te, dell grysav** 'There's not a drop of milk to make tea as I believe', instead of **My a grys nag eus ...** This usage is particularly common after **pysi** 'ask, pray', instead of the regular **may** with a verb: **My a'th pys ty a ri** (= **may rylli**) 'I ask you to give'; **Gans ow holonn y pysav mos a wredh** (= **may hwryllowgh mos**) 'With my heart I ask you to go'; **My a bys re dhannvonno negys dhymm** (= **may tannvonno**) 'I pray he may send a message to me'.

(5) Direct speech. The words of a speaker may be directly quoted in one of several ways.

(a) The quotation and a form of **yn-medh** 'say, said' (§219). **Yn-medh** precedes, interrupts or follows the quotation: **Yn-medh Mtr Kest, "Ass yw splann an gewer!"** 'Said Mr Keast, "How splendid the weather is!"'; **"A Powl!" yn-medhav. "An dornskrif ma yw gwell"** '"Ah, Paul!" I said. "This handwriting is better."'; **"Ny'gan beus pluvennow," yn medhons-i, "ytho ny yllyn skrifa"** '"We haven't any pens," they said, "so we can't write"'; **"My a vynn mos genes," yn-medh hi** '"I will go with you," she said'.

(b) The quotation with some other verb of saying. There are three constructions in common use:

Quotation - subject - particle - verb: **"Piw osta?" an skrifennyades a wovynnas** '"Who are you?" the secretary asked'.

Subject - particle - verb - quotation: **Ena my a grias, "Na wra!"** 'Then I cried out, "Don't!"'

Quotation - particle - verb - subject: **"Hemm yw re dhrog," a leveris an perghenn** '"This is too bad," said the owner'.

In these three cases the quotation is the direct object of the verb.

§337 The noun clause as complement of *bos* A noun clause in any of its forms can serve as the complement of **bos**: **An ken a veu y fistenas re** 'The cause was that he hurried too much'; **Y breder a vydh nevra bos ladron owth entra dh'y ji** 'His worry is always that thieves are/will be entering his house'; **Konter an tybyans na yw an eghenn dhe vywa orth losow** 'The opposite of that opinion is that the species lives on plants'.

For noun phrases after certain prepositions forming adverbial clauses of time, place and cause, see under these headings below.

§338 Sequence of tenses The action described in the subordinate sentence takes place in relationship to the action described in the principal sentence, being future to, contemporary with, or prior to, that action.

This relationship is shown by the choice of tense in the subordinate sentence. The sequence of tenses which thus arises is shown in the following table where the abbreviation f. indicates 'future', cty. 'contemporary' and pt. 'past'

Principal sentence   Subordinate sentences

Tense	*Pres./fut.* *f., cty.*	*Pres.perf.* *cty., pt.*	*Imperfect* *pt.*	*Preterite* *pt.*	*Pluperfect* *pt.*
Pres./fut. **Ev a lever** He says (that)	**y hwel** he sees	**re welas** he has seen	**y hweli** he used to see	**y hwelas** he saw	**re welsa** he had seen
Pres.perf. **Ev re leveris** He has said (that)	**y hwel** he sees	**re welas** he has seen	**y hweli** he used to see	**y hwelas** he saw	**re welsa** he had seen

Principal sentence   Subordinate sentences

Tense	*Imperfect f.*	*Preterite cty.*	*Pluperfect pt.*
Imperfect **Ev a leveri** He used to say (that)	**y hweli** he would see	**y hwelas** he saw	**re welsa/ y hwelsa** he had seen
Preterite **Ev a leveris** He said (that)	**y hweli** he would see	**y hwelas** he saw	**re welsa/ y hwelsa** he had seen
Pluperfect **Ev re lavarsa** He had said (that)	**y hwel** he sees	**re welas** he has seen	**y hweli** he used to see

§338 Subordinate Sentences

The present/future and the present perfect are followed by any of the five tenses of the indicative. The imperfect, the preterite and the pluperfect are followed by one of three tenses as shown.

The pluperfect in subordinate clauses may be introduced by **re** (§228(5)).

The negative subordinating conjunction is **na** (§291).

In direct quotation of a speaker's words the original tense used in the statement remains, of course: **Ev a leveris, "My a welas Yowann"** 'He said, "I saw John"', which in indirect statement would become: **Ev a leveris re welsa/y hwelsa Yowann** 'He said (that) he had seen John'.

When the verb in the subordinate sentence is to be in the subjunctive the sequence of tenses is as follows:

The present/future or the present perfect in the principal sentence is followed by the present subjunctive: **Hi a ergh/re erghis an flogh mayth effo an leth** 'She orders/has ordered the child to drink the milk'.

The imperfect, the preterite and the pluperfect tenses in the principal sentence are followed by the imperfect subjunctive in the subordinate sentence: **Hi a erghi/erghis/re arghsa an flogh mayth effa an leth** 'She used to order/ordered/had ordered the child that it should drink the milk'.

ADJECTIVAL CLAUSES

Relative sentences describing a noun or a pronoun in the principal sentence have the function of an adjective.

§339 In Cornish there are two types of relative sentence, the direct relative in which the particle represents the subject or the direct object of the verb, and the oblique relative in which the particle has some other relationship with the verb.

The direct relative particles are **a** (§278) and the negative **na(g)** (§276(6)).

The oblique relative particles are **may(th)** and the negative **ma na(g)** (§291).

§340 **The direct relative sentence**

(1) The relative particle stands as subject in the subordinate sentence: **Diskwedh dhymm, mar pleg, an den a'm kuhudhas!** 'Show me, please, the

§340(6) Subordinate Sentences

person who told tales about me!' **Gyllys yw an men a sevi a-rag an daras** 'Gone is the stone which stood before the door'.

The verb remains 3s. whatever the person and number of the antecedent: **Ni a'th weres yw dha gowetha** 'We who help you are your friends'; **Ple'ma an brybours a'n gwrug?** 'Where are the villains who did it?' **Teg yw an bleujennow a dyv ena** 'Fair are the flowers which grow there'.

(2) The relative particle stands as the direct object to the verb in the subordinate sentence: **My a re dhis an lyver a dhewisydh** 'I shall give you the book which you choose'; **Hemm yw an chi a garav** 'This is the house which I love'; **Piw yw an soedhek a welis vy?** 'Who is the official whom I saw?'

In this case the verb will be in the person and number appropriate to the subject (§303(2)).

(3) The relative particle is sometimes used without an antecedent and will then mean 'the one who/whom, that which', etc.: **A aswonn an fordh, kevarwoedhes ev an bagas!** 'The one who knows the road, let him show the group the way!; **My a glyw a wredh** 'I hear that which you do'.

(4) The relative particle is not used after the perfective particle **re** (§279): **Hemm yw an gour re'm gweresas** 'That is the man who has helped me'; **Bedhes an jydh re dhewissons i!** 'Let it be the day which they have chosen!' **Nyns o an venyn re dhothya hy modrep** 'The woman who had come was not her aunt'.

(5) The conjunction **ha(g)** 'and' can be put before the particle and this makes the relative more distinct: **Kemmer an radyo hag a veu ewnys de!** 'Take the radio which was repaired yesterday!' lit. 'and the one which'. This usage makes it possible to distinguish the true relative from a nominal sentence based on the relative (§303).

(6) In speaking of persons the pronoun **neb** (§72(7)) can be used either independently or in apposition with a previous noun or pronoun, singular or plural: **Neb a'n dyghtyas yndella yw dhe vlamya** 'The person/Whoever treated him thus is to blame'; **Hware i a lettyas neb a veu dannvenys di a wul y soedh** 'Straight away they prevented the person who was sent there from doing his job'; **Yma y'n lowarth neb a gerydh** 'In the garden there is someone whom you love'; **An menyster neb a yll gorthybi a vydh genen skon** 'The minister who can answer will be with us quickly', lit. 'The minister, someone who ...'; **Ytho y hwelav an den neb a gampoellsys** 'So I shall see the person

§340(6) Subordinate Sentences

(the one) whom you mentioned'; **An Bardh Meur yw neb a led** 'The Grand Bard is the one who leads'.

(7) In speaking of things the phrase **an pyth** 'the thing' can be used, either independently or referring to a previously mentioned object: **Meth a's tevo a'n pyth a wrussa hi** 'She was ashamed of what she had done'; **An droglamm, an pyth a'n lettyas a dhos, o bos difyk yn y garr** 'The mishap, (that) which prevented him from coming, was (that) there was a fault in his car'.

(8) As well as **neb**, certain other indefinite pronominals are followed by a relative construction: **seul** 'such, as many' (§72(13)); **myns** 'as much, all who' (§72(5)); **kemmys, kekemmys** 'as many, all who/which' (§72(2)); **keniver** 'as many, all who/which' (§72(4)); **pynag, pypynag** 'whatever'; **pyneyl pynag** whichever one'; **piwpynag** 'whosoever, whomsoever' (§72(11)).

Because of the element of indefiniteness in such sentences, the subjunctive mood is frequently used: **Pypynag a hwarvo, y savav omma** 'Whatever may happen, I'll stand here'; **Kemmer myns a vynni!** 'Take as much as you will!' **Piwpynag a wrella henna, nyns o my** 'Whoever might have done it, it was not me'.

(9) The subjunctive is also used with the ordinary relative particles when there is some idea of indefiniteness: **Na wra gorra dhyn a skonnyo a gesoberi!** 'Don't send us anyone who may refuse to co-operate!' **Eus ser prenn hag a vo skentel lowr dhe wuthyl an gador?** 'Is there a craftsman in wood who would be skilful enough to make the chair?'

(10) These indefinite pronominals may be preceded by prepositions while themselves remaining in a direct relative sentence as subject or as object: **Kows dhe neb a'n gwrug!** 'Speak to whoever did it!' **Dhe vyns a vo dh'y alloes, sur ev a wra** 'As much as he may be able to do, he will surely do'; **Ke yn keniver chi a gyffi!** 'Go into as many houses as you may find!'

In the texts are examples of a preposition governing the particle **a** when used as a pronoun: **Molleth Dyw war a'th treylyas!** 'The curse of God on whoever converted you!' **awos a ylli dhymm gul** 'in spite of what you may be able to do to me', BM. 3557.

(11) When **na** introduces a negative relative sentence the verb of that sentence is in the appropriate person and number:

§341(5)   Subordinate Sentences

1s.	**My na gewsyn ger vydh a veu kuhudhys**	'I who used not to say a word was accused'
1p.	**Ni yw na wodhon konvedhes an styr**	'We it is who cannot understand the meaning'
2s.	**Ty na veus genen re gollas dha wober**	'You who were not with us have lost your pay'
2p.	**I a'gas gorr na'gas beus lywyas**	'They will take you who cannot drive'
3s.:	**Nyns eus den y'n bys na gammdyb treweythyow**	'There is no one at all who does not occasionally think mistakenly'
3p.	**Yma meyn nag yns a'n keth gweli**	'There are stones which (they) are not from the same stratum'

§341 The relative with the verbs *bos* 'be' and *mos* 'go'

(1) The relative particle is omitted before parts of **bos** 'be' which begin with a vowel. Thus **yw, usi, eus, o, esa** mean in relative constructions '(who/which) is, (who/which) are, (who/which) was, (who/which) were'. **Yma** is not used in relative sentences (§332(1)).

(2) Negative forms are: **nag yw, nag usi, nag eus, nag o, nag esa** meaning '(who/which) is not, (who/which) are not, (who/which) was not, (who/which) were not'. Examples: **My a gar flogh yw nebes tont** 'I like a child who is a little bit cheeky'; **Plos o an leurlennow esa y'n chi** 'Dirty were the carpets which were in the house'; **Eus lyver omma nag yw skwerdys y folennow?** 'Is there a book here without torn pages?' lit. 'which is not torn its pages?' **Mowes a driga gansa nag e yn-mes yn fenowgh** 'A girl lived with them who did not go out very often'.

(3) The form **usi** is used with definite antecedents: **Kyrgh dhymm an venyn usi ow leverel hemma!** 'Bring me the woman who is saying this!' **A aswonnydh jy den nag usi owth oberi war neb fordh?** 'Do you know anyone who is not working in some way?'

(4) The form **eus** is used with definite or indefinite antecedents but in Modern Cornish is confined to the latter: **My a dhe le eus yn Kernow** 'I shall go to a place which is in Cornwall'; **Kempennyn an amari usi/eus y'th chambour!** 'Let us tidy the cupboard which is in your bedroom!' **Alena y tremenowgh war aswa nag eus yet dhedhi** 'From there you pass on by way of a gap with no gate'.

(5) Parts of the verb **bos** which begin with **b-** retain the relative particle **a** and are constructed regularly: **Ott! an den a veu ordenys aga skrifennyas** 'Look!

§341(5)

the man who was appointed their secretary'; **I o tus re bia shyndys** 'They were people who had been injured'.

(6) The verbal phrase **y'm beus** 'I have', etc. (§198) is constructed regularly also: **An lyver a'm bo o koth** 'The book which I had was old'; **Yn hwir yth yns marnoryon na's teves kok** 'Really they are sailors who have not got a boat'.

(7) The particle **a** is not used with **mos** 'go': **Kyns yth esa maw e dhe skol gans y hwoer** 'Once there was a boy who used to go to school with his sister'. **Neb** and **ha(g)** can be inserted into the construction: **Kyns yth esa maw neb e/hag e** (§340(5)(6)). This remark applies also to the anomalous forms of **mos**, the perfect and the pluperfect (§205(2a)): **Den gallas re goth ny yll bos esel** 'A person who has become (has gone) too old cannot be a member'; **Yth esa losower galsa dhe Amerika Dheghow** 'There was a botanist who had gone to South America'.

§342 The oblique relative expresses relationships between the antecedent and the verb of the relative sentence which are other than those of subject or direct object. In English such relationships are denoted by the use of an adverb of place: 'where, whither, whence'; an adverb of time: 'when, (until) when, (by) when'; or through a preposition: 'to whom, by whom, in whom, through which, over which, by which', etc.

(1) The oblique relative particle or conjunction is **may(th)**, negative form **ma na(g)** (§291). May requires an antecedent: **Yma skavell boblek war an lann may tyv an kegis** 'There is a public bench on the bank where the hemlocks grow'.

(2) 'Where' etc.: **Birmingham yw an tyller may ma ev owth oberi y'n eur ma** 'Birmingham is the place where he is working now'; **Nyns eus ke ma nag eus skovarn na goen ma nag eus lagas** 'There is no hedge where there is not an ear nor down where there is not an eye'; **Loundres yw an sita may teuth hi** 'London is the city from which she came'; **My a aswonn an chi ma'n dannvonas** 'I know the house where he sent it'.

(3) 'When', etc.: **Devedhys yw an eur mayth yw res mos** 'The time has arrived when it is necessary to go'; **Lavar dhodho an jydh ma'n gwelydh!** 'Tell him the date when you will see him!' **An nessa blydhen a vydh an vlydhen ma na vydh kuntelles** 'Next year will be the year when there will not be a meeting'.

§343(2) Subordinate Sentences

Note that **ple, py** 'where' and **p'eur** 'when' are interrogative and are used in direct and indirect questions (§326). **Pan** 'when' is adverbial and has no antecedent (§295).

(4) Other relationships are equivalent to a preposition with a pronoun: **An ser prenn may feu gwrys an gador o skentel dres eghenn** 'The carpenter by whom the chair was made was exceptionally skilful'; **Homm yw an estyllenn may hworris an seth** 'This is the shelf on which I put the jar'; **Neb may fo moyha gyvys a gar moyha** 'The person to whom most is forgiven, loves most'; **A nyns yw gwir y vos gour ma na yllir krysi?** 'Is it not true that he is a man whom one cannot believe?' or 'in whom one cannot believe?' (**gava** and **krysi** govern through the preposition **dhe**, (§141(15d, h)); **Bysi yw gul kusul may hwellhyn an dre** 'It is important to make a plan by which we shall improve the town'; **Eus nebonan ma na'n ros yn tokyn a'y gres ynno?** 'Is there anyone to whom he did not give it in token of his faith in him?'

The relationship may be more precisely defined or reinforced by the inclusion of an appropriate prepositional phrase in the relative sentence. Thus in the above examples: **an ser prenn may feu gwrys an gador ganso**; **an estyllenn may hworris an seth warnedhi**; **neb may fo moyha gyvys dhodho**; **a nyns yw gwir y vos gour ma na yllir krysi dhodho/ynno?**; **bysi yw gul kusul may hwellhyn an dre dredhi**; **eus nebonan ma na'n ros dhodho?**

This prepositional phrase may exceptionally be put before the particle for special effect: **Bysi yw gul kusul dredhi may hwellhyn an dre** 'It is important to make a plan by which we shall improve the town' (§330).

§343 In some cases the relative sentence refers to or describes only part of or one aspect of the antecedent. The part or aspect to be referred to is mentioned in the relative sentence and a possessive adjective links it with the antecedent. This usage applies as follows:

(1) As the equivalent of the English 'whose, of which': **An gour a veu shyndys y arr** 'The man whose leg was injured', lit. 'who was injured his leg'; **Ottena an chi a goedhas y jymbla!** 'See there the house the chimney of which fell', lit. 'which fell its chimney'; **Yma genen an venyn a leveris hy mab na vynnas oberi** 'With us is the woman whose son said that he did not wish to work'. Note by contrast to this last example: **Yma genen an venyn a leveris na vynnas hy mab oberi** 'With us is the woman who said that her son did not wish to work'. Cf. §254 and 'Attendant circumstances', §351.

(2) When the verb of the relative sentence is in the compound construction as an auxiliary verb (§304(2b)): **Honn yw bre a vynnav hy yskynna** 'That is a

§343(2)

hill which I will climb', lit. 'a hill which I will its climbing'; **Dr Skott yw medhyk a wren ni y skonya** 'Dr Scott is a doctor whom we avoid', lit. 'whom we do his avoiding'; **dowr a yllir y eva** 'water which one can drink', i.e. 'drinkable' (§307(2)). As indicated above, the negative uses the particle **na(g)**: **pow na wrons i y weles** 'a country which they are not going to see'; **tesenn na vynnir hy dybri** 'a cake which one will not eat'.

(3) As an alternative to the oblique relative with **may** described in §342: **Piw yw an venyn a skrifsys dhedhi?** 'Who is the woman to whom you wrote?' in place of **Piw yw an venyn may skrifsys dhedhi?**

ADVERBIAL CLAUSES

Adverbial clauses define the circumstances of the main action. They are described under the headings:

Conditional clauses (§344)
Concessive clauses (§345)
Causal clauses (§346)
Temporal clauses (§347)
Local clauses (§342)

Comparative clauses (§348)
Final clauses (§349)
Consecutive clauses (§350)
Attendant circumstances (§351)

§344 Conditional clauses

(1) A conditional clause is one which states the circumstances under which the statement in the principal sentence was, is, will be, might be or may be true.

The conjunctions used are **mar/mara/mars/maras, a** 'if'. Negative forms are **mar ny(ns), na** 'if not' (§292).

There are two types of construction. The first treats the statements as facts and merely states the connection between them. The second type implies a judgement on the part of the speaker as to the truth, probability or possibility of the condition.

(2) Factual statements. The principal statement has for its verb the present/future, the future (**bydh, gwra, mynn**), the preterite, the imperative, the optative (**re** + present/future subjunctive). The place of the principal sentence may be taken by an exclamative phrase, e.g. **Gwynn vys!** 'It is good!' **Go-ev!** 'Unlucky for him!'

§344(2) Subordinate Sentences

The subordinate sentence has for its verb any appropriate tense of the indicative mood: present/future, future (**mar pydh, mar kwra, mar mynn**), preterite (which can have the meaning of the perfect in 'have, has') and, less commonly, the imperfect or the pluperfect with its meaning of prior time, 'had'.

Either the principal sentence or the subordinate sentence may come first, according to the emphasis to be given to one or the other. In the examples however the principal sentence is put first for ease of comparison.

Present/future **Fatell allav vy glanhe an karr,** 'How can I clean the car,	*Present* **mar ny'm beus an termyn?** if I have not the time?'
Future **Ny vynnav gul ken,** 'I will not do otherwise,	*Present/future* **mars yw henna y vodh.** if that is his wish.'
Present/future **Mighal a aswonn an benneglos,** 'Michael knows the cathedral,	*Imperfect* **mar triga ev yn Truru.** if he lived in Truro.'
Future **My a'n talvydh dhis,** 'I will repay it to you,	*Future* **mar pydhydh omma bys y'n eur na.** if you will be here then'
Preterite **Prag na'm pyssons a styrya an mater dhedha,** 'Why did they not ask me to explain the matter to them,	*Preterite* **mar ny'n konvedhsons?** if they did not understand it?'
Preterite **Ny dylsys namoy,** 'You did not owe any more,	*Pluperfect* **mar talvies pymthek peuns dhodho seulabrys.** if you had repaid him fifteen pounds already.'
Imperative **Gas e a-ji,** 'Leave him inside,	*Present* **mars usi ev ow koska!** if he is sleeping!'
Imperative **Kerdhyn a'n tu na,** 'Let's walk in that direction,	*Present* **mars eus hyns der an koes!** if there is a way through the wood!'
Optative **Re sewenno** 'May he succeed,	*Present/future* **mara tewl ev dhe vones tramor!** if he plans to go overseas!'
Exclamative **Gwynn vys,** 'Fine,	*Future* **mar mynnowgh gortos gensi!** if you are going to wait with her!'

§344(3) Subordinate Sentences

(3) **Contingent statements**

(a) If the speaker introduces into the statement a judgement as to whether or not what is described in the conditional clause is true, then the subordinate 'if' clause has its verb in the imperfect subjunctive. The conjunction is **mar**, etc. (negative **mar ny**) if the judgement is confined to whether or not what is described is true or not: **mara pen tre** 'if I were at home' implying that I am not at home, contrasting with **mars esov tre** 'if I am at home' in which there is no such implication. **Mar ny ve Peder skwith** 'if Peter were not tired' similarly implies that in the judgement of the speaker Peter is in fact tired, contrasting with **mar nyns yw Peder skwith** 'if Peter is not tired' which contains no such judgement.

(b) The conjunction **a** 'if', negative **na**, is used if the implication is not merely that the statement is not true but that it is improbable or even impossible: **a pe Maria an vyghternes** 'if Mary were the queen', which implies that the speaker knows that Mary is not the queen and also that it is very improbable that she could be: **na wrella hi glaw arta bys gorfenn bys** 'if it were not to rain again until the end of the world', a state of affairs known to be impossible but assumed as an hypothesis.

(c) In both cases the principal sentence has its verb in the pluperfect with its conditional meaning (§228(6)): **Y firsen orth an bellwolok, mara pen tre** 'I would watch the television, if I were at home'; **Peder a allsa mos yn-mes dhe dhonsya, mar ny ve skwith** 'If Peter were not tired, he would be able to go out dancing'; **Maria a wisksa kurun a adamantow, a pe hi an vyghternes** 'Mary would wear a crown of diamonds, if she were the queen'; **Gorfenn an bys via, na wrella hi glaw arta bys gorfenn an bys** 'It would be the end of the world, if it were not to rain again until the end of the world'.

(d) English has circumlocutions which give a past, present or future to this kind of conditional statement: 'if it were to have rained; if it were raining, if it were to rain'.

Cornish has only one type of statement and the context determines the relative time of the presumed occurrence: **Mars ellen ni tramor mis Me a dheu, ni a assa an gath genes** 'If we were to go abroad next May, we should leave the cat with you'. This in the indicative would be: **Mars en ni tramor, ni a as an gath genes** 'If we go, we shall leave the cat with you'; **My a sorrsa, mar tiwettha an fylm dygynsete** 'I should have been angry, if the film had ended the day before yesterday'.

§344(4) Subordinate Sentences

In these following examples the parallel forms with the indicative are given for comparison where applicable.

With **mar** (3a):

Ev a gavsa goemmon lowr, mar tiyskynna dhe'n treth a-vorow a-varr 'He would find enough seaweed, if he were to go down to the beach tomorrow early'. (He is unlikely to do so.)
Ev a gyv goemmon lowr, mar tiyskynn dhe'n treth 'He will find enough seaweed, if he goes down to the beach' (factual).
Ny'th hassa, mara pe ev lel goweth dhis 'He would not leave you, if he were a loyal friend to you' (but this is in doubt).
Ny'th has, mara pydh ... 'He will not leave you, if he is ...' (factual).
Ny allsen pesya gans an hwel, mar ny'm skoetthya hi 'I would not be able to continue with the job, did she not support me' (she does).
Ny allav pesya, mar ny'm skoedh 'I cannot continue, if she does not support me' (factual).
Ny's drosen, mar ny ve onan 'vas 'I would not have brought it, if it had not been a good one' (some uncertainty).
Ny'n dren (imperfect indicative), **mar nyns o onan 'vas** 'I did not bring it, if it was not a good one' (factual).

With **a (na)**:

My a werthsa ow chi ha prena tylda yn y le, a pe ev haval orth y ji eev 'I would have sold my house and bought a tent in its place, were it like his house' (but it could not possibly be so).
My a werth, mars yw ... 'I shall sell, if it is ...'.
Piw a's sawsa, na's gweressa an withysi als? 'Who would have saved them, had not the coastguards helped them?'
Piw a's sawyas, mar ny's gweresas? 'Who saved them, if they (the coastguards) did not help them?'
Ny vien ni yn fyw, na vens i 'We should not be alive, were it not for them' (lit. 'if they did not exist').

(4) The pluperfect is often used in principal sentences with its conditional meaning without any accompanying subordinate clause expressed.

This is the case when the condition is general, implicit in the situation or assumed to be known: **A vynnses jy kavoes hanafas te (mar pareussen onan)?** 'Would you wish to have a cup of tea (if I were to make one)?' **My a vynnsa y weles (mar kaffen kummyas)** 'I would like to see him (if I could get

§344(4) Subordinate Sentences

permission)'; **Meth via ni dh'y asa yn-mes (mara'n gwrellen)** 'It would be a shame to leave him out (if we were to do it)'.

(5) Mar in its several forms is used in indirect questions with the meaning 'if, whether' after verbs of seeing, asking, finding out, etc.: **gweles mar** 'see if'; **aspia mar** 'observe, see whether'; **govynn mar** 'enquire if'; **previ mar** 'prove whether'; **hwilas mar** 'find out whether'; **dannvon mar** 'send to find out whether'; **mires mar** 'look to see if'; **godhvos mar** 'know if'.

Examples: **My a vynn mos dhe aspia mars eus leth lowr** 'I will go to see whether there is enough milk'; **I a wovynnas orthiv mar mynnen** (imperfect indicative) **ledya an kana** 'They asked me if I would lead the singing'; **A-dhistowgh y tannvonas ev mar tothyens dhe-dre** 'Straight away he sent (to find out) if they had arrived home'; **Prov, mars yw da genes, mar nyns yw an sagh leun a dewes!** 'Test, if you like, whether the sack is not full of sand!'

Mar is sometimes omitted after **godhvos**: **Ny wonn eus koffi gesys** 'I don't know (if) there is any coffee left'.

With an expression of the sort mentioned above to be understood or implicit in the situation, **mar** is also used before **bos** 'be' and **galloes** 'be able' to mean 'to see or to find out if something is so or is possible': **My a di mar kallav y gavoes** 'I shall go there (to see) if I can get it'; **Galw an fleghes mar kyllons y wul!** 'Call the children (to find out) if they can do it!' **Res yw hy gorra dhe'n medhyk mar kyll hi bos sawys** 'It is necessary to take her to the doctor (to find out) if she can be cured'; **Profyn an stylyow mars yns kompes dhe'n fosow!** 'Let us offer the beams (to see) whether they are even to the walls!'

The subjunctive expresses a doubt: **Der unn skochfordh y poenyas kavoes hy mab mar kalla** 'Through a certain short cut she ran (to see) if she might find her son', MC. 164.5/6.

(6) **Mar** is used after verbs of saying, telling, relating, etc. to introduce indirect questions with the meaning 'if (it is the case that)': **Lavar dhymm mars yw hemma gwir!** 'Tell me if (it is the case that) this is true!' **Ny dherivsons mara piens lowen warbarth** 'They did not say if (it was the case that) they had been happy together'; **A vynn'ta diskwedhes dhodho mar kodhes nivera yn Kernewek bys yn kans?** 'Will you show him whether (it is the case that) you know how to count in Cornish up to a hundred?'

(7) If a principal sentence with a conditional clause in the subjunctive (3) is put into indirect statement, both verbs revert to an appropriate tense of the

§345(3) Subordinate Sentences

indicative. However an imperfect indicative may replace the pluperfect conditional as the 'future in the past' and the imperfect subjunctive may remain in the 'if' clause. Thus **Y tothya mar kalla ev** 'He would come if he could' or 'He would have come if he had been able' becomes **Ev a lever y teu** (present/future) **mar kyll** (present/future) 'He says that he will come if he can'; **Ev re leveris y teu mar kyll** 'He has said that he will come if he can'; **Ev a leveris y to** (imperfect) **mar kallas** (preterite) 'He said that he would come if he could' but **Ev a leveris y to** (imperfect) **mar kalla** (imperfect subjunctive) 'He said that he would come if he were able'.

The verb of saying may exceptionally be followed by a direct statement: **Ev a leveris my a via wolkumm, mar omjunnyen gans an gowethas** 'He said I would be welcome, if I joined the club' in place of the regular **Ev a leveris y fedhen, mar omjunyen** 'He said I would be, if I were to join'.

§345 **Concessive clauses** concede that a situation normally inconsistent with that described in the main clause of the sentence is, may be, or might be, true.

(1) The conjunction used is **kyn(th)** 'though, even though', negative **kyn na(g)** (§293). The main clause, the principal sentence, uses any appropriate tense of the indicative, including the pluperfect in its conditional sense. The imperative mood is also found.

The subordinate clause uses both the indicative and the subjunctive moods.

(2) If the clause makes a statement of fact, the indicative is used: **Kyn hwoer hi Kernewek, hi a skon a'y usya** 'Although she knows Cornish, she refuses to use it'; **Deber e, kyn na'n kerydh!** 'Eat it, even though you don't like it!' **Kynth yw an gewer teg y'n eur ma, fur yw doen glawlenn** 'Even though the weather is fine at present, it is wise to take an umbrella'; **Kyn kenwerthens ganso, ny'n gwelens nammenowgh** 'Though they had commercial dealings with him, they did not see him often'; **Ny gewsyn orto, kyn y'n gwelsyn** 'We didn't speak to him, even though we saw him'.

(3) If the subordinate clause makes a supposition, the present/future or the imperfect of the subjunctive is used with an appropriate tense of the indicative in the main clause: **Kyn lavarro yndella, ny grysav dhodho** 'Though he may say so, I do not believe him'; **My a'n kar, kyn na'n kyrri** 'I like him, even though you may not like him'; **Kyn fo an tonnow ughel, na dhout!** 'Though the waves may be high, do not be afraid!' **Den, kyn fe ow kerdhes dew our, ny allsa bos omma** 'Though a person should be walking (for) two hours, he could not be here'; **Kyn fo an gwerthji igor bys dhe naw eur, ny yll ow**

§345(3)   Subordinate Sentences

gwreg drehedhes di 'Though the shop may be open until nine o'clock, my wife cannot get there'; **Y vab, kyn lavassa mos yn-rag, ny vydh eev hardh dhe wul henna** 'His son, even though he dare to go on, he will not be bold enough to do that'; **Gortewgh ena, kyn fo an chi gwag!** 'Wait there, even though the house may be empty!' **Kyn lamma dres an fos, ny dhianksa** 'Though he were to jump over the wall, he would not escape'.

The use of the imperfect subjunctive in the subordinate clause with the pluperfect in its conditional sense in the main clause is parallel to the usage discussed in §344(3) but as the examples show, the accompanying tense in the main clause is not confined to the conditional pluperfect.

§346 **Causal clauses** are those which assign a reason for the state or the action described in the main clause. There are two types of construction:

(1) A subordinate clause with a finite verb in either the indicative or the subjunctive mood.

The conjunctions used are: **pan** in its special sense of 'since' and **a-ban** (= a + pan) 'since'. Negative forms are: **pan na(g)** and **a-ban na(g)** 'since not' (§294): **Aga maga gwra pan y's teves edhomm a voes!** 'Feed them since they have need of food!' **Ny grys dhodho pan lever ev pypynag a bleg dhodho!** 'Do not believe him since he says anything he pleases!' **Fatell yllir y witha pan na vynn omwitha?** 'How can one look after him since he does not look after himself?' **Gortyn a-berth y'n chi hedhyw a-ban usi an glaw ow koedha maga tynn!** 'Let's wait inside the house today since the rain is coming down so sharply!'

(2) A noun clause in one of the forms described in §334(2)(3). The conjunctions used are **rag, drefenn, awos**, all with the meaning 'because'. In the negative **rag na, drefenn na** (not *awos na) introduce a verbal sentence (§302(8)): **An dus a dyb yndellma awos aga bos toellys** 'The people believe so because they are deceived'; **Rag ev dhe vos peskys re, y ferwis an konin** 'Because it was overfed the rabbit died'; **Gasa tre a-varr ev a vynnas drefenn ev dhe dewlel towl a wul meur a hwel** 'He wished to leave home early because he planned to do a lot of work'; **Ny dheber an gath rag nag yw hi nownek hwath** 'The cat does not eat because she is not hungry yet'; **Trigoryon an tyller ma a dhrehav aga chiow war an treth drefenn nag eus spas leven lowr a-berth y'n tir** 'The inhabitants of this place build their houses on the beach because there is not space level enough inland'; **Ny wodhons i Kernewek rag na vynnens pesya orth y studhya** 'They do not know Cornish because they were not willing to continue studying it'.

§347 **Temporal clauses** define the time at which or during which the action described in the main clause takes place. As with the causal clauses mentioned above (§346), there are two constructions possible:

(1) A subordinate sentence with any tense of the indicative, or with the present subjunctive to show an uncertain or indefinite future, is used with one of the following conjunctions: **pan, may(th)** 'when'; **pan na(g), ma na(g)** 'when not'; **a-ban** 'since'; **a-ban na(g)** 'since not'; **erna(g), bys pan, bys may(th)** 'until'; **bys pan na(g), bys ma na(g)** 'until not'; **hedra** 'while'; **kettell** 'as soon as'.

For the various forms of these words and the mutations they cause see §295.

The following points may be noted here:

Erna(g) 'until', **hedra** 'while', **kettell** 'as soon as', have no negative form and a negative, if needed, is supplied by another word or by a circumlocution.
May(th) 'when' is, as noted above §342(1), a relative and requires an antecedent, whereas **pan** 'when' is adverbial and has no antecedent.
Hedra 'while' is only used with the b- tenses of **bos** 'be' and parts of **bywa** 'live'.

For the use of **ha(g)** to show attendant circumstances see §351.

Examples: **Pan boenyas gour y'n chi own hi a's tevo hware** 'When a man ran into the house she was alarmed straight away'; **Y'n jydh may taskorro ow fythow, my a av dhodho** 'The day on which (= when) he returns my property I will forgive him'; **Ny vynn an pennarghanser leverel nahen erna vova parys** 'The bank manager will not say differently until he is ready'; **Piw a yll ankevi an gwel na hedra vywo?** 'Who can forget that sight while he lives?' **I pan nag esa boes dhe dhybri a ladra** 'They, when there was no food to eat, would steal'; **Res porres dhedha gortos bys pan na wrello hi glaw** 'They will have to wait until it is not raining'; **An fardell pan y'n igoras hi o gwag** 'The parcel when she opened it was empty'; **An perbrenn re devis meur a-ban y'n plansas ev nans yw diw vlydhen** 'The pear tree has grown a lot since he planted it two years ago'; **An gevarwoedhoryon a omdenn bys ma's galwo an skrifennyas** 'The directors will withdraw until the secretary calls them'.

The phrase **bydh pan** 'whenever, as soon as ever' generalises **pan**, see §258(8) under **bydh**: **Bydh pan enttro, ev a esedh** 'Whenever he comes in, he sits'.

(2) One of the noun phrases described in §334(2)(3) is used. The

§347(2) Subordinate Sentences

conjunctions are: **kyns** 'before' (§150), **war-lergh** (§163), **wosa** (§166), 'after': **Soudoryon ens kyns aga bos dyskadoryon** 'They were soldiers before they were teachers'; **War-lergh bos an bellwolok ewnys y fyllis arta** 'After the television was mended, it broke down again'; **Wosa hwi dhe vos kuhudhys ny worthybsowgh. Praga?** 'After you had been accused you did not reply. Why?' **An gan ma, kyns hy dh'y hana, ny via klywys nep-prys a-rag tus** 'This song, before she sang it, had never been heard in public'.

There are no negative forms and the want of these is supplied by circumlocutions: **wosa ev dhe fyllel a wul** 'after he had failed to do' = 'didn't do'; **wosa hi dhe besya difun** 'after she had stayed awake' = 'not slept'.

Because of its comparative sense **kyns** can be followed by **(ag)es** 'than': **kyns es goslowes orthowgh** 'before listening to you, rather than listen to you'. This phrase is then followed by **dell** to connect it to a finite verb: **kyns ages dell dhegeydh an daras** 'before you shut the door'.

For local clauses denoting the place where the action occurs see §342.

§348 **Comparative clauses** offer a standard by which the statement made in the principal clause can be judged.

(1) The conjunctions are: **dell** 'as'(§297), **par dell, kepar dell, kepar ha dell** 'just as'; **kepar ha pan** 'just as though'. Negative forms are: **(kepar) dell na(g); kepar ha pan na(g)** 'just as though not'.

The perfective particle **re** (§279) can follow **dell** to give the meaning 'as have/has/had'.

There may be a demonstrative adverb in the main clause to correspond to the comparative statement. Examples are included below.

All the conjunctions listed above introduce a verbal sentence in which either the indicative or the subjunctive mood is used, the latter when the action is judged uncertain or improbable, or impossible of fulfilment but assumed to be true.

(2) With the indicative: **Gyllys yw dell dhesevav** 'She is gone as I suppose'; **Kepar dell heveli dhyn, yndella o yn hwir** 'Just as it seemed to us, so it really was'; **Gwynn aga bys mara pes y'n termyn a dheu kepar dell yw hi lemmyn** 'They will be lucky if it continues in the future just as it is now'; **Nyns o ev maga fel dell re bia seuladhydh** 'He was not so crafty as he had been formerly'.

(3) With the subjunctive: **Henna gwra dell y'm kyrri!** 'Do that as you love me! (= pleas)' **An flogh a wra y berthi mar hardh dell allo** 'The child will bear it as bravely as he can'; **Ty a yll gul par dell vynni** 'You can do just as you will'; **Orto y firas par dell ve ankoth** 'He looked at him just as though he were a stranger'; **Ha'n howl a splann nosweyth kepar ha pan ve hi an jydh** 'And the sun shines at night just as though it were the day'; **Dybri a wrug an maw kepar yn bys ha pan na wodhve leverel, 'Lowr!'** 'The boy ate for all the world as though he did not know how to say, "Enough!"'

(4) As mentioned in §347, the phrases **kyns (ag)es, kyns es dell**, although temporal in basic meaning, have come to have a secondary meaning, 'rather than, in preference to': **Gwell via genen gul tro y'n pow kyns (ag)es mos dhe'n dre** 'We would prefer take a trip in the country rather than go to town'; **Kyns es dell ello hi hy honan, ni a gensi** 'Rather than that she should go by herself, we shall go with her'.

(5) A superlative adjective followed by a tense of the subjunctive without a verbal particle has a comparative (equative), adverbial meaning: **My a'n gwra gwella gylliv** 'I shall do it as best I can'; **I a ganas hwekka godhvens** 'They sang as sweetly as they knew how'.

§349 **Final clauses** In a final clause the aim or the purpose of the action of the principal sentence is stated. The subjunctive is the appropriate mood because the aim is not yet realised and may not be:

The conjunctions are: **may(th)** 'so that', **rag may(th)** 'in order that'; negative forms are: **ma na(g), rag ma na(g), rag na(g)** 'in order not to' (§154(2b)).

Examples: **Keffrys an chi ha'n lowarth hi a gempennas ma's degemmerra dell dhesedh** 'Both the house and the garden she tidied so that she might receive them fittingly'; **Igor dhymm daras an karrji, mar pleg, rag may lywiv an karr a-ji!** 'Open the door of the garage, please, so that I may drive the car in!' **Y leverir an ost dhe dhowrhe an korev may pessyo pella** 'It is said that the landlord waters the beer so that it may last longer'; **My a gews dhodho mar deg na skonnyer pandr'a wren ni** 'I will speak to him so fairly that there be no objection to what we do', PD. 189-190.

§350 **Consecutive clauses** define the consequences of the action described in the principal sentence. Since they are factual in nature the indicative mood is used. The conjunction is again **may(th)** with the meaning 'that, so that'. The preposition **bys** (§140) 'until' is added to give precision to the conjunction.

§350   Subordinate Sentences

Negative forms are **ma na(g)**, **bys ma na(g)** 'until not'.

The principal sentence may have a demonstrative adverb referring to the subordinate sentence: **Wostalleth y trigen ni yn rannji byghan may hyllyn kuntell nebes arghans** 'At first we lived in a small flat so that we were able to accumulate some money'. If the subjunctive had been used here the meaning would have been 'so that we might be able' (§349). **Mar dhrog o studh an leur may teuth dillas an babi ha bos plos** 'So bad was the state of the floor that the baby's clothes became dirty'; **Kabol an devnydhyow bys mayth yns kowal kemmyskys!** 'Stir the ingredients until they are thoroughly mixed!'

§351 **Attendant circumstances**   The co-ordinating conjunction **ha(g)** 'and' introduces a phrase without a finite verb which describes the circumstances in which the main action takes place. Such phrases have a noun or a pronoun as a subject and, as complement, an adjective, a past participle, the present participle construction, a prepositional phrase or an adverb of place. The English equivalent usually starts with 'while' or 'with'.

Examples: **Na gows ha my skwith!** 'Don't talk while I am tired!' **Salow on ha'n daras ha'n fenestri oll prennys** 'We're safe with the door and windows all secured/while the door and windows are all secured'; **Ha'n howl ow splanna mar deg, fatell yllydh jy gortos a-ji?** 'While the sun is shining so beautifully, how can you stay indoors?' **Yma mowes yn-hons ha gensi tri hi** 'There is a girl over there with three dogs/who has three dogs'; **Y teuth troesyer ha dhodho kota pilennek** 'There came a pedlar with a ragged coat/who had a ragged coat/whose coat was ragged'. Cf.§343(1); **Teyr eur yw hi ha'n lien hwath war an voes** 'It's three o'clock and the cloth is still on the table'; **Ny vynnas entra dhe'n lowarth ha'n ki ena** 'He did not wish to enter the garden while the dog was there'. See also §300.

❖ ❖ ❖ ❖ ❖

INTERJECTIONS

§352 Simple imitative sounds, single words which are nouns, adverbs, parts of verbs, whole phrases, sometimes contracted, provide the range of exclamations, greetings, calls and so on which may be called interjectional. Some of those mentioned below are not in modern use but are given for the sake of completeness. Some interrogative pronominals have an exclamative use: **pandra!** (§73(1) and **piw!** §74(4)). See also the use of the exclamative adjective in §88 and of **ass!** in §281.

(1) Assent and dissent: **ya!** 'yes!' not as a reply to a direct question for which see §321, but in agreement, encouragement: **My a grys an framm ma dhe vos krev lowr. Ya!** 'I believe that this frame is strong enough. Yes!' **gwir, yn gwir, yn hwir, dhe-wir!** 'truly!' **yn hwir yn ta, dhe-wir yn ta, pur wir, pur wir yn ta!** 'very truly!' **devri, yn tevri!** 'certainly, indeed!' **yredi!** 'readily!' **yn surredi!** 'very readily!' **sur!** 'surely!' **sertan!** 'certainly!' **heb fall, heb falladow!** 'without fail, certainly!' **heb wow!** 'surely, indeed!' **heb dhout!** 'without doubt, certainly!' See also §265. Negative: **na!** 'no!', not as the reply to a question but to show disagreement: **Gwell via komptya an niverennow arta. Na!** 'It would be better to reckon the numbers again. No!'

(2) Regret: **eghan!** 'alas!' **go!** 'alas, woe!' (for the use of this word with pronouns and the constructions involved see §68); **tru!** 'alas, what a pity!' **soweth!** 'alas, bad luck!' **ogh!** 'oh, ah, alas!' **out!** 'oh!' (dismay, dislike); **welawo!** 'woe is me!' **ellas!** 'alas!' **harow!** 'alas, help!'

(3) Disapproval: **dar, ow dar, ay dar!** 'what, why!' (surprised enquiry); **Dar! Nyns yw hi gyllys?** 'What! Hasn't she gone?' **tetivali!** 'tut tut!' (impatience, contempt); **pla!** 'plague, what a nuisance!'; **mal!** 'pest!'; **malbew!** (softens, §23) 'plague take!'. Thus **malbew damm/vanna/onan!** 'not a plaguey bit/drop/one!'; **fi!** 'fie!'; **agh!** 'fie, ah!'; **jowl!** '(the) devil!'; **dhe'th kregi!** 'hang you!'

(4) Oaths: **re!** 'by!' (§156), **re Varia!** 'by Mary!' shortened to **'aria!**, **re Vighal!** 'by Michael!' **re'm lowta!** 'by my troth!' **ren ow thas!** 'by my father!' **re'm fay!** 'by my faith!' **re Jovyn!** 'by Jove!' **tann ow fydh!** 'by my faith!' (§159); **dh'y lawa!** 'praise him (God)!' **Dyw yn test!** 'God as witness!' **Dyw dhe'm selwel!** 'God save me!'

(5) Commands: **hala!** 'heave!' **war, waryewgh!** 'be careful!' §224), **darwar!** (§214) 'be forewarned!' **oyeth** 'hear, listen', **oyeth sy** 'hear here',

§352(5) Interjections

oyeth or! 'hear now!' (these from Old French); **dhe-dre!** 'home with you!' **ho!** 'stop!' **yn sol!** 'up on your feet!' **tann! tannewgh!** 'take!' (§223).

(6) Joy, satisfaction: **gwynnvys!** 'how lucky, fortunate!', lit. 'fair world' (§88(3)); **pur dha!** 'very good!' **brav!** 'fine, well done!' **gwrys yn ta!** 'well done!' **gwrys fest yn ta!** 'very well done!' **bryntin!** 'splendid!'

(7) Address: **a!** (softens, §23) 'o!' in addressing someone. The mutation affects common nouns and the adjective preceding them, but not usually proper names. This seems to be a matter of discretion. So in the salutation of letters: **A goweth/gowethes ker!** '(O!) dear friend' but **A Mighal ker!** '(O) dear Michael!' or **A Vighal ker!**.

The same considerations apply in the use of the vocative **ty, hwi!** 'you!' **Ty dhen!** 'you man!' **Ty venyn!** 'you woman!' **ty wokki!** 'you foolish (person)!' **hwi Gernewegoryon!** 'you Cornish speakers!' **ay, hou!** 'oh, hi!' **otta, awotta!** 'see, look, behold!' **ottomma!** 'see here!' **ottena!** 'see there!' **ott an ...!** 'see the ...!' (§67); **Ott(a) ha fethus yw hi!** 'See how beautiful she is!' (§287).

(8) Greetings: **hayl!** 'hail, hullo!' **ow!** 'ho, hullo!' **gromersi!** 'many thanks!' **meur ras!** 'thanks!' **meurastajy!** s., **meurastahwi!** p. 'thank you!' cf. §141(15e); **praydha!** 'I pray you!' **farwel!** 'farewell!' **Dyw genes sy/genowgh hwi!** 'goodbye!' **dursoenno dhis/dhywgh!** 'God bless you, God prosper you!' **durdala dhis/dhywgh!** 'God repay you!' **dydh da!** 'good day!' **durdadhajy/durdadhyhwi!** 'Good day!' **durnosta dhis/dhywgh!** 'good night to you!' The syllable **dur** is a contraction of **Dyw roy!** or **Dyw re!** 'God grant!' (§208(2a), §229(1)). **jevodi!** 'tell you, I say!' (French *je vous dis* through Middle English). In toasts, etc.: **Yeghes da!** 'Good health!' **Sewena!** 'Success!'

(9) Calls to animals, etc.: **prouyt!** to cattle; **tubby!** to pigeons; **war yew!** 'on yoke!' to oxen to take up the strain, also more usually as an encouragement to begin a task (§16l(1)); **hevva!** 'a shoal!', the hewer's cry on sighting a shoal of pilchards.

❖ ❖ ❖ ❖ ❖

INDEXES

Items are arranged in a word-by-word order. Cornish words are in italics and are only entered if there is a grammatical aspect to be mentioned. English equivalents to Cornish words are given only when there are similar entries, e.g. *ken* 'cause' and *ken* 'other'. References are to sections and main references are in bold type. Subsections are in parentheses. Repetition of a word is marked by a line (-). In multiple entries the arrangement is by principal words, thus:

a prep.23(1) **126**
  with adjective as noun 90
  forming adjectives 78
  forming adverbs 126(4)
  in composition 57, 58
  departure 126(2)
  with *deur* vb. 246(3)
  'in respect of' 126(8)
  location 126(4)
  etc.

GENERAL INDEX

a interr. part. 23(1), **277**, 320
  a ny neg. interr. 320
a = *vy, ty, ev* pers. pron. 64(3)
a prep. 23(1), **126**
  with adj. as noun 90
  forming adjs.78
  forming advbs. 126(4)
  in composition 57, 58
  departure 126(2)
  with *deur* vb. 246(3)
  'in respect of' 126(8)
  location 126(4)
  material 126(5)
  movement 126(1)
  with numbers 105(3)
  with ordinals 108(2)
  origin 126(7)

  partitive 126(6)
  sensation 255
  source 126(3)
  value 126(9)
  with verbs of emotion 126(8d)
a rel. part. 23(1), **278**
  as object 278(2)
  as subject 278(1)
a sub. conj. 'if' **292**, 334(3)
a voc. part. 23, 352(7)
a-ban 23(1), **294**, 295
  causal 346, 347(1)
a-barth 127
a-barth a-wartha 259(1)
a-barth a-woeles 291(1)
a-bell 259(1)
a-bervedh 259(1)
a-ble/a by le **74(13)**, 259(3), 326
a-boynt 258(5)
a-brys 258(4)
a bub tu 259(1)
a-dal 128
a-denewenn 259(1)
a-der 129
a-derdro 259(1)
a-dermyn 258(4)
a-dhann 23(1), 169
a-dheghow 259(1)
a-dheghowbarth 259(1)
a-dhelergh 259(1)
a-dherag see *a-rag*

a-dhesempis 258(5)
a-dhia 23(1), 130, 259(3)
a-dhifun 260
a-dhihons (dhe) 259(3)
a-dhihwans 258(1)
  see also *dihwans*
a-dhistowgh 258(5)
a-dhiwar see *diwar* and 259(3)
a-dhiwedhes 258(4)
a-dhiworth see *diworth*
a-dre 259(1)
a-dreus (dhe) **131**, 259(2)
a-dro 259(1)
  a-dro dhe 132
a-droes 260
a-dryv **133**, 259(1)
a-esedh 259(2)
a-gledh 259(1)
a-gledhbarth 259(1)
(a) govis 134
a-gynsow 258(4)
a-is 259(1)
a-ji 259(1)
  a-ji dhe 135
  a-ji dhe our 258(1)
a-les 260
a-rag/a-dherag/derag/dherag **155**, 259(1)
a-sav 259(2)
a-ugh **136**, 259(1)
a-vann 259(1)
a-varr 258(4)
a-ves 259(1)
  a-ves dhe 137
a-vorow 258(2)
a-wartha 259(1)
a-wel 260
a-woeles 259(1)
a-wosa **138**, 258(6)
a-wrowedh 259(2)
a'n eyl tu 259(1)
a'y oes 258(8)
a-y wosa 258(6)

-able, translation of 79(4), 343(2)
abstract nouns, see nouns, abstract
accent, see stress
addition 110(1)
adjectival clauses (relative) **339-343**
adjectival phrases 89
adjectives
  as adverbs 91, 257(3)
  comparative & superlative 82, 83(8)
    with subj. 348(5)
  derived 78, 79
  of English origin 80
  equative 84
  gender and number of 81
  in compounds 61(1g), 83(4b)
  mutation of 23(3), 83(2), 96
  as nouns 90
  position of 83
  possessive 51
-adow suff. 31(1), 79(4)
adverbial clauses 344-351
adverbial pres. part. const. 243(5), 243(6)
adverbs 257 - 267
  additive 262
  affirmative 265
  causal 264
  comparative 261
  concessive & conditional 263
  degree 267
  equative & manner 260
  negative 266
  place 259
  time 258
aga poss. adj., see poss. adjs. and 51(8)
agan poss. adj., see poss. adj. and 51(7)
agas poss. adj., see poss. adjs. and 51(7)
age 114
agency
  with *dre* 142(4)
  with *gans* 147(6)
  nouns of 33

ages, see *es*
ahanan 259(3)
ahwer 12(1), 256
alemma 259(3)
alena 259(3)
alphabet 2
an def. article 'the' 23(2), 50
  with *ma, na* 50(5)
  mutation after 50(3)
  shortening of 50(2)
a'n eyl torn 258(1)
an- pref. 269
an re ma, an re na dem. pron. 69(2)
androw 12(1)
androweyth 258(2)
animals, familiar 42(2)
  plurals of 43(8)
ankoth 12(1)
ankres 12(1)
answers, see questions and answers
anticipatory object 63(4), **302(6)**, 317, 334(3)
anticipatory subject 302(6), 316, 331(4aii), 332(2), 334(3)
anvenowgh 258(7)
apposition, genitive of 23(3i), 55
  with *a* prep. 'of' 57, 58
  range of ideas 56
apposition, simple 59
  conventional phrases 59(3)
  materials 59(4)
  names of places 59(1)
  personal names 59(2)
  with *oll* 72(8)
ar- pref. 272
arader 12(2)
aradror 12(2)
arall/erell 70(2)
  an arall 70(3)
argh- pref. 268
arithmetical operations 110
as- pref. 270

-as suff. '-ful' 36(2)
assa verb. part. 23(1), 88(1), **281**
assimilation 18, 19
attal 12(1)
attendant circumstances 300, 351
auxiliary verbs 225 - 227
  in compound constructions 304-317
avel 12(1), 84, 260, 261
avi 265
aweyl 12(1)
awos prep. **139**
  cause 255
  'for the sake of' 139(8)
  'in spite of' 139(9)
  with infinitive 139(5)
  intentiion 139(7)
  with v.n. 139(4)
awos sub.conj. 294, 346(2)
awotta see *ott(a)*

banna m. 266
banow f. 42(2)
(hy) ben 70(2)
benow, denoting females 42(4)
bern m. 147(5b)
berr adj. 83(4)
bilen adj. *bileni* f. 23(4)
bo conj. see *po*
boban m. 12(1)
bogh m. 42(2)
boghes- pref. 267, 269
boghesvenogh adv. 258(7)
boken conj., see *poken*
bos vb. **197**
  expressing possession 253
  in sentences 331 - 333
  and see entry in index of verbs
bras, brassa adjs. 82(4), 83(4)
brav interjection 352(6)
bri (vri) m. 23(3)
broder m. 42(1)
bugh f. 42(2)

bulhorn m. 12(1)
bydh suff. 'any' 20(3), 49(3), **266**, 258(8)
bydh moy 258(8), 266
bydh onan 266
bydh pan 347(1)
bydh well 266
byghan, byghanna adjs. 82(4)
bykken adv. 258
bynari adv. 258(8)
bynner re 229(1), 258(7), **279(13)**
bys prep. 23(2), 140
bys di/ti adv. 259(3)
bys may(th) sub. conj. 347(1), 350
bys nevra adv. 258(8)
bys omma adv. 259(3)
bys pan sub. conj. 258(8), **295**, 347(1)
bys vykken adv. 258(8)
bys vynari adv. 258(8)
bys vynytha adv.258(8)
bysi adj. 237(1), 246(2)
bysmer m. 12(1)
bythkweth adv. 258(8)
byttegyns adv. 12(1), 263
byttele 12(1), 263
byttiwedh adv. 258(8), 259(3)
byttiwettha adv. 263
byttydh *(bydh yn dydh)* adv. 258(8)

causal clauses 346
cause
  with *awos* 139
  with *drefenn* 143, 294
  with *gul* 141(7)
  with *rag* 154(2)
  with *war* 161(5)
circumstances, referring pronouns 71(3b)
collectives, see nouns, number
comparative adverbs 261
comparative clauses 348
comparison
  adjectival forms 82
  constructions 83(8), 85

equative 84, 63(8)
  with *ha* 287
complement, see under *bos* vb.
  independent prons. as 63(5)
compound constructions 304, 329
  with *galloes* 307
  with *godhvos* 308
  with *gul* 305
  with *mynnes* 306
compound words 60, 83(4b)
  see also nouns, compound
  close 61(1), 83(4b)
  improper 60, 83(4b)
  loose 60, 61(2)
  proper 60
  stress in 19, 60(1b), 61(2a)
concessive clauses 345
conditional clauses 344
  with pluperfect 228(6)
conditions, referring pronouns 71(3b)
conjunctions 282-300
  stress in 8(6)
  co-ordinating **282-289**
  additive 283
  adversative 286
  alternative 285
  comparative 287
  consequential 289
  separative 284
  subordinating **290-300**
  attendant circumstances 351
  causal 294
  comparative 297
  concessive 293
  conditional 292
  consecutive 299
  consequential 289
  final 298
  with *go* 'woe' 68(1)
  local 296
  temporal 295
consecutive clauses 350

consonants 6
  loss of final 13
  unvoicing/voicing of 20
contempt 246(5)
count nouns, see nouns, count

da 82(4), 147(5a),
  an da 90
danjer 256
dar interj. 352(3)
dar- pref. 272
das- pref. 270
date 111
dative, see indirect object
davas, an dhavas/an navas 27
day 111(2)
de- pref. 268
de 'yesterday' 258(2)
decimal fractions 109(4)
decimal numbering 122
defective verbs, see verbs, defective
definite article *an* 8(1), 23(2), **50**
definitiion 48
deg(ow) m. 106
degynsow adv. 58(4)
degys past part. 244(4)
dell sub, conj. 23(1), 279(8), **297**, 332(7), 348
demmas m.12(1)
demonstrative pronouns
  alternative 70
  with *gans* 147(9)
  independent 69
  reference of 71
der see *dre* prep.
derag, see *a-rag*
derived adjectives, see adjectives, derived
descriptive phrases 63(7)
desempis adv. 258(5)
desta vb. 23(4)
determiners 50 - 58
devar m. 248(4)

devedhys past part. 244(4)
devri 12(1), 265
dew/diw '2' 23(1), 96
dha poss. adj. 23(1), 51(3), and see poss. adjs.
dhe prep. 23(1), **141**
  with adjs. and past parts. 141(18)
  advantage 141(5)
  causing 141(7)
  compl. of *bos* vb. 141(17)
  conformity 141(10)
  destination 141(2)
  with displaced obj. 141(16), **304(2a)**
  exclamative 141(20)
  'happening to' 141(6)
  indirect obj. 141(14)
  infinitive const. 141(19)
  likeness 141(9)
  position 141(11)
  progression 141(3)
  proximity 141(8)
  purpose 141(13)
  recipient 141(4)
  stress 8(7)
  time 141(12)
  with verbs 141(15)
dhe-denewenn adv. 259(3)
dhe-dre adv. 259(3)
dhe-hys adv. 258(6)
dhe-ves adv. 259(3)
dhe-wari adv. 259(1), 260
dhe-wartha adv. 259(3)
dhe-wir adv. 265
dhe-woeles adv. 259(3)
dhe'n dre adv. 259(3)
dhe'n leur adv. 259(3)
dherag adv. , see *a-rag*
dhiworth, see *diworth*
di 'house', see *ji*
di pref. 269
di/dhi adv. 'thither' 259(3)
dibarow adv. 260

dibarth f. 12(1)
dihwans/a-dhihwans adv. 12(1), 258(5), 260
diminutives 35
diphthongs 5
direct object of verb 302(5), 303(2)
direct speech 336(5)
dis- pref. 269
dison adv. 260
distance 116
distowgh 258(5)
division
  arithmetical 110(4)
  into parts 178(4)
diw '2', see *dew*
diwar/a-dhiwar prep. 162
diwor' an nos adv. 258(2)
diworth/a-dhiworth/a-dhiworth prep. **153**
  with abstract nns.153(3)
  movement from a person 153(2)
  movement from a place 153(1)
  time 153(4), 258(2)
dohajydh adv. 12(1)
(an) dor m. 27
dorn m. in composition 61(1e)
dour adv. 260
dout m. 126(8d), 255, 256
dowr m. in composition 61(1e)
dre- pref. 268
dre/der prep. **142**
  agency, means 142(4)
  adverbial 142(6)
  figurative 142(3)
  in passive const. 142(5)
  spacial relationships 142(1)
  time 142(2)
dredhi adv. 142(6), 264
drefenn prep. 143
drefenn sub. conj. 294, 346(2)
dremas m. 12
dres past part. 244(4)
dres prep. **144**
  excess 144(4)
  'other side of' 144(2)
  'over' 144(1)
  time 144(3)
drog adj. 82(4), 83(4), 147(5a)
(an) drog 90
drogatti m. 12(1)
dual, see noun, number
dughan m. 255
dur = *Dyw re/roy* 208(2a), 352(8)
durdala 352(8)
dustunya vb. 23(4) and see entry in index of verbs
duty 248
Dy' 24(4) and see *dydh*
Dy' Gwener dhe nos, etc. 258(2)
Dy' Gwener dohajydh, etc. 258(2)
Dy' Gwener vyttin, etc. 258(2)
dydh m. 'day'
  in dates 111(2)
  mutation of 28
  stress 9(9)
dygynsete adv. 12(1), 258(2)

e = *ev* 64(1), 66(5)
edhomm m. 126(8d), 255
edrek m. 126(8d), 147(5b), 255
eghan interj. 12, 352(2)
ellas interj. 352(2)
ena adv. 258(1), 259(1)
eno/enos adv. 259(1)
equative 84
  superlative adj. and subj. mood 348(5)
er prep. **145**
  attachment 145(1)
  concern 145(2)
erbynn prep. **146**
  attitude 146(2)
  contrary action 146(3)
  meeting 146(1)
  point in time 146(4)
erell adj./pron., see *arall*

erna(g) sub. conj. 23(1), 295, 347(1)
es/ages comp. adv. 12, **85**, 261
es- pref. 269
ethves/ethes num. 107(6)
eur f. 112
eus vb. 'is' 197(2b) and see *bos*
euthek adj. 267
ev pers. pron. see pronouns, personal
ewl f. 255
ewn adj. 83(4)
ewnter m. 42(1)
exclamatives 73, 74(4), **88**, 126(8f), 281, 352
(an) eyl pron. 70(1)

facts, referring pronouns 71(3a)
fals adj. 83(4)
fatell interr. adv. 23(1), **77**, 147(5c), 260, 323, 332(7)
fatla interr. adv. 260
fekyl adj. 83(4)
feminine nouns, see nouns, gender of
fest/fast adv. 91, 267
final clauses 349
flour adj. 83(6a)
-fold 121(2)
fors m. 246(4)
fractions 109
   decimal 109(4)
future
   of *bos* 333(1a)
   'future in the past' 228(4)
   with *gul* 305(1)
   indefinite 228(1)
   with *mynnes* 306(5)
   with *-vydh* 197(2f)

gallas, gallsa, see *mos* vb.
'gan poss. adj., see *agan*
gans prep. **147**
   accompanying circumstances 147(3)
   agency 147(6)

   close possession 147(2)
   with *dyski* vb. 147(7)
   feelings, opinions 147(5)
   with *hemma, henna* 147(9)
   instrument, means 147(4)
   with *klywes* vb. 147(7)
   'in presence of' 147(1)
   with *skornya* vb. 147(8)
garow adj. 82(2)
garwa comp. adj. 82(2)
'gas poss. adj., see *agas*
gasa vb. in 1s. imperv. 183(1)
gast f. 42(2)
gaver f. 42(2)
gender of adj., see adjs., gender of
gender of nouns, see nouns, gender of
gene' = *genev* 13
genitive of apposition, see appositional genitive
gerundive 79(4)
gew m. 23(4)
(y) gila pron. 70(2)
glan adj. as adv. 267
gnas m. 22 note
go m. 'woe' 68, 352(2)
go- pref. 269
godhor f. 12(1)
godhvedhes past part. 244(4)
godhvos vb. expressing thanks, see under 'thanks' and in index of verbs
godramm m. 12
goedhvil m. 42(2)
goeldheys m. 12(1)
gohydh f. 42(1)
gor- pref. 268
gordhiwedh adv. 258(6)
gorow adj., denoting male 42(5)
gorsedh f. 23(4)
gorth- pref. 272
gorthugher m. 258(2)
gour m., denoting male 42(6)
govis prep., see *a-govis*

gow m. 83(4)
gras, grassys, see under 'thanks'
gryll m. 42(2)
gul vb. **225**
  as auxiliary vb. 304, 305
  causing, with *dhe*
  exclamative 281
  with *fors* 246(4)
  expressing future 305(1)
  as imperative 305(4)
  with *orth* 152(4)
  replacing other vbs. 305(3)
  with two objects 305(7)
  and see entry under Verbs
gul vri 23(3d), 246(5)
gwann adj. 83(4)
gwas m., in composition 61(f)
gwaytya vb., with subj. 229(3i)
gwell, gwella comp. adj. **82(4)**, 147(5a), 237(1)
  with *mil* 121(4)
gwelvydh vb. 197(2f)
gweres vb., with *orth* 152(4)
gweth, gwettha comp. adj. **82(4)**
  with *mil* 121(4)
gweyth f. 'time' 36(3)
  in composition 61(1f)
  in adverbial numbers 121(1)
gweyth m. 'work' 36(4), 61(1f)
gwir adj. 83(4)
gwreg f. 42(1)
gwrys past part. 244(4)
gwynnvys exclam. 88(3), 352(6)
gyllys past part. 244(4)
gyw m. 23(4)

ha(g) conj. **283**, 287
  addition 110(1)
  attendant circumstances **300**, 351
  in comparisons 287
  in descriptive phrases 63(7)
  linking adjs. 83(1)

  with numerals 104
  in relative sentences 340(5)
  ha ... ha 283
hager adj. 83(4)
hakkra comp. adj. 82(2)
hala interj. 352(5)
haneth adv. 258(2)
  - *dhe nos* 258(2)
  - *yn nos* 258(2)
hanter m.109(1)
  hanterdydh 109(1)
  hanterkans 101(3)
  hanternos 109(1)
harow interj. 352(2)
haval adj.
  - *dhe* 141(9)
  - *orth* 152(3)
hayl interj. 352(8)
he- pref. 273
-he v.n. suff. 9(13), 187
heb prep. 23(2), **148**
  'be without' 148(3)
  neg. of v.n. 149(4), 242
heblydh adj. 273
hedhyw adv. 258
  hedhyw y'n jydh, y'n jydh hedhyw 258(2)
  hedhyw vyttin 258(2)
hedra sub. conj. 23(1), **295**, 347(1)
hegar adj. 273
hemm see *hemma*
hemma dem. pron. **69(1)**, 70(2)
  with *gans* 147(9)
hen adj. 'old' 83(5a)
henn see *henna*
henna dem. pron. **69(1)**
  with *gans* 147(9)
hepken adv. 148(6)
herwydh prep. 149
hevlyna adv. 258(2)
hi, hyhi pers. pron., see personal pronouns
hir adj. 83(4)
hireth m. 'longing' 255

304

hirethek adj. 163(4)
hirneth f. 'long time' 258(8)
hogen adv. 263
homm see *homma*
homma dem. pron. 69(1)
honan pron. 95
honn, see *honna*
honna dem. pron. 69(1)
hons 259(1)
hordh m. 42(2)
(an) huni 72(1)
hwans m. 126(8d), 255
hware adv. 258(5)
hwarvos vb. **202**
  with infixed pronoun as ind. obj. 65(7c)
  and see entry under Verbs
hwarvedhys past part. 202
hwath adv. 258(8)
hweger f. 42(1)
hweves, hweghes, hweffes num. 107(5)
hwi, hwyhwi pers. pron., see under
  personal pronouns
  as vocative 352(7)
hwoer f. 42(1)
hwygron m. 42(1)
hwymm-hwamm adv. 260
hy poss. adj. 51(6) and see under
  possessive adjs.
hy ben dem. pron. 70(2)
hys ha hys adv. 259(3)

i pers. pron. 62 and see under
  personal pronouns
-ible E. suffix 307(2)
imperative mood
  uses 230
  verbal suffixes of 183
imperfect indicative 228(4)
imperfect subjunctive
  general 229
  in conditional sentences 344(3)
impersonal forms of verb, uses of 231

importance 246
increase of quality 86
indefinite pronominals 72
  governed by preps. 340(10)
  in relative sentences 340(8)
indefiniteness 48, 49
indicative mood
  use of tenses 228
  verbal suffixes of 180
  see also under names of tenses
indirect object
  after *dhe* 141(14)
  of *gweres* 141(15g)
  with *hwarvos* 202(2b)
  infixed pronouns 65(7)
indirect questions 322, 344(5)
indirect speech/statement
  see noun clauses
infinitive construction 141(19), 334(3)
  with *awos* 346(2)
  with *drefenn* 346(2)
  with *gwynnvys* 88(3d)
  with *kyns* 347(2)
  with *mynnes* 306(2)
  with pronouns as subject 63(6)
  with *rag* 346(2)
  with *war-lergh* 347(2)
  with *wosa* 347(2)
  in nn. clauses 334(3)
infixed pronouns 62, 65
  with *dell* 297
  as indirect object 65(7)
  with *kettell* 295
  with *kyn* 293
  with *may(th)* 291
  in nominal sentences 303(3)
  with *ny* 275
  with *pan* 294
  with *piw* 'own' 252(1)
  as object of imperative 66(3c)
  with *re* perf. part. 279
  re-inforced 65(6)

in relative sentences 278(2c)
instrument, nouns of, see
  nouns, instrument
instrumental case 47(4)
interjections 352
interrogative pronouns 73 - 77
  exclamative use of 73(1), 74(3), 73(4)
  in nominal sentences 327
  personal 73
irregular verbs, see verbs, irregular
is, isa comp. adjs. 82(4), 272
isel, isella adjs. 82(4)

james adv. 258(8)
ji (ti, di) m. 'house'
  as suff. 34(2), 61(1f)
jowl interj. 352(3)
jy suff. pron. 64(1)
(an) jydh m. 28

kamm, kabm adj. 27, 83(4)
kammenn adv. with neg. 266
kans num. 101(6), 106
karow m. 42(2)
ke- pref. 9(5), 271
keffrys, kekeffrys (ha) 262, 287
kehys (ha) 261, 287
kekemmys, see *kemmys*
kelegel m. 12(2)
kemmys, kekemmys **72(2)**, 261, 348
  in compounds 121(3)
  kemmys ha 287
ken m. 'cause' 148(2)
ken adj. 'other' **72(3)**, 83(5b), 148(6), 260
kenderow m. 12(2), 42(1)
kenedhel f. 12(2)
keniterow f. 12(2), 42(1)
keniver adj. **72(4)**, 340(8)
  keniver ha 287
kepar ha 260, **287**
  kepar ha pan 297, 348
kes past part. 244(4)

kes- pref. 271
(an) keth adj. 23(2), 69(3), **83(5c)**
  an keth ha 287
  stress in compounds 9(6)
kettell sub. conj. 23(1), 258(3), **295**
kettep adj. 83(5d)
kettoeth (ha) adv. 258(3), 287
kev- pref. 271
ki m. 42(2)
kinship 42(1)
klabytter m. 12(2)
kom-, kon- pref. 271
konter, kontrari adv. 260
korr- pref. 273
kott adj. 83(4)
kov m. 256
kowal, kowl adv.267, pref. 268
kulyek m. 'cock' to denote masc. 42(7)
kummyas m. *(a, dhe)* 126(8d)
kuv adj. 83(4)
kwartron, kwarter, kwartenn m. 109(2)
kyn sub. conj. 'before' 295
kyn(th) sub. conj. 'though' 26, 274(8a),
  293, 345
kyns, kynsa comp. adj. 70(2), **82(4**,
  107(1),
  258(4), 347(2)
  kyns oll 267
  'rather than' 348(4)
kyns, kyn prep. 150
  as pref. 272
kyns (es) sub. conj. 295

-la suff. 34(3)
lakka comp. adj. 82(4)
le comp. adj. 'less' **82(4)**, 120(7), 267
le m. 'place' 34(3)
lel adj. 83(4)
lelduri m. 12(2)
lemmyn adv. 285(1)
  with *nans* 280
len adj. 83(4)

lenduri m. 12(2)
lenition, see mutation, soft
lenn f. in compounds 61(1f)
les m. 'plant' in compounds 61(1f)
les- pref. 273
leun adj. 83(4), 126(5)
lies adj. 83(5e)
 - *torn* 258(7)
local clauses 342
lower adj. 'many' 83(5f)
lowr adj. 'enough' **83(6b)**, 267
lust m. 255
lyha comp. adj. **82(4)**, 267

'm poss. adj. 52(1)
ma enclitic 8(5), **50(5)**
 with adj. 83(3)
ma = vy suff. pron. 64(3)
mab m. 42(1)
 - *dha dhama, - dha vamm* 49(5)
maga adv. 'so, as' 26, **84**
 - *ta* 261
mal interj. 352(3)
malbew interj. 23(1), 352(3)
mall m. 126(8d), 147(5b), 255
mamm f. 42(1)
 in compounds 61(1e)
mann m. **94**, 266
mar adv. 'as' 23(1), **84**, 260
 - *ha* 287
mar/mara/mars/maras sub. conj. 'if'
 25(2) **292**
 in indirect questions 344(5)
margh m. 42(2)
marnas/ma's conj. 286
marnas/ma's prep. **151**
 in clock time 112
 in subtraction 110(2)
marow adj. 244(4)
martesen adv. 263
marth m. 126(8d), 147(5b), **255**
marthys adj. 91, 267

masculine nouns, see nouns, gender of
mass nouns, see nouns, number
may(th) sub. conj. 26, 274(8b), **291**,
 332(7)
 purpose 291, 298, **349**
 result 299, **350**
 'when' 295
 'where' 296
 with verbs of willing 336(3)
measurement
 distance 116
 linear 115
 with *orth* 152(3)
 price with *a* 126(9)
 size 118
 square 117
 volume 118
menowgh adv. 258(7)
mercy on 126(8e)
mes conj. 'but' 286
(yn) mes a prep. 175
meth m. 126(8d), 147(5b), **255**, 256
meur adj. 23(2), **57(2a)**, 82(4), 83(4)
 meur ras, etc. 352(8)
mil num. 23(1), **103**, 106
milyon num. 106
'mine' etc. 254
mir (ha) 287
mis m. 111(2)
mixed mutation, see mutation, mixed
modrep f. 42(1)
month 111(2)
mood of verb, see verb, mood
mor m., in compounds 61(1e)
moy, (an) moyha comp. adj. **82(4)**, 91,
 120(7)
 forming comp. of adjs. 267
multiplication 110(3)
mutation 21 - 29
 breathed 24
 causes of 2nd state 23
 in compound words 61(1d)

hard 25
irregular 29
mixed 26
nasal 27
table of 22
my pers. pron., see personal pronouns
myghtern 12(1)
myns m. **72(5)**, 340(8)
myrgh f. 42(1)
- *dha dhamma/- dha vamm* 49(5)
mys- pref. 269

'n infxd. pron. 65
na = neb 24(3), 83(7)
na enclitic 8(6), **50(5)**
  with adjs. 83(3)
na(g) co-ord. conj. 284, 285
na hwath 263
na interj. 'no' 352(1)
nal(g) neg. rel. part. 23(1), **276(6)**
na(g) neg. verb. part. 23(1), 276
  agreement with neg. command 276(3)
  before imperv. 276(1)
  in negative replies 276(2)
  re-inforcing 276(4)
na(g) sub. conj. 23(2), 276(5), 291
nafella adv. 83(7)
nahen 12(1)
nameur 12(1), 258(7), 266
nammenowgh adv. 258(7)
nammnygen adv/ 12(1), 258(4)
namna(g) 23(1), 267
namoy adv/ 12(1), 266
naneyl adj. 12(1), 284
nans verb. part. 280
(an) navas f. 27
neb pron. 72(7)
  = 'a certain' 49(2)
nebes adj. 57(2b), **72(6)**, 82(4), 267
necessity 247
negys m.,with orth 152(4)
nes, nessa comp. adjs. 70(2), **82(4)**,

107(2), 177(2), 266
nev m. 40(4)
nevra adv. 258(8)
neyth f. 42(1)
ni pers. pron., see personal pronouns
niver m. 119
nominal sentences, see sentences, nominal
(an) nor, norvys m. 27
nosweyth adv. 258(2)
'nought' 94
nouns
  abstract 31, 32, 240(4)
  object of 240(4)
  case 47
  collective 44, 71(2)
  compound 23(3), 61
  count 46
  definite with *an* 'the' 50
  definition of 48
  diminutives 35
  dual 45
  familiar animals 42(2)
  feminine 39
  forms of 30
  indefinite 49
  instrument and agency 33
  kinship 42(1)
  masculine 38
  mass 46
  miscellaneous forms 36
  number 43 - 46
  place 34, 43(9)
  plurals 43, 71(2)
  singulatives 44
noun clauses (subordinate sentences)
  as complement of *bos* 337
  as indirect statement 336(4)
  as object 336
  as subject 335
nown m. 255
nowydh 'newly, just' 258(4)

noy m. 42(1)
number
 of adjectives, see adjectives, number
 of nouns, see nouns number
numbers
 accompanying nouns 105
 adverbial 121
 cardinal 93 - 106
 complex 104
 compound 9(3), 101(4)
 decimal system 122
 fractional 109
 ordinal 107, 108
numerical expressions
 adverbial 121
 miscellaneous 120
ny(ns) neg. verb. part. 23(1), **275**
(yn) nyhewer gorthugher adv. 258(2)

oaths 352(4)
 with *re* 156
 with *tann* 159
object of verb
 anticipatory 302(6)
 direct 302(5), 304(1)
 displaced 141(16), **304(2)**
 of imperative 66
 indirect = dative 47(3), 65(7), 141(14)
object of preposition 63(9)
oblique relative, see relative, oblique
oes m. 114
ogas adv. 82(4), 83(4), 120(6), 259(1)
 - *(ha)* 258(8), 287
 - *di/ogasti/ogatti* 267
ogas omma 259(1)
ogh interj. 352(2)
oll adj., pron. 57(2c), **72(8)**
om- pref. 9(12), 273
omma adv, 259(1)
onan num. 72(9), 95
 - *hag onan* 120(1)
optative

re with pres. subj. 229(1), 250(6), 279(12), 279(13)
 sense of imperfect 228(4)
orth prep. **152**
 attachment 152(5)
 emotions 152(8)
 expressions 152(9)
 guarding against 152(7)
 measure 120(8), 152(3)
 position 152(1)
 pres. part. construction 152(10), 243
 resistance 152(6)
 temporal 152(2)
 with verbs 152(4)
otta/otta (a-wott/a-wotta) 67
 - *(ha)* 287, 352(7)
ottiwedh 258(6)
our m. 112
ow poss. adj. 51(1) and see poss. adjs.
ow/owth pres. part. particle 152(10)
 243(1), 251 and see orth prep.
own m. 126(8d), 255, 256

pals adj. 83(6c)
pan interr. pron. 'what' 23(2), **74(2)**, 328, 332(7)
pan sub. conj. 'when' 23(1), **294**, 295, 346(1), 347(1)
pana interr. pron. 23(1), **74(3)**, 328, 332(7)
 - re 74(6)
pandra interr. pron. **74(4)**, 327, 332(7)
par adv. 260
 - *dell* 260
parallel increase 87
particles, verbal 274 - 281
 a interr. 277
 a rel. 278
 assa 281
 nans 280
 ny 275
 re 279

y(th) 274
stress 8(2)
parys past part. 244(4)
passive sense 147(6), 245(3b), 333(1c)
past participle
  complement of *bos* 'be' 332(3)
  forms of 244
  with imperf. tense 245(3a)
  with *moy, le* 245(5), 267
  with pret. tense 245(3b) as passive
  syntax 245
  with *yn* 245(6)
peder num., see *peswar*
pedn = *penn* 27
pell adj. 258(8)
penn m. in compounds 61(1e)
'per' 120(10)
percentages 109(5)
personal pronouns 62 - 64
  with *go* 'woe' 68
  with imperative as subj. , obj. 66
  independent 63
  infixed 65
  with *ott* 'see' 67
  with preps. 124(3)
  suffixed 64
  with *war'tu ha* 'towards' 164
  with *ynter* 'between' 178
pes interr. pron. **76**, 267, 328
pes past part. 244(4)
peskweyth interr. pron. **76**, 258(7), 274(7), 324
pestermyn interr. pron. **76**, 258(8), 274(7), 324
peswar m. num., *peder* f. num. 98
peub pron. 72(10)
p'eur interr. adv. 26, **75(15)**, 258, 326
phonetic system 1
'pity on' 126(8e)
piw inter. pron 'who' **73(1)**, 327, 330
piw vb. 'own' **73(2)**, 199, 252
piwpynag 12(1), 72(11)

pla interj. 352(3)
place, position 259
ple(th) interr. adv. 26, **74(12)**, 259(1) 274(8c), 326, 332(7)
plegadow vb. adj. 141(15i)
pluperfect tense
  endings of 180
  uses of 228(5)
plural, see nouns, plural
po co-or. conj. 285
pobel f. 7(3b), 40(2)
poes adj. 147(5a)
poken adv. 12(1), 260, 285
por- pref. 268
poran adv. 120(9), 267
porres adv. 265
position, see place
possession 47(2), **249**, 256
possessive adjectives
  contracted 52
  with displaced obj. 304(2b)
  distributive sense of 53
  forms of 51
  reference of 71
  repetition of 54
  stress 8(3)
possessive prons. 254
prag interr. adv. **74(16)**, 264, 324, 325, 332(7)
praga interr. adv. 264
prefixes 23(2), 23(3c), **268 - 273**
  asssociative 271
  intensive 268
  negative and privative 269
  positional 272
  repetitive 270
  stress with 19(1)
  temporal 272
prepositions 123 - 178
  forms of 123
  government of 124
  personal endings of 125

present/future indicative 228(1)
present/future subjunctive 229(1)
present participle construction 243
present perfect 228(3)
preshyous adj. 260
prest adv. 258(5)
preterite 228(2)
prevection, see mutation, hard
price 126(9)
pronominals 72
pronouns 62 - 77
  alternative 70
  demonstrative 69
  with the imperv. 66
  independent 63
  infixed 65
  interrogative 73
  personal 62
  reference of 71
  suffixed 64, 83(3),
  stress in 8(4), 9(7)
pronunciation 2
personal names (proper nouns) 23(3b), 59(2)
prys (a) 126(8d)
pub adj. 72(10), 120(4)
pub blydhen 258(7)
pub dydh 258(7)
pub eur 258(7)
pub mis 258(7)
pup-prys adv. 258(7)
pub Sadorn, etc. 258(7)
pur adv. 23(1), 83(4), 91
purpose 154(2b)
py conj. see po
py interr. adv. 'where' **75**, 326, 332(7)
py interr. pron. 'what' **74(1)**, 328
py eghenn **74(11)**, 327
py kinda 74(11), 327
py kost, py le, py plas, py tyller **74(14)**, 259(1), 274(7), 324, 325
py le pynag 72(11)

py lies 74(9), 327
py lies gweyth 258(7)
py lies termyn 258(7)
py lies treveth 258(7)
py par **74(11)**, 327
py re **74(6)**, 327
py seul **74(10)**, 327
py sort **74(11)**, 327
pygans interr. pron. 12(1)
pygemmys interr. pron. 74(8), 327
  - *termyn* 258(8)
pylepynag interr. adv. 72(11)
pympes num. 107(4)
pynag, pypynag interr. pron. 12(1), 49(4) 72(11), 340(8)
pyneyl interr. pron. **74(7)**, 328
  - *pynag* **72(11)**, 340(8)
pyth interr. pron. **74(5)**, 327
(a*n) pyth*, rel. use of 340(7)

questions and answers 320 - 330
  indirect 322
  oblique 330

rag co-ord. conj. 288
rag prep. 68(4), **154**, 346(2)
  'for the sake of' 154(3)
  with may 154(2b)
  as prefix 272
  position 154(1)
  protection 154(4)
  reason 154(2)
  thanking 154(2a)
  time 154(5)
rag sub. conj. 294
rann f. 109(3)
ras, rasow m. 141(15e)
re adv 'too' 23(1), 267
re optative part. 23(1), 250(1), **279(12)**
re perf. part. 23(1), 197(2e), 205(2c), 278(1e), **279**, 348(1)
re prep. 'by', in oaths 23(1), 52, **156,**

352(4)
re pron. 'some' 72(12)
reason
  rag 154(2)
  war 161(5)
reciprocal verbs 232
redi, see y*redi*
reflexive verbs 232
relatives, in indefinite statements 340(7), 340(8)
relative clauses
  direct (adjectival) 340
  indirect (oblique) 342
  particles
  a 278
  na(g) 276
  with *bos, mos* 341
remoter object 304(2)
ren, see *re* prep.
replies, see questions and answers
res adj., vb. 'necessary' 221, 237(1), **247**
res past part. 'given' 244(4)
res perf. part., see *re* perf. part.
reydh 'sex, kind' as suffix 36(5)
rivers, reference to 39(10), 71(3b)
ro/roy opt. of ri vb. 'give' **208(2a)**, 352(8)
ryb prep. 157

's infix. pron. 65
sarf f. 42(2)
saw prep., conj. 158, 286
  - *unnsel* 267
segments, addition, change and ommision of 17
semi-vowels 4
semli 260
sentences 301 - 333
  nominal 303
  subordinate
  as adj. clauses 340
  as adv. clauses 344 - 351
  as nn. clauses 334 - 337

verbal 302
sequence of tenses, see tenses, sequence of
sertus 265
settlements, reference to 71(3b)
settya vb. in valuation 246(5)
seul pron. 23(1), **72(13)**, 340(80
seulabrys adv. 12(1), 258(4), 258(8)
seuladhydh adv. 12(1), 258(4), 258(8)
seythves/seythes 107(6)
sians 255
singulatives, see nouns, singulative
size, see measurement
skant adv. 267
skantlowr adv. 267
sket adv. 258(5)
skon adv/ 258(5)
skyll- pref. 269
soweth excl. 12(1), 352(2)
speshyal adv. 260
spiration, see mutation, breathed
stark 260
stress 8
  with adj. 9(2), 10
  in compounds 9
  in genitive const. 11
  irregular 12
  with prefixes 9(1), 9(5), 9(6)
  with suffixes 9(4)
subject
  anticipatory 63(2)
  of infinitive const. 63(6)
  of imperv. 66
  pronoun as 63(2)
subjunctive mood
  sequence of tenses in 338
  uses of 229
  verbal endings of 181
subordinating conjunctions, see conjunctions, subordinating
subordinate sentences, see sentences subordinate

subtraction 110(2)
suffixed pronouns 64
  with adjs. 83(3)
  after dhe 141(1)
  double 64(2)
  with long forms of *bos* 332(2)
  object after vbs. in *-ya* 188(3)
  object of imper. 66(3)
  object of *y'm beus* 250(3)
  reduced forms 64(3)
  re-inforcing infxd. pron. 65(6)
  single forms 64(1)
  stress in 8(4)
  subject of imperv. 66(1), 66(2)
suffixes
  forming adjectives 79
  forming nouns 30 - 36
  affecting stress 9
sur, yn sur 265
synsi vb. in valuation 246(5)
syghes m. 255
synsys past part. 141(15k)

ta = *ty, jy* suff. pron. 64(1), 64(3)
tamm (vydh) 266
tann prep. 159, interj. 352(4), 352(5)
tarow m. 42(2)
tas m. 42(1)
tebel adj. 83(4)
teg as adv. 267
temporal clauses 347
tenses of verbs
  sequence of 338
  uses of 228
  and see separately under
  names of tenses
ter- pref. 270
termyn m. 'time' with ord. num. 121(5)
ternos vyttin 258(2)
tetivali interj. 352(3)
teyr num., see *tri* num.
'th infixd. pron. 26, 65(2)

'th poss. adj. 51(4) and see poss. adjs.
thanks 126(8c), 141(15e), 141(15k)
  352(8)
ti m., see *ji* m.
time
  of day 112
  duration of 113
  at which, etc. 112, 141(12)
  'n' times 121(1)
  reference to 71(3b)
toch (vydh)(adv. 266
toeth bras 260
toetta adv. 12(1) 260
towns, reference to 71(3b)
tra f. 40(1), 71(3b)
trank heb worfenn 258(8)
tre adv. 'at home' 259(1), 259(3)
tre- pref. 268 and see *ter-* pref.
trenja adv. 258(2)
tressa num. 107(3)
treus adv. 260, pref. 272
treweythyow adv. 258(7)
tri, teyr nums '3' 24(2), **97**
tro ha(g) prep. 160
tru interj. 352(2)
trysa 107(3)
tu ha tre 259(3)
tulyfant m. 12(2)
tus pl. 40(3)
ty pers. pron., see personal prons.
  in vocative 23(1), 352(7)
tys ha tas 260

ugens-ow num. 106
ugh- pref. 268
unn num. '1' 23(2), **95(3)**
  'a certain' 49(1)
unnek num. 27
unnweyth adv. 266
usi vb. 'is', see bos vb.
uskis adv. 258(5), 260

313

value with a 126(9)
vas = *mas* adj. 83(2d)
verbal action 73(3)
verbal noun 235 - 242
  with adj. 235(4), 235(5)
  in compounds 235(5)
  with definite article 235(2)
  endings
  in -*a* 185, 233(1)
  in -*as* 233(8)
  in -*el* 180(4a, b), 191(3), 191(4), 191(5a), 233(6),
  in -*es* 233(6), 233(7)
  in -*he* 187, 233(5)
  in -*i* 233(3)
  in -*ia* 186
  in -*wel* 193
  in -*ya* 188, 233(2)
  as complement of *bos* 239
  forms of 233
  gender of 235(3)
  in idioms 237
  from intransitive verbs 240(2)
  negative of 242
  as object 238, 315
  object of 240(1)
  as passive 239(2)
  in place of verb 241
  with prep. 235(6)
  as subject 236, 237
  subject of 240(1), 240(2)
  syntax of 235
  from transitive verbs 240(1)
verbal particles, see particles, verbal
verbal sentences, see sentences, verbal
verbs 179 - 256
  auxiliary 225 - 227
  classes of 184
  defective 213 - 224
  forms of 179
  imperfect ind. in -*i* 180(5)
  irrregular 197 - 212

  modification of stem in subj. 182
  moods 179(3)
  persons 179(1)
  preterite in -*is* 180(4)
  regular in -*a* 185
  - in -*he* 187
  - in -*ia, -ias* 186
  - in -*ya* 188
  suffixes of imperative 183
  - of indicative 180
  - of subjunctive 181
  with two objects 305(7)
  tenses of 179 and see under names of tenses
  with vowel added 193 - 195
  with vowel affection 189 - 191
  with vowel narrowed in 3p.s. of pres./fut. 192
  with vowel omitted 196
vil adj. 83(4)
vilen, vileni m. 23(4)
vocative 352(7)
volume, see measurement . cubic
vowels 3
  addition of 17(4
  affection of 14
  in vbs. 189
  length of 7
  omission of 17(1)
vri (bri) m. 246(5), 126(8b)
vy = *my* pers. pron. 64(1)
vydh (bydh) adj., see bydh

war adj. 83(4)
war, waryewgh interj. 352(5)
war yew interj. 352(9)
war prep. 161
  advantage 161(4)
  'against' 161(3)
  cause 161(5)
  direction 161(7), 259(3)
  inclination 161(8)

method 161(10)
numbers *(warn)* 161(6), 101(4)
position 161(1)
prayer 161(9)
rate 161(11)
time 161(2)
topic 161(12)
war-barth ha 12(1), 260, **287**
war-gamm 161(11), 260
war hemma*, *war henna 258(3)
war-lergh adv. 258(6), 347(2)
war-lergh prep. **163**
  'according to' 163(3)
  following 163(3)
  longing 163(4)
  position 163(1)
  time 163(2)
war-lergh sub. conj. 295
war neb kor 260
war-not adv. 258(3)
war-nuk adv. 258(5)
war tu delergh 259(1)
war-tu ha 164
war-ves a 165
war-wartha 161(3)
warlyna adv. 258(2)
warn prep., see *war*
weather 71
welawo interj. 352(2)
- ***weyth*** f. 'time', see *gweyth* f.
'whose' 343(1)
word order 309 319
  in affirmative sentences 309 - 313
  with aauxiliary vbs. 315
  in neg. sentences 314
  object emphasised 317
  subject emphasised 316
  verb emphasised 312
wortalleth ha wor'tiwedh 258(7)
worth*, *wor', see *orth* prep.
wor'tiwedh 258(6)
wosa prep. 166, 347(2)

with infinitive cons. 347(2)
wosa sub. conj. 295
wostalleth adv. 258(4)
wostiwedh 258(6)

y poss. adj. 23(1), **51(5)**
y(th) vb. part. 26, 274
  introducing sub. nn. clause 334
  omission of 274(2), 274(3), 274(4), 274(5)
  supporting infxd. pron. 274(9)
  with sub. sent. 291
y gila pron. 70(2)
ya interj. 352(1)
year 111
yma vb. 'is', see *bos*
y'm beus vb. **198**, 250
  with vb. nn. 238(3)
ymons vb. 'are', see *bos*
yn adv. part. 92, 257(3)
yn- pref. 272
yn prep. **167**
  with abstract nns. 167(6)
  in adverbial pres. part. const. 167(9)
  'in' 167(3)
  'inside' 167(1)
  instrumental 167(8)
  'into' 167(2)
  manner 47(4), 167(7)
  'on' 167(4)
  time 167(5)
yn-bann adv. 259(3)
yn chi adv. 259(1)
yn-dann prep. 23(1), 168
  in pres. part. const. 168(3), 243(6)
yn despit prep. 170
y'n dre 259(1)
y'n eur ma/na 258(1)
yn fenowgh 258(7)
y'n gwella/gwettha prys 260
yn herwydh prep. 171
yn hons 259(1)

315

yn hwir/gwir 265
yn kerdh 259(3)
y'n keth maner ma/na 260
yn kettermyn 258(3)
yn kever prep. **173**
  behaviour 173(1)
  concerning 173(2)
yn kosk 260
yn kyrgh 259(3)
yn kyrghynn prep. 172
yn le prep. 174
yn leur 259(3)
yn-medh vb. 'says, said' 219, 336(5a)
yn-mes a prep. 175
yn mysk prep. 176
yn nans 259(3)
yn nes 259(1)
yn ober 47(4), 260
yn-ogas 177
  position 177(1)
  social relationships 177(2)
yn pell 259(1)
yn priva/privedh 260
yn rag 259(3)
yn skon 258(5)
yn sol interj. 352(5)
yn sur 265
yn ta 262
yn tevri, see *devri*
y'n tor ma/na 258(1) 260
yn tre 259(1)
yn unn adverbial pres. part. const. 23(1), **167(9)**, 243(5)
y'n vlydhen a dheu 258(2)
yn y oes 258(8)
yndella/yndellma 260
yredi 265
ynter/yntra prep. **178**
  in division 178(4)
  position 178(1), 178(3)
  relationship 178(2)
ynwedh adv. 12(1)

ytho conj. 12(1), 289

zero 94

INDEX OF VERBS

Type verbs are entered in upper case letters. The verbal noun ending is separated by a hyphen for ease of reference. Some verbs are also entered in the general index.

AFI-A flee **186**
akord-ya 'agree' - with *gans* 147(8), with *orth* 152(4)
ambos-a 'promise' - with *orth* 'to' 152(4)
amm-a 'kiss' 141(15a), 181(5b), 189(3)
ankev-i 'forget' 190(3)
arveth 'hire' 233(13)
aspi-a 'espy' 152(4), 186(3)
astell 'discontinue' 233(13)
aswi-a 'make a gap' 186(3)
aswonn 'know' 180(4b), 180(5b), 233(13)
attyl-i 'repay' 180(4b), 191(3), 201

benyn-a 'womanise' 234(1)
bern-ya (ny vern) 'it does not matter' 213, 246(1)
BERR-HE 'shorten' **187**
BOS 'be' 23(3f), **197**,
  'b' tenses of 333
  with past part. 332(3)
  expressing possession 253
  in sentences 331 - 333
  pres. and imperf. long forms 332
  pres. and imperf. short forms 331
bost-ya 'boast' 196(2)
brew-i 'break' 181(4b)
bryj-yon 'boil' 189(5), 233(12)
byw-a 'live' (*orth* 'on)

chast-ya 'chastise' 186(3)

daffar 'provide' 233(13)
dagrew-i 'weep' 181(4b), 19l(1)
dalleth 'begin' 180(5b), 190(4), 233(13)
dampn-ya 'damn' 195(3)
dannvon 'send' 189(7), 233(13)
 - *a* 'send to' 126(8c)
darbar-i 'prepare' 272
daromres 233(11)
darvos 'happen' 65(7c), 203
darwar 'forewarn' 214, 352(5)
daskni-as 'ruminate' 186(3)
daskorr 'give back' 189(7), 233(13)
dassen-i 'resound' 190(3)
dassergh-i 'rise again' 190(3)
dedhew-i 'promise' 180(4b)
dedhw-i 'lay eggs' 190(3), 190(5), 191(4), 193(4)
defi-a 'defy' 186(3)
dege-a 'shut' 244(4)
deghes-i 'fling' 161(4)
degoedh 'be due' 12(1), 248(1)
 and see *koedh*
dehwel-es 'return' 180(4b)
delivr-a 'deliver' 194(3)
delledh 'it is proper' 216, 248(2)
demmedh-i 'marry' 180(4b)
dendil 'earn' 233(13)
denew-i 'pour' 180(4b), 191(4), 212
dens-el 'gnaw' 191(3)
deriv-as 'report' 180(4b)
 - *orth* 'to' 152(4)
dervynn 'demand' 180(5b), 233(13)
desedh 'fit, befit' 248(3)
deskern-i 'snarl' 152(9)
dest-a 'witness' 23(4)
deur 'it concerns' 65(7b), 217, 246(3)
devess-a 'look for sheep' 234(2)
dewan-a 'penetrate' 268
dewis 'choose' 180(5b), 233(13)
diank 'escape' 12(1), 180(4b), 191(3),

233(13)
diberth 'part' 12(1), 180(5b), 190(4), 233(13)
difenn 'forbid' 180(5b), 229(3f), 233(13)
 with *orth* as direct obj. 152(4)
dinew-i 'pour' 180(4b), 191(4), 191(5), 212
dineyth-i 'give birth' 180(4b)
diskrys-i 'disbelieve' 180(4b)
diskwedh-es 'show' 212
distru-i 'destroy' 180(4b)
diswul 'undo' 269
diwisk-a 'undress' 196(2)
DOEN 'bear' 180(5b), **207**
dolos 'pretend' 12(1), 233(13)
domhwel 'overthrow' 181(4b)
DOS 'come' **206**
drehedh-es 'reach' 268
drehev-el 'build' 191(3), 191(5)
DRI 'bring' **209**
dustun-ya 'witness' 23(4)
dybr-i 'eat' 180(4b), 191(5), 194(5a)
dyerbynn (*-a*) 233(13), 268
dyffres 'protect' 233(13)
dyght-ya 'deal with'
 with subj. 229(3b)
DYLL-O 'issue' **211**
dynnergh-i 'welcome' 191(3)
dysk-i 'learn, teach' 196(2), 240(5)
 with *dhe* 141(15b)
 with *gans* 147(7)

entr-a 'enter' 195(3)
ERGH-I 'order' 180(4b), **191**
 with *a* 126(8c)
 with subj. 229(3e)
 similar verbs 191(3), 191(4), 191(5)
ev-a 'drink' 192

fagl-a 'flame' 194(5a)
fast-a/ fast-he/fast-ya 'fasten' 152(5)
fekl-a 'flatter' 194(5c)

317

fi-a 'flee' 186(3)
fols-a 'split' 192
fyll-el 'fail' 126(1), 141(15c), 191(3)

GALL-OES 'be able' 180(5b), 192, **227**, 307
gas-a 'leave' 183(1)
gav-a 'forgive' 141(15d)
ged-ya 'guide' 192
GELW-EL 'call' **193**
  similar verbs 193(3), 193(4)
gi-a 'spear' 186(3)
glen-a 'stick' 152(5)
godhav/godhev-el 'endure' 180(4b), 191(3) 191(5), 233(12)
GODHVOS 'know' **200**, 308
godr-a 'milk' 194(5a)
godros 'menace' 233(13)
gohol-es 'shun' 269
goli-a 'wound' 186(3)
gonis (gonedh) 'work' 233(14)
gorgul 'do strictly' 268
gorhemmynn 'order' 233(13)
  with subj. 229(3e)
gormel 'praise' 233(13)
gorowr-a 'gild' 268
gorthyb-i 'answer' 180(4b)
gort-os 'await' 212, 233(10)
goslow-es 'listen' with *orth* 'to' 152(4)
govynn 'ask' with *orth* 'of' 152(4) 180(5b) 233(13)
gowli-a 'lie' 186(3)
grass-a 'thank' 141(15e)
grev-ya 'trouble' 141(15f)
grommyal 'growl' 233(13), also *gromm-ya*
gront-ya 'grant' 229(3h)
gryghi-as 'neigh' 186(3)
GUL 'make, do' **225**, 305
  with *dhe* and subj.141(7)
  with *orth* 152(4)
gustl-a 'riot' 195(3)

gwandr-a 'wander' 195(3)
gwari 'play' 186(3), 233(13)
gwayt-ya 'expect', with subj. 229(3c,i)
gwedhr-a 'wither' 194(5a)
gweres 'help' 141(15g), 233(13)
  with *orth* 152(4)
gwesk-el 'strike' 191(3), 191(5), 192, 196(2)
gweyth-a 'work', with *orth* 152(4)
gwi-a 'weave' 186(3)
gwibess-a chase gnats' (= waste time) 234(2)
gwisk-a 'dress' 196(2)
GWYSTL-A 'pledge' **195**
  similar vbs. 195(3)
gwith-a 'guard'
  with *orth* 152(7)
  with *rag* 154(4)
  with *war* 161(8)
  with subj. 229(3f)
gwri-as 'sew' 186(3)

handl-a 'handle' 195(3)
hebkorr 'renounce' 233(13)
hedh-i 'stop' 180(4b)
hembronk 'lead' 180(5b), 233(13)
henw-el 'call' 193(3)
hevel-i 'seem' 180(4b), 191(3)
hunros'dream' 233(13), also *hunros-a*
HWARVOS 'happen' 65(7c), **202**
hwedhl-a 'tell tales' 194(5a)
hwel-es 'turn' (only in compounds) 218
hwerthin 'laugh' 180(5b), 190(4), 233(12)
hwil-as 'seek', with orth 152(4)
hwiless-a 'hunt beetles' 234(2)
HWITHR-A 'look at' **194**
  similar vbs. 194(5a)
  with *orth* 152(4)
hwyrn-i 'hum, buzz' 194(5a)
hwystr-a 'whisper' 195(3)

IGER-I -'open' **190**,

similar vbs. 190(3), 190(4), 190(5)

kagl-a 'void excrement' 194(5)
kammwonis 'bungle' 233(14)
kannmeul 'praise highly' 233(13)
kav-oes 'have, find' 192, 251
kell-i 'lose' 190(3), 192
kelm-i 'knot' 190(3)
kemmer-es 'take' 251
kemmyn 'bequeath' 180(4b), 233(13)
kenki-a 'contend' 186(3)
kentr-a 'nail' 152(5), 195(3)
kentrew-i 'nail' 180(4b), 191(4)
kesk-i 'exhort' 190(3)
kest-ya 'trick' 196(2)
keunyss-a 'gather firewood' 234(2)
kevarwoedh-a 'signal' 271
kevelekk-a 'hunt woodcock' 234(2)
kews-el 'speak' 191(4)
   with *gans* 147(8)
   with *orth* 152(4)
KLYW-ES 'hear' **204**
   with *gans* 147(7)
kni-as 'gnaw' 186(3)
KOEDH and *degoedh* 'be due' **215**, 248
koel-a 'trust', with *orth* 152(4)
kommond-ya, with subj. 229(3e)
koniness-a 'hunt rabbits' 234(2)
kontradi-a 'contadict' 186(3)
kovi-a 'cherish' 186(3)
krampoeth-a 'go begging pancakes' 234(1
kreg-i 'hang' 190(3)
kregynn-a 'look for molluscs' 234(2)
kreun-i 'accumulate' 180(4b)
kri-a 'cry' 186(3)
kryghyll-i 'jolt, rattle' 233(11)
krys-i 'believe' 141(15h)
kudh-a 'hide' 154(4)
kuntell 'gather' 233(13)
kusul-ya 'advise'
   with *a* 126(8c)
   with subj. 229(3g)

kynnik 'offer' 233(13)
kynyew-el 'dine' 191(4)
kywni-a 'become mossy' 186(3)

ladr-a 'steal' 194(4), 194(5)
las-ya 'lash', with *orth* 152(5)
lavas-os 'dare' 180(5b)
legess-a 'hunt mice' 234(2)
lemm-el 'jump' 191(3)
lenw-el 'fill' 193(3)
   with *a* 'fill with 126(5)
lesk-i 'burn' 190(3), 196(2)
LEST-A 'prevent' **196**
   similar vbs. 196(2)
lett-ya 'prevent' 126(1), 152(7)
   with subj. 229(3f)
lever-el 'say' 191(3)
   with *orth* 152(4)
li-a 'take an oath' 186(3)
lymn-a 194(5a)

marghogeth 'ride' 233(12)
medh-es 'say, said' 219, 336(5a)
medr-a 'aim, notice' 194(5a)
meg-i 'smoke' 190(3)
mel-a 'gather honey' 234(1)
melhwess-a 'hunt slugs' 234(2)
merw-el 'die' 193(3)
mes-a 'gather acorns' 234(1)
meskl-a 'gather mussels' 234(1)
methrin 'rear' 194(5a)
met-ya 'meet'
   with *gans* 147(8)
   with *orth* 152(1)
minhwerth-in 'smile' 180(5b), 190(4)
mir-es 'look', with orth 152(4)
moldr-a 'murder' 195(3)
molleth-i 'curse' 191(4)
MOS/MONES 'go' **205**
most-ya 'befoul' 196(2)
MYNN-ES be willing' **226**, 229(3a), 306
   indication future intention 306

with infinitive const. 306(2)
with *may* and subj. 306(3)
with *orth* 152(4), 306(4)

niver-a 'count' 119

omberth-i 'balance' 232
omdhal 'quarrel' 232, 233(13)
'omdhoen 'bear a child' 232
om'dhoen 'behave oneself' 232
omglyw-es 'feel' 204(2d), 232
omguntell 'meet' 233(13)
omladh 'fight' 180(5b), 232
omladh-a 'kill oneself' 232
omwen 'wriggle' 233(13)
omweres 'help oneself' 232
omwovynn 'ask oneself, wonder' 232
omwul 'make oneself out to be, pretend' 225(2e), 232
ordn-a 'arrange', with subj. 229(3b)
ost-ya 'lodge' 196(2)

pareus-i 'prepare' 244(4)
pargh/paragh 'endure, last' 220
pe 'pay' 233(13)
pedr-i 'rot' 190(3), 194(5a)
perghenn-a 'own' 251
perth-i 'bear' 190(3), 232
  with nouns of feeling 256
pesk-i 'graze' 190(4), 196(2)
PIW 'own' 73(2), **199**, 252
pleg-ya 'bend' 141(15i), 147(5d)
pob-as 'bake' 192
POEN-YA 'run hard' **188**
powes 'rest' 233(13)
preder-i 'think' 180(4b)
pregowth-a 'preach' 189(6), 233(13)
PREN-A 'buy, pay for' **185**, 248(5f)
prev-i 'prove' 190(3)
provi-a 'provide' 186(3)
pryvess-a 'hunt vermin' 234(2)
pys-i 'pray, ask' 180(4b)

with *a* 126(8c)
with *diworth* 153(2)
with subj. 229(3d)
pyskess-a 'fish' 234(2)

rask-a 'plane' 196(2)
ravn-a 'ravish' 194(5a)
rekn-a 'reckon' 194(5a)
renk-i 'snort' 190(3)
res 'it is necessary' 221
res-ek 'run' 233(12)
resn-a 'reason' 194(5b)
restr-a/restr-i 'arrange' 195(3)
rest-ya 'rest' 196(2)
RI 'give' **208**
  valuation 246(5)
rost-ya 'roast' 196(2)

sakrifi-a 'sacrifice' 186(3)
selw-el 'save' 193(3)
sen-i 'sound' 190(3)
serr-i 'be, make angry' 190(3)
sett-ya 'set', in valuation 246(5)
sev-el 'stand' 191(3)
sevi-a 'pick strawberries' 186(3), 234(1)
si-a 'buzz' 186(3)
skil-a 'mean' 222
skon-ya, with *a* 'refuse to' 126(1)
skorn-ya 'scorn' 147(8)
sokr-a 'succour' 194(5b)
sommys 'flit' 233(13)
sompn-a 'summon' 195(3)
sotl-a 'use artifice' 194(5a)
sugn-a 'suck' 194(5a)
syns-i 'hold', in valuation 246(5)

takk-ya 'nail' 152(5)
takl-a 'trim' 194(5c)
talk-ya 'talk' 189(4)
talvos 'value' 201(2a)
tann 'take!' 223
tardr-a 'bore holes' 195(3)

TAV-A 'touch' **189**
tell-i 'bore holes' 190(3)
tempr-a 'tame' 195(3)
terlentr-i 'glitter' 195(3)
terr-i 'break' 190(3)
test-a, see dest-a
tev-i 'grow' 192
tew-el 'be silent' 191(3)
TI 'swear' 210
ti 'roof' 186(3), 210(5c)
tregh-i 'cut' 190(3)
trest-ya 'trust' 196(2)
trobl-a 'trouble' 194(3a)
tustun-ya, see *dustun-ya*
TYL-I 'pay, owe' 180(4b), 191(3), **201**, 248(5)
tynkyal 'tinkle' 233(13)

war 'take care' 224

ydhyn-a 'hunt birds' 234(1)
yes 'confess' 233(13)
yeun-i 'yearn', with *war-lergh* 163(4)

NOTES

NOTES

NOTES

NOTES

NOTES

NOTES

NOTES